LIVE & WORK IN

ITALY

LIVE & WORK IN
ITALY

Victoria Pybus

Distributed in the USA by
The Globe Pequot Press, Guilford, Connecticut

Published by Vacation Work, 9 Park End Street, Oxford
www.vacationwork.co.uk

LIVE AND WORK IN ITALY
First edition 1992 Victoria Pybus & Rachel Robinson
Second edition 1998 Victoria Pybus
Third edition 2002 Victoria Pybus & Huw Francis
Fourth edition 2005 Victoria Pybus

ISBN 1-85458-332-8

Publicity: Charles Cutting

Cover design by mccdesign

Title page illustration by Mick Siddens

Text design and typesetting by Brendan Cole

Cover photograph: gondolas in Venice

Printed and bound in Italy by Legoprint SpA, Trento

CONTENTS

SECTION 1
LIVING IN ITALY

RETIREMENT

SECTION II
WORKING IN ITALY

EMPLOYMENT

FOREWORD

Live and work in Italy is part of a successful series of books providing essential information and advice for those thinking of moving abroad, planning to move abroad or already living abroad. These country specific guides cover the modalities of life in each country, as well as work opportunities for foreigners, information on starting a business, buying a business or retiring there. *Live and Work in Italy* is divided into two sections, *Living in Italy* and *Working in Italy* respectively. These two sections cover the essential aspects of moving to Italy, including how to open a bank account or arrange an Italian mortgage, the legalities of renting an apartment or house, employment regulations and opportunities, sources and ideas for setting up a small business and the finer points of Italian etiquette, language and culture.

Over 100,000 Britons live in Italy, of whom around two thirds are homeowners there. The majority of homeowners have set up home in the rolling hills of Tuscany and Umbria, and increasingly, Le Marche. There are others to be found in less publicised regions like Liguria, Piedmont, Puglia and Sardinia. Rural lifestyles contrast greatly with the urban ones led by expatriates who live in the big cities of Milan, Turin, Florence and the capital Rome and may suit some but not others.

It is not just the climate that attracts foreigners to Italy – the reasons for moving there are as varied as the regions of Italy itself. Some will be posted there by international companies, some have a deep-seated love of the country and its people and wish to immerse themselves in Italian culture, and some will have spotted a gap in the commercial market and a way to make a living in Italy and put down roots there.

Despite its disorganised and notoriously corrupt state bureaucracy, Italy boasts one of the most dynamic and efficient business areas of Europe, mostly in northern Italy. The Italians are friendly and hospitable host nationals, and Italy has a cultural heritage that is the cornerstone of Western civilization and it would be hard to tire of its fascination.

The cost of property in northern Italy and the popular, idyllic regions of Tuscany and Umbria now equates to the UK, though it is cheaper than in the big cities of North America. However, there are still bargains to be found in other regions where expatriates have just begun to make inroads such as Abruzzo and Puglia. In cities property prices can be much higher than rural areas, especially in fashionable areas the northern metropolises. There are also wide differences in the cost of renting accommodation. The landlords of Naples charge less than those of Florence and Rome and more than those of small towns. The cost of living is noticeably higher in Italian cities e.g. Rome, Milan, Bologna etc. than in the UK and North America, but so is the quality of life.

Until the 1990s, Italy's economy was one of the fastest growing in Europe.

This was followed by several years of recession, and political upheaval as corruption scandals swept away the Christian Democrat party, which had held the balance of power for nearly fifty years. By all accounts, Italy is far from putting its traditional political and economic problems and scandals behind it despite its wholehearted enthusiasm for the EU. Italy now has a growing deficit and minimal economic growth, and a government based on personal leadership backed by enthusiastic media and vast amounts of money. Despite his reputation for being survivor in the notoriously fickle world of Italian politics, Berlusconi has failed to deliver on his 2001 election promises and his star might have waned; his coalition received a drubbing in the 2005 spring local elections from Romano Prodi's centre-left party and the Berlusconi coalition itself collapsed a few weeks later causing Berlusconi's resignation (in order to re-form his government without calling a general election). The next general election is due in 2006. The split between north and south is very marked, though there are areas of the south that are doing well economically. Unemployment in the north is as low as 5%, while it is still over 20% in the south.

Although known for their parochial outlook, the continued growth of their export economy, closer ties with Europe and a relaxation of currency restrictions has woken Italians up to the potential of international investments such as property and there is a huge market for international consultants. Other areas of particular demand for foreign expertise include teachers of English language, dental practitioners, high technology experts and financial services providers, particularly of insurance and pensions. There is no doubt that opportunities will continue to increase for foreigners wishing to live and work in Italy, while high tech communications will make it easier to keep in touch with friends and family at home.

The bulk expansion of the EU in May 2004 to 25 member countries is set to open up the Italian economy to outside investment. Italy is well placed for trading with some of the new members such as Slovenia. Italy is one of the keenest European Union members and supported the European Constitution in 2005); it also perceives its own economy will be boosted by close links with well-established ones.

This book is applicable and useful to international residents, whether they are from inside the EU, or from other nations. There are complications inherent in setting up a new home and starting a new job and/or life simultaneously in a country which has different laws and procedures to those with which you are familiar. However, by using *Live and Work in Italy*, you will be able to take this giant step briefed with the knowledge of what to expect. This knowledge should make the process of moving internationally much smoother and less stressful for you and your family.

Victoria Pybus
May 2005

ACKNOWLEDGMENTS

The author and publisher would like to thank the following, in no particular order, for their invaluable help in compiling this book: Gordon Neale for his contributions to Setting up Home and Daily Life, Alessandra Dolloy of Fondazione CENSIS Rome, Barry Walker of the Italian Chamber of Commerce in London, Francesca Piovano of FILEF, Linda Travella of Casa Travella, Morfa Downs of The British Chamber of Commerce in Milan, the Reverend Richard Major of St Mark's, Florence, Gerald Smith of Piedmont Properties and Joel Tortolero of www.recruitaly.com. Also, Charles Butterno, Erin McCloskey, Maria Makepeace, Georgina Gordon-Ham, John Matta, Roger Warwick and Sarah Rasmer for providing us with histories of their own experiences of living and working in Italy.

Special thanks are due to Fabio Ausenda of Green Volunteers for his exhaustive reading of the text and his suggestions, corrections and additions throughout the book.

We are also grateful to Dott. Paulo di Filippo LL.M, Managing Director of the Internet Group for his invaluable help with the chapter on *Starting a Business*.

TELEPHONE NUMBERS

Please note that the telephone numbers in this book are written as needed to call that number from inside the same country. To call these numbers from outside the country you will need to know the relevant international access code; these are currently 00 from the UK and Italy and 011 from the USA.

To call Italy: dial the international access code + 39 + the complete number as given in this book.

To call the UK: international access code +44 + the complete number as given in this book – *but omitting the first 0 in the British number.*

To call the USA: international access code +1 + the complete number as given in this book.

Section 1

LIVING IN ITALY

GENERAL INTRODUCTION

RESIDENCE AND ENTRY REGULATIONS

SETTING UP HOME

DAILY LIFE

RETIREMENT

General Introduction

CHAPTER SUMMARY

- Italy has only existed as a unified country since 1861, and most Italians feel a loyalty to their region rather than their nation.
- Italy has an artistic and archaeological heritage second to none.
- There are marked differences between the more prosperous industrial north and the less affluent agricultural south of the country, but the Italian government offers incentives to attract foreign investment into the south.
- **Climate:** winters can be cold in the north but are generally mild in the south; however, the far south and Sicily can be uncomfortably hot in summer.
- **The way of life:** Italians have a relaxed approach to doing business and frequently mix business with pleasure, with working suppers and weekend meetings.
- English is not widely spoken so knowledge of Italian is nearly essential, especially when tackling the Byzantine bureacracy.
- **Politics:** Italian politics is confusing, with a large number of parties broadly divided into two coalitions.
  - Silvio Berlusconi's *Casa delle Libertà* (House of Freedoms) coalition of centre-right parties makes up the government. The next general election is due in 2006.
- **Geography**: The European fault line runs through Italy north-south and 70% of central and southern Italy is susceptible to earthquakes.
  - Italy has a population of 58 million, and for administrative purposes it is divided into twenty regions and 106 provinces.

DESTINATION ITALY

As the European union dismantles economic and trade borders between its member states, an increasing number of EU citizens are contemplating joining thousands of their counterparts already living and working in another member country. Now that the euro is in people's pockets it is even easier to cross from one country to another. The Schengen Agreement means that border posts between Austria, Belgium, Denmark, France, Germany, Greece, Italy, Luxembourg, Netherlands, Norway, Spain, Sweden and Portugal have been removed and those allowed to enter the thirteen countries listed above can also enter Iceland without requiring a visa or passing through customs checks. With the recent expansion of the EU, more people will move between countries to work and companies will increasingly look to hire staff from anywhere within Europe.

As the European economy becomes increasingly united it also becomes more attractive to non-EU companies and greater numbers of organisations from North America, South America and the Asia Pacific Rim will send staff to Europe. As Italy has historically had one of the lowest rates of inward investment within the EU, it is going to become an increasingly popular target for takeovers and exports as organisations turn to less saturated markets, resulting in more expatriates being sent to Italy.

The prospect of being sent abroad is growing for many professionals, though qualified workers are more likely to be sent than unqualified ones due to the restrictions placed on unskilled foreign workers by many governments. It is possible for EU nationals, to practice their profession or skills anywhere in the European Union through a comparison system for different national qualifications, which is becoming more familiar to employers. The EU directives concerning the recognition of most academic and professional qualifications gained within the EU have been in place since 1993. Likewise, prospects for setting up a business abroad are expanding enormously as the governments of EU nations vie with each other to offer the most attractive incentive packages to foreign investors.

As a country in which to live and work, Italy is considerably more complex, and is probably less well understood than many other European countries. Italy as a unified country did not exist until 1861 and most Italians have a regional loyalty before a national one. Long-established stereotypes of Italians are, as stereotypes usually are, mostly wrong, but they have had a trivialising and/or damaging effect on the world's view of Italy and Italians. According to popular caricature Italians eat vast quantities of pasta, and (if they are male) worship their mothers, pinch bottoms and sing Verdi in the street. The Mafia is also considered to run everything. The reality is somewhat different, not least because there are many different kinds of Italians. Although the sinister brotherhood's influence is pervasive in politics and commerce, the Mafia does not actually run

Italy. Mafia influence is, however, distinctly powerful in its traditional fiefdoms of Calabria, Naples and much of the island of Sicily. The Mafia indirectly makes it presence felt in other parts of Italy too, though to a much lesser extent.

The perception of Italy as a country of two parts has been enhanced in recent years by the leader of the Northern League (*Lega Nord*), Umberto Bossi, who has been calling for an independent state to be created in the north. The Lega Nord has gained up to 5% of the vote nationally and currently has three ministers in the government as it is part of the Berlusconi coalition. Though the likelihood of a split is remote, the differences between the north and south of Italy are marked. In the north the inhabitants are generally, more serious, industrious and prosperous, while the south, the *Mezzogiorno*, is traditionally poor, violent and ruled by the Mafia. However, it would be an error to write off the *Mezzogiorno* as an area in which to live and work, since the Italian government is offering huge financial incentives for foreign business interests investing in certain areas like Puglia, Molise, Campania and Abruzzi where in consequence, prosperity is increasing. SviluppoItalia (Agency for Economic and Entrepreneurial Development, ☎06 421 60939-43-45; investinitaly@sviluppo italia.it; www.sviluppoitalia.it) now run adverts highlighting the tax breaks and incentives available for investors in magazines like *The Economist* to attract new foreign investment.

PROS AND CONS OF MOVING TO ITALY

Those seeking employment or business opportunities in Italy will find that the country has much to offer: the presence of many major Italian and international companies offers a huge range of possibilities for employment and also opportunities for consultancy and other freelance work. There is a dynamism about northern Italian business people which puts some of their fellow Europeans to shame. However, Italians do not like to be hustled and will strictly observe the necessary social and business etiquette before clinching a deal. Italians work late but quite often mix commerce with pleasure: a working supper or weekend meetings with business colleagues being common occurrences. Though different to UK and North American business practices, many expatriates find that they adapt quickly to this style of business and find they enjoy the Italian working style when compared to those of other countries and enjoy working with Italians more than other nationalities. However, many will find the laid back style and apparently relaxed way of doing business frustrating, especially when it eats into evenings and weekends that are usually thought of as free time or family time.

Those who might be concerned that they are moving to a country where living standards and infrastructures leave a lot to be desired and where the government is inherently unstable will find only a few of their worst fears justified. Italy is a highly developed country where even the farmers have the latest model Lancia or Audi tucked away in a barn, and where workers know the exact market value of their skills in the work place. The Italian postal system, especially for internal services, was generally regarded as very inefficient, but in recent years has been completely modernized as has the telephone system and the Italians have embraced the mobile phone like no other nation. The national road system, which owes its origins to the Romans, Mussolini and in modern times, the charging of staggeringly high tolls, is one of the best in Europe. The much publicised fifty plus changes of government since the end of the Second World War, amount to little more than reshuffles as Italy was dominated by the same political party, the Christian Democrats, for fifty years. Ironically, this made Italy one of the more politically stable countries in Europe.

Pros:

o   There are favourable employment prospects for skilled workers and professionals.

o   Industry is very advanced and successful, particularly in the north of Italy.

o   The Italians have a strong economy that is paying dividends to foreign investors: many of the most profitable companies in Italy are foreign owned.

o   Housing and public transport are considerably cheaper than in the UK.

o   Managerial salaries are around 30-35% higher in Italy than in the UK.

o   The climate in most regions is marvellous and Italy has some of the most beautiful landscapes in Europe.

o   Italy has one of the greatest art and architectural heritages of any European country.

o   Italy has much to offer by way of lifestyle and living standards.

o   Italians are extremely receptive to foreigners.

Cons:

o   Knowledge of Italian is essential to conduct business in Italy as state bureaucrats and most Italian business people speak virtually no English.

o   Large parts of southern Italy are unsuitable for foreign business ventures thanks to the influence of the Mafia.

o   There are enormous differences in business practices between northern and southern Italy.

o   Italy has a Byzantine bureaucracy that is notorious for being a source of aggravation to both Italians and foreigners.

o   Start up costs for businesses in northern Italy can be horrendously high.

o   Employers pay very high employee social security contributions (as they do in much of Europe when compared to the USA and the UK).

o   Italian social behaviour and customs can seem totally at odds with the British and American way of doing things.

Italy has made well-advertised efforts to clean up politics in recent years by weeding out the corruptors and corrupted and prosecuting them where necessary and/or possible. Similarly, there has been a concerted move to bring the big Mafia bosses to trial and bang them up for long jail sentences. But the Mafia is a hydra-headed monster; cut off one head and two new ones grows in its place: apparently in some cases, Mafia women have been running things while the men folk are in jail.

One of the disadvantages for foreigners wishing to set up businesses, especially in northern Italy, is that costs are extremely high: office space and service costs etc. seem disproportionate to other factors, including official salary levels which are lower than in the UK and much lower than in the US. Actual levels of individual income are, can be hard to assess, as nowhere in Europe is the pastime of tax evasion practised with such verve, especially amongst small and individual business owners. Employees, who have tax deducted from the salary, and large companies are less likely to be able to fiddle their taxes. In the 1990s the Italian Inland Revenue estimated that nine out of ten taxpayers were dodging at least some of their dues. In part, such large-scale evasion derived from the fact that many Italians in the South of Italy have several jobs if they can manage it, as poverty is rife. However, unemployment there is a much bigger problem than tax evasion. So, while the level of salaries does not correspond to the otherwise obvious prosperity of many Italians, the fact is, they manage have more spending money than their counterparts in France and the UK. Admittedly, some aspects of life in Italy are cheaper than in the UK, notably excellent public transport, but affordable housing is greatly lacking in large towns and cities which causes problems for both foreigners and Italians.

Italy has a marvellous climate, which is a distinct advantage in the eyes of Britons contemplating setting up home there. However, the glorious cities which are a main attraction for tourists and foreign residents alike, often seem to be cared for indifferently by their citizens: traffic problems, pollution and a shortage of funds have all conspired to make many cities, even the historic ones, look dilapidated. Though with such an enormous heritage of art and architecture it is hardly surprising that there is insufficient money to cover the maintenance of all such treasures.

Moving from the UK to Italy inevitably involves some language problems. Unless you are already proficient in Italian it is essential to take an Italian course as otherwise you will be at a disadvantage in a country where business and social life are virtually intertwined. Furthermore, unlike some Europeans, notably the Scandinavians and Germans, Italians are not noted for their fluent grasp of English. While this situation has been remedied to certain extent by the inclusion of English in the school curriculum, it should nevertheless be unthinkable for foreigners to live in Italy without learning Italian.

HISTORY, POLITICS AND ECONOMIC STRUCTURE

History

There is not space here to do justice to Italian history, which is, in effect, the history of the former kingdoms, states and duchies that now make up Italy. However, it is necessary to have a basic knowledge of the country's recent past including *Il Risorgimento* (The Unification), in order to understand Italy and Italians today. It could be argued that the first proponent of a unified Italy was Napoleon I who, during the years of French occupation from 1796 to 1814, managed to set up a modern, meritocratic civil service regulated by the Code Napoléon. Unification proper took place in stages beginning with the annexation by Count Camillo Cavour (Italy's answer to Bismarck) of most of northern and central Italy during 1859 and 1860. Meanwhile the popular hero and guerrilla fighter, Giuseppe Garibaldi (1807-82) joined Cavour's Piedmontese northern alliance and conquered the entire south of Italy, which was then united with the north under the Piedmontese king, Vittorio Emanuele II. The remaining pieces of the Italian jigsaw, Veneto (the region around Venice) and Lazio (the region around Rome) were added in 1866 and 1870 respectively. During the process of Risorgimento the seat of government moved three times: until 1865 it was in Turin, followed by a six-year sojourn in Florence before finally settling in Rome in 1871.

In the aftermath of the First World War Italy was in a demoralised and confused state beset by crippling strikes, accompanied by a breakdown of law and order. There was the very real possibility of a communist revolution. Enter Benito Mussolini, a former socialist journalist, who managed to exploit fear of the communists on the part of the wealthy and middle classes sufficiently to win himself and his Fascist Party 35 seats in the 1921 Parliament. Later the same year the government collapsed and Mussolini staged his famous 'March on Rome' when, accompanied by 30,000 supporters known as *camicie nere* (blackshirts) he entered Parliament and convinced the government and the King that in the absence of any other competent powers he should be awarded outright dictatorship. The King and parliament agreed, initially for a one-year period, which in the event extended to 21 years of Fascist rule – much the same as the dictator Sulla did in Roman times. Under Mussolini the Italians were probably more organised than they have ever been since the Romans – an era constantly evoked in Mussolini's military iconography.

At home, Mussolini drained the Pontine Marshes, made the trains run on time, and instigated the Lateran Pact with the Vatican, thus creating a workable relationship between Church and State for the first time in Italian history. Abroad, the Italian Empire of East Africa was created following the shockingly brutal take over of Abyssinia in 1935. Mussolini contributed greatly to the restoration of national pride, at the expense of almost all civil liberties, but he managed to avoid most of the unspeakable excesses of the parallel regime in Germany. Italy was allied to Germany in 1939 when Mussolini signed the Pact of Steel with Hitler.

Following the collapse of his regime towards the end of the Second World War, Mussolini and the die-hard remnant of his supporters fled Rome, which fell to the Allies in 1943, and set up the Independent Republic of Salò in the northeast corner of Italy. The Mussolini era was brought to an ignominious end on April 28, 1945 when 'Il Duce' was captured and executed by partisans and hung upside down alongside his mistress, Claretta Petacci, and his leading supporters from a lamp post in Milan's busiest square, the *Piazza Loreto*. The fact that Mussolini was executed by Italian freedom fighters and that Italy suffered Nazi occupation, meant that she was not penalised nearly as much as Germany after the War; a fact that contributed greatly to the rebirth of national pride.

In May 1946 Italy held a national referendum to decide whether to retain the monarchy or institute a republic. The republic won and the last king of Italy, Umberto II, went submissively into exile. Elections followed for the Constituent Assembly whose function was to decide what kind of constitution Italy would have, and then draw it up. Two years later, in 1948, the first parliamentary elections of the new republic saw the Christian Democrats romp home to victory and begin their lengthy domination of parliament which lasted for almost 50 years until their demise, mainly through corruption scandals, in 1994.

POLITICAL STRUCTURE

At the pinnacle of the state is the President of the Republic, who also controls the armed forces and the Judiciary and is elected for a seven-year term by both chambers, plus 58 regional representatives. Next in the hierarchy is the President of the Senate and third comes the President of the Chamber of Deputies. The powers of the President, currently Carlo Azeglio Ciampi, correspond approximately to those of the British monarch, i.e. they are mainly ceremonial and include dissolving parliaments, approving or vetoing the appointing of Prime Ministers and the signing or vetoing of new laws. The seat of government is in Rome, the capital of Italy. Parliament is made up of two chambers, the *Camera dei Deputati* (Chamber of Deputies) and the *Senato* (Senate). Since neither of these chambers takes precedence over the other, frequent conflicts over parliamentary bills are the norm. The *Camera dei Deputati* comprises 630 members housed in the *Palazzo di Montecitorio*. The *Senato* meanwhile occupies another building, the *Palazzo Madama*, and has around 326 members some of whom are elected for life. Proceedings in both chambers are generally conducted less boisterously than in the notoriously noisy House of Commons in the UK. Women made up 9.2% of members in both houses after the 2001 election, which is less than after the 1996 election.

The Italian voting system is immensely complicated, involving hundreds of candidates per electoral region. Since most of the candidates are unknown to the voters, a system has evolved whereby major political figures put forward their names for several constituencies simultaneously and then stand down in favour of lesser-known candidates allowing them to sail home on their votes. This is perfectly legal and readily employed.

The proportional representation system has been gradually reduced so that nowadays, three quarters of candidates are chosen on a first past the post system and the rest by proportional representation. In the past, proportional representation has meant an average of around twenty-five parties being represented in Parliament, so Italy can only be ruled by a coalition of parties who are broadly banded into centre-left or centre-right groupings. After the 2001 election 15 parties were elected to the senate and chamber of deputies. They were mainly grouped into two coalitions, The House of Freedoms (*Casa delle Liberta*) and Olive Tree (*L'Ulivo*).

The fashion of adopting celebrity candidates is, like many things Italian, done more flamboyantly than elsewhere, for example the election of the porno-actress Ilona Staller ('*La Cicciolina*') – somehow Glenda Jackson and Clint Eastwood do not have quite the same ring! Alessandra Mussolini, niece of Sophia Loren, granddaughter of Benito Mussolini, and glamorous but forceful politician, was elected as an MP for Naples and Ischia in 1992. She was for a time a front member of the right wing *Alleanza Nationale* from which she broke away to form her own party *Alternativa Sociale* which gained about 2% in the last regional elections. As well as celebrity candidates, Italy also has extreme left and right wing parties which are basically communist and fascist; these parties (e.g. the neo-Fascist *Alleanza Nationale, Lega Nord*) are sometimes part of the government.

Italy changes Prime Minister approximately once every nine months. This pattern changed after the 2001 election won by Silvio Berlusconi. Berlusconi, who leads the Forza Italia has lasted longer than any of his post-war predecessors have done. He resigned in April 2005 because he lost the local elections and wanted to test his majority in Parliament and to know if he could stay in power to the end of his term (May 2006). A few days after resigning he reformed his government after shuffling a few ministers around.

Political Parties

Foreign observers of Italian politics usually find it difficult to spot any discernible differences between many of the political parties. In common with many highly developed countries, Italy has experienced the increasing prosperity of the once poorer classes, which has resulted in a corresponding decrease in extremism that once characterised the leftist parties. In Italy this means that the *Partito Comunista*

Italiano (Italian Communist Party) has all but ceased to exist. In the early 1990s when it splintered three ways into the DS Democratic Left (20% of the vote), Rifondazione Comunista (8% of the vote) and the rump Comunisti Italiani (only 2% of the vote). As demonstrated, Italian political parties tend to splinter into *correnti* (factions), which gravitate around the more powerful political leaders. Therefore, to achieve any kind of political power, tactical manoeuvring of the most Machiavellian kind is required. Strategic alliances are formed and broken on purely opportunistic grounds. The lengths to which party leaders will go to win the loyalty of the local electorate, particularly in the South, deepens the opacity of Italian politics.

Italian political parties are funded to a staggering extent by the state. In 1999 the Italian parliament voted in a new law that provides a subsidy of approximately US$2 per voter, that is divided among political parties who received more than 1% of the vote in the last election. With such funds the political support of whole southern villages and communities could be bought on the promise of extra jobs through the creation of an entirely useless state office or wing of a hospital for which fictitious wages and even false pensions will be paid. This system known as voto di scambio (votes in exchange) has been greatly reduced since the end of the Christian Democrat era about a decade ago. After the 2001 election, two main coalitions were elected:

The House of Freedoms (Casa delle Liberta) Coalition: led by Silvio Berlusconi and his *Forza Italia* party, it gained 177 seats in the senate and 368 seats in the Chamber of deputies. The coalition included the following parties:

Forza Italia (Forwards Italy). As a young party, with a businessman as its leader, it remains to be seen how *Forza Italia* will develop. In its own words *Forza Italia* is: '...a party with a very simple name. Its substance is to be 'the people's party', the party of those with goodwill and common sense, the party of the Italians who love other people as well as their own country, the party of the Italians who love freedom. *Forza Italia*: force of freedom.

Alleanza Nazionale (National Alliance). Formed when the *Movimento Sociale Italiano* (MSI) was dismantled in 1994. The MSI was a Neo-Fascist party founded just after the Second World War. There has always been a certain amount of nostalgia for Il Duce (Mussolini) and the recruitment of Alessandra Mussolini, his granddaughter, to party ranks helped turn the fortunes of the MSI around as did its new name the *Alleanza Nazionale*. The old MSI-DN also included sympathisers of the deposed Bourbon royal dynasty and some right-wing thuggery in the form of extremist youth movements. They now have a credible leader in the smooth-talking Gianfranco Fini. The Alleanza Nazionale has been trying (with some success) to drop its neo-fascist image – Alessandra Mussolini left the party to start her own and Gianfranco Fini has been sent to Israel a few times as foreign minister and has been a fierce supporter of the Bush administration and the war in Iraq.

Lega Nord (Northern League). In the May 1990 local elections, a new political party of the right, the Lega Lombarda was voted in. Other similar regional parties in northern Italy, notably the Lega Veneta, did not do as well but these two have now combined into the Lega Nord. The Lega Nord and other right wing political organisations throughout Europe attract a disproportionate amount of publicity and probably does not represent a marked increase in extreme right wing support. In the 2001 elections *Lega Nord* support was sufficient for them to wind up as part of the Berlusconi coalition and they have three ministers in government.

Centro Cristiano Democratico (Christian Democratic Center). Formed by splitting away from the old Christian Democrat party just as it was crumbling in the wake of the massive corruption scandals in the early 1990s. Nominally a Catholic party, the Christian Democrats took a hard line on abortion and divorce (both of which had been already legal for about two decades) but a liberal line on most other issues including the treatment of terrorists. It has about 5% of the vote.

Partito Socialista Italiano (Socialist Party). The Socialist Party is no such thing, being vehemently right wing and incorrigibly corrupt. When he was leader of the party, Bettino Craxi was Prime Minister for four years. The SPI has historically received about 14% of the national vote but a disproportionate share (30%) of the administration. Therefore it was able to manipulate the Christian Democrats which needed the co-operation of the PSI to stay in power. Its power has since waned and it currently gets about 2% of the vote.

The Olive Tree (L'Ulivo) Coalition: led by Romano Prodi, former prime minister and EU President and pretender to Berlusconi's crown, this main opposition grouping gained 125 seats in the senate and 242 in the Chamber of Deputies. The coalition included the following parties:

Partito Democratico della Sinistra (Democrats of the Left). This is the former *Partito Comunista Italiano* (Italian Communist Party). The PDS was the traditional main opposition party, but during the years of Italian prosperity has become the virtual equivalent of the Christian Democrats except that it portrays itself as the (only) party free from corruption. Its main base and spiritual home is the supremely wealthy city of Bologna. The PDS won 34% of the votes in 1976 (when it was still the PCI) and in 1997 was the single biggest party in the 'Ulivo' (Olive Tree) government of Romano Prodi. In the 2001 election their percentage of the vote dropped to 16.6% – the second largest percentage in the election.

La Margherita is a grouping of four centre left parties, which are: *Partito Popolare Italiano* (Italian People's Party), *I Democratici* (Democrats), *Rinnovamento Italiano* (Italian Renovation) and *Unione Democratici per l'Europa* (Democratic

Union for Europe). These parties themselves are made up of separate groups from various cities around Italy.

Partito dei Comunisti Italiani (Italian Communists Party). Founded on October 11, 1998, the party is made up of members who split from the *Rifondazione Communista* for ideological and political reasons.

I Verdi (Greens). The Greens and the Rainbow Greens (*Verdi-Arcobaleno*) merged to form the Federazione dei Verdi and have seats in both the Italian Parliament and the European Parliament. The Greens are gaining popularity in Europe, especially Italy and Germany where they have been part of both governments.

Partito Socialdemocratico Italiano (Italian Democratic Socialists). With very little going for them political, the party is, however, notoriously adept at buying votes – to the tune of 3% of the electorate.

Outside of the two coalitions, the Communist Refocundation Party (PRC), led by Fausto Bertinotti also won 3 seats in the Senate and 11 in the Chamber of Deputies. The *Rifondazione Communista* is a hard line leftist party which formed part of the centre-left coalition of Romano Prodi's 'Ulivo' government elected in the early summer of 1996. *The Radical Party*, led by Emma Bonino lost the one seat they held in the senate as did the *Fiamma Tricolore* led by Pino Rauti.

ECONOMY

Italy's post-war economic aims are to a large extent responsible for today's massive division between north and south. The powers of the time decided to open up Italy's economy and go for an international export market rather than concentrate on restructuring production for self-sufficiency at home. This was about the extent to which the Italians went to plan a post-war economy and up until quite recent times policy in this area can best be summed up as *laissez-faire*. In other words, production was allowed to rally to the demands of the open market with virtually no controls or restraints. Such an economic 'policy' was to a great extent dictated by circumstances, namely that Italy possesses few of the resources (e.g. iron, coal & oil) essential for most industrial processes. Italy's main markets have traditionally been Western Europe and North America. Rather than pour money into quickly modernising agricultural production methods, which would have resulted in mass unemployment in the south, most resources were directed into expanding the industries of the north. As agriculture slowly modernised and therefore required a smaller labour force, the unemployed farm-workers of the south were used as a cheap source of labour for the expanding factories of the north – which helped offset the cost of importing the resources necessary for the manufacturing processes.

The years between 1958 and 1962 were years of thriving economic growth for Italy. However, with their economy so closely linked with the USA, the lira, which was pegged at 625 per dollar until 1971, collapsed along with the whole system of fixed exchange rates when America devalued the dollar. Italy's economy stayed weak up to the beginning of the 1980s and Italy was well known as the poorest of Western European countries. In the 1980s the economy took off again at breakneck speed. However, there was a downside to the rapid economic growth. As a result of having had no clear discernible economic policy for years, the national debt had now grown to the extent that it exceeded Gross Domestic Product and stood at 123% of GDP. By raising VAT (sales tax) rates in 1997 and exercising great budget discipline, which verged on austerity measures, the budget deficit, which was running at 6%, was reduced to 2.8% and Italy managed to meet the strict requirements of the European Union for entry into European Monetary Union.

Italy's economy grew faster than most others in Europe in 2000 and early 2001, but its growth had stopped by the middle of 2001. The growth in the economy has raised the per capita GDP to around US$21,000, but this figure is misleading as to the general wealth of the country because of the disparity between the north and south of the country. This slowdown, coupled with increased public spending (big pay rises for public servants) and a cut in income taxes in 2005, means that the budget deficit for 2005 will rise to 3.8%, which is above the EU guidelines for Eurozone members. Berlusconi's government specializes in providing a lot of fluff but few hard details on how they will fulfil their election promises and it remains to be seen how the Italian economy will cope. GDP growth is predicted to rise to just under 2% in 2006.

Stringent budgets are the solution to one of Italy's economic problems and the Berlusconi government has been forced into a modicum of crisis management in this direction, but there is another great problem. The workforce of the north is highly motivated (some say by runaway hedonism) which makes it an excellent area of Europe for those thinking of living and working abroad. In economic terms, Italy claims to have done better at reducing its budget deficit than either France or Germany – though this seems to be an optimistic claim. If it were true about the budget deficit, then it means that Italy is in a better state to succeed in the single currency than either France or Germany, which does not bode well for the euro. However, such a claim is belied by the enormous national debt, 9% unemployment and the enormous drain on government resources caused by the demands of welfare system. Also, in the ten years to 2000 the Italian GDP was the slowest growing (in percentage terms) when compared to the USA, UK, Spain, France and Germany. The only good news was that Italy reduced inflation from double figures at the end of 1980s to around 2% in the mid 1990s, though it is now back up to 2.2% – higher than the EU average.

One factor that is not usually taken into account when assessing the state of the Italian economy is the amount of revenue lost through tax evasion. This is despite the fact that taxation accounts for approximately 43.4% of GDP

– second only to France at 44.2% and compared to the US at 25.4%. One of the most recent targets of the tax authorities has been Italians living abroad who are suspected of fiddling the residence criteria to avoid paying the motherland's taxes. The Italian tax authorities also have to power to levy taxes on perceived wealth – such as the Ferrari parked in the garage of a poor tradesman.

Milan is the home of the Italian stock market (Consiglio Di Borsa, Plazza degli Affari 6, Milan, Italy 21033; ☎ 39-2-724-26-336; fax 39-2-724-26-336; www. borsaitalia.it) and therefore Italy's financial capital. The Milan stock market (*la borsa*) is small, with only 278 companies listed in 2005, compared with 2,500 in London and over 3,000 in New York (including 400 non-US companies). The Italian *borsa* has been run for decades by the same families and insider dealing was legal until quite recently. Italian stockbrokers are doubtful that recent legislation against insider dealing will be effective against a practice that is so engrained and difficult to prove. Italian companies also tend to be much smaller than their European and US counterparts – of the top 500 European companies only 7% are Italian.

The 'borsa' was privatised in 1997 under Italy's big sell off of state assets and from 1998 the government attempted to entice small companies to be quoted by offering generous tax incentives, as well as encouraging larger companies to reinvest profits in the market by cutting tax on them by nearly 50%.

Securities trading companies are known as *Societa di Intermediadiazone Mobiliare* (SIM) and are the sole stock market intermediaries.

Italy in the Future

Despite the difficulties with its economy already mentioned above and a decline in Italians' optimism about their future, the country continues to attract a steady amount of foreign investment and to encourage business and commerce in the regions through its Sviluppo Italia programme. The amounts of foreign investment are however miniscule compared to the UK which attracts around 30% of all inward EU investment. Italian economists have traditionally been pessimistic; in their view the economy was like the Titanic – heading full steam toward disaster. This is probably why the Italians were so enthusiastic about European monetary union and the stabilising effect of the European Union generally. There is no doubt that government faces economic problems including a large amount of debt and the fact that one mainstay of the economy, the Italian fashion industry, has been greatly undermined by the upsurge of designers in countries which have traditionally bought Italian clothes (i.e. Germany). The undercutting of the fashion market by designers who have clothes made up in the Far East will continue to be problematic for the Italian economy and the opening up of Chinese textile products has been disastrous to the Italian textile industry. But some of the old problems have at last been tackled: lack of transparency and the massive bureaucracy have both been improved; corruption possibly less so. However, Italy still imports 80% of its oil while having voted in a national referendum to phase out the entire Italian nuclear power programme. Also, the separation between the highly developed north and the poor south will continue to be exacerbated by the ongoing economic success of the north at the expense of the south, unless action to encourage investors (both foreign and domestic) to look at areas they have previously discounted continues to show progress.

GEOGRAPHICAL INFORMATION

Mainland and Offshore Italy

Italy occupies an area of 116,000 square miles (301,278 sq km). As well as the long peninsula which, as most schoolchildren learn, is shaped like a boot, Italy's offshore elements include the island of Sicily situated off the toe of the boot across the Strait of Messina, the islands of Pantelleria, Linosa and Lampedusa which lie between Sicily and Tunisia, the island of Elba located off Tuscany, and the rocky, barren island of Sardinia which lies west of Rome and south of Corsica. The Tyrrhenian Sea bounds the south west of the peninsula, with the Ionian Sea under the sole of the boot. The Adriatic Sea lies on the eastern side between Italy and former-Yugoslavia. Italy shares borders with France, Switzerland, Austria and Slovenia.

Main physical features include the Alps, which form much of the northern border with Slovenia, Austria, Switzerland and France. Also in the north are Italy's main lakes: Garda, Maggiore and Como. An offshoot of the Alps curves round the Gulf of Genoa and runs spine-like down the peninsula to form the Appenines. The longest river, the Po, lies in the north and flows from west to east across the plain of Lombardy and into the Adriatic. On Sicily, the still active volcano, Mount Etna rises to 10,741 feet (3,274 m). Etna has been very active during 2001 and some experts were predicting a major eruption.

Earthquakes & Volcanoes The European fault line runs right through Italy from north to south. The main risk areas for quakes are central and southern Italy where about 70% of the region is susceptible. Tremors are quite common in Umbria and the Appenines. Seismologists claim that the number, strength and frequency of quakes hitting central Italy is increasing. Following an earthquake there is usually a drop in tourism and house buying by foreigners. Over 2000 minor tremors a year occur in Italy, the majority of them below Magnitude 4 (on a scale of 10). Italy's last epic earthquake flattened Messina in 1908, killing 84,000 people and causing the shoreline to sink by half a metre overnight. Other serious ones were Friuli (1976), Irpinia (1980), and Umbria (1997) – the most memorable recent quake caused severe damage to the Church of Asissi in front of the television cameras.

As if this were not geological excitement enough, Italy has three well-known active volcanoes. The most famous of these is Vesuvius near Naples, which buried 2,000 inhabitants in their hedonistic city of Pompeii in AD79. These days the volcano's rumblings are under continuous monitoring so there should be plenty of warning before it pops again. The other volcanoes are off the mainland: Etna on Sicily and Stromboli on a small island off the western coast of southern Italy. Up-to-date information on seismicity in Italy can be found at the US Geological Survey site (www.neic.usgs.gov/neis/world/italy/).

REGIONAL DIVISIONS

For administrative purposes Italy is divided into twenty regions, five of which have special autonomy, 106 provinces and more than 8000 comunes. The regions (listed northwest to south) and their respective provinces are as follows:

AOSTA VALLEY (Val d'Aosta) Aosta.
PIEDMONT (PIEMONTE) – Alessandria, Asti, Biella, Cuneo, Novara, Torino, Verbano-Cusio-Ossola.
LOMBARDIA (LOMBARDY) – Bergamo, Brescia, Como, Cremona, Lecco, Lodi, Mantova, Milano, Pavia, Sondrio, Varese.
TRENTINO-ALTO-ADIGE – Bolzano, Trento.
VENETO – Belluno, Padova (Padua), Rovigo, Treviso, Venezia (Venice), Vicenza, Verona.
FRIULI-VENEZIA GIULIA – Gorizia, Pordenone, Trieste, Udine.
LIGURIA – Genova, (Genoa), Imperia, La Spezia, Savona.
EMILIA ROMAGNA – Bologna, Ferrara, Forli-Cesena, Modena, Parma, Piacenza, Ravenna, Reggio Emilia, Rimini.
TUSCANY (TOSCANA) – Arezzo, Firenze (Florence), Grosseto, Livorno, Lucca, Massa-Carrara, Pisa, Pistoia, Prato, Siena.
UMBRIA – Perugia, Terni.
MARCHE - Ancona, Ascoli-Piceno, Macerata, Pesaro-Urbino.
LAZIO – Frosinone, Latina, Rieti, Roma, Viterbo.
ABRUZZO – L'Aquila, Chieti, Pescara, Teramo.
MOLISE – Campobasso, Isernia.
CAMPANIA – Avellino, Benevento, Caserta, Napoli (Naples), Salerno.
PUGLIA (APULIA) – Bari, Brindisi, Foggia, Lecce, Taranto.
BASILICATA – Matera, Potenza.
CALABRIA – Catanzaro, Cosenza, Crotone, Reggio Calabria, Vibo Valentia.
SICILY (SICILIA) – Agrigento, Caltanissetta, Catania, Enna, Messina, Palermo, Ragusa, Siracusa, Trapani.
SARDINIA (SARDEGNA) – Cagliari, Nuoro, Oristano, Sassari (and four new provinces Sulcis-Iglesiente (main town Iglesias), Medio Campidano (main town Sanluri, Ogliastra (main town Lanusei) and Gallura (Ollbia).

Population

Italy's population numbers approximately 58.1 million, a little less than that of the UK and approximately a quarter of the US. However, the Italians have more elbow room than Britons with 190 persons per square km compared with 232 in the UK. Until the 1980s Italy had been a country of emigration rather than immigration. The waves of emigration were: from the 1890s to 1930s to Argentina and the United States; from the 1950s to 1970s to Australia, Canada, Germany and Switzerland. From the end of communism around 1989 there has been huge immigration into Italy from old Eastern Bloc countries. Surprisingly for a country traditionally associated with large families, Italy has one of the lowest birth rates in Europe with many couples choosing not to have children and those that do having a single child. This low birth rate and restrictions on immigration from outside the EU has led to fears that the population will shrink so much that there will be a severe labour shortage in the future that will ruin the economy.

Immigration from outside the EU. Already, the population includes a large number of immigrants; some are from ex-colonies, including Somalia, Libya and Eritrea. Most of the immigrants have arrived within the last twenty years as a result of Italy's liberal entry regulations. These have, however, been tightened up under the Schengen Agreement because of fears from other EU countries that Italy would become a stepping stone for massive numbers of immigrants. There are also significant numbers of Eastern Europeans, Filipinos and Brazilians in the country. There is no official census of the number of immigrants, though around half a million have arrived through official channels. The majority of immigrants remain illegal (aided by Italy's 8000 km long and difficult to patrol coastline) and the vicinity of Italy to the coasts of Albania and Tunisia. The total number is believed to exceed two million. Naples now has a large African population while Rome has become home to a wide variety of ethnological backgrounds amongst its population of nearly four million. The most recent influx of immigrants and refugees to Italy has come from the stricken country of Albania. An estimated 200,000 Albanians have entered Italy both legally and illegally, amongst them a ruthless criminal element, who are rumoured to be more deadly than the Mafia whom they are replacing in some areas, particularly Milan.

THE POPULATIONS OF THE OTHER LARGEST ITALIAN CITIES	
City	**Population**
Milano	1,724,557,
Napoli (Naples)	1,214,775.
Torino (Turin)	1,181,698,
Palermo	996,000,

Genova (Genoa)	787,011,
Bologna	493,282,
Firenze (Florence)	441,654,
Venice	305,000,
Verona	255,000

States within the State

Within its borders Italy contains three micro sovereign states, the most famous of which is the Vatican City; no less arcane, but wielding considerably less temporal power, are San Marino and the Knights of Malta. Each of these three states has its own government, head of state and car licence plates:

The Vatican City: The Vatican City (area: 116 acres; population: 730;), has been a sovereign state since the Middle Ages, but was reduced to its current miniscule plot within the boundaries of Rome when it was conquered by the newly formed Kingdom of Italy in 1870. It signed an agreement with the Italian state in 1929 and established formal diplomatic relations between the two states. Its high walls enclose all the apparatus of a mini-state: the secret archives, Radio Vatican, Vatican Television, the Vatican bank, the Vatican Museums, the Vatican Newspaper (*L'Osservatore Romano*) and a legion of staff including accountants, Swiss Guards, Vatican Police, the Palatine Guard and even its own football league made up of teams from each of these. It is small wonder that the Vatican is considered to be less of a spiritual entity than a political one, the Catholic Church being as faction ridden as any Italian political party. During a period of liberalisation in the sixties and seventies under popes John XXIII and Paul VI many intellectuals of a progressive outlook were elected to positions of power in the Church and its associated lay organisations such as the *Azione Cattolica*. This move towards liberalization has been firmly stamped on by the two most recent popes for whom conservative is probably an understatement and their 'presage-of-doom' view of mankind's future need no further elaboration here.

Saint Peter's Church and parts of the Papal Palace designated Vatican Museums are open to the public and the website is www.vatican.va.

San Marino: The largest of the micro states, San Marino covers an area of 24 square miles (61 square kilometres) and has a population of 28,500. It is well-known for its large and colourful postage stamps and big losses in international football matches. San Marino lies between the regions of Emilia Romagna and Marche about fifteen miles inland from Rimini and has been in existence since the Middle Ages.

The Knights of Malta: The Knights have several enclaves which, like the Vatican City, are located within the boundaries of Rome. The venerable Knights are an international brotherhood led by a Grand Master who is seventy-eighth in a line dating back to the Middle Ages. The KOM website is www.orderofmalta.org.

AVERAGE TEMPERATURES				
City & Province	Jan °F/°C	Apr °F/°C	July °F/°C	Nov °F/°C
Ancona (Marche)	42/6	56/14	77/25	55/13
Bari(Puglia)	46/8	57/14	77/25	59/15
Bologna (Emilia Romagna)	37/3	56/15	78/26	50/10
Florence (Tuscany)	42/6	55/13	77/25	52/11
Genova (Liguria)	46/8	56/14	77/25	55f/13
Milan (Lombardy)	36/2	55/13	77/25	48/9
Naples (Campania)	48/9	56/14	77/25	59/15
Palermo(Sicily)	50/10	61/16	77/25	50/16
Rome (Latium)	45/7	57/14	78/26	55/13
Trieste (Friuli-Venezia)	41/5	55/13	75/25	52/11
Venice (Venetia)	39/4	55/13	75/24	52/10

Climatic Zones

The climate of Italy shows the kind of regional variation one would expect from a country with its head in the Alps and its toe in the Mediterranean. At the foot of the Alps in the north is the flat and fertile Plain of Po, which is also one of the main industrial areas. Cold and wet in winter, those who find themselves living and working in the north can escape to different climatic regions to rejuvenate themselves. There are the cold, dry Alps further northwards for winter sports. The Italian Riviera (Liguria), which is pleasantly mild in winter. Or there is the south, including Sicily, where the winters are even milder and typically Mediterranean. In summer and winter, the middle regions of Tuscany and Umbria, which are home to many expatriates, have the best of both worlds: neither too cold in winter nor too parched in summer. However, the higher areas of even these favoured regions can be cold and snowbound in winter. The far south and Sicily are generally considered too hot for comfort in summer.

REGIONAL GUIDE

Historically, Italy as a unified country has existed for little more than a hundred and thirty-seven years. Before the *Risorgimento* (unification) the whole region was a collection of city-states, kingdoms, duchies and the republics of Venice, Naples, Lombardy, Florence, Piedmont and Sicily. The result of such a relatively recent union is that Italians have not really had time to adjust to the concept of national identity and instead consider themselves Neapolitan, Piedmontese etc., and only Italian as an afterthought. This regionalism is expressed by the word *campanilismo*, from the word for a bell-tower (i.e. a village). Thus, in a slightly derogatory way, Italians express their obsession with discussing the finer points of the differences in character and culture of the inhabitants of the many different regions that make up the country.

In view of the separate historical development of the Italian regions it comes as little surprise that not only do the customs and outlook vary considerably amongst them, but also the language spoken. Dialects abound in every province and are a source of pride to Italians as a way of defining their identity.

In France and Spain there are areas favoured by expatriates who are looking to set up a second home or a permanent one if they are retired. This is no less true of Italy where hilltop dwellings in Tuscany and more recently Umbria, have been selling steadily to the Brits, the Dutch, Swedes and Germans, among others. Professional expatriates with full-time jobs are, on the other hand, more likely to find themselves based in the bigger cities: Milan, Florence, Genoa, Turin, Naples or the capital, Rome. It is, however, becoming more common for expatriates to find themselves in almost any city from Como to Cagliari.

Information Sources

An excellent starting point for information is the national Italian tourist organisation *ENIT* which supplies free maps and brochures and can provide information on everything from how to get an audience with the Pope to where to go for Italian courses. The ENIT website (www.enit.it) provides much information, in a number of languages or you can e-mail italy@italiantouristboard.co.uk. In Italy itself every regional capital city has its own tourist board called either: *Azienda Promozione Turistica (APT)*. For specialist maps such as the large-scale road maps or maps for hiking, contact Stanfords (address below).

Useful Addresses & Website

*Ente Nazionale Italiano per il Turismo (ENIT):*1 Princes Street, London W1R 8AY; ☎020-7408 1254; fax 020-7399 3567; e-mail italy@italiantourist board.co.uk; www.enit.it.

Ente Nazionale Italiano per il Turismo (ENIT): 630 Fifth Avenue, Suite 1565, 10111 New York, USA; ☎212 245 5618/245 4822; fax 212 586 9249.

Italia.gov.it: Italian government portal *(Il Portale Nationale del Cittadino),* to all kinds of information from Italian petrol prices, regional information and job opportunities.

Stanfords: 12 Long Acre, Covent Garden, London WC2 9LP; ☎020-7836 1321; fax 020-7836 1321; e-mail sales@stanfords.co.uk; www.stanfords.

co.uk. Perhaps the best-known map and travel book shop in London.

Touring Club Italy: www.touringclub.it. Non-profit organization with half a million members. Has excellent maps and excellent guides in English.

THE NORTH WEST

Regions: Piedmont, Lombardy, Liguria, Val d'Aosta.

Main cities: Turin, Genoa, Aosta, Milan.

In the north west corner of Italy the two regions of Piedmont (Piemonte) and Val d'Aosta are probably the two least Italianate; at least to foreigners with the Tuscan or Mediterranean idyll in mind) regions of Italy. Tiny Val d'Aosta is wedged between France and Switzerland and is a mountainous, bilingual (in French and Italian) area. Peaks picturesquely ring the regional capital, Aosta, and as you would expect ski resorts are plentiful.

Until the end of the nineteenth century the Piemontese were also French-speaking. In the eleventh century Umberto Bianca-mano founded the kingdom of Savoy-Piedmont, which included the Val d'Aosta. Unfortunately situated on the invasion route from France, the kingdom suffered its fair share of intrusions over the years. However, a successful swipe at the French on their way to Lombardy to fight the War of the Spanish succession enhanced the prestige of Duke Vittorio Amadeo II of Savoy-Piedmont, who not only gained Sicily but was also elevated to kingship at the Treaty of Utrecht (1714). Turin (Torino), the main regional city, has the distinction of being at the centre of the drive for Italian unity and was home to the first Italian Parliament in 1861 when unification of the greater part of Italy had been achieved. The giant automotive corporation FIAT (*Fabbrica Italiana di Automobili Torino*) and Olivetti have their headquarters in Turin; the former company since its founding in 1899. The Turin area is also famous for its good quality wines particularly Barolo and Barbera, and the internationally known aperitifs Cinzano and Martini, which are produced there. Wealthy Turin is not immediately attractive as a place to live and work, but it is handy for the Alps, France and the Italian Riviera and much less atmospherically polluted than Milan.

Throughout history Lombardy has dominated northern Italy and continues to do so. Not only is it the most commercially and industrially successful area but it is also the country's financial powerhouse. It is the most heavily populated region of the country with 9,347,456 (August 2004) inhabitants, many of them workers from the south. The heavily industrialised area around Milan produces around 40% of Italy's GNP and Milan is easily the most expensive and luxurious city in the country. Historically, Lombardy is one of the great battlefields of Europe – most noticeably perhaps during the Thirty Years War (1618-48), when the French, Spanish and Austrians were simultaneously rampaging over the landscape in a dispute over Valtellina. The resulting privations led to a long period of economic decline in Lombardy, which was reversed in the more constructive period of the eighteenth century. This welcome respite from war lasted until the return of the French under Bonaparte in 1796, which culminated in his coronation as King of Italy in Milan (1805). Following Napoleon's defeat, the Kingdom of Lombardy-Venetia was absorbed into the Austrian Empire until the unification of the greater part of Italy with Piedmont was achieved in 1861.

The Liguria region, also called the Italian Riviera is a coastal strip that follows on eastwards from the French Riviera and is centred on the ancient trading port of Genova (Genoa) which was one of the five great maritime republics of Italy in the thirteenth century. Successively invaded by the French and the Austrians during the seventeenth and eighteenth centuries, the port of Genoa suffered progressive economic decline. During the period leading up to the Unification, the area became a haven for political refugees and the popular hero of the Italian liberation movement, Garibaldi (1807-82), came from the region. In the nineteenth and twentieth centuries an economic resurgence in the form of heavy industry made Genoa Italy's third most important industrial centre. Its fortunes have since taken a nosedive with the decline of heavy industries like steel production, thus forcing many of the region's one million, seven hundred thousand inhabitants to move to other areas of Italy in search of work.

The majority of the foreign business community in Italy are based in the north, particularly Milan, rather than Rome as one might expect. Though there is a large expatriate community in Rome, including many diplomats, as can be seen from the number of International schools there. Those who live in the north and can afford it may have a city flat and a weekend house at one of the nearby lakes.

THE NORTH EAST

Regions: Trentino Alto-Adige, Veneto, Friuli-Venezia-Giulia, Emilia Romagna.
Main Towns: Bolzano, Trent, Udine, Trieste, Cortina, Verona, Venice, Parma, Ferrara, Bologna, Ravenna.
The first two of these regions contain the beautiful scenery of the Dolomite mountains, which run along the north-eastern edge of Italy and form a natural border with Austria. Justly famed for its wine producing qualities, this landscape is usually only visited by foreigners in search of mountain holidays, notably winter sports. Trentino-Alto Adige was part of the Austrian Empire until 1918 and German is still spoken there. The large autonomous region of Alto Adige has a German majority and linguistic squabbling between German and Italian speakers in the region is an on-going source of tension there. Ethnic Germans aggrieved that they were 'Italianised' by Mussolini, while rival factions like the Ladins, who claim their origins and language go back to the Romans, want their Italian lan-

guage rights protected. The result is that place names are in Italian and German. The region has a population of around 800,000.

Friuli-Venezia Giulia, which has a population of just over a million, also came within the ambit of the Habsburgs in the nineteenth century. Later, in the chaotic aftermath of the Second World War it was partitioned between Italy and Yugoslavia. The last dispute between the two countries over the area was not settled until the 1970s. As a legacy of its turbulent history the region is ethnically mixed and more eastern European than typically Italian. Trieste is the regional capital and projects into Slovenia and does not have the appearance of an Italian city at all. Historically, Trieste was one of three great cities of the Austro-Hungarian Empire – Vienna and Prague being the other two. These days it is being revitalised by a more open Europe and is being increasingly used as a base within the EU to do business with Slovenia, Croatia and the Czech and Slovak Republics. The main problem of Trieste is that the majority of its population are elderly people. However, positioned as it is, Trieste will have plenty of opportunity to reinvent itself.

The Veneto region is one of the undisputed treasure houses of Europe. In addition to Venice, the cities of Verona, Vicenza and Padua are also of great cultural interest. By the year 1000, Venice had become powerful in the region through commerce and maritime prowess, which enabled her to be the main conduit for trade between Europe and the Orient. This supremacy lasted until the mid-thirteenth century when the Black Death swept across Europe. In the twelfth century, when the German Kings were making unrealisitic claims to the Veneto, the first Hohenstaufen Emperor, Barbarossa (red beard) had already conquered Milan. Then the Trevisan League of cities, with Venice at their head, routed his army and negotiated with Barbarossa to be the sole supplier of the imperial armies on their future sorties in Italy. During the fifteenth century, the existence of Venice was threatened by the rival state of Genoa. These being two great maritime republics, the contest naturally took place on the seas and resulted in victory for the Venetians. Venice reached its *terra firma* limits with the conquests of Brescia and Bergamo in the first half of the fifteenth century. The long decline of Venetian greatness was heralded by the fall of Constantinople (1453) with whose fortunes those of Venice were inextricably linked. During the sixteenth century the policy of the Venetian Republic proceeded along defensive lines, treading a delicate path of diplomacy amongst the expansionist powers of the time – the Hapsburg Empire and France. There was also the added irritant of political interference by the Pope. However, by far the main threat to the Venetians were the Turks, who were in the process of usurping the supremacy of Venetian trading interests. It was this struggle, principally a maritime one, which gradually enfeebled Venice and left a vacuum for the ascendancy of the old archival, Genoa. In 1797 Venice took up Bonaparte's unrefusable offer to become part of the Austrian Empire and officially ended the Venetian Republic. After crowning himself Emperor of France in 1804, Bonaparte returned to Italy to organise its reconstruction. The result was a kingdom of Italy, which included Lombardy and Venice. Having more pressing matters to attend to, Napoleon left his stepson, Eugéne Beauharnais, in charge of the Kingdom as its Viceroy. After Napoleon's defeat, Venice became part of Austria-Hungary until 1859.

For all its incomparable glories, Venice is notoriously foggy in winter and smelly in summer which may be a reason, along with the high prices and excess of tourists, why its native population has shrunk by two thirds in the last 20 years. Within the same period the prosperity of the Venetian hinterland has been considerably revived with the creation of many new companies producing small, high-quality goods including shoes, medical equipment, spectacle frames and machine components. Treviso is also host to the headquarters of the Benetton group. If it were not for the dismal winters many more foreigners would probably choose to settle in this commercially upbeat region – though expatriates will continue to be sent there and be able to enjoy the aesthetic beauty if not the weather and the aroma.

Emilia Romagna takes its name from the ancient Roman road to Rome, the Via Emilia, and Romagna, the name of the former Papal State which covered the area of what are now the provinces of Forli and Ravenna. The northern part of the region is characterised by a flat and featureless wheat prairie, while the south takes in the foothills of the Appenines. An extremely prosperous region, its main town, Bologna experienced an economic boom in the eighties largely through the development of high-tech industries. As a place in which to live and work, Emilia Romagna has obvious attractions, especially its beautiful towns and a rich gastronomic heritage; Bologna is also the seat of Europe's oldest university. However the main problem for foreign residents is the expense: the cost of daily living in Bologna matches, if not exceeds, that of Milan or Florence. Properties in the region are, however, reasonably priced but are not much sought after by either foreigners or Italians and so foreign residents can feel isolated unless they like peace and quiet, or are near enough to Bologna to make use of the social life there. There is a small community of foreigners in Bologna who speak highly of their adopted home and find it lively, congenial, cultivated and relatively tourist free. There are also possibilities for teaching English as a foreign language in the region (see the chapter *Employment*).

THE UPPER CENTRE

Regions: Toscana (Tuscany), Umbria, Marche.
Main cities: Pisa, Florence, Siena, Orvieto, Perugia, Urbino.
Of all the regions of Italy, Tuscany and Umbria continue to attract the most foreign residents who are looking to buy property and/or live in Italy, but who do

not require employment. The superlatives of best climate, best scenery, best cultural heritage, etc. continue to draw foreigners looking for archetypal Italy. The region is so popular that the International School in Florence receives thousands of unsolicited applications from foreign teachers every year, despite the relatively few vacancies that occur. Parts of the western, central region of Tuscany are now 'colonised' by foreigners including Britons, Northern Europeans, and Irish. While the Brits continue to flock to Tuscany (there are currently around 8,000 permanent residents and many more holiday-home owners), the Italians are streaming out. The two trends are not necessarily connected. The departure of the Italians has more to do with the economic depression of the area than a wish to flee from the delights of 'Chianti-shire'. Even this beloved region of hilltop villages, vineyards and files of cypress trees is not without its drawbacks: water and electricity supplies are a problem in the remoter regions and tourists overrun the principal attractions, Florence, Siena, Pisa and the coast, for six months of the year. Originally a marquisate under Matilda of Tuscany, the area became prosperous through the woollen and cloth industries in the fourteenth centuries. The history of the region is essentially centred on Florence, which was the focus of the Renaissance and existed as a republic under the Medicis in the fifteenth and sixteenth centuries. Cosimo Medici then made himself the first Grand-Duke of Tuscany in 1570. Tuscany remained an independent Duchy and was simply annexed to Italy (Piedmont) in 1860 when the Risorgimento was in progress. There was, however, a brief fifteen-year interlude under French rule during the Napoleonic era.

Despite its propensity for earthquakes, the landlocked region of Umbria has become the other 'in-place' for foreign residents to set up home – though property sales slump after every reported tremor. With a smaller population than Tuscany, and somewhat overshadowed by the spectacular glories of that region, Umbria nevertheless has some lures for the prospective foreign resident. Most attractive of these are the property prices, which are about half those of Tuscany. However, the rapidly growing popularity of the region with both foreigners and Romans means that this financial advantage may quite soon evaporate. The main problem for foreign residents appears to be that communications are not brilliant. Rome airport is reasonably convenient for those living in the southern part of Umbria: Rome to Perugia takes about three hours by road (two and half hours if you have an Italian driver). For those in the north coming from Pisa airport, it takes considerably longer.

The region's attractions include Assisi, an important destination for pilgrimages dedicated to Italy's patron saint, St Francis, and the walled town of Spoleto. Sadly, the earthquake that hit the region in 1997 destroyed much of the renowned frescoes in Assisi's Basilica of St Francis and highlighted the fact that Europe's fault line runs down almost throughout the centre of Italy. Restoration of the frescoes was begun with a grant from the Vatican and was completed within three years. The Umbrian city of Foligno was also badly hit by the quake which bought down the cathedral's bell tower. Umbria also has a Foreigners' University (*Universita italiana per gli stranieri*) based in Perugia, to which students from all over the world come to take courses on Italian art, culture and language. This institution would be extremely useful for foreign residents keen to absorb Italian culture and make the most of their stay in the country.

Marche, situated between Umbria and the Adriatic, is a mountainous but varied region almost unknown to foreigners. Not many expatriates will be posted to the region either, as there are few large cities that play host to international organisations in the region. Italians flock to its coastal strip where resorts such as Pesaro and Senigallia in the north and San Benedetto del Tronto (also an important fishing port) in the south are the playgrounds of northern Italians throughout the summer. As a result, property prices on the coast are pushed high by the demand for summer flats. The hinterland is just beginning to attract foreign buyers but the remoteness of the region is regarded as something of a drawback. Communications with the north are excellent from the coast and once the region opens up, are likely to improve in the hinterland. The southern part of Marche used to be regarded as part of the Mezzogiorno but owing to increasing prosperity it has now had its financial benefits withdrawn by the government. Historically, Marche made a major contribution to civilisation through Frederico da Montefeltro, whose patronage of some of the greatest artists and architects to build and embellish his palace at Urbino, made it one of the most aristocratic and civilised courts of the Renaissance period. Ascoli Piceno is another large town that flourished in the same period.

THE LOWER CENTRE AND SARDINIA

Regions: Lazio (Latium), Abruzzo, Molise.
Main cities: Rome, L'Aquila, Isernia.
The region of Lazio encompasses Rome, the Italian capital, which as the centre of the former Roman Empire shaped much of Western civilisation. However it seems more through geography than suitability that Rome found itself the capital of modern Italy. Following full unification in 1871, Rome appeared ideally situated between northern and southern Italy. She was however far from being the largest or most important city of the time: the claims of Milan, Turin and Naples were greater since they had been administrative centres or capitals for centuries. In contrast, Rome had nothing to offer but glorious and symbolic antiquity and the Vatican. The ruinous expense of building her up into a capital city of appropriate grandeur lasted well into Mussolini's time. Nowadays Rome is notorious amongst other things for being the headquarters of the state apparatus whose thousands of functionaries drive anyone who has dealings with them to distraction with their legendary inefficiency and political corruption; the predominant

characteristics of the national administration. Many of these state employees are from the south of Italy, which aggravates the northerners' contempt for Rome and the south. The perception is of Rome squandering the hard-earned wealth of the north on the lazy and unproductive south. Since the 1980s Rome's slightly backward reputation has diminished thanks to industrial expansion particularly in the high technology field; the reality is however that it still lags behind Milan and Turin in the league table of industrial cities.

Georgina Gordon-Ham found Rome an attractive place to live
Apart from July and August when it is very humid, the climate is very pleasant and mild, especially in winter. The area around, particularly the hills are beautiful and in winter you can go skiing for the day at Terminillo and Campo Felice about one and half hour's drive away. The sea is also close and there are some lovely resorts such as Sperlonga, Circeo, Friggene, Santa Marinella.

However exciting the prospect of living and working in Rome and its environs may seem, there are considerable drawbacks in doing so. These include the difficulty of finding accommodation and the traffic congestion, which has reached unendurable limits while it fills the narrow, high-sided streets with noxious fumes that cannot disperse. To reduce both the atmospheric pollution and noise pollution of Rome, the traditional two-stroke mopeds (including the Vespas made famous in numerous movies) were banned on Friday and Saturday nights in certain streets. However, for all its faults and frustrations Rome is a city that fosters deep fascination, not the least of which is the pleasure of living in an atmosphere created by two thousand years of occupation, power, wealth and history.

After Milan, Rome has the second largest community of foreigners living and working in the city and its environs. Formerly the Abruzzi, the region east and south of Rome was partitioned into the two regions of Abruzzo and Molise in 1963. Both areas are mountainous and sparsely populated and to many foreigners they seem wild and forbidding. Folk traditions, which have faded out in the more developed areas of Italy, survive here among the hilltop villages along with witches and wolves. The latter can be found in the Parco Nazionale dell'Abruzzo along with brown bears and chamois. In recent years Abruzzo has grown wealthier than poverty-stricken Molise by taking full advantage of government incentive schemes for businesses and proving that factories in Abruzzo can operate as efficiently and productively as anywhere in the north of Italy. The Abruzzese have also been quick to develop the potential of their Adriatic seaboard and in particular Pescara, which has become a popular holiday spot for Italians. The main town of Abruzzo, L'Aquila (eagle), has a 99-spout fountain (one for every village from which the city's original population is reputed to have been formed), and a brooding sixteenth century castle built by the Spaniards during their 150 year period of influence in Italy. Abruzzo has also poured investment into Green Tourism thanks to its National Parks, and well organised protected areas. The earthquakes that occur periodically have also helped ensure a rush of public funds to renovate houses for hosting tourism. Prices in Abruzzo are still very affordable and if you are thinking of going into the tourism business, it might be worth considering.

Poor and backward Molise, which is about half the area of Abruzzo, is where the south really begins. The entire Abruzzi area is an earthquake zone that places a dampener on the real estate market there, while the main town of Molise, Isernia, is still propped up by scaffolding from the quake of 1984. It is not too far across the Adriatic to Albania and Croatia and the connections between the regions are evident in the customs and dialect of the region. There is a young coastal resort at Termoli.

Sardegna (Sardinia)

Sardinia, the Mediterranean's second largest island after Sicily, has long been on the periphery of Italian affairs. At one time in the possession of the Spanish, the Dukes of Savoy took it over in 1718. The barren and harsh landscape of the island is capable only of subsistence agriculture. The islanders speak Sardo (see *The Italian Language, Daily Life*). A small community, which speaks undiluted fifteenth century Catalan, is an even more curious linguistic anachronism. The available options for working in Sardinia are mostly limited to tourism-related jobs and English language teaching. The only big employer is Tiscali, a large multinational internet and telecommunications company founded by Sardinian Renato Soru, who is now president of the region. He is an environmentalist and a fierce opponent of Berlusconi's privileges regarding his properties on the island. Tiscali's European headquarters are in the island's main town, Cagliari. There is also millionaires' row on the Costa Smerelda in the north-east. For retiring to the island has its charms, notably some incredible scenery, though it may be too quiet for many people outside the holiday season when considering the legendary insularity of the Sardi.

THE SOUTH AND SICILY

Regions: Campania, Apulia (Puglia), Basilicata, Calabria.
Main cities: Naples, Amalfi, Lecce (Lucca), Bari, Brindisi, Reggio.
It is a widely-held belief that the South of Italy is penurious throughout and crawling with gun-toting mafiosi who will knee-cap or assassinate anyone who seems to threaten their interests. If this were the case, the possibility of any normal business activity would be nil. In fact there are pockets of wealth and industry in the south, e.g. in Puglia and Sicily, which rival anything in the north. Such development has

been greatly encouraged by enormous financial incentives offered by the Italian government (see the Chapter, *Starting a Business*). However there are areas where the risk of Mafia interference should be taken extremely seriously: these include virtually the whole of Campania, the toe of Calabria and much of Sicily. As the home ground of the various brotherhoods: the *camorra*, 'ndrangheta' (the Calabrian Mafia), and the Sicilian Mafia (*Cosa Nostra*), these are regarded as virtual no go areas, particularly for small businesses which are less resilient to threats than the large corporations which can hope to shrug them off. It is estimated that 80% of shops in Palermo and Catania pay protection money.

The crackdown on Mafia activity paid dividends in the late 1980s and early 1990s. However, it seems that Mafia activity is again on the increase despite Silvio Berlusconi's party winning most of the Sicilian parliamentary seats in the 2001 election where Mafia controlled candidates usually win.

Campania

Campania is dominated by the city of Naples, which represents the south in much the same way that Milan represents the north. The region was called *Campania Felix* by the Romans, whose elite built their palatial villas along the Riviera of the bay of Naples. The Roman idyll is in stark contrast to the Naples coastline of today, which is blotted with the smokestacks and industrial installations of the city's more recent heritage. Naples is largely neglected by foreigners who perhaps fear the reputation of its pickpockets, its *bassi* (slums), and its notorious rubbish disposal problem – the result of the chronic inefficiency of the local council. Naples' tourism heyday was probably the eighteenth century when it was an obligatory stop on the English gentleman's Grand Tour of Europe. Influenced by the Spanish for 300 years, it passed to the Bourbon French in 1734. Famed for its Roman ruins, in particular nearby Pompeii and Herculaneum in the shadow of Vesuvius, Naples acquired a reputation for its courtesans when ruled by the French. The city remained a hit with the British until the killjoy Victorians denounced it as a latter day version of Sodom and Gomorrah. After the end of the Kingdom of Naples in 1860 the city became rapidly provincialised, a process which was accelerated when Rome became the capital of a united Italy.

Foreigners are unlikely to choose Naples as a place to live unless they are offered employment there, though Positano and Amalfi are very desirable places to live. The endemic problems include extreme poverty, and the petty crime and organised criminal activity that go with it. Naples comes under the domain of the *camorra* (the Neapolitan version of the Mafia). In addition, the reputed anarchic driving habits of Italians generally, have reached their ultimate manifestation in the Neapolitans who are oblivious to all road signs and traffic signals giving an entirely new slant to Goethe's dictum 'see Naples and die'.

Positano, Sorrento, Amalfi, Capri and Ischia islands are mainly Camorra –free, but outrageously expensive to settle in. Property on the three islands in the Bay of Naples – Ischia, Capri and Procida – rarely comes on the market. On the mainland the most attractive coastal areas are Sorrento, Amalfi, Positano and Ravello, but one has to run the gauntlet of Neapolitan motorists on the precipitous cliff roads to get to them. Inland, property prices fall dramatically. However, there is an inherent danger in the area from earthquakes – the earthquake of 1980 devastated the area behind Salerno. In acknowledgement of the poverty of the extreme south, all the *autostrade* south of Salerno are toll free.

Despite the infamous poverty and high unemployment in the city, Naples is Italy's largest trading port and commerce is very important for the local economy. As an industrial city, Naples is home to engineering, petrochemical, shipbuilding and other heavy industries; the fashion industry is, however, also present too.

Apulia (Puglia)

The olive and wine-producing area of Puglia is a long strip that stretches for over 250 miles (400 km) along the heel of Italy. The Normans invaded Southern Italy, including Puglia, in the eleventh century (thus ousting the Ottoman armies). The Normans left behind many fine cathedrals including those at Trani, Barletta, Bitonto, Ruvo di Puglia and Bari. The main city, Bari, is situated about halfway down the Adriatic coast of Puglia, and is one of the showcases of the south owing to an economic boom from high tech and service industries. The other main industrial area is located around the ancient port of Taranto, which has long been given over to steel production. The upper part of the region, *il Promontorio del Gargano* (the Gargano Promontory), which juts into the Adriatic is considered one of the most attractive parts of Puglia with its wooded hills and stunning views of the sea. The area was once rich with religious sanctuaries and Monte Sant'Angelo, where the archangel Michael put in an 'appearance' in AD490, has long been a point of pilgrimage. Between Taranto and Bari are numerous *trulli* (circular, dry-stone built houses with conical roofs) and you can see a whole town of them at Alberobello. While you may hear that they were prehistoric dwellings, it is generally accepted that they represent an early form of tax evasion from the Spanish invaders' tax on bricks and mortar in the 16th century. Lecce, in the far corner of Puglia is usually regarded as the architectural gem of southern Italy – it is built in a particularly refined baroque style. Galatina is the home of the dance *tarantella* that is celebrated annually in a medieval festival. The dance, named from the tarantula spider, is supposed to reflect the writhing of those bitten by the deadly arachnid. The Isole Tremiti (Tremiti islands) 25 miles off Gargano, were once the Devil's Islands of Italy. The presence of prisoners has long since been replaced by that of tourists estimated figure 100,000 during August (many of them day trippers) who far outnumber the few hundred permanent inhabitants.

A number of foreigners have found the charms of Gargano irresistible and made their homes in these pleasant surroundings. Anyone thinking of retiring there could probably rent a holiday villa in the area while they carry out a reconnaissance. Unlike Campania, there is little organised crime in Puglia (at least outside the towns of Bari and Foggia which is where the criminal elements are concentrated). From the ports of Otranto and Brindisi there are ferries to the former Yugoslavia, and Greece.

Basilicata (Lucania) and Calabria

The two most southerly regions of Basilicata and Calabria are the poorest and most underdeveloped in Italy and best epitomise the plight of the Mezzogiorno. The traditional migration of southerners from these regions to the north in search of jobs continues apace, despite government efforts to bring industrial development to the south. In an effort to deal with the prosperity imbalance between north and south the Italian government set up a development fund, *La Cassa del Mezzogiorno* in the 1950s, which has since been superseded by various other bodies with specialised responsibilities. Massive government resources have been poured into the south to fund irrigation projects, an improved infrastructure, modern communications and industrial and tourism development. However, the area has suffered from corruption on an unprecedented scale and this, coupled with gross inefficiency and the lack of an overall investment plan, has resulted in most of the money being squandered on political patronage. Much of the money has thus ended up in private bank accounts and the coffers of the 'ndrangheta'. From 1992, the EU Regional Investment Fund took over the organising of funding the Mezzogiorno.

The dramatic decline of the populations of Basilicata and Calabria is the result of the constant migration of those desperate to escape poverty. Add to this the mountainous and inhospitable landscape and the undercurrent of criminality, and there does not seem to be much here to appeal to many foreign residents. Basilicata's main city is Matera, which has acquired some tourism clout since standing in for Jerusalem in Mel Gibson's controversial but very commercially successful film *The Passion of the Christ* shot in 2004. Prominent features of the landscape in the region are the *Sassi* cave dwellings, where until very recently peasants slept in the same accommodation as their animals. Basilicata has lately been experiencing a development boom as companies are taking advantage of the government's funding and Basilicata's relatively crime free reputation.

Calabria, which forms the 'toe' of Italy, has the attraction of its beautiful Tyrrhenian coastline, which draws a regular summer tourist trade. This would not have been possible if the mosquitoes that plagued the coast up to the early twentieth century had not been eliminated. In the eighth century the Greeks flourished in Calabria and this was probably the high point of Calabrian history which has, from some perspectives anyway, been downhill since then. Firmly part of mafia territory, Crotone, the birthplace of Pythagoras, and Reggio Calabria have a pretty evil reputation. From the promontory of Tropea in the south west of Calabria you can see the Lipari islands and even Stromboli (whose last reported bout of volcanic eruption was in 1971). The main problem for anyone with major assets thinking of living in Calabria is the risk of kidnapping. Calabria is notorious for the practice and the wild and difficult terrain makes it easy for local gangs who know their way around to hide and avoid capture. It is reported that local shepherds have in the past been sent into the mountains to locate carabinieri who have become lost while attempting to find kidnappers' hideouts there. Owing to a dearth of Calabrian industrialists, the kidnappers prey on the professional classes and their offspring. The kidnappings tend to be family affairs and well organised. Ransoms used to end up in the pockets of the local drug barons or the construction industry, which is known to be rife with *malavita* throughout most of southern Italy. There was even a rather macabre custom in Calabria of nicknaming hotels and apartment blocks after those whose ransom money has paid for them. However, kidnappings have been reduced to one every couple of years since the government adopted the policy of freezing kidnappers' assets. Foreigners are not generally regarded as prime targets since the ensuing publicity in the foreign media would put the Italian government in a position of ridicule and draw unwanted international attention on the kidnappers. Furthermore, such goings on would have a devastating effect on much-needed tourism in Calabria. The region is not a great place to settle as signified by the fact that honest Calabresi tend to leave it too; if they are able.

SICILY (SICILIA)

Main towns: Palermo, Messina, Catania, Syracuse.
Population: Five million.
The island of Sicily which lies off the toe of Italy is a *regioni a statuto speciale* meaning that it has a greater degree of autonomy than most of the other twenty regions. This status has less to do with the fact that Sicily is the home of the *Cosa Nostra* (Mafia) who *are* a law unto themselves, and more to do with historical and ethnic differences. Nonetheless, to many people the name of Sicily is synonymous with the dark force of the Mafia. The origins of this brutal brotherhood are obscure; some claim that the Mafia have existed for two thousand years as a kind of freemasons' organisation. It is evident, however, that the end of the nineteenth century marked the onset of their notoriety. During the 1920s the fascists under Mussolini lost no time in stamping out such an undesirable phenomenon – they

were competition in the quest for power and wealth. The responsibility for their revival in Sicily after the Second World War can be laid at the door of the American military and the predecessor of the CIA. Having successfully invaded Italy during the Second World War, they implanted several veteran Mafiosi from New York to counteract and combat the spread of Communism that they feared would take over Italy. Unfortunately, the cure turned out to be much more deadly than the disease.

There is no way of estimating the Mafia's clandestine wealth world-wide, but in Italy their turnover is estimated to be 12% of the GNP. Until the 1960s the Mafia area of operations was largely confined to Sicily, since then there are few areas of Italian commercial life which it has not penetrated and its multinational operations have made it probably the richest and most powerful criminal organisation in the world. The Mafia was turning guns into ploughshares long before the Cold War ended by investing their ill-gotten wealth in legal enterprises.

Palermo, Sicily's main city, has the infamous distinction of being a world centre of the illegal drugs and armaments trade. With this awesome power over life, death and the economy it comes as little surprise that there are few who will stand up to the Mafia, though there are some notable exceptions among the judicial profession. One example of those who stood up to the Mafia was the young Sicilian judge Giovanni Falcone who conducted the much publicised *maxi-processi* (mega-trials) of Mafia luminaries, which put several, including Michele Greco the leader, behind bars. The price Falcone paid for his courage was to be the Salman Rushdie of Sicily, guarded round the clock by twenty-five armed bodyguards. These were not sufficient protection from the (some say inevitable) assassination that ended his life in 1992. The Mafia, like the Mounties it seems, always get their man. However, there was such an outcry over the murder of Falcone and another judge, Paolo Borsellino, that the Mafia went quiet for a while and began working in a much more unobtrusive way. The man reputedly responsible for the murder of the two judges, Benedetto Spera, was eventually captured just outside Palermo in 2001.

Sicily is slowly modernising itself; there is even a Europe Office in Palermo offering information in English. It is perfectly feasible to buy a house in Sicily, and many foreigners do have holiday homes there. Despite unemployment of 23% amongst the local population, it is possible for foreigners to find work on the island: there are opportunities for English teaching in Messina and Siracuse and there are foreigners working for the oil companies at Gela. There is also the American Air Force base on the island, which has a school that employs teachers with American citizenship and certification. The island has many attractions including beautiful scenery and Greek ruins (Siracuse was the second largest city of ancient Greece). Trampled by other invaders, including Roman, Ottoman, Norman, French and Spanish, the island of Sicily is a fascinating mixture of styles as is the capital Palermo, where Arab architecture meets Baroque. Another of the island's famous sights is Mount Etna, which lies in the north-east between Messina and Catania. Etna erupted in 1983 and again in 2001, when it threatened a number of villages and the experts forecast an even bigger eruption to come.

The railway from Palermo to the other major town, Catania, remains single track though the new motorway from Messina to Palermo will make that journey quicker. Silvio Berlusconi says he will build the long talked about bridge linking Sicily to the mainland, but many other governments have said that before and Sicily is still an island. Work has been about to start on the bridge for over thirty years, but successive governments have never quite managed to get things moving. Stretching across the Straits of Messina from Villa San Giovanni to Messina, the planned road and rail bridge will be two miles long, 195 feet wide and building it will take many years. The designers claim it will withstand winds of over 200 m.p.h and more importantly that it will be earthquake proof. The straits are one of Italy's seismic hotspots, most notably when the town of Messina was flattened by the big quake of 1908. The bridge will be funded internationally and it is expected to pay for itself in tolls after ten years.

GETTING TO ITALY

By Air

High Street travel agents, the travel pages of most national newspapers and nowadays mainly the internet, are obvious sources of discounted fares to Italy and there is plenty of choice. Non-stop flights are available from the UK to over 30 Italian cities. If you change to a domestic flight at Milan or Rome, you can reach still more. Due to the constantly changing nature of the airline industry and the spreading network of the budget airlines, it is likely that origin and destination airports will change, and airlines will disappear (like British Airways' budget airline Go, which was absorbed by EasyJet in 2002 and Buzz which was taken over by Ryanair in 2003. Italy's very own budget airline, Volare folded at the end of 2004 and its routes were snapped up by other airlines including Ryanair and EasyJet. The information below is therefore for guidance only and should be checked on the internet, or direct with the airline well in advance of your departure and before you make concrete travel plans.

Internet tools that regularly scan airlines' websites and download details of fares from different airlines and compare them can be useful. www.skyscanner. net and www.aerfares.net and www.easyvalue.com are such tools, and cover most budget airlines, while Austrian Airlines website has a comprehensive interactive flight planner that allows travellers to find details of most scheduled flights, on any airline, in the world: www.aua.com. It is getting hard for Americans to find cheap flights direct to Italy. Promising websites for bargains include www. airtravelcenter.com and the Dutch-based website www.etn.nl. Americans also have the option of getting a cheap flight to London and then picking up an ex-UK, no frills fare, to Italy from there.

Milan Linate is 10 km east of the city and Milan Malpensa is 46 km north-west of the city. Malpensa to Milan is by Malpensa Express (train) and the Malpensa Shuttle coach.

A reliable, independent booking service for low cost flights on scheduled and charter services to Italy is available from *Flightclub*, who are members of ABTA. Telephone 0845 880 1808 or book online at www.flightclub.co.uk.

Most of the airlines listed below allow passengers to book flights online.

Useful Contacts – Airlines & Charter Flights

Avro: (☎0870 458 2841; www.avro. co.uk). Charter flights to Italy.

Aer Lingus: (☎0818 365000; www. aerlingus.com). Flies direct from Dublin to Bologna and Milan from £34.

Air Malta : (☎0845 607 3710; www.airmalta.com). Flies London Gatwick to Catania via Malta.

Alitalia: (☎0870 544 8259; www. alitalia.co.uk and in Ireland ☎01 677 5171). Flies from main UK cities to most cities in Italy.

Air Berlin: (☎0870 738 8880; www. airberlin.com). German airline that flies direct from Stansted to Milan

and Rome and Manchester to Milan.

BMI: (☎0870 607 0555; www. flybmi.co.uk). Flies from Heathrow to Milan, Naples and Venice.

British Airways: (☎0870 850 9850; www.ba.com). Uses Heathrow and Gatwick.. Sample fares: Gatwick to Turin and Bari from £64.40 return.

Charter Flight Centre: (☎0845 045 0153; www.charterflights.co.uk).

EasyJet: (☎0870 600 0000; www. easyjet.com). Flies Bristol and East Midlands to Venice and Rome and Newcastle to Rome; Gatwick to Milan, Venice, Rome and Olbia;

Luton to Cagliari and Turin; Stansted to Bologna and Naples and some other destinations from the UK.

Eujet: (☎0870 414 1414; www.eujet. com). Flies to Turin from Kent International Airport.

Excel Airways: (☎08709 989898 ; www.excelairways.com). Flies to Rome.

Flightclub, Guildbourne Centre, Chapel Road, Worthing, West Sussex BN11 1LZ; ☎0845 880 1808; www.flightclub.co.uk. Member of ABTA.

Globespan: (☎0870 5561 522; www.flyglobespan.com). Low fares operator based in Scotland flies Glasgow Prestwick to Rome (Fiumicino) and Edinburgh to Rome (Fiumicino) and Venice. Fares from about £60. Also flights from Canada to Scotland.

Jet2: (☎0871 226 1737; www.jet2. com). Flies from Manchester to Pisa and Venice.

Meridiana: (☎020 7730 3454; www. meridiana.it). Italian domestic carrier but also flies from London Gatwick to Cagliari, Olbia and Florence. Special offer flights from £29 (London to Florence without taxes).

Ryanair: (☎0871 246 0000; www. ryanair.com). Based at Stansted. Flies to many Italian destinations including Alghero, Ancona, Bari, Brescia, Brindisi, Cagliari, Genoa, Milan, Palermo, Pescara, Pisa, Rome, Trieste, Turin and Venice.

Thomsonfly: (☎0870 190 0737; www.thomsonfly.com). Flies from Coventry to Naples, Pisa and Venice and from Doncaster and Bournemouth to Pisa. One-way flights from £16.

Virgin Express: (☎0207-744 0004;www.virgin-express.com). Belgian airline that flies from Brussels and Amsterdam to Rome (Fiumicino) and Milan (Linate).

Airlines offering direct flights to Italy from the USA and Canada

Air Canada: (☎800; www.aircanada. ca).

Alitalia: (☎800 223 5730; www. alitaliausa.com).

Delta: (☎800 221 1212 in USA and Canada; 800-864 114 (in Italy; www.delta.com).

NorthWest: (☎800 447 4747; www. nwa.com).

Approximate Flight Lengths

London to Rome – two and a half hours
New York to Rome – ten hours
Los Angeles to Rome – Fifteen and a half hours
Sydney to Rome – just over twenty-four hours

By Rail

For those who don't care to fly, getting to Italy from Northern European stations such as Paris and Calais can be a doddle on a direct through train. It is however expensive compared with no frills airfares. There are also sleeper services from Paris and Calais (contact Citalia ☎0870-9014013; www.citalia.co.uk or Rail Europe ☎0870 5848848). If you want to take the car but not drive it to Italy, you can use the Motorail service from Denderleeuw in Belgium. Denderleeuw is about a 100-mile drive from Calais and the route goes through Belgium, eastern France and Switzerland. Once in Italy the route goes through Milan and terminates at Bologna. A useful contact is Railsavers; ☎0870-750 7070; www.railsavers.com.

By Road

You can enter Italy by road from France, Switzerland and Austria. The routes from Austria and France are open year round. From Switzerland access is via the Mont Blanc tunnel from Chamonix (France) to Courmayeur in Italy. If you have a tunnel phobia then from Switzerland access is via the Grand St. Bernard pass, which can be dodgy in winter when you will almost certainly need snow chains on your tyres.

Residence and
Entry Regulations

CHAPTER SUMMARY

- Any non-Italian – including a national of another EU country – planning to stay in Italy for over 90 days must apply for a *permesso di soggiorno* (permit to stay).
- Those not from EU countries must apply for the *permesso di soggiorno* and a work visa *before* they enter Italy.
- All those planning to take up employment – including EU nationals – also need to obtain a *libretto di lavoro* (worker registration card) from the town hall; this will be held by your employer.
- Once you have the *permesso di soggiorno* and have moved to an Italian address you should obtain a residence permit (*certificato di residenza*): this is not compulsory for EU nationals, but is useful as proof that you have settled in Italy. Self-certification (a declaration that you are a resident) is now permitted for many formalities which previously required a certificato di residenza.
- All Italian residents, whether native or foreign, must have a *codice fiscale* (tax code number) even if they are not subject to Italian taxation.
- All Italian residents, whether native or foreign, must carry an identity card (*Carta d'Identità*) with them at all times.
- Italy is currently tightening its immigration laws for all non-EU citizens (which has fallout for North Americans), to combat a rising flood of illegal immigrants (*clandestini*) from eastern Europe and Africa.

THE SCHENGEN ACCORD

Before discussing the visa regulations for Italy, it is important to understand the implications of the Schengen Accord. The introduction of new immigration laws (see below) and the extra vigilance at vulnerable border areas in Italy is not unrelated to the Schengen Accord – introduced in Italy in October 1997. At the time of writing there are fifteen countries in the Schengen group: Austria, Belgium, Denmark, Finland, France, Germany, Greece, Iceland, Italy, Luxembourg, Netherlands, Norway, Portugal, Spain and Sweden. The United Kingdom and Ireland, who have limited border controls between their two countries, have declined to participate in the Accord because they (especially the UK) believe that they are the final targets of most illegal immigrants and so wish to maintain border controls.

The Schengen countries have generally eliminated passport and baggage controls except for general airport and airline safety in the airports of their countries. In some cases this has meant modification of existing airports like the Malpensa 2000 airport in Milan to accommodate increased traffic. It is now possible to travel around much of Europe and only be aware that a border has been crossed when the street signs change language and car number plates change style.

The main fear of other Schengen countries, particularly France and Germany, has been that illegal immigrants will still find it easier to enter Italy, which has 8000 miles of coastline, than other countries and will then pass through Italy to the other European countries. Additionally, the coastlines of both Spain and Italy are separated by just a few miles of sea from North Africa (the source of many illegal immigrants) and in Italy's case also Albania. The Schengen agreement has been suspended more than once and temporary border controls implemented because of fears of a sudden major increase in illegal immigrants from Italy; and also most notoriously, before the G8 Summit debacle in Genoa in 2001.

The Schengen agreement also allows nationals of countries from outside the EU to enter a member country through the normal passport controls on a visa issued by that country and then move around the Schengen Accord countries freely without further passport checks. To counteract possible abuse by the criminal fraternity and those that have been deported from one country and try to return through another, the member countries came up with the 'Schengen Information System' (SIS). This connects consulates and embassies worldwide to a centralised data bank in Strasbourg where the names and details of all known criminals will be stored. Apart from at embassies and consulates, the information can be accessed from terminals at first points of entry to the Schengen Area. Under the protection of personal data regulations, private citizens are allowed to check information relating to them that is stored in the system.

VISA AND RESIDENCY INFORMATION
All Nationalities

For stays of longer than 90 days all nationalities of visitor require a *permesso di soggiorno* (permit to stay), which must be applied for within eight days of arrival. EU nationals, whose passports are not usually stamped on arrival will not have to worry quite so much about this timescale as non-EU visitors whose visas will be checked and their passport stamped at the port of entry. With the Schengen Accord in place, passports of non-EU nationals will only be checked when they first enter Schengen area and the Italian authorities may use this date when calculating the 90 days.

Citizens of the following countries do not require visas for Schengen area countries when visiting for business or tourism, though technically they need to register for the residency permit (*permesso di soggiorno*) within eight days of arrival in Italy: Andorra, Argentina, Australia, Brazil, Canada, Chile, Cyprus, Czech Republic, Ecuador, Estonia, Hungary, Israel, Japan, Latvia, Lichtenstein, Lithuania, Malta, Mexico, Monaco, New Zealand, Paraguay, Poland, San Marino, Singapore, Slovakia, Slovenia, South Korea, Switzerland, USA, Uruguay, Vatican City.

Citizens of the following countries do not require visas when entering Italy for business or tourism for 90 days or less: Bolivia, Bulgaria, Costa Rica, Croatia, El Salvador, Guatemala, Honduras, Malaysia, Nicaragua, Panama, Venezuela.

Up to date visa information can be found on the Italian Embassy in Washington website (www.italyemb.org), though visa applications must be made to the consular office whose jurisdiction covers the region or country in which the applicant lives (see end of this chapter for contact details).

Applications for all visas must be made in person and the length of time that the application takes to be processed ranges from twenty-four hours to five weeks. It is usually best to assume the longer timescale to ensure your visa arrives in time for your departure, especially during the busy summer months.

European Union Nationals

In theory, one of the touted advantages of the creation of a European Union is the melting away of internal borders as far as the free movement of EU nationals within the EU is concerned. Any EU national, has a basic right to live and work in other EU countries. However, there is still red tape to get through for EU nationals (but not nearly as much as there is for non-EU nationals) who want to stay longer than 90 days in Italy. The difference for EU nationals is that there is an obligation to allow them to remain in Italy long-term, even though they still have to apply for a residence permit. The possession of a residence permit (*permesso di soggiorno*) is essential to get access to public services such as health care and utilities contracts. The bureaucratic rigmarole involved with residing in Italy is almost without exception complicated and time consuming. The regulations concerning residence permits are dealt with in detail below and, in theory, the procedure for obtaining them should be the same everywhere in the country. In practice there may well be differences depending on the *comune* in which you are living and your particular circumstances. The main thing to bear in mind as you struggle with the bureaucratic insanity, is that it is as much a bugbear for the Italians themselves, as it is for the foreigners staying in their country.

Non-European Union Nationals

For non-European Union nationals the process is much more involved as their right to stay and work in Italy is not assumed from the outset. A non-EU national must apply for their work visa and visitor's visa *before* entering Italy. For some nationalities it is also necessary to apply for, and receive the visas through the Italian embassy in their home country, though it will often be possible to apply for a visa in the area where you are permanently resident. For long-term expatriates this usually means that they can apply for their visa in the country where they are currently living, especially if they have a residence permit or other official documentation to prove they live there full time. It is also necessary to have employment before applying for the visas. Work permits for non-EU nationals will be issued only to people outside Italy, and only for jobs where the provincial Office of the Ministry of Labour is satisfied that no Italian can do the job.

The Italian employer must apply for an *Autorizzazione al Lavoro* which must then be presented by prospective employee at the Italian Embassy in the applicant's home country or place of residence. In recent years large numbers of non-EU citizens have been given work permits, mainly because of the skills shortage in the north created by the booming economy in the area. Skilled workers, especially in electronics and other high-tech industries, and those looking for work in an area where a skill such as native English ability or a skill only possible to obtain on another country is necessary will be most likely to secure a work permit. It is not possible to convert a tourist visa to an employment visa inside Italy – i.e. tourists must leave the country, apply for a work permit and then return once they have it. For those who want to try and work illegally, renewal of a tourist visa is possible, but not guaranteed. Proof of funds and a good reason for the extension (other than a nice job) are essential if one is to be obtained.

The Permesso di Soggiorno

EU Nationals: EU nationals who arrive in Italy with a job already arranged must apply at the *ufficio stranieri* (foreigners office) of the *questura*, (police station) or the *comune* in smaller towns, for their *Permesso di Soggiorno – motivi di lavoro* (sometimes also known as a *Carta di Soggiorno*), within eight days of arrival. Reports vary as to how long it takes for the *Permesso di Soggiorno* to be issued, but three months is the official delay. Having a job in Italy is not prerequisite for getting a permesso di soggiorno.

Requirements for the *permesso di soggiorno* may vary. In many cases you will be required to produce proof of financial solvency, of having some kind of income and be able to name your intended profession while in Italy, if this is relevant. There are reports that EU nationals applying in the north for the Permesso di Soggiorno have only had to show a passport and supply four photographs. The soggiorno is free of charge and has to be renewed periodically, either every five or ten years. Note that failure to renew the document can result in a substantial fine. Renewals are made through the *comune*, or the *questura* in large towns and cities. The *Permesso di Soggiorno* has to be renewed every five years, no matter how long you live in Italy. All renewals must be made on special document paper, *carta bollata*, which can be purchased from most tobacconists (*tabaccherie*) currently for €11. Depending on your status, the *permesso di soggiorno* will have a different suffix, for example: employee, student, tourist, student, spouse, foreign spouse of an Italian, etc.

Non-EU Nationals: all non-EU nationals *(extracomunitari)* intending to live in the country must have received the necessary visas before arrival otherwise they will have little or no chance of regularising their paperwork with the authorities. The best chance of this is if they are dual nationality Italian/American or if they have a firm offer of a job in Italy. This means that their employer in Italy has to obtain an authorisation to work, issued by the Ministry of Labour or a provincial office of labour (*ufficio provinciale di lavoro*), which in the time-honoured multi-layered manner of Italian bureaucracy then gets sent to the Rome office for approval, then returned to the provincial labour office for their authorisation, then returned to the employer, who can then send it to the prospective employee in their home country, who can then enter Italy with the permit and apply at the for a stay permit. The originals of these together with the applicant's passport and a photograph should be sent to the nearest embassy or consulate. There is a useful publication for Americans, which has guidelines on how to deal with Italian bureaucracy, *Living, Studying and Working in Italy* by Travis Neighbour Ward and Monica Larner ($17 from Owl Books 2003, or for less on Amazon).

Italian Fabio Ausenda, explains how North Americans have fallen foul of the new, tougher laws on immigration in Italy
Unfortunately, for non-EU citizens the already lengthy bureaucratic process has got longer because of the attitude of the current political leaders towards immigrants. The Bossi-Fini law (July 2002) named after the leaders of the Northern League

and National Alliance (which by definition are anti-immigration parties) which form part of Berlusconi's rightist coalition, has made citizens of the USA and Canada end up being treated the same as Albanians who want to stay in Italy. This law reduced the duration of the permesso di soggiorno *to one year for non-EU applicants thus increasing the bureaucratic workload. When the comuni asked if they could issue the permesso di soggiorno instead of the questure (police stations), so that the police could spend more time on fighting crime, the government refused because they claimed that leftist comuni would issue too many permessi di soggiorno. Mind you, the process for Italians wanting to emigrate to the USA is just as time consuming and complicated; the difference is that in Italy the bureaucratic process is exacerbated by the underlying political stance.*

All Nationalities: When making an application for a *permesso di soggiorno* it is advisable to take every document required at the time of application to make a return visit unnecessary, or worse, prevent having to repeat the entire process of waiting and the aggravation that goes with it. The list below is guide to what many people have been requested to present, though the list should be checked at the office you will apply to as local requirements may vary, especially between EU and non-EU nationals.

- A valid passport. Most countries require your passport to be valid for six months or more beyond your intended stay and Italy is no exception. A photocopy of the relevant information pages, including your visa, will also be required.
- Up to four black and white passport-sized photos.
- A tax stamp *(marca da bollo)* of the correct value (check what is required at the local *questura*).
- For employees, a letter of employment is necessary.
- For the self-employed, proof of registration with the Chamber of Commerce and VAT certificate (or exemption) is required.
- For students a letter from their institution is required.
- For retired/non-working people proof of financial resources is needed.
- Proof of health insurance or coverage by social security system of Italy or another country.
- Marriage/divorce certificate.
- Passports of children to be included on the *permesso di soggiorno*, if the children are not on the parents passport, plus the birth certificates of the children.

It is necessary to have notarised translations of certain documents and have others provided in Italian – check with the office where the application will be made for current requirements. Official translations of the marriage, divorce and birth certificates, as well as the letter of employment in Italian will probably be required. Translations should be done by an official translator and enquiries should be made at an Italian Embassy or at the *questura* where an application is to be made.

Libretto di Lavoro

Many employees, including EU citizens, are also required to apply for a worker registration card (*libretto di lavoro*). This is obtained after the *Permesso di Soggiorno*, from the local job centre *(centro per l'impiego)* or in small towns and villages, by the comune. The *libretto di lavoro* is valid for ten years and once obtained will be held by the employer. During any periods of unemployment it will be kept by the *centro per l'impiego* .

Autocertificazione (di Residenza)

Once you have obtained a *permesso di soggiorno* and moved into your new Italian home, you can use the new autocertificazione system to self-certify your residence status. You achieve this by signing a declaration (bearing in mind it is a criminal offence to falsely self-certificate yourself). You sign this when you apply for health care, a driving licence, send your children to school, open a bank account and ship your personal effects to Italy. This replaces the previous requirement to apply for a residence certificate, *certificato di residenza* and also cuts down on the bureaucracy. Now all you need is the permesso di soggiorno, a codice fiscale, and a declaration of residency to gain all the vital privileges that you previously had to have a *certificato di residenza* for.

Codice Fiscale (Tax-code Number)

After getting a *permesso di soggiorno*, all nationalities including Italians have to obtain a tax-code number, whether or not they are liable for Italian taxes. The reason for this is that the codice fiscale is essential for most of the practices that living and working in Italy entails including opening a bank or postal account, signing any official contract (e.g. lease, utilities, insurance), buying a Vespa or motor vehicle, and of course working. You will have to visit the Provincial Tax Office (taking your stay permit and passport/ID) to get your tax-code number which should be allocated on the spot.

Entering to Start a Business

EU Nationals. Those EU nationals who wish to enter Italy to start up a business are free to do so and no prior authorisation is required (further information is given on this in the chapter, *Starting a Business*). Anyone in this category should apply for a *permesso di soggiorno* in just the way described above. However, if you have received a *permesso* as an employee it is necessary to have it amended to reflect your change in circumstances. Proven experience of three years in the field of the intended business and registration with the Chamber of Commerce is necessary as is obtaining a VAT number, or an exemption. Registration with the Chamber of Commerce is relatively simple, though obtaining the tax papers can be more difficult and many expatriates employ a specialist company to help them through the process. Starting work before completing the registration process is not recommended as it is technically against the law and can lead to fines and confiscation of equipment. There are a number of incentive programmes available in Italy that include low-interest loans and tax rebates.

More information on starting a business regulations can be found in the chapter *Starting a Business*.

Non-European Union Nationals: For those without right of abode in the EU who wish to enter and start a business a visa is necessary, for which proof of qualification to do so to do so in Italy is required. To obtaining the visa it may be necessary to obtain documentation from Italian organisations in Italy (e.g. Chamber of Commerce), sometimes it is necessary to obtain the documentation from the local of office in the area where the business will be located. Advice should be sought from an Italian Embassy and other Italian oriented trade organisations.

Entering with Retirement Status

Anyone intending to retire to Italy must be able to show proof of funds with which to support themselves in order to obtain their *permesso di soggiorno*. Depending on nationality, the residence permit must be renewed at varying intervals from one to five years and continuing proof of funds must be provided each time. Non-EU nationals must also furnish proof of health insurance that covers them in Italy. Further information regarding residence regulations for those retiring to Italy is given in the *Retirement* chapter.

The Carta d'Identità

All residents, native and foreign, are required to carry an identity card (*Carta d'Identità* with them at all times. This is a regulation that the majority of Italians comply with, without feeling that it is any kind of infringement of their personal liberty. Apart from the UK (yet), most European countries require people to carry some form of identity at all times, as do the majority of countries around the world – the premise being that if you have nothing to hide why should you worry if the police want to know who you are. Permanent residents are issued with an identity card that includes the holder's nationality and is valid for five years. The card should be bought from the *comune*. However, only Italian nationals can use their Italian identity card as a travel document in lieu of their passport.

Registering with the Embassy

Expatriates are advised to register with their Embassy or Consulate in Italy – US, Canadian and British offices are listed below. This registration enables the Embassy to keep their nationals up to date with any information they need to be aware of and also enables the Embassy to trace individuals in the event of an emergency. The Consulates can also help with information regarding their nationals' status overseas and advise with any diplomatic or passport problems. They may also be able to help in an emergency such as the unfortunate event of the death of a relative. However, the Consulates do not function as a source of general help and advice, nor act as an employment bureau and they make this quite obvious in response to any such appeals. Some embassies run social clubs for their nationals and the nationals of friendly countries may be allowed to join too. Apart from being a good place to meet fellow nationals and other expatriates, these social clubs can be useful places to network for employment and business opportunities.

Italian Citizenship

Residency is not synonymous with citizenship and those who wish to be adopted as a citizen of Italy may find that they have some difficulty in doing so. There are however various ways to gain Italian citizenship, some of which are easier to complete than others, these include:

- By descent (if one or more parent or grandparent were Italian).
- By marriage to an Italian, after six months of residency in Italy or three years of marriage.
- Through residency of more than two years in Italy (see www.escapeartist. com/efan/living-in-italy.htm or www.lainet.com for the story of a US national trying to obtain Italian citizenship).

However, for EU nationals it should be no inconvenience to retain your current nationality, as you will have most of the rights, and also obligations, of an Italian national – expatriates can even vote in local elections. In January 2005 Italy abolished compulsory military service in favour of voluntary signing up for the armed forces, which used to be a consideration for those taking Italian citizenship, although national military service personnel were not usually sent to combat zones.

Immigration

Italy is currently tightening its immigration laws in an effort to restrict the flood of immigrants (legal and illegal) from Eastern Europe, particularly Albania, the numbers from North Africa and the sub-Sahara are also causing concern. These immigrants form Italy's 'underclass' and are the main pillar of Italy's flourishing black economy. The *clandestini* as they are known, work without being registered, so apart from being able to pay lower wages, their employers save up to 50% of their usual labour costs as there are no social security or holiday benefit payments to be made. Although the official immigration figure for Italy currently stands at around a million, the true figure is probably double that. To combat this problem, immigration legislation has been introduced, visa controls are being imposed and large numbers of police and military units have been deployed along the country's massive land frontiers and coastline in a concerted effort to repel the swelling ranks of Italy's illegal immigrants. Most recently there has been an influx of Kurdish refugees from Turkey and Iraq. Areas where vigilance has been especially concentrated are Sicily, Calabria and Puglia in the south and Friuli in the north.

The problems of illegal immigration are not limited to volume, but include organised crime. Either the illegal immigrants end up working for the Mafia or, as in the case of Albanians, they take over from them as they turn out to be more deadly than the indigenous Mafia whom they have managed to intimidate and supplant in northern cities like Milan.

One of the new Immigration Laws enables the Italian state to deport any *clandestino* found guilty of committing a crime on Italian territory. The same applies if they are found to have a previous criminal record, or they refuse to produce proper identification. If a *clandestino* is unable to produce identification, he or she can be held at a detention centre for a maximum of 30 days while identification is being sought.

On a number of occasions Italy has allowed *clandestini* already living in the country without valid documents to apply for their situation to be regularised. If they can show good reason why they should be allowed to stay, they are almost always allowed to do so. In such cases proof of work and housing is usually required and the employer has to pay social security payments due. A blanket amnesty of this sort is unlikely to happen under the present rightist government.

Sources of Information

Before getting too far into planning any move to Italy, all and every piece of information should be checked and double-checked – including information in this book. Italian Embassies and Consulates in whose jurisdiction you live and your own Embassy in Italy are the best places to get information, though they might not always respond quickly.

Inhabitants of Rome, its province or region, who are floundering helplessly in a sea of incomprehensible bureaucracy can try one of the websites aimed at expats in Italy such as *The Informer* (www.informer.it), which operates by subscription with basic information available free to all, or www.romebuddy. com which is free. These are online guides to living in Italy which carry useful information and forums on how to handle the paperwork involved in getting various *certificati* and *permessi*, which you now find you need. Alternatively, try the Comune di Roma website pages www.commune.roma.it/info_cittadino/schede/index6.htm or their telephone helpline 060606 which gives information (in several languages), about the services provided by Rome city and is manned Mon-Sat, 4pm-7pm. There is a free public service known as Socialtel, provided by a local government, university, trade union and telephone company amalgamation, formed in response to the numerous calls incited by the Italian bureaucratic system and you can find it in the telephone directory. Last but not least, browse the expatriate websites for Italy as they can be a very useful source of information from the sharp end. A list of some of them can be found in the *Daily Life* chapter.

Useful Contacts – Information & Help with Italian Bureaucracy

Italian Bureaucratic Help Service Centre; tel/fax +39 (0)6 7236559; mobile +39 347 0603556; e-mail cristina.nucci@tiscali.it; www.icaro. it/bureaucratic.service/. Will get all kinds of bureaucratic papers from permesso di soggiorno, and help with opening a bank account and much more. 20-7312 2200; fax 020-7499 2283; www.embitaly.org. uk.

www.stranieriinintalia.it - website portal for foreigners in Italy that gives useful information for everyday life including updates on Italian legislation and practical advice.

www.clandestinos.itdocumentitaliani. it.asp - site giving details of all the main *documenti italiani* and how to get them and renew them (in Italian).

Other useful information about Italy including embassies, universities and comunes and everything required to legalise your stay.

Expatriate Websites for Italy – Useful Forums Include Bureaucratic Matters

www.expatsinitaly.com – run by American Cristina Fassio who lives in Italy. Very informative and constantly expanding site.

Expatsinitaly@groups.msn.com –very useful message board for expatriates in Italy.

www.intoitaly.it – Yellow Pages for Italy, directory and useful information resource for Anglo-phones living and working in Italy.

Useful Addresses

Italian Embassies and Consulates in the United Kingdom:

Italian Embassy: 14 Three Kings Yard, Davies Street, London W1Y 2EH; ☎020-7312 2200; fax 020-7499 2283; www.embitaly.org.uk.

Italian Consulate General: 38 Eaton Place, London SW1 8AN; ☎020-7235 9371; fax 020-7823 1609; e-mail itconlond_visti@btconnect.com; www.ambitalia.org.uk/visainfo.htm.

Italian Consulate General: Rodwell Tower, 111 Piccadilly, Manchester M1 2HY; ☎0161-236 9024. Easier to get through to than the London Consulate. For latest regulations send a request and a stamped addressed envelope to the Visa Department.

Italian Consulate General: 32 Melville Street, Edinburgh EH3 7HW; ☎0131-226 3631; 0131-220 3695; e-mail consedimb@consedimb.demon.co.uk.

Italian Vice Consulate: 7-9 Greyfriars, Bedford MK40 1HJ; ☎01234-356647; consulat@netcomuk.co.uk. Operates 9.30am-12.30pm Monday to Friday.

Italian Embassies and Consulates in the United States of America:

Italian Embassy: 3000 Whitehaven Street NW, Washington DC 20008; ☎202-612-4400; fax 202-518-2154; www.italyemb.org.

Italian Consul General: 690 Park Avenue, New York, NY 10021, USA; ☎212-439 8600; fax 212-249 4945; www.italyconsulnyc.org.

Italian Consul: 2590 Webster Street, angolo Broadway, San Francisco; ☎415-292-9210/931 ; visa enquiries; www.italconsfrisco.org.

Italian Consul: Boston - www.italiansonsulateboston.org/English/visti.html.

Italian Consul: Chicago – www.italconschicago.org.

Other Italian Embassies and Consulates:

Italian Embassy: 21st Floor, 275 Slater Street, Ottawa, Ontario, KIP 5H9; ☎613-232 2401; fax 613-233 1484; www.italyincanada.com; ambital@italyincanada.com.

Italian Consul General: 136 Beverley Street, Toronto (ON) M5T 1Y5, Canada; ☎416-977 1566; fax 416-977 1119; www.toronto.itconsulate.org; www.italconsulate.org.

Embassy of Italy: 12 Grey Street, Deakin A.C.T. 2600, Australia, ☎621-6273 3333; fax 612-6273 4233; www.ambitalia.org.au.

Embassy of Italy: 63 Northumberland Road, Dublin, Eire; ☎01-6601744; fax 01-6682759; e-mail info@italianembassy.ie; www.italianembassy.ie.

British Embassies and Consulates in Italy:

British Embassy: Via XX Settembre 80a (Porta Pia), 00187 Rome, Italy; ☎064-220 0001 (8am-1pm & 2-4pm); www.britain.it.

British Consulate General: via S. Paolo 7, 20121 Milano, Italy; ☎02 723001; fax 02-864 65081.

British Consulate: Via Dalmazia 127, 70121 Bari; ☎080-554 3668.

British Consulate: Viale Colombo 160, 09045 Quartu S Elena, Cagliari, Sardinia; ☎070-828628; fax 070-862293; e-mail britcon. cagliari@tiscali.it.

British Consulate: via Verdi 53, 95100 Catania; ☎095 7151864; fax 095 7151503.

British Consulate: Palazzo Castelbarco, Lungarno Corsini 2, 50123 Firenze; ☎055-284133; fax 055-219112; e-mail consular.Florence@fco.gov.uk.

British Consulate-General: Via dei Mille 40, 80121 Napoli; ☎081-423 8911; fax 081-422 434; e-mail info.naples@fco.gov.uk.

British Consulate: Via Cavour 121, 90133 Palermo; ☎091 326412; fax 091 584240.

British Consulate: via Madama Cristina 99, 10126 Torino, Italy; ☎011-650 9202; fax 011-669 5982; e-mail bcturin@yahoo.com.

British Consulate: via Roma 15, 34132 Trieste; ☎040-3478303; 040-3478311; e-mail jododds@tin.it.

British Consulate: Piazzale Donatori di Sangue 2/5, 30171 Venezia-Mestre VE; ☎041-5055990; fax 041-950254.

Other Consulates are listed on the UK Embassy website www.britain.it.

United States Embassies and Consulates in Italy:

Embassy of the United States of America: via Vittorio Venetto 119/A, 00187 Roma Italy; ☎06-467 1; fax 06-4882 672 or 06-4674 2356; www. usembassy.it.

US Consulate General: Lungarno Vespucci, 38, 50123 Firenze, Italy; ☎055-239 8276; 055-284 088.

US Consulate General: Via Principe Amedeo, 2/10 – 20121 Milano, Italy; ☎02-290 351; fax 02-2900 1165.

US Consulate General: Piazza della Repubblica – 80122 Napoli, Italy; ☎081-5838 111; fax 081-7611 869.

American Embassy to the Holy See: via dell Terme Deciane 26, 00162 Rome, Italy; ☎06-4674 3428; fax 06-575 8346.

Canadian Embassy and Consul in Italy:

Canadian Embassy: Consular Section, Via Zara, 30, 00198 Rome, Italy; ☎06-445 981; fax 06-445 98 3750; e-mail rome@international. qc.ca; www.canada.it.

Canadian Consulate General: Consular Section, Via Vittor Pisani,19, 20124 Milan, Italy; ☎02-67581; fax 02-6758 3900.

SETTING UP HOME

CHAPTER SUMMARY

○ Tuscany, Umbria, Marche and, increasingly, Puglia are the favoured regions for British expatriates wanting to settle in Italy.

○ **Property prices:** Away from the famous cities and Tuscany and Umbria, property is generally cheaper, but there will be fewer expatriates to socialise with.

○ **The Italians and housing.** Traditionally the supply of single accommodation was scarce as Italians tend to live in large family groups. However with one of the lowest birth rates in Europe this is changing, though it can still be hard to find somewhere to live on your own.

 ○ Italians themselves prefer to buy privately from vendors, but it is difficult even for Italians, if they don't have the contacts, so many end up using an estate agent.

 ○ Those letting out property back home may find employing a letting agent a worthwhile investment.

○ **Buying property.** Italian banks have speeded up their mortgage approval procedures which now take about two weeks (half the time it took a few years ago) and there are many more banks promoting mortgage packages to foreigners.

 ○ British mortgage lenders will not normally lend money to buy property in Italy, but you may be able to raise money by re-mortgaging your UK property.

 ○ Foreigners not familiar with Italian property buying procedures may find it useful to employ an *avvocato* (lawyer) to represent them.

 ○ Surveys are not compulsory but are advisable, especially for older property.

○ **Renting Property.** Renting an apartment can provide a base from which to try the way of life of a region while you look for your ideal home.

○ **Utilities.** Check that electricity, gas (in towns) and telephone are connected before moving in as having these installed/ being connected to the mains can take time and a lot of money.

OVERVIEW

Italy was among the first group of countries to use the euro in January 2002, along with Austria, Belgium, Finland, France, Germany, Ireland, Luxembourg, The Netherlands, Portugal and Spain. Denmark, Greece, Sweden and the United Kingdom have not yet joined and it is unclear at this point whether/when they will join the club.

As the European nations continue their progress towards political and economic union, thousands of Europeans are relocating to new jobs, homes and countries to set up home. France, Italy, Spain, Greece and Portugal are the most popular destinations for UK citizens moving abroad, and Italy has long been a favourite of North Americans, as can be seen from the number of American schools in Rome and other Italian cities. Over the past three decades Italy has been the dream destination of thousands of Europeans wishing to escape the northern European winters and who also have a passion for Italian landscape and culture.

Those who do not need to work have set up home in assorted properties including converted convents, shepherds' cottages, farmhouses, seaside flats, Renaissance villas and 18th century *palazzi*, with the favoured regions being the picturesque provinces of Tuscany, Umbria, Le Marche and increasingly, Puglia. The number of British expatriates resident in Italy is in the tens of thousands with many thousands more owning holiday homes there. The British Prime Minister, Tony Blair, holidayed in Chiantishire, Hollywood celebrities including George Clooney buy Italian properties and, Italy's popularity is sure to grow further. However France and Spain each have more than twice as many British foreign residents as Italy does; some might say this shows the exclusivity of Italy, while others would point to the potential risks to property that may be subject to whims of the European fault line that runs through the country. The fault line causes reasonably frequent tremors to occur in Umbria, Tuscany and elsewhere and serious damage does occur at not too lengthy intervals, as shown by the 1997 earthquake in Umbria.

For working expatriates the north of the country is most likely to be their destination, especially Milan and Bologna. Rome is, of course, home to many expats. There is no disputing that Italy has glorious scenery, an impressive cultural heritage, and a relaxed lifestyle. In theory, it is of course possible to live anywhere in the country, but in reality, it will depend on commuting times, Italian language ability (or the availability of English-speaking estate agents and other expats to socialise with), budget limitations, and how anxious the prospect of living in an earthquake zone makes you.

When buying property, Umbria and Tuscany have been popular with overseas house buyers for so long it is probably easier to find an English-speaking estate agent in those areas (even if the supply of cheaper properties has been almost entirely used up). However, it may be possible to find English speaking agents in other areas (see list of *Estate Agents in Italy below).*

For expats who have been posted to a city by their employer, or have secured a job with a new employer, there is no choice but to buy or rent somewhere close enough to the office to make commuting times acceptable. There are also local weather conditions to consider too; Bologna and Ferrara suffer from fog during the four months from November to February, so it can be better to live closer to work and avoid the inevitable accidents and delays of commuting.

BUYING PROPERTY

Away from Umbria and Tuscany you can find many other parts of Italy where the aesthetic attractions are as plentiful; these include Le Marche (pronounced markay) and north-eastern Puglia (pronounced poolia), Piedmont and Calabria, and the large island of Sardinia. British-based estate agents barely cover these other regions, with the exception of Brian A. French and Associates (☎ 0870 7301910; fax 0870 7301911; louise.talbot@brianfrench.com; www. brianfrench.com: Italian office 075 9600024 or mobile 340 341 5667, Mr. Steve Emmett), Liguria specialist, Casa Travella (www.casatravella.com) and Piedmont Properties (www.piedmont.co.uk). Another source of property for sale is the internet and a search using any of the leading search engines will find numerous online agencies. There is also the Shop Casa section on the home page of Yahoo! Italia – where property in most regions is advertised. If you cannot find a property you want in the area of your choice through an international estate agent or the internet, you will have no option but to make several trips to the region to find an agent in the locality of your choice or to deal directly with a vendor. Unless you have a thorough knowledge of the region in which you are interested, have Italian friends and contacts, and/or you speak fluent Italian, the latter option would be like jumping overboard at shark feeding time. In other words, getting through the buying procedure in one piece would be *un miracolo* and this is not the recommended way to buy Italian property. Properties are advertised for sale in all the main Italian newspapers, but they tend to be city properties. Few expatriates are interested in city properties as short term residents would be unlikely to find it financially worthwhile to buy property whose value rises slowly and costs a lot to buy in bureaucratic charges.

For a large company that expects to send a steady stream of expatriates to Italy a purchase may be worthwhile as it will save the repeated charges of estate agents when the new expat rents an apartment upon arrival. It will also save the initial hotel bills while the new expat is searching for somewhere to live. On the downside, successive expats may not find the accommodation suitable for their varying family circumstances, i.e garden, parking, location of schools, etc.

Buying property in a foreign country is always different to doing it in your home country. Therefore, unless you have the money to pay for the best legal advice and have someone else take responsibility for buying a property that matches your requirements and produces no surprises after the purchase, it will take a lot of effort on your part to complete a satisfactory purchase. Although this chapter explains the main processes involved, it is essential that professional advice applicable to both your home country and Italy be taken before any financial commitments are made. It is necessary to seek legal advice both at home and abroad as property purchase and setting up home in a foreign country often affects your residency and tax situation. Such advice is easily obtainable from property agents and lawyers in the UK, US, Canada and Italy, and personal recommendations can be obtained from those who have already set up home in Italy. However, it is important to make sure that advice is taken from a reputable and reliable expert with specialist knowledge of Italy and your home country – most embassies hold lists of local lawyers who also speak the language of their country.

The Price of Property

In the popular region of Tuscany pricetags can start at around £90,000 (approximately US$172,000) for a derelict farm house requiring three times that amount to restore it. However, more typical prices are £240,000+ (US$458,000) for a farmhouse ready for occupation with three acres of land, and up to £1.3 million for a dilapidated eighteenth century villa with twenty-five bedrooms and 350 hectares of land. Properties in need of restoration and those located far from the telephone, gas and electricity mains are always cheaper. Umbria is slightly cheaper than Tuscany and some say, just as beautiful. Properties in Le Marche are cheaper all round: a habitable, three-bedroomed house could cost about £80,000 (US$153,000) and a typical farm house with a little land and in need of restoration would be in the region of £90,000 (US$172,000) to £120,000 (US$229,000) – though as little as £30,000 is possible for something that needs a lot of work. Away from Tuscany and Umbria country purchases are cheaper and Puglia is now becoming popular because of its cheaper properties. Note that in many of the remoter areas there are few foreigners for expat retirees to socialise with, which can mean life is lonely for non-Italian speakers.

How do the Italians Live?

To understand the Italian property market and the availability of certain types of accommodation, it is necessary to understand how Italians live and the sort of accommodation they prefer. The Italian concept of home is virtually inseparable from the family. A high proportion of Italians tend to live in a large family *appartamento* in a *palazzo*, which can mean a palace but is more likely (depending on the circles you move in) to refer to a fairly modest block of flats. Even when children do move out of the parental apartment, usually to get married, they may voluntarily take a flat in the same neighbourhood or even block as their parents and continue to live as part of the family. Another reason for Italians continuing to live at home until they get married is the shortage of well paid jobs for young graduates who therefore may not be able to rent a flat of their own. Despite families living on top of each other in this fashion, there are surprisingly few social problems, which may come as a surprise to Anglo-Saxons and many North Americans with their cherished belief that everyone needs their own personal space in which to develop and relax.

However, in some areas this family proximity reaches extremes. In Naples, for instance, overcrowding resulting from poverty and an acute housing shortage means that sprawling families live in large single-room apartments, the notorious slums (*i bassi*) of that city. As a result of the way Italians live, irremediably bonded in tight family units, bachelor apartments or single accommodation (i.e. small flats) can be extremely difficult to find, especially at affordable prices.

Another aspect of Italian life that is liable to come as a shock to an unsuspecting foreigner is the noise level in and around apartment blocks and other residences. Italians do not live quietly and though a lively and vibrant city can be exciting and enjoyable when on holiday, living in a traditional Mediterranean country, with its late nights and voluble people, can take a lot of getting used to for quieter Northern Europeans and North Americans.

Italians, and Europeans in general, take much longer than North Americans to become friends with someone – though they will be very friendly and polite to newly arrived expatriates. It can take quite a while before new friends are invited to visit the home, as this is an honour reserved for family and close friends. Just because you work with someone does not mean they consider you their friend. Initial socialising is likely to be done in restaurants and bars, until Italians consider they know you well enough or like you enough, to invite you to their home.

Owing to the ever-worsening traffic and public transport problems, there is a trend towards city-centre dwelling, usually in the old part (*centro storico*) which most Italian cities of any note possess. Thirty years ago the old quarters in many European cities were invariably overcrowded, rundown or plain slum areas. Nowadays they are turning into chic residential districts popular with the young, trendy and artistic members of the community. In Italy the areas just outside the centre are known as *il semicentro*, where most of the purpose-built palazzi are located. The suburbs, (*periferia*) are where the least well off generally live, though new American-style housing estates, sporting detached homes and gardens are appearing – Silvio Berlusconi made a fortune by building one of the first in Italy.

Council accommodation (*le case popolari*) does exist in Italy but it is an administrative disaster area and is nowhere near as widespread as in the UK or other EU countries. Council tenants are charged *equo canone* (fair rents) which is in some cases an understatement, since many have not been increased since the 1960s. In any case the question of council rents is an academic one since a high percentage (20% in Milan; more in poorer areas) of tenants have not paid any rent at all for the last decade. Around 78% of Italian families are owner-occupiers, one of the highest rates in Europe; the rest live in the limited rented accommodation (*un appartamento in affitto*) that most working expatriates will have to compete for.

Rich Italians looking for a second or holiday home in their own country are less likely to go for the type of quaint, rustic property favoured by foreign retirees and those dreaming of moving to a life of ease in the Italian countryside. Italians are more likely to buy or rent a luxury seaside flat or a house in the mountains. However this is now changing and in some areas there is equal competition between Italians and foreigners for picturesque properties.

Estate Agents and Other Property Advisors

Whenever there is a boom in demand for Italian property, estate agents seem to leap out of nowhere, hit the ground running and then disappear or switch to another area of Europe when things go quiet. The real Italy specialists are likely to manage the leaner years by letting out Italian property, and improving their contacts ready for when the next boomlet occurs. They may be based in Italy or have long-standing contacts based there. The Federation of Overseas Property Developers and Consultants – FOPDAC (3rd Floor, 95 Aldwych, London WC2B 4JF; ☎020-8941 5588; fax 020-8941 0202; www.fopdac.com; info@fopdac.com) is an association of English speaking estate agents, lawyers and other specialists in the property field who work with people looking to buy European property in a country other than their own – companies must meet very strict criteria for membership.

Italian estate agents (*agenti immobiliari*) used not to be numerous as Italian buyers used local contacts that enabled them to buy privately from the vendor, thus saving the agency commission of about 3%. This has gradually been changing and it is virtually impossible to locate properties without using an agent in popular holiday areas. It is a legal requirement that all estate agents, whether Italian or foreign, register with their local chamber of commerce. Gerald Smith of Piedmont Properties advises: 'it's a good idea to check that any estate agent you deal with is registered there'.

The Italian association of real estate consultants is the *Associazione Italiana Consulenti e Gestori Immobiliari* (Via Nerino 5, 20123 Milan; ☎02-720 10974; fax 02-86452597; www.aici-italia.it) while the Federazione Italiana Agenti Immobiliari Professionali (FIAIP) represents over 20,000 estate agents and 7000 estate agencies and has dozens of regional branches.

Foreign estate agents selling property in Italy usually operate in conjunction with local associates in Italy who may be either English or Italian.

Estate Agents in the UK & FOPDAC:

Brian A. French and Associates: ☎0870-7301910; fax 0870-7301911; louise.talbot@brianfrench.com; www.brianfrench.com: Italian office: sales@brianfrench.com; ☎075-9600024 or mobile 340-341 5667, Mr. Steve Emmett). Offers a wide range of areas including Tuscany, Umbria, Le Marche, Como and Liguria.

Casa Travella; 65 Birchwood Road, Wilmington, Kent DA2 7HF, England; ☎ 01322-660988; fax 01322-667206; www.casatravella.com; e-mail casatravella. com. Sells in a wide selection of areas in Italy including Sardinia and will help with relocation, restoration, etc.

Elma Homes:127 High Road, Leavesden, Herts, WD25 7AP; ☎01923-893764; e-mail flavio@caseasole.com; www.caseasole.com. Finds homes in Tuscany, Sardinia and Puglia and provides comprehensive advice and assistance with all matters connected to buying, renovating, furnishing, translating etc.

Homes in Italy: 22, Irongate, Derby DE1 3GP; ☎01332-341146; fax 01332-348676; www.homesinitaly.co.uk; e-mail mark@homesinitaly.co.uk. Covers

Marche, Tuscany and Umbria.

Knight Frank; Head Office, 20 Hanover Square, London W1S 1HZ, ☎020-7629 8171; info@knightfrank.com; www.knightfrank.com an international agency with associates in Tuscany and North America (*Grub & Ellis*; 800-877-9066; www.grubb-ellis.com; with offices across America). Mainly Tuscan properties.

Piedmont Properties: Gerald Smith, 17 Llanvair Close, Ascot, Berks SL5 9HX; ☎01344-624096; www.piedmont.co.uk; specialise in marketing villas and vineyards in the Monteferrato and Langhe regions of Piedmont (around Asti and Alba).

Undiscovered Tuscany: Linda Travella, Woodstock, Forest Road, East Horsley, Surrey KT24 5ES; ☎01483-284011; fax 01483-285264. Started in 1987. Deals with property mainly in the Lake Como area and the lakes region as well as Liguria and Tuscany. Can arrange long and short term rentals and provide full property purchasing service.

Estate Agents in Italy: In addition to the addresses listed below, online agencies can be found via websites such as www.findaproperty.com and www. accommodation.com.

Azur Assistance: via Masaccio 21, 50136 Firenze; ☎+39 055 246 64 92; fax +39 055 200 10 29; www.azurassistance.com; Italia@azurassistance.com. Property in **Tuscany.**

Casaitalia International: Piazza della Vittoria 26, 06049 Spoleto (PG); ☎+39 0743 220122; fax +39 0743 220182; www.casait.it; info@casait.it. Rentals and sales in Latium and Abruzzo, Tuscany, Umbria and Marche, Sardinia and the rest of Italy.

Concept Italia: via Vittorio Emmanuelle II 54, 55100 Lucca; ☎0338-7127122; fax 583-32740939. Contact: Sally Adams. **Tuscany.**

D'Amico: Via Maggia, 4 Casarano (LE); ☎ +39 0833 504327; www.damioimmobiliare.it; damico.fabrizio@libero.it. Salento (**Puglia**) properties.

Garda Homes: ☎+0700 5947 137; freephone 0800 011 2127; www.gardahomes.co.uk; info@gardahomes.co.uk. **Lake Garda** specialist in sales and rentals.

Giorgio Vigano: 003914. Milan estate agent deals with property all over Italy.

Il Trovacasa: Viale Roosvelt 3, 67039 Sulmona (AQ); ☎+39 0864 33271; fax +39 0864 206273; www.agenziatrovacasa.com; info@agenziatrovacasa.com. Properties in **Abruzzo**.

Immbobiliare Menaggio: Via Como 6, 22017 Menaggio (CO); ☎+39 0344 30167; fax +39 0344 30181; www.immobiliaremenaggio.com; e-mail immo bilaremenaggio@virgilio.it. **Lake Como**.

Inter Italia: Via de Gasperi 22, 73020 Uggiano La Chiesa (LE); ☎+39 328 7445847; fax +39 0836 801848; e-mail interalia@libero.it. **Puglia** property.

La Porta Verde: Villa Rosa, Madonna delle Grazie 77, Castello delle Forme, Perugia

06055; ☎+39 075 878 4296; www.laportaverde.com; Linda@laportaverde.com. Properties and holidays in **Umbria**.

La Rocca: Louise Rocca di Vecchi, via Torino 51, 20123 Milan; ☎02-7252141; fax 02-89010909. Covers all regions of Italy.

Marcheshire.com: Piazza V Emanuele no. I, Palazzo del Cassero, 62020 Gualdo (MC); ☎+39 0733 667091; www.marcheshire.com; lemarcheshire@tiscali.it. Properties in **Marche**.

Michael Goodall: ☎0577-941703. Property agent.

Paradise Possible: v Ufficio Turistico, Via Marconi 5, 60048 Serra San Quirico; ☎+39 0731 880601; www.paradisepossible.com; e-mail mail@paradisepossible.com. **Marche** properties.

Pure Puglia: ☎+39 3395757367; in the UK 07796204962; www.pure.com; info@purepuglia.com. Properties in **Puglia**.

Tailor Made Italia: via Dante 2/77, 16121 Genova; ☎+39 3474 182336; www.tailormadebv.nl; varaldo@tailormadebv.com. Tuscany, Piedmont, Liguria, Lago Maggiore, Marche, Umbria.

Tombolesi: Via Papa Giovanni XXIII, Pergola (PU), Marche; tel/fax +33 0721 734669; e-mail info@tombolesi.com. **Marche.**

Trullitalia: ☎+39 080 4321392; fax +39 080 4327826; www.trulitalia.com; pino@trullitalia.com. Properties in **Puglia**.

Villaman: Via di Cecina 610, 55029 Ponte a Moriano, Lucca; tel/fax 583-404066. Properties in **Tuscany**.

Voltaia: Via di Voltaia nel Corso 32, Montepulciano (Siena); ☎+39 333 6712434 (English spoken); www.immobiliare-voltaia.it; voltaia@immobiliare-voltaia.it. **Tuscany** and **Umbria**.

Welcomeservice in Umbria: Via S. Maria 62, 06059 Todi (PG); ☎+39 339 6531677; fax +39 075 8944531; e-mail info@welcomeservice.it; www.welcomeservice.it. Villas, farmhouses, apartments and plots for sale. Also holiday rentals and property management.

Useful Publications & Miscellaneous Contacts

Italy Assist: 26-28 Addison road, Bromley, Kent BR2 9RR; ;e-mail italyassist@email.com; www.italyassist.com. Can help with building renovation in Tuscany, Emilia Romagna, Marche and Umbria and will consider other areas of Italy. Contact Matthew Church.

Porta Portese: comes out in Rome on Tuesdays and Fridays and contains a useful accommodation section.

Ville & Casali: Edizioni Living International (ELI) SpA, Via Anton Giulio Bragaglia, 33-00123 Rome; ☎06-30884122; fax 06-30889944. Ville & Casali is a national property and decoration magazine in Italian, the classified property advertisements are listed in both Italian and English.

La Dolce Vita: important Italian property and lifestyle festival held at Earls Court Exhibition Centre. New event (2005) will be held annually in springtime. Contact www.ladolcevitaevent.co.uk or contact the organizers Beat Ltd. (☎0207-307 0020; info@beatcapital.com) for 2006 dates and London venue.

HOME SWAPS

If you are not sure which region you would like to buy a property in, would like to 'try the region out', or have a base from which to look around for a suitable property, a home swap can be an economic way to do this. There are branches of the main home swap organisations in Italy, which are listed here:

Family Links: Via Brescia 34, Rome; tel/fax 06 85354524.

Green Theme International: Euroculture, Via A Rossi 7, 36100 Vicenza; www. gti-home-exchange.com. Home swaps for those who care about the impact of tourism on the environment and the culture of the country they are visiting who want to swap homes with like-minded travellers.

Homelink International: Casa Vacanze, Campiello del Duomo 7/8 31046 Oderzo (TV); www.homelink.org. Worldwide organisation with branches in 32 countries. Founded in 1952.

Intervac International Home Exchange: www.intervac.com. Private organisation started in 1953 to give people the change of affordable holidays and to enable them to have a true experience of other ways of living.

Latitudes Home Exchange: Home Exchange.com Inc. POB 787, Hermosa Beach, CA 90254, USA; ☎310-798-3864; toll free ☎800-877-8723; fax 310-798-3865; www.home-swap.com. Over 6,000 listings worldwide.

LETTING PROPERTY IN YOUR HOME COUNTRY

For those who own accommodation in their home country, letting it while they are away can be a good way to maintain a source of income whilst living in Italy. However, it should be born in mind that being an absentee landlord is not always easy and the income not always reliable – tenants do not always pay the rent and it can be hard to find a replacement when living in another country or if your visits home are infrequent. Estate agents often act as letting agents too and will manage property for absentee landlords. For expatriates, utilising a local agent to manage their property, rather than a friend or family member, can be well worth the agency fees; 10% of the income is not much for relieving the stress and worry of managing rental property in another country and lessening the likelihood of falling out with friends or family if the tenant damages the property or skips with the deposit.

Some expats specifically buy property in their home country to rent while they live abroad. This can be to generate income, as a form of investment, or be the intended place of retirement at the end of an international career. Recommended reading on this subject is listed below.

FINANCE

Mortgages with Italian Banks

Italians often buy their apartments by outright purchase in one go, though all the family will probably chip in. A mortgage (*un mutuo*) can be arranged with the majority of Italian banks in Italy and interest rates in Italy remain historically low at around 4%-5%, but bear in mind that they will probably not stay that way. Traditionally financial sector services in Italy operate in a moribund fashion (see *Banking* in *Daily Life*). For instance, it takes a minimum of five days to get a mortgage approved with a UK building society or bank, compared with a minimum of one month with an Italian bank or financial institution. The main reason for this difference is that the client vetting procedures of the Italian banks are extremely cumbersome. However, increased competition from foreign organisations has compelled Italian banks and finance institutions to streamline their procedures and the procedure can be carried out in two weeks.

Historically Italian banks granted relatively low percentage mortgages (i.e. around 75% mortgage or less) on a property ready for habitation. This is now changing though as those banks that have specialist foreign buyers departments such as Unicredit Banca per la Casa (which bought Abbey National Italy) and Banca Woolwich offer up to 85% on some types of mortgage and local lenders are trying to remain competitive. Banca Intesa (www.bancaintesa.it) offers up to 90% mortgages. A few banks offer a *mutuo per ristrutturazione* (a mortgage for properties requiring restoration) of 80-90%. Currently Unicredit are offering rates of 5.30% and 5.75% on ten and 20-year fixed rate mortgages while mortgage specialists Micos Banca has a rates from 3.40% on variable rate mortgages. Many Italian banks offer a choice of fixed or variable interest mortgages, *tasso fisso* and *tasso variabile* respectively. Some banks in the

Mezzogiorno and Sardinia offer reduced interest rates (*abbattimento tasso*) in order to attract buyers to certain areas. Such banks include *Banco di Sardegna* and the *Cassa Risparmio di Calabria*. Most banks do not have an upper limit (*importo massimo*) on the amount of the mortgage.

Specialist mortgage departments in Italian financial institutions have become more common in recent years as have online banks and mortgages. The Dutch bank ING have had great success since offering services to Italians at www.ingdirect.it with their online bank account, Conto Arancio and their Mutuo Arancio Orange Mortgage (the advertising symbol is an orange pumpkin). The online account pays 3% interest and the mortgage rate is very competitive.

Italian banking institutions can provide up to 80% mortgages over a fifteen year period, which would be attractive for expatriates earning an Italian salary. Non-residents are normally treated with more caution than Italian residents. Italian residents can have up to a 30-year mortgage depending on their age.

What Kind of Mortgage?

Fixed rate	– if you want to be sure of the exact amounts and the end total, in advance, and if you foresee growing inflation.
Variable rate	– if you foresee a drop in inflation, have a medium to high income and like taking risks.
Mixed rate (renegotiable every 24 months)	– if you are unsure of the present state of the economy and want to have the option of adapting to more advantageous conditions in the future.
Capped rate	– if you want to keep to a flexible rate whilst limiting the risks, and at the same time retain the guarantee of a fixed rate without the extra costs.
Balanced rate	– if you have a feel for market movements and like to manipulate the balance between fixed and variable rates.
Interest only	– if you expect to be able to pay off the capital sporadically.

Banks sometimes offer cheap promotional introductory rates for a brief initial period (3-6 months).

Typical Mortgage Conditions

Purpose of mortgage:	primary or secondary residence for purchase, renovation or completion, or for other stated purpose.
Types of repayment:	fixed, variable, mixed or capped rates, or interest only. (see below)

Sum available:	up to 80% of the value of the property – 60% for non-residents. NB. valuations are conservative.
Duration:	normally 5, 10, 15, 20 years but up to 25 or 30 years.
Age limit:	mortgage to expire at age 65, 70, 75, or as long as you are able.
Frequency of repayments:	Monthly, quarterly or biennially.
Setting up expenses:	typically 0.20% of the sum borrowed, but variable.
Valuation expenses:	typically €300, but variable, sometimes free.
Occasional expenses:	typically €1,29 for every communication or €1,00 for each repayment.
Insurance cover:	insurance is compulsory, in favour of the bank, against the risk of fire, lightning, gas explosions, possibly also against the risk of impact of vehicles or aircraft, 'socio-political events', 'atmospheric events' burst pipes etc. Insurance premium to be paid in a one-off *una tantum* payment. Premium typically 0.21% of value of property for 20 year contract. A life assurance policy guaranteeing repayment in the event of your death, accident, illness or loss of job is optional.
Penalties for early redemption:	typically between 0.5% and 3% of residual capital, depending on the timescale.
Penalties for late payment or default:	late payments, *ritardati pagamenti,* are defined as ones made 30-180 days after the due date. They incur the application of interest on arrears, *interessi di mora.* If you are more than seven times late with your repayments – not necessarily consecutively – the bank can repossess the property. The bank will also foreclose on you if you fail to make a repayment within 180 days of the due date.
Collateral guarantees required:	A first degree state-registered mortgage, *ipoteca di primogrado,* of the property. Some banks accept – in addition or as an alternative – a life insurance policy, stocks and bonds, and the transfer to them of rental contracts. A third person can also give a guarantee, *fideiusussione.*
Conditions:	You might have to open an account in the mortgager's bank. Sometimes it is a condition that the property be a first home *primaria abitazione* or that it only be used for residential purposes.
Evidence of income:	bank guidelines require proof that your repayments are not more than 35% of your disposable income.

There is an excellent Italian website dedicated to mortgages and loans for instant competitive quotations online: www.mutuionline.it.. There are over 20 banks, mostly Italian to compare on the website.

Useful Addresses – Italian Banks and UK Mortgage Brokers

Banca Intesa: www.bancaintesa.it has branches in most regions of Italy and one in London and in New York.

Banca Nazionale del Lavoro: Direzione Generale, Via Vittorio Veneto 119, 00187 Rome; www.bnl.it.

Banca Woolwich SpA: Milan Regional Office: Piazza della Repubblica 8, 20121 Milan; ☎02 290401; fax 02 290 40619.

Banca Woolwich SpA: Via Pantano 13, 20122 Milano; ☎02-58 488309; fax 02-58488511; www.bancawoolwich.it.

Casa Travella: (www.casatravella.com) ☎01322-660988) is a property agent that may be able to give assistance with obtaining mortgages with some banks, for instance Banca Popolare di Sondrio in Como, or Banca di Toscana depending on the region and the branches.

Woolwich Europe Ltd: 30 Erith Road, Bexley Heath, Kent DA7 6BP; ☎020-8298 4771; fax 020-8298 5315.

Conti Financial Services: 204 Church Road, Hove, E Sussex BN3 2DJ; ☎01273-772811; fax 01273-321269; www.mortgageoverseas.com. Conti have many years of experience arranging finance for clients (both UK and non-UK nationals) purchasing properties overseas and is an independent mortgage broker.

Istituto Monte dei Paschi di Siena: U.S.I.E. Sett. Serv. V.le Toselli 60, 53100 Siena

Kevin Sewell Mortgages: 7a Bath Road Business Park, Devizes, Wiltshire SN10 1XA; ☎01380-739198; www.internationalmortgages.org; ksewell@netcomuk.co.uk. International mortgages.

Micos Banca: www.micosbanca.it. Specialist house mortgage bank.

Unicredit Banca per la Casa: via Orefici 10, centre zone, Milan; ☎02-8545651; fax 02 85456508; www.bancaperlacasa.it. Branches also in Bergamo and Brescia, northern Italy (took over Abbey National Italy).

Documents for Bank Mortgage Approval

In order to consider your mortgage the bank will require the following documentation, which it will photocopy:

- ◑ The preliminary sale documents, the *compromesso* or *preliminare di vendita,* between you and the vendor of the property in question, or a land registry proof of your title.
- ◑ Your passport.
- ◑ Your Italian fiscal code number, *codice fiscale.*
- ◑ Your most recent tax returns (at least three).
- ◑ Your most recent bank statements (at least three months).
- ◑ Any other documents proving your income.

The bank will also require documentation on the property itself, which only your surveyor, *geometra,* can supply:

- ◑ *La provenienza del bene* – The provenance of the property.

O *Il certificato storico ventennale* – a twenty-year retrospective certification
of the property.

Non-residents may find it difficult to obtain a mortgage to buy a dilapidated or
isolated rural property, but easier to buy it first and then obtain a mortgage for
renovation. The bank will normally require at least four weeks to process your
application.

Offshore Mortgages

Another option open to expatriates is to take out an offshore mortgage. For
convenience and tax-free interest on their savings, expatriates often utilise offshore
banking and financial services. Jersey, Guernsey and the Isle of Man are the prime
offshore banking centres in Europe, along with Switzerland, Liechtenstein and
Luxembourg for those with a lot of money. Banks in Jersey, Guernsey and the Isle
of Man operate under UK banking rules and offer reliable and efficient banking
and financial services, including euro mortgages for buying property in Europe.

Offshore mortgages work slightly differently to standard mortgages and
potential mortgagees should investigate them thoroughly before taking one
on. Articles on offshore mortgages and details of providers can be found in
expatriate magazines such as *FT Expat, Nexus* etc. Independent mortgage brokers
who advertise in the expatriate magazines should also be able to advise you on
offshore financial services. International Mortgage Plans ☎ 01932-830660;
e-mail info@international-mortgageplans.com; www.international-mortgage-
plans.com) is an offshore mortgage broker.

Importing Currency

When buying property in Italy, you will, under normal circumstances have to
pay in euros, the local currency. Thanks to the Single Market, you can take as
much cash as you like with you, but there is no advantage in doing so, and it is
certainly risky. If you take more than €10,330 (about £7,068) in cash with you
into Italy, you are required to declare it to customs. Taking a large amount of cash
is not only risky, but you could be suspected of being a drugs dealer or terrorist by
Italian customs if they find out.

Currency is nowadays normally sent using electronic transfer; the SWIFT
system is the most well-known. There are charges involved at both ends so you
need to know who is paying for them, and how much the receiving bank in Italy
is likely to charge. Most big banks will do a transfer. The receiving bank in Italy
should charge very little. The use of banker's drafts is not recommended as they
are far too slow, and there is a risk of losing the draft.

Since the UK is not part of 'euroland', anyone buying property abroad is confronted with the painful possibility that a percentage of their money is going to disappear into the coffers of a high street bank. Fortunately, this need not be the case, since a number of specialist companies have started up to lessen the financial penalty of the transaction.

A specialised company such as market leader Currencies Direct (www. currenciesdirect.com), also PropertyFinance4Less (www.propertyfinance4less. com; ☎020 7594 0555), Moneycorp (www.moneycorp.com), HIFX, Currencies4Less, World First (www.worldfirst.com) and other similar companies can help in a number of ways, by offering better exchange rates than banks, without charging commission, and giving you the possibility of 'forward buying' – agreeing on the rate that you will pay at a fixed date in the future – or with a limit order – waiting until the rate you want is reached. For those who prefer to know exactly how much money they have available for their property purchase, forward buying is the best solution, since you no longer worry about the movement of the pound against the euro working to your detriment. Payments can be made in one lump sum or on a regular basis. It is usual when building new property to pay in four instalments, so-called 'stage payments'.

There is a further possibility, which is to use the services of a law firm in the UK to transfer the money. They can hold the money for you until the exact time that you need it; they will use the services of a currency dealer themselves.

THE PURCHASING AND CONVEYANCING PROCEDURE

PROFESSIONAL ASSISTANCE

The sale of real estate in Italy (*La compravendita di un immobile*) is governed by the Civil Code articles 1754-1765 and also by laws (*leggi*) *39 of 3 feb 1989 and 452 of 21 dec 1990. It consists of two stages:*

(a) The *Compromesso*, the preliminary contract or *preliminare di vendita*, whereby the buyer pays a deposit called a *caparra*, or earnest money, on an agreed price on a specified property, the contract to be completed by a specified date. It can be a privately signed deed between the buyer and vendor, but it is recommended that it should be done with a notary, publicly registered, and regarded as seriously as a final contract. If the buyer fails to complete he forfeits his deposit. If the vendor pulls out of the contract he must pay back the buyer double his deposit.

(b) Il rogito – the final contract and transfer of title, registered in the Land Registry office (*Ufficio del Registro* or *Catasto*) by the *notaio*.

Before you sign anything remember that an estate agent, however honest, is not guaranteed to be impartial. You are advised at this stage to get the help of a lawyer or a notary.

O an *avvocato civilista* – of the status of the international practitioners mentioned above.

O a *notaio*. Employ a *notaio* from the very beginning, and you will get the documentation and the wording right, and avoid possible complications. A *notaio* is professionally qualified to make all the necessary checks that are required for the filing of a contract.

O The *Compromesso* is the important and binding part of this contract.

Who Does What

The official usually appointed to handle a property sale is a *notaio* (public notary) who in Italy acts for both the vendor and the purchaser; a similar system operates in other European countries such as France. There are also some lawyers (*avvocati*) who are not qualified to handle property transactions but who are expert in property legislation and can advise you about legal issues that may arise. Foreigners, who are generally not versed in Italian property buying procedures, may wish to appoint both a *notaio* and an *avvocato*. This way, an expatriate can have a competent professional who works for them directly explain the process to them fully and completely, and not someone who is supposed to be an impartial administrator. Italian lawyers based in the UK can represent expatriates in Italy (see addresses below) when you are buying Italian property, alternatively your embassy or regional consular office should be able to supply a list of local lawyers who speak your language. The *notaio* is responsible for gathering together all the necessary documents, checking that the title deeds are in order, that the property is legally registered and that it has no illegal buildings on it. Having ascertained that this is the case, the next step is for the purchaser and vendor to sign a preliminary contract of sale.

You may also want to call on the services of a surveyor (*geometra*) to check the soundness of the building, point out any structural defects and estimate the cost of putting them right. Unlike in Britain, however, surveys are not compulsory and many Italians do not bother with them. For foreigners buying older buildings, especially those in need of restoration, a survey is almost certainly essential to prevent post-sale surprises.

A *geometra* can draw up contracts, carry out land searches and also monitor building work and make orders to suppliers if restoration is needed once the sale is completed.

Fabio Ausenda, an Italian who has bought several properties, explains why he thinks using professionals is necessary when buying property in Italy

A lawyer can verify that the property you are buying is free from rights by other neighbouring properties, for example, rights of way, right to use the waters etc . If you buy farmland, verify that no one else has acquired the right to use your property because they have already been using it for over 20 or 30 years ...in other words a lawyer can tell you aspects that the sale agent may not know and the vendor may hide, or be unaware of because he has never investigated these rights, or they may be written on the deeds but not that evident. The notaio *should inform you when he reads the deeds, but if he does not speak English, or if the student interpreter you have taken along does not understand limitations on property these things may not come to light until later.*

It is also wise to check with an architect or geometra what the neighbours' building rights are, and what is the maximum height a building near yours can be built....All the zoning laws are known to these professionals and they are in the best position to tell you what can happen around your home in future, based on the local town zoning laws. Moreover, they are also able to tell you what you can do to renovate a building. It may be that you cannot install new windows or alter the walls. All these rules are known as vincoli *and* vincoli storici *or* artistici *and they can be very strict. Living in a house that cost a fortune and being forced to live with tiny mediaeval windows which were meant to keep the house warm in winter, may not be your idea of heaven.*

Lawyers

It is a matter of choice whether you use a locally based lawyer (as many house purchasers recommend) as they will have the best knowledge of the area where you are buying and the problems likely to arise with a particular property. Using a local lawyer has the advantage that it also helps you to make friends in the area where you will be living i.e. If you use a non-local lawyer it might be inferred that you do not really trust Italian lawyers. The obvious problem with using a local lawyer is that they may not speak English, which is fine if you trust your house agent, or some other interpreter to be your means of communicating with them. However, it is better to deal with someone with whom you have a language in common. It is not impossible to find an Italian lawyer outside Tuscany, Rome or Milan who speaks good English and you can get a list from the regional consular office or from your Embassy. Your estate agent should also know if there is an English-speaking lawyer locally.

Fabio Ausenda offers suggestions on finding an Italian-speaking lawyer

If there is no lawyer locally who speaks English, go to the nearest large town, for instance the Capoluogo di Provincia *(the provincial capital). It is important that the lawyer is local enough to know the region and that he or she is expert in Italian property legislation and is able to interpret local zoning laws. A local lawyer, if you can find one would be better and cheaper. Alternatively, you can choose the notary yourself. The notary is always paid by the buyer and although he is impartial, if you are the party who chooses the notary you can ask the notary (with an interpreter if needed) to certify that the property is* libera da vincoli *(free from obligations). You should not have to pay any extra charges for this beyond what you have to pay the notary anyway. Every time I have bought a property I have always used my notary, who though impartial is still paid by me and so has worked for me.*

There are also Italian lawyers based in the UK who can represent expatriates in Italy (see below), and English legal firms with specialist property lawyers for different countries (also see below).

Specialist lawyers based in the UK:

Bennett & Co: D144 Knutsford Road, Wilmslow, Cheshire, SK9 6JP; ☎01625-586937; www.bennett-and-co.com; international lawyers@Bennett-and-co.com.

Claudio del Giudice: Avvocato and Solicitor, Rivington House, 82 Great Eastern Street, London EC2A 3JF; ☎020 7613 2788; e-mail delgiudice@clara.co.uk; www.delgiudice.clara.net. Specialises in Italian property work and conveyancing.

Giambrone & Law: 9 Gunnery Terrace, Royal Arsenal, London SE18; ☎020-8301 8671; fax 0208-301 8149; www.giambronelaw.co.uk. Italian lawyers with expertise on property law of both the UK and Italy.

Giovanni Lombardo Dobson & Sinisi, 1 Throgmorton Avenue, London EC2N

2JJ; ☎020-7628 8163; fax 020-7920 0861. No lawyers in the London office but they will provide contact to their Italian office.

Pini, Bingham & Partners: 30 St. John's Lane, London EC1M 4NB; ☎020-7689 2000; fax 020-7689 2001; www.pinilaw.co.uk. Strong in international and commercial law. Can advise on both Italian and English law. Links with firms throughout Italy.

The International Property Law Centre: Unit 2, Waterside Park, Livingstone Road, Hessle, HU13 OEG; please contact Ugo Tanda, Italian Avvocato, on ☎0870-800 4591 (e-mail ugot@maxgold.com); or Stefano Lucatello, Italian Solicitor on ☎0870-800 4565 (e-mail Stefano@maxgold.com); fax 0870-800 4567; general e-mail internationalproperty@maxgold.com; www. internationalpropertylaw.com. Specialists in the purchase and sale of Italian property and businesses, wills and probate, and litigation.

James Bennett & Co: Nightingale House, Brighton Road, Crawley, West Sussex, RH10 6AE; ☎01293-544044; www.jamesbennett.co.uk; info@jbb-law. co.uk.

John Howell & Co: The Old Glassworks, 22 Endell Street, Covent Garden, London WC2H 9AD; ☎020-7420 0400; fax 020-7836 3626; e-mail info@europelaw.com; www.europelaw.com. Law firm specialising entirely in foreign property purchase.

Italian Lawyers in Italy

Avv. Fabio Pucciarelli: Via Migliorati 7, 63021 Amandola (AP) Le Marche, Italy; ☎+39 333 2045500 mobile; tel/fax +39 0736 847692; www. propertyadviceitaly.com. English-speaking Italian lawyer provides legal advice to clients for the purchase of property in Le Marche, Abruzzo, Lazio, Molise, Tuscany and Umbria and deals with inheritance questions.

For Italian lawyers in Italy who are members of the British Chamber of Commerce in Milan, see list of *Major Employers* in the *Employment* chapter.

LOCAL PROFESSIONALS

The key local professionals indispensable to the purchase of a property in Italy are the surveyor *(geometra)* and the notary *(notaio)*. The *geometra* performs the functions, which we associate with an architect, – making drawings and specifications, supervising work etc. Architects *(architetti)* also exist in Italy, and it is worth explaining the difference between an *architetto* and a *geometra*.

Comparison of Geometri and Architetti

A *geometra* does all the work we expect of an architect, up to a certain level. An *architetto* has a more prestigious title and operates on a higher plane both financially and artistically. A *geometra* qualifies by passing the requisite high school exam, and then, following another exam after two years of apprenticeship, he is fully fledged at twenty-two. But an *architetto* has to do a five-year university course and is usually 28 before qualifying. The result is that *architetti* know a lot about the artistic and theoretical but little about the practical side of building; they charge much more, seldom visit sites – and the *geometri* get most of the work. There is a state of mutual hostility between these two branches of the same profession. *Architetti* often exploit *geometri* and *geometri* are resentful of this.

The *geometra* is now a threatened species; the system is changing in Italy to conform with the rest of Europe: they will all become *architetti*. As it stands, you would only consult an *architetto* if you were involved in a large project or on a listed building, or if you were looking for an artistic modern treatment for the interior of an ancient building. *Architetti* are employed by the Fine Arts Commission (*la sovrintendenza delle Belle Arti*) of the Province, which is a sort of local style-police appointed by the Culture Ministry of Rome (*il Ministero dei Beni Culturali*).

THE GEOMETRA

An alert and vigilant *geometra* should pick up on any faults in a building, which might be used if possible to negotiate a lower price. But certain considerations which are important in the British Isles, such as rising damp, woodworm or rotten timbers, are taken for granted in unrestored properties in Italy, where the price is dictated by the broader picture – the rarity value or the location or the beauty of the environment.

The *geometra* is familiar with both the legal and technical aspects of land and buildings, and it is vital to have him check all the points listed below before you arrange for the legal side of your purchase, for which you will require the services of a notary or *notaio*, and more checks.

Checklist for the Geometra

So, at the normal domestic level of house buying you would employ a *geometra* for the purpose of inspections or surveys. A site visit is called a *sopralluogo*. A technical survey is called a *perizia*. A checklist for an apartment or town house should include the following points:

- ◯ architectural drawings? (*La planimetria*)
- ◯ floor space in square metres? (*i metri quadri*)
- ◯ type and number of rooms? (*tipologia e numero vani*)

- year of construction? (*anno di costruzione*)
- which floor? (*piano*)
- type of condominium (*tipo condominio*)
- lift? elevator? (*ascensore*)
- porter/janitor? (*portineria*)
- utilities and services ok? (*impianti a norma*)
- garage? how big? (*box*)
- parking space? (*postauto*)
- cellar? how big? (*cantina*)
- store room? how big? (*ripostiglio*)
- balconies? how big? (*balconi*)
- terrace? how big? (*terrazzo*)
- doors and windows? in what state? (*infissi*)
- floors? in what state? (*pavimenti*)
- plumbing and bathrooms? in what state? (*sanitari*)
- leaks? (*infiltrazioni*)

A checklist for a country property should add the following points:
Access roads? (*strade di accesso*) (What are they like in winter? How much to repair and maintain? Whose responsibility? Normally they are *strade vicinali* neighbourhood roads, but don't count on the neighbours making a contribution to any repairs.

- electricity (see *ENEL* in *Services* chapter).
- water (*acquedotto*) (see *Services* chapter)
- gas (*gas metano*) (see *Services* chapter)
- cracks? (*crepe*)
- subsidence? (*assestamento*)
- roof? (*tetto*)
- rotten beams? (*travi marce*)
- rights of way? (*diritti di passo*)
- earthquake risks? (*rischio seismico*) (what architectural reinforcements are required by local building codes?)
- Radon gas risks? (*rischio gas radon*) (this applies to the Dolomites and other granitic areas, Tufa areas might be at risk. Remedial architecture is available.)
- flooding risk? (*rischio allagamento*)
- landslide risk? (*rischio frana*)
- If you are putting in a bore-hole for water (*pozzo artesiano*) or an in-ground swimming pool your *geometra* must obtain a *svincolo idrogeologico* or a hydrogeological clearance from the provincial authority.
- sewage (*fognatura*) Is it mains (*comunale*) or a private septic tank? (*fossa*

biologica) Does it need repairs or replacement? Periodic emptying?

Checklist For The Buyer

Verbal agreements. No verbal agreement has any value in Italian law. Handshakes in the market place belong to a past age.

Inspection of Property. Don't accept the definition of property 'as seen' (*visto e piaciuto*), and do not accept it 'in the state of fact and law in which it is at present found' (*nello stato di fatto e diritto in cui attualmente si trova*) without visiting and carefully checking everything.

Appurtenances. In particular check that all appurtenances (*pertinenze*) are specified, such as cellars, attics, garages and sheds. Attach a *geometra's* drawing of the property to the contract, signed by both parties and specify such appurtenances in writing.

Utilities and Services. Examine the utilities and services with the help of an expert. Water, gas, electricity, oil, boilers, pumps – (*impianti*). Yearly service contracts and guarantees should be obtained from the vendor. Details such as whether or not the gas pipelines arrive at the building can make a huge difference to the cost of heating bills. Remote areas may not be connected to DSL lines which may be crucial for those wanting to work from their nice Tuscan home, e.g. a web designer.

Furniture and Fittings. Make an inventory (*elenco*) of all the items you and the vendor are agreed on for you to keep. Check that all rubbish and all the items you do not want are removed before the sale. Some unscrupulous owners remove all fittings, door handles, switches, radiators, boilers, etc. To avoid this, include them in the inventory. As an extra precaution, arrange with the owner for a final check-up on the day or the day before the final contract. The same argument applies to plants, shrubs, olive trees, tubs and planters etc., which you might or might not want to keep.

Mortgages. Mortgages (*ipoteche*). Be aware of the fact that even if you buy a property on which the previous mortgage has been completely paid off, this does not mean it has been officially cancelled. You need to know how much the necessary formalities would cost to cancel the mortgage in the land registry (*La conservatoria dei registri immobiliari*).

Alternatively you can take over the vendor's existing mortgage (see *Mortgages*). The notary will be able to advise you on this: you can take on the remaining mortgage if the bank agrees to let you do this. You will thereby save on the *perizia,* the official valuation of the house for the bank for example. Your bank will still negotiate a new mortgage with you, and would want all the usual proof of income etc. and the new mortgage with a new mortgage lender would be written into the deed by the notary.

PRELAZIONE – THIRD PARTIES RIGHT TO BUY

Il diritto di prelazione – pre-emptive rights, designed to protect the small working farmer of yesteryear, are still available to people who are officially registered as *coltivatori diretti,* literally direct cultivators, who are *confinanti,* contiguous neighbours, giving them the right of first refusal on any non-urban land adjacent to their own. They are entitled to buy this at the declared price.

Sitting tenants and individuals, who are conducting a business in the property also have a right to buy.

The state – or the *comune* or other state bodies also have the right to buy, or requisition in certain cases, for example, in the case of an archaeological find, and in the case of listed buildings in the *beni culturali* category.

To avert this threat you have to obtain a disclaimer (*rinuncia*) from any interested party. For this you need the co-operation of the vendor, or of your own professional, *geometra* or *avvocato.*

Inherited or Donated Property. Beware of property acquired by donation or inheritance. A group of siblings often inherit a property, which they decide to sell, but at the last minute one of them refuses to sign. This is often used as a ruse to jack the price up, and is a frequent cause of disappointment for buyers. The only solution to this problem is for the *notaio* to assemble all the owners of the property at the early *compromesso* stage and obtain their signatures on the *compromesso.*

A *certificato di provenienza* – a certificate of provenance such as a will or a donation attests to the legal owners of such property.

Vacant Possession. Check that there are no tenants or squatters in a property supposed to be vacant, including the owner himself. It takes six to ten years to evict a tenant or squatter, going through the Italian legal process. Make sure that all goods and chattels not required by you are removed from the premises.

Tenanted Property. If the property is tenanted it can be as much as 30% cheaper than an untenanted property and could be regarded as an investment.

It is advisable to talk to the tenant and find out his intentions. You have to give him six months written notice to get him to leave. If he decides to stay, the Italian legal system will take an average of six to ten years to evict him.

You must get from the vendor: the tenancy lease, the tenant's deposit money and any advance rent already paid (*il contratto di locazione, il deposito cauzionale,* and *i canoni anticipati*).

Restrictions and Limitations on the Property. Itemise all restrictions (*vincoli*) and limitations (*servitù*), rights of way (*diritti di passo*) and other burdens (*oneri*) on the property. Make the vendor responsible for any expenses required for eliminating any declared or undeclared restrictions.

Planning Regulations. The validity of a property sale contract in Italy requires documents proving that any illegal improvements have been sanctioned. The local council (*comune*) can issue a document specifying all the permissions they have granted to the property, although not many councils are aware of this. The sanctioning of illegal work is called a *condono edilizio*. Building permission is: *concessione edilizia*.

Imminent Planning Threats. If possible go with your *geometra* or an interpreter to the *Ufficio Tecnico* (planning office) of your local Council (*Comune*), which is normally open to the public two mornings a week.

Ask to see the PRG, the master zoning plan, (*piano regolatore generale*) to check the scenarios: housing estates (*zone edificabili*), industrial developments: (*zone industriali*), quarries, clay pits (*cave*), roads (*strade*), roundabouts (*rotatorie*), overpasses (*sopraelevate*), railways (*ferrovie*), dumps (*discariche*), composting plants (*impianti di compostaggio*) and golf courses (*campi da golf*). There are many long term projects, such as the *Grosseto-Fano* road link, which has been long in abeyance, but is apt at any moment to bring large scale road works to the most hidden valleys of Tuscany, Umbria and the Marches.

The *ufficio tecnico* can provide you with copies of its plans, and the status of your target property, whether it is listed (*schedata*) and what the neighbours might be up to. The word *zoning* has entered the Italian language.

These researches are not automatically carried out in Italy, certainly not by lawyers or notaries. The key professional to commission for the task is the local *geometra* who will be familiar with the *comune* involved.

WHAT MONEY CAN DO

Some house-owners in Italy, when they find their property is threatened by certain municipal planning use their resources and resourcefulness to get things changed. Methods include:

Road Diversions. Roadside houses can be given the priceless advantage of privacy by diverting the road to by-pass the property at a distance. You can only do this if you own, or can buy, the land on which to locate the new road; and then only if the old road is a *strada bianca* – a dirt road, literally a 'white road'. You have to negotiate with the local council if the road is a *strada comunale* (a road which is the responsibility of the *comune*). A *strada provinciale* (provincial road) is not normally negotiable, but if you were to have a go it would be with the provincial planning office.

An unthinkable amount of political clout would be required to change the course of a *strada statale* (a road which is the responsibility of the state). On the other hand a *strada vicinale* – a neighbourhood road – would only require the assent of the neighbours who used that road, plus the planning consent of the local council.

Burying Electricity or Telephone Wires. There are three types of electricity cable *alta, media* and *bassa tensione* (high, medium and low). *Alta tensione* pylons are impossible to move but *media* and *bassa* are no problem, and indeed encouraged for aesthetic reasons. You simply apply to the Electricity board, the ENEL, who will do the work for you. The conduit alone costs €3,000 per 100 metres. To bury *media tensione* cable costs €140,000 per 250 metres. For telephone lines apply to the telephone company, usually Telecom Italia.

Improvements Without Planning Consent. Many house owners carry out improvements regardless of planning permission. They simply pay the fine when challenged, and get the work *condonato* (amnestied) at a later date. Be aware that Councils have been known to issue legal injunctions to stop or demolish *abusivo* work, in particular when they have received complaints from the public, and especially in the case of swimming pools. To achieve your objectives in all these cases you need the services of a *geometra* who is familiar with the planning offices involved. You will also need plenty of money (*un sacco di soldi*).

In the Event of any Dispute. It is wise to put into the contract an agreement to settle any eventual disputes with a neighbour by means of a preferably quick and cheap arbitration. If you have a litigious neighbour, it could be long and costly and not necessarily end in victory for you. Avoid if at all possible a a dispute with the comune as this will be the longest and costliest of all. A notary (*notaio*) can be appointed for this task; it is his job to be impartial. Alternatively the local *Tribunale* or law court can be named. This arrangement is called *una clausola arbitrale*.

Beware of the Vendors. Establish first that the vendor(s) have the right identity, and that they own the property. Is the vendor of sound mind? Is he under age? Is there a spouse lurking in the background with a claim to the property? Is he bankrupt?

If he goes bankrupt within two years of selling the property, the property reverts to his estate, on which you will figure as one of the creditors.

If you buy from a company it is even more imperative to check – in the local chamber of commerce – whether the company is still registered or struck off, or encumbered with debt or insolvent (*fallito*). Bankruptcies (*fallimenti*) are common. You and your professional advisers have to be extremely vigilant.

Fraud (*Truffa*). Beware of con men (*imbroglioni*). A single property was once sold to three different buyers on the same day at different notaries. The first notary to register the property in the *catasto* yielded the only legal owner.

In Bologna two flats were rented out to 26 different tenants at the same time, at a deposit of €43.8 per head, which the fake estate agents pocketed and then disappeared into thin air. The gang was recognised by one of the victims when its leader appeared on a TV quiz show.

That particular gang consisted of Italians and Colombians – but the con man could equally be British or German or American, preying on his own compatriots.

THE NOTARY

The *notaio* is a representative of the state whose duty it is to register all contracts, deeds, and titles in the appropriate registry office, and collect all appropriate taxes and duties on behalf of the state; responsible, if in default, for making good any deficit out of his or her own pocket. Women are increasingly evident in the profession. A *notaio's* office is an august and serious place and much dignity and prestige is attached to the profession. Beware of being late or casual with your appointments, and always be sure to bring all your documents and identifications. Despite this dignified appearance fees are negotiable and notaries compete for business. Many prefer to be paid in cash (*contanti*).

The buyer has the right to choose the notary. Normally the agent (*mediatore*) will supply one, your friends in the district will recommend one, or you can find one in the yellow pages. Not many notaries speak English – despite the high academic qualifications that are required for the job, so bring an interpreter if you don't speak Italian.

By law, the notary must be sure that you understand Italian, i.e. that you understand what you are signing in the contract. If he thinks you do not understand, a notarised translation of the contract must be supplied. The notary himself will arrange this for you at a cost.

Power of Attorney, Proxy (procura, delega)

If the vendor has a power of attorney, it needs careful checking by the *notaio*. Is it original? Is it a properly notarised copy? What powers does it confer? Is it of recent date?

If you require a power of attorney yourself, i.e. someone to sign for you, the two main requirements are that he should be (a) trustworthy and (b) understand what he is signing, i.e. an Italian speaker you know and trust.

The drawing up of a proxy document can be done at the *notaio's* office or in an Italian consulate anywhere. You need a valid passport or ID and if possible an Italian *codice fiscale* number. The following information is also required:

⊙ personal details about the procurator (name, surname, place and date of birth, address and occupation, nationality);
⊙ list of functions the procurator is to perform (e.g. buying or selling property), this can either be specific or general. A specific proxy deals with a specific transaction – in the case of property the land registry details should be given.

Powers of attorney in English can be translated and authenticated by the Consulate.

Documents required from the Vendor by the Notary

⊙ Deed of provenance (*atto di provenienza*). This is normally the previous contract of sale (*rogito precedente*), but could be a will or a donation.
⊙ Land registry details (*scheda catastale*): ground plans, plot numbers etc. These should be checked thoroughly in the inspection of the property to ensure that they correspond with the reality.
⊙ Land registry tax certificate (*certificato catastale*). This gives details which include the rateable value (*la rendita catastale*).
⊙ Condominium rules (*regolamento condominiale*) – if applicable.
⊙ A photocopy of the passport or ID and *codice fiscale* – Italian tax code number of the vendor(s).
⊙ Any planning sanctions and permissions (*condono fiscale*), if applicable.
⊙ Marital status document (*estratto per sunto degli atti di matrimonio*) issued by the vendor's Comune. This document is necessary if the owners are in a nuptial joint ownership regime, whereby the sale is invalidated if one of them refuses to sign.
⊙ Any rental contracts (*contratti di locazione*) or recent cancellations of same.
⊙ The latest income tax return of the vendor, (*dichiarazione dei redditi*) proving that the property has been declared to the tax authorities.
⊙ Further documents: certificate of habitability (*certificato di abitabilità*), heating and electrical certificates (*certificati impianti*).

Documents you need for the Notary

○ Passport or other valid ID.
○ Italian civil code number (*codice fiscale*).
○ If you have obtained an Italian residence you will also need a residence certificate (*certificato di residenza*) in order to avail yourself of certain tax reductions. Passport or other valid on a prima casa, the house where you are resident you pay only 4% taxes instead of 10% if it is not your primary residence.

THE CODICE FISCALE

Any contract or official transaction in Italy requires, along with your identification details, an Italian tax code number (*codice fiscale*) which is made up according to a formula of letters and numbers taken from your name, date of birth, birthplace and sex. Plastic *codice fiscale* cards are issued by your local comune or tax office (Ufficio delle Imposte Dirette). They can also be obtained through Italian consulates. Numbers can be worked out for you on the internet (www.codicefiscale.com).

Deposits (*acconto-anticipo-caparra*)

The first deposit (*acconto*) you will be asked to pay is by the estate agent for his so-called 'irrevocable proposal to buy' *proposta irrevocabile d'acquisto* or *prenotazione*. This has the merit of showing that you are not a time waster (*perditempo*), it engages you to the agent and prevents you from any collusion in a private deal with the vendor, but it is no guarantee that you have secured a property. Its purpose is to give the agent a fixed amount of time, normally a month, to obtain an agreement from the owner to sell you the property. If this agreement is not forthcoming your deposit is refunded.

Agents have been known to collect several deposits from different candidates for the same property and then proceed to an auction, awarding the property to the highest bidder. To avoid falling into traps like this and to limit the risks, four precautions are recommended:

○ Get the 'irrevocable proposal to buy' drawn up by the notary who you have engaged to handle the conveyancing. In fact this proposal must contain all the details of the definitive contract.
○ Limit the period in which the proposal is irrevocable to 24 or 48 hours maximum, This is quite enough time for the agent to contact the owner of the property.
○ Make this deposit minimal: a hundred odd euros. The real deposit will be paid later, at the *compromesso* (preliminary contract). No deposit should

be made out to the agent, but to the vendor direct.

O   Get the agent to specify his commission and/or expenses on a separate sheet; they are nothing to do with the deposit. The true deposit in the contract is called a *caparra*, which is governed by the civil code. It is normally 10% – 30% of the final price.

If the buyer is in default (i.e. doesn't pay by the scheduled day, or backs out) he loses his deposit. If the vendor fails to complete or does not complete by the scheduled date he is supposed to refund the buyer double his deposit. Both parties can take the other to court to enforce the contract.

There are two kinds of *caparra*: *caparra confirmatoria* and *caparra penitenziale*. The *caparra penitenziale* allows for either party to withdraw from the deal on their own terms, jointly agreed, and the contract is not enforceable.

It is advisable to pay any deposits by banker's draft or non-transferable cheque (*assegno non trasferibile*) and to keep a photocopy of the cheque(s).

Full Declaration versus Under-declaration

Under-declaration of the price is common practice in Italian conveyancing deeds. The lowest you can get away with (*il minimo consigliabile*) is quantified at 100 times the figure given for the *rendita catastale* in the *certificato catastale* (the rateable value in the land registry document). Declare any less than this and you will attract the attention of the tax assessors, who have three years in which to re-assess your declared valuation.

The advantage of this practice is that you pay less tax on the sale. Before the abolition of Capital Gains Tax (INVIM) in 2002, the tax evaded was much greater. But the practice is still embedded, as part of the Italian way. Indeed you can consult with your notary as to the correct figure to declare.

The disadvantages of underdeclaring the value – apart from the inconvenience of carrying banknotes around in brown envelopes are: the minor risk of tax reassessment at a future date, and the risk of falling prey to any party who might have a right to buy (*diritto di prelazione*) at the declared price. This could be a tenant of the property, a neighbouring 'farmer' (*coltivatore diretto*) or the state itself. (see *Checklist for Buyer 6, Prelazione*). In a recent case in Southern Tuscany, a Sardinian shepherd's wife – whose husband had signed a disclaimer (*rinuncia*) – made such a claim – and had to be paid off for a large sum.

As for declaring the full value, the law (30/97) enabled compromessos to be registered by a notary at the land registry (*conservatoria dei registri immobiliari*). Lawyers and estate agents encourage this 'correct' way, which safeguards the buyers from other purchasers, prevents any price increase and gives you peace of mind if there is going to be a long gap between the *compromesso* and the final contract (*rogito*) as the registration is valid for up to three years.

The framers of the new land registry system (the N.C.E.U or *Nuovo Catasto Edilizio Urbano*) which came into force on 1 January 2000 instructed their tax assessors to base the rateable valuation of real estate on current market prices, which, when it happens, will remove this anomaly.

The Dangers of Under-declaring the Purchase Price

There are inherent dangers in under-declaring the amount you are paying for your property, which is sometimes advised by notaries as it enables you to pay less money in notarial fees and taxes associated with purchasing. However, if you sell the property within five years, and you have under-declared on the purchase price you will end up paying higher taxes on the *plusvalenza* (value added to the property by the time you sell) (see *Tax on* Plusvalenza).

There is also the shock of under-declaring at the *compromesso* stage and then finding yourself paying nearly double the amount you expected at the *rogito* (final act of purchase) stage. This is what happened to Mr. B. He was advised by a notary to declare a price of sixty thousand euros on the property he was buying. However, he wrote cheques to the value of one hundred and forty thousand euros. At completion (the *rogito*), the notary acting pointed out the difference between the declared price and the actual price as denoted by the cheques and Mr B. found himself paying the equivalent of €17,400 instead of the €8,000 purchase costs, that he had been expecting to pay. The moral of this story is that if you do under-declare then your cheques must correspond to the amount you have declared. Note that cheques can be traced by the tax police (*guardia di finanza)* should they wish to take a special interest in your financial affairs.

Whatever value you decide to declare it should not be less than 100 times the annual taxable value of the property. If there is a dispute later, this will give you some protection.

The Compromesso

The *compromesso* or preliminary sale agreement outlines the conditions of purchase and any get-out clauses for the prospective purchaser, which may be applicable in some circumstances. These may include planning permission not being granted or failure of the purchaser's mortgage application. The *compromesso* also sets a date by which the transfer of property will be completed. Alternatives to the *compromesso*, the *Promessa d'Acquisto* (purchase proposal) or the *Promesso di Vendita* (promise of sale) are sometimes used.

Once one of the above documents has been authenticated, the purchaser then pays a deposit (*caparra*), which is usually about 10% of the sale price but can be up to 30% of the purchase price. The *caparra* is forfeited if the purchaser backs out of the agreement for a reason not covered by the *compromesso*. Likewise, if the vendor backs out of the sale, or does not hand over the property by the date given in the *compromesso*, then he or she is legally obliged to reimburse the vendor with double the amount of the *caparra*. The *caparra* is of course deductible from the purchase when the remainder of the money is paid.

Completion Date

Stipulate a completion date (*data del rogito*) as soon as possible after the *compromesso*. Two or three months is the normal time. Anything could happen in between. If the time has to be longer it is all the more imperative that you have a properly notarised and registered *compromesso*. Even then the vendor might be tempted by a higher bidder *and* afford to give you back double your deposit.

The Rogito Notarile

The *Rogito* – or final contract – is the Big Day for which the *compromesso* has been a rehearsal. The time and date will have been booked well in advance. All you will need are your identity documents and the money.

It is advisable to book the *rogito* appointment for the morning or early afternoon while the banks are open, just in case there is a hitch with the payment formalities, which a trip to the bank might immediately rectify. All parties have to be present, naturally, to sign the contract. The estate agent or *mediatore* will also probably be there (with his hand out) and it is advisable to have an interpreter to help you check all the details of the contract, which the *notaio* will read out, (unless you have previously arranged for an official English translation).

Ask the *notaio* to reassure you that he will file the contract in the Land Registry without delay – it is only then that the title officially changes hands. The Land Registry will then take about two months to furnish a certificate of your title.

MONEY TO COMPLETE THE PURCHASE ETC.

Make sure to give yourself plenty of time, months not weeks, to transfer the necessary funds to a local bank in Italy. See the section *Importing Currency* for the different ways of doing this. It is wise to have a chequebook and to get the notary to write out the cheques you have to sign on completion day, with his prior agreement. In many cases wads of banknotes are required – even for the notary – combined with banker's drafts (*assegni circolari*). It is always preferable to pay by personal cheque rather than carry large sums in brown envelopes. In Italy you can make out a cheque to yourself and countersign it on the back, which is as good as cash and does not name the recipient. You should not exceed €10,000 for each cheque.

When larger sums are deposited they are subject to the strictures of the anti-money laundering measures (*anti-riciclaggio*) put in place to combat organised crime.

TAXES AND FEES

Taxes and duties vary on a property sale:

If the house is to be a principal residence and the vendor is a private individual (prima casa).
O Registry Tax – (*imposta del registro*) 3%
O Fixed mortgage tax – (*imposta ipotecaria fissa*) 129.11 euros
O Fixed Land Registry Tax – (*imposta catastale fissa*) 129.11 euros

If the property is a second house (seconda casa) the total tax is 10%
O Registry tax – 7%
O Mortgage tax – 2%
O Land Registry tax – 1%

If it is a primary residence being bought by a developer the taxes are:
O IVA (Value added tax) – 4% for a primary residence; otherwise 10%.
O Fixed mortgage tax – €129.11
O Fixed Land Registry tax – €129.11

The above taxes are levied on the value declared in the deed of sale. This value cannot be less than the rateable value (*valore catastale*), which is obtained by multiplying the *rendita catastale* by 100.

Typical notary's fee (*onorario*); depending on property:

Value of property	Fee
€50,000	€1,400
€250,000	€2,000
€300,000	€2,200
€500,000	€3,000

increasing by €100 for each additional €25,000 of value. This is the fee on the *rogito*. The fee on the *compromesso* is 50% of the above.

In addition the notary will charge for the following:

O accessory rights (*diritti accessori*)
O indemnities (*indennità*)
O searches (*visure*)
O authentications (*autenticazioni*)

○ expenses (*rimborso spese*)

It is essential to ask the *notaio* for an estimate of his charges at the very start. His fees may be fixed, but with all those extras he has plenty of room to negotiate. In a typical transaction the total notarial expenses will be between €1,500 and €,2000 for a *rogito notarile* depending on the cost of the property.

POST-COMPLETION FORMALITIES

It is the duty of the notary to file and register the transfer of title and pay all taxes due, with all possible speed. Within 48 hours the local police – the *carabinieri* in a *comune* – or the *questura* in a provincial capital – must be informed of the change of ownership. The notary can do this himself or supply you with the relevant form. You will also want to transfer the utilities into your name, (electricity, water, telephone, gas, etc.) and arrange for new contracts (*volturazione delle utenze*), for which a photocopy of your contract will be useful.

LAND REGISTRY (ACCATASTAMENTO)

The *catasto* is an official register, created for taxation purposes, which files details of ownership, boundaries, mortgages and rateable values.

This register is divided into two parts:

○ *Nuovo Catasto Terreni* (N.C.T.), New Land Registry.

○ *Nuovo Catasto Edilizio Urbano* (new urban building registry).

The new system came into force on 1 January 2000 by presidential decree. Each census zone of the national territory is divided into 'microzones', and each property is classified in categories. Valuations are based on current market values, and revaluations are possible after any permanent 'socio-economical, environmental or urbanistic' change. The system, recently digitalised, is still in the throes of computerisation.

In theory anyone can apply for a search in any registry office on payment of a search fee (*visura*) of about 6 euros. Generally this search is done by the *geometra*, the *notaio* or their minions. But if you are doing the search yourself remember to start early and be prepared to shuttle from one office to another as is the case in all bureaucratic endeavours in Italy. Searches via the internet are becoming the norm for accredited professionals and their associations. (www.visurmet.com).

REAL ESTATE GLOSSARY

Abitabilità	literally 'habitability' certificate issued by the Comune ensuring that ceiling heights, window, safety regulations etc. are complied with.
Agente immobiliare	Estate Agent.
Acconto	Refundable deposit.
Bucalossi	A tax on renovation work named after the minister who introduced it in 1977 which is not refundable.
Buona fede	Good faith (ignorance of encroaching on another's right).
Caparra	non-refundable deposit – essential guarantee of a sale contract.
Catasto	Office of the Ministry of Finance which acts as a Land registry for updating land maps and plans of real estate.
Catasto certificate	Certificate giving land registry details, ownership, rateable value.
Catasto categories	Buildings are classified by letter:- A. Dwellings B. Collective institutions such as barracks or schools C. Commercial buildings such as shops D. Industrial buildings E. Special buildings Under categories:- A1. de luxe, A2 civil, A3 economy, A4 popular, A5 ultrapopular, A6 rural, A7 small house, A8 villa, A9 historical building.
Centro storico	The ancient centre of a town or city. Often used as a reference point.
Clausola penale	Penalty clause specifying amount payable for defaulting party.
Compromesso	Preliminary sale contract.
Comuncazione di cessione d fabbricato	Document which must be presented within 48 hours of purchase or rental of a property, to the Comune or Carabinieri.
Comunione dei beni	Joint ownership in the case of a married couple.
Concessione edilizia	Planning permission from the comune essential for any building work.
Condómino	Owner of property in a condominium.
Condono edilizio	Amnesty, by payment, for legalising past illegal building work, essential for the validity of the sale contract.
Conduttore	Tenant of a rented property .(legal word)
Delega	Power of attorney.
Dichiarazione ici (see ici)	Declaration to the Comune for tax purposes to be made by June 30 of any acquisition of a property.
Diritto di abitazione	Right to live in a house – limited to a person or family. No sub-letting or sale allowed.

Diritto di uso	Right to use a property – mainly in an agricultural context, limited to the needs of a particular farmer or family.
Diritto di usufrutto	Right of usufruct – which does not exceed the life time of the beneficiary – but can be tranferred.
Fallimento	Insolvency, bankruptcy.
ICI	Imposta Comunale Sugli Immobili. Council (Comune) tax on property, levied according to the Catasto value of the property.
Imposte	Registration
Ipoteca	Mortgage on a property.
Ipotecarie di registro e catastali	taxes payable by the buyer at the moment of sale, according to the catasto value of the property.
Inquilino	Tenant of a rented property (normal word).
IRPEF	Imposta sui redditi delle persone fisiche; Income tax payable on the catasto value of the property – or on the rent, if rented, even if the rent is not collected.
Libero al rogito	'Free on completion' – meaning the property will be freed of its occupants on completion of the sale.
Locatario	Tenant of a rented property.
Locatore	Landlord contract for a property.
Locazione	Rental contract for a property
Mutuo	Long-term loan or mortgage.
Multiproprietà	Time sharing.
Ónere	Burden, limitation.
Percentuale	Percentage – commission.
Perizia	Technical survey.
Permuta	Exchange – or house-swapping – governed by articles 1552-1555 of the civil code.
Pertinenze	Appurtenances – such as garage, attic, cellar or outhouse – belonging to an apartment or house.
Piano regolatore	Development plan drawn up by the Comune for zoning the district into building, industrial, green etc. areas.
Procura	Power of attorney.
Preliminare di vendita	The same as compromesso or preliminary contract of sale.
Provvigione	Commission.
Rendita	Annual rateable value for a property established by the Ufficio tecnico erariale or Tax office.
Ristrutturazione	Renovation, rebuilding.
Rogito notarile	Notarial deed signifying the final contract.
Separazione dei beni	Separate ownership (of married couples).
Sopralluogo	Site visit.
Supercondominio	Complex of more than one building with shared facilities such as access road, car parking, garden etc.
Tabella millesimale	'Table of thousandths', showing the exact share of the expenses of a condominium for each member.

Trascrizione	The public registration of any real estate contract, governed by article 2643 of the civil code and lodged in the local land registry (Ufficio dei Registri Immobiliari).
Trattative	Negotiations.
Ute	Ufficio Tecnico Erariale – the tax office which gives a rateable value to real estate.
Valore catastale	Catasto value – obtained by multiplying by 100 for dwellings, by 50 for offices and by 34 for shops, the basis for the calculation of the sale and ICI taxes.

RENTING PROPERTY

Some expatriates have their accommodation arranged for them as part of their job package, though many have to arrange their own accommodation on the spot once they arrive. Finding property to rent in most big Italian cities will be like trying to do so in any other big metropolis around the world – time-consuming, tiring, stressful and requiring large outlays of money. Renting accommodation in a foreign country with its different procedures in a foreign language and in an unfamiliar city adds additional problems. Although not high by British and American standards, rents in Italy can be expensive, especially when measured against Italian salaries, so for many finding reasonable rents can be very difficult. As already mentioned, Italians tend to live in large family apartments and so contribute their share to the pot with many contributors. For single foreigners the main difficulty is finding single accommodation, which is comparatively scarce except perhaps in the big cities where there are studio flats (at a price). You can get round this by staying as a lodger with an Italian family. However, this will involve becoming a part of the family, which can be claustrophobic and tiring for those who are used to having their own space with peace and quiet – though it will speed up the rate at which language fluency is achieved.

A few tips from Property International before you sign a rental contract:
- Check the notice period. The 6-month break clause can be negotiated to 3 months.
- Make sure an inventory list is drawn up noting any previous to furniture, floors etc.
- Return the property properly cleaned otherwise owners will keep money back from the deposit.

Those intending to buy property in Italy in order to become resident on a long-term or permanent basis will probably want to rent a villa, farmhouse or apartment to use as a base from which to look for a property to buy. This provides the chance to decide which area appeals the most and determine any local conditions that might explain why certain properties are much cheaper than similar ones in the neighbourhood. There are a number of firms offering holiday rentals and a full list may be obtained from the Italian State Tourist Office (see below). Alternatively, rental websites abound on the internet.

A pre-relocation visit is well worth the effort and cost even if your employer will not pay for it, as accommodation can be arranged to be available when you do actually relocate. It can take some time to find accommodation and it would be advantageous for your employer or a contact to set up estate agents or a relocation agent in advance of your arrival to begin showing you potential accommodation shortly after you arrive in Italy. A translator would also be very useful if you do not speak Italian, as the intricacies of Italian rental contracts can be unfathomable to the uninitiated.

One expat has the following to say on renting an apartment

My husband and I took over an apartment from a couple moving back to the U.S. and did not look for one on our own. The couple we took over the apartment from said that it is better to find a furnished (ammobiliato) *apartment because an unfurnished* (non ammobiliato) *apartment might not have kitchen cupboards, light fixtures, etc. I know that they also hired a translator to assist them in their search. It is also essential to have the lease agreement translated, before signing it. We did not realise we were supposed to have the furnace inspected each fall (which is required under Italian law) and that we were responsible for paying for the inspection – it was, however, in our lease agreement, in Italian. It is also a good idea to establish up front who will be paying for any maintenance done to the apartment.*

The website www.wantedinrome.com has listings of accommodation for rent and links to relocation agencies in the Rome area.

Useful Contacts – Rentals and Relocators

Accademia Realty: Palazzo Frescobaldi, Via S. Spirito, 11, 50125 Firenze; ☎ +39 055 26 70 331; fax +39 055 26 47 322; www.accademiarealty.com. Real estate sales and rentals throughout Tuscany.

Arias SRL Real Estate Agency: via Caradosso 11, 20123 Milan; ☎ 02 481 6005; fax 02 481 65241787-479191; e-mail ariassrl.it; www.ariassrl.it. Lets, Arranges rentals and letting of properties in Milan. Also purchase and sales.

At Home, Specialty Relocation and Real Estate Services, via del Babuino 56, 00187 Rome; ☎ 06 321 20102; fax 06 178 274 0479; www.at-home-italy.

com.

Casapiu Real Estate: via Dante Alighieri n.11, Levanto (SP) cap 19015; ☎0187-802059; fax 0187-803400; e-mail info@casapiu@tin.it; www.casapiuonline.com. Vacation rentals and sales in Liguria, near Levanto.

Hello Italy: ☎0 870 0272373 and 01483-419964; fax 01483 414112; www.helloit.co.uk. Letting agent for Lunigiana, northern Tuscany (about 30 minutes from the Ligurian coast), also Florence, Siena, Rome and more. Can provide introductions to purchasing contacts in the area, help with restoration and building, and sales after care. Many clients who buy, have then used Hello Italy as a letting agent.

InFlorence: In Florence is an agency that specializes in apartment rentals in Florence short-term and up to a year (www.inflorence.co.uk).

Italian State Tourist Office: 1 Princes Street, London W1R 8AY; ☎020-7408 1254; www.italiantouristboard.co.uk. Can supply details of holiday rental companies with whom it may be possible to negotiate cheaper rates for a longer period during winter.

Klemm Real Estate Agency: www.klemm.it. Based in Rome. Offers leases and sales.

Professional Relo: Via Cesare Battisti 10, 20041 Agrate Brianza (Milan); ☎+39 039 63 460 260; e-mail getinfo@professionalrelo.com; www.professionalrelo.it. Assists only corporate people relocating on behalf of their companies to Rome, Milan, Turin and Modena.

Property International: Via Correggio 55, 20149 Milan; Milan office ☎+39 02 49 80092; fax +39 02 48 194170; e-mail property@tiscali.it; Rome office ☎+39 06 5743170; fax +39 06 5743182; e-mail property.rm@flashnet.it. Handles corporate and individual relocations to Italy. Rentals in Rome and Milan areas. Can also find places to buy. Contact Deirdre Doyle.

Studio Papperini: via Capo Peloro 27, 00141 Rome, Italy; ☎+39 06-868 95810; fax 06-86896546; www.studiopapperini.com; info@studiopapperini.it. A comprehensive relocation service headed by Giovanni Papperini a solicitor specialising in immigration and nationality law. Based in Rome, but operates throughout Italy. Offers a pre-move service and cost effective, tailor-made package to suit employer or employee.

Suzanne Pitcher; Via Pietro Thouar 2, 50122 Florence; ☎+39 055 234 3354; fax +39 055 234 7240; www.pitcherflaccomio.com. Based in Florence. Offers short and long-term rentals in Florence and Tuscany.

Vacanze in Italia, c/o Carl Stewart, 22, Railroad Street, Great Barrington, MA 01230, USA; ☎413-528 6610; fax 413-528 6222; info@homeabroad.com; www.homeabroad.com. Several hundred properties covering most areas of Italy, but concentrated in Tuscany and Umbria. Rentals for one or two weeks, or longer. Sister company MyHome4Yours.com organizes home exchanges between the USA and Italy.

Welcomeservice in Umbria: Via S. Maria 62, 06059 Todi (PG); ☎+39 339 6531677; fax +39 075 8944531; e-mail info@welcomeservice.it; www. welcomeservice.it. Rentals and property management, also villas, farmhouses, apartments and plots for sale.

GLOSSARY OF RENTAL TERMS

un appartamento ammobiliato: a furnished apartment – more expensive than an unfurnished (*da ammobiliare*) one, though possibly ending up cheaper and almost certainly more convenient than having to buy a lot of furniture for a short stay.

attico: it may be an attic in the country, but in the city it means a penthouse.

il bagno: bathroom.

il balcone: balcony – also called *la terazza.*

Il bilocale: two-room apartment

Il canone mensile: monthly rent

Il conduttore: tenant

Il contratto di locazione: rental contract

la cucina: kitchen

dare la disdetta: to give notice of termination of rental contract

deposito cauzionale: deposit against damage

un giardino: garden. Not many flats or palazzi have these, even on the ground floor

l' inquilino: tenant

il locale: room

il locatario: tenant

monolocale con servizi: one-room with kitchen and bathroom. Average price around £400 a month but difficult to find

mora: in arrears

I patti: stipulated agreements

piano: floor: *primo/secondo/terzo piano* = first/second/third floor *il pianterreno:* ground floor

piano terra: ground floor

il portiere: doorman/janitor in charge of a block of flats

il risarcimento danni: payment for damage

il riscaldamento: central heating

la sala da pranzo: dining room.

il salotto: (sitting-room). For many Italian families this doubles as an extra bedroom.

i servizi: kitchen and bathroom. Advertisements do not include these when giving the number of rooms.

stanze: room. Un appartamento di due/tre/quattro stanze = a two/three/four-roomed flat.

stanze da letto: bedroom

sublocare: sub-let

le utenze: utilities

un villino: cottage.

Where to Look for Accommodation

Apart from following up *affitasi* (to let) signs outside *palazzi*, the other obvious place to look for accommodation is in the classified sections headed *appartamenti da affittare* (flats to let), of main local papers. There is the daily *Il Messagero* in Rome, the bi-weekly publication and website *Seconda Mano* (www.secondamano. it) Mondays and Thursdays) in the Milan area and most major cities also have free newspapers. For other papers see the section, *Media and Communications* in the chapter, *Daily Life*. You may also wish to consult one of the relocation specialists that offer accommodation services to individuals. Another possibility would be to consult university notice boards and even the notice boards of large international companies and organisations, where adverts for accommodation are displayed, primarily for the benefit of staff, but potentially useful to outsiders brazen enough to use them *in extremis*. Expat websites including www.hellomilano.it, www. italymag.co.uk, www.theinformer.it, www.romebuddy.com, www.expats initaly. com also carry adverts for rentals.

Tenancy Laws

Obtaining a tenancy agreement is undoubtedly easier if you are a non-resident since anyone with *residenza* status is protected by state laws from being evicted (*sfrattato*). The length of rental contracts varies but is normally for four years and if it is not a holiday rental then property owners usually prefer a minimum period of a year though six months is possible especially in metropolitan areas. For periods of less than six months major cities have residences/hotels where rooms with kitchenettes can be rented by the month. In some popular places like Rome and Tuscany there is a thriving short-term rental market. In out of the way countryside places you may be able to negotiate to rent for a few months at a favourable price as the custom is not as prolific. For formal tenancies, when the landlord or lady (*padrone/padrona*) wishes to have the property back the tenant (*inquilino*) will be sent a notice to quit.

As a tenant you will also have certain responsibilities, such as obtaining an annual certificate to confirm your central heating boiler and gas heaters conform to EU requirements. The tenant is liable for the cost of the certificate. The tenant is also expected to maintain the property (except for major repair work) and to return it to the landlord in the condition it was handed over.

Check with other expats as well as your landlord exactly what is expected of you and what the landlord is responsible for as local conditions and rental contracts vary – as does the quality of landlord.

Belinda Scaburri who moved to the Marche from the UK with an Italian husband still had initial difficulties renting

Despite there being an enormous demand for rental properties, the laws are still such that landlords are not protected and are therefore nervous and reluctant to enter into rental agreements which, in many instances, end in the law courts. We imagined that we would appear the ideal tenants – a mummy, a daddy and two adorable children. In actual fact, we presented the very worst type of tenant risk. We were not employed, we 'claimed' to be looking for a house to buy and, being foreigners (my husband, being a northern Italian, constituted as much of a foreigner as myself), we could say we had nowhere to go should we decide to stay at the end of the tenancy. A combination of luck, timing and a telephone number spotted on an internet site meant that we did find ourselves a house to rent, but it is by no means the hassle-free, legally sound procedure to which we have all become accustomed in the UK.

Rubbish Tax

The occupant of a flat or house has to register at the local municipal tax office for payment of the tax for household rubbish removal. The cost is calculated on the size of the building and the number of occupants living in it. The cost is paid by the occupant either twice yearly, or yearly.

Communal Apartment Blocks

In Italy, a communal apartment block is known as a *condominio*. As virtually all Italian property is sold freehold, it is not necessary to pay ground rents to the leaseholder as well as rent to the building landlord who is responsible for the upkeep of the building. In Italy, the Civil Code states that the tenants are responsible for the upkeep and repairs caused by day to day usage requirements such as electricity, rubbish removal (from the building to the collection point outside), maintaining elevators, cleaning communal hallways and stairs, central plumbing and heating etc and are jointly responsible for the costs (*spese*). The landlord/owner is responsible for big renovations and insurance of the building as well as any major maintenance such as roof repairs. If you are renting a flat in a condo you should make sure that you have a copy of the agreement about who is responsible for what and how much you have to pay towards the communal charges set out in the building's covenant. Important decisions concerning the future running of the building are made by the landlords/owners at annual meetings (*riunione di condominio*), which are held at not less than one year intervals.

In blocks of flats containing five or more apartments it is obligatory for the owners to appoint an agent *amministratore del condominio* to manage the property on behalf of the owners.

INSURANCE

Italy has a bad reputation for petty crime – burglary, pick pocketing and theft. However, this is much worse in the cities than in country areas and villagers often leave their homes unlocked. The rates of crime detection are appalling – less than 10% of burglaries are solved. As a result, insurance premiums are high and because it is expensive to insure house contents, most Italians do not bother. Foreign residents from Britain will find that insurance quotes from Italian firms are at least double what they would expect to pay in the UK and North America – Turin and Milan, two of the most likely destinations for expatriate workers, also have some of the highest premiums in Italy. Italian insurance companies are also notoriously slow about settling claims.

Estate agents sometimes offer house and contents insurance at competitive rates to their clients and it is worth asking them about this. For owners of second homes, an alternative to an Italian insurer is to use a British company such as those listed below, who will insure rural properties in Italy. Annual rates vary depending on the extent of the cover but are roughly £5 per £1,000 of the house value and £10 per £1,000 of the contents value. It is important to note that if you are moving to the earthquake zone, most insurance policies exclude earthquake damage.

Owing to the expense of insuring city apartments, it is prudent to take anti-burglar precautions – multiple locks and bars on ground floor windows are two of the basic requirements and an obvious deterrent to any prospective burglar.

Useful addresses

Copeland Insurance: Roy Thomas (Managing Director), 230 Portland Road, London SE25 4SL; ☎020-8656 8435); fax 020-8655 1271; service@andrewcopeland.co.uk; www.andrewcopeland.co.uk. Provides insurance for both holiday homes and permanent residents.

Harrison Beaumont Insurance Services: 2 des Roches Square, Witney, Oxon. OX28 4LG; ☎0870 1217590; fax 0870 1217 592; www.hb2.hbinsurance. co.uk/holiday_homes/; info@hbinsurance.co.uk. Holiday homes abroad insurance.

Insurance for Holiday Homes: 28 Waterloo Street, Weston-super-Mare, BS8 1LN; ☎01934-424040; fax 01934-424141. Holiday home abroad insurance.

Intasure: Phoenix House, 11 Wellesley Road, Croydon CRO 2NW; ☎0845-111 0680; fax 0845 111 0682; e-mail enquiries@intasure.com. Holiday home abroad insurance.

O'Halloran and Co: St James Terrace, 84 Newland, Lincoln LN1 1YA, England; 01522-537491; fax 01522-540 442; tpo@ohal.org. Will arrange cover for holiday homes in Europe.

Lark Insurance: www.larkquickquote.co.uk/overseas.phtml. Holiday homes abroad insurance.

Property Insurance Abroad: P O Box 150, Rugby CV22 5BR, England; ☎01788-550294; fax 01788-562579. Will provide a free quote.

Schofields: ☎01204-365080; www.schofields.ltd.uk. Insures holiday homes in Italy, let or unlet.

Woodham Group Ltd.: 17 Fircroft Close, Woking GU22 7LZ, England; ☎01483-770787; www.woodhamgroup.com.

WILLS

Under Italian law a foreigner's will drawn up outside Italy is deemed to be governed by the laws of the foreigner's country. If the will is straightforward, i.e. the property goes directly to the surviving spouse or the children there will be no problem. However, theoretically, problems could occur when English Common Law clashes with Roman Law as practised in Italy. In English law, executors are appointed by the deceased to administer the will according to his or her wishes. Under Italian law the death duties paid on the estate are minimal on bequests to next of kin and swingeing on distant or non-relatives. The concept of intermediary ownership as practised by English executors does not exist and it therefore poses a problem for Italian lawyers who must reach some kind of compromise. In order to keep complications to a minimum it is advisable to have a will drawn up by a lawyer with experience of both the Italian system and the legal system of your country.

UTILITIES

It is important for anyone contemplating a move to Italy to be aware that if their property is not already connected to the gas or water mains or is without electricity, they may have a long wait in store before these services are connected. Also, the further away the property is from the nearest telephone line or mains, the greater the cost of linkage. Such costs can add considerably to the price of an Italian property and you should therefore expect to pay a lower price for property without utilities than would be asked for a property with them.

In Italy it was the custom to peremptorily cut off those who delayed paying their utility bills without any preamble. Now, as in many countries it is customary for service providers to send a reminder notifying their customers that they have fallen behind with payments. Legally, providers are not entitled to cut off your electricity just because you have not paid your bill on time.

Electricity

The national electricity company is *Ente Nazionale per l'Energia Elettrica* commonly referred to as ENEL (www.enel.it). Before you can be plugged into it an ENEL inspector will have to ascertain that the wiring you have had installed meets ENEL specifications. Make sure that all electrical work is carried out on your property by a fully qualified electrician (*elettricista*). The electrician should be registered at the local Chamber of Commerce (*La Camera di Commercio*). It is important that if your property is being wired for the first time, the electrician is aware that you wish to be connected to the national supply, as some householders prefer to run a private generator and in such cases the wiring may be done to a lower standard.

Taking out a contract with ENEL. Once the ENEL inspector is satisfied you will be allowed to take out a contract with the electricity company on a non-resident or a resident basis. The latter is preferable as non-residents pay a premium rate. In order to obtain a resident's contract one needs to produce a residence certificate (see *Residence and Entry Regulations* chapter).

After purchasing your property and if the estate agent hasn't arranged for the electricity to be transferred to your name, you will have to sign a new contract *(volturazione delle utenze)* at the local ENEL office. You need to bring identification with you either your passport or residence permit (see the *Residence and Entry Regulations* chapter) the registration number of the meter and the previous owner's paid electricity bill. If the supply is already connected you can also do this by telephone.

Billing and Paying. Enel monitors your consumption of electricity every two months and sends estimated bills (*bollette*): your bill is adjusted twice a year when meters have been read. Bills show your account number (*numero utente*), amount payable (*importo euro*) and due date (*scadenza*). You can pay your bill at the bank, post office or the electricity board's own offices but the easiest way to pay bills is by direct debit from your bank. You can read your own meter and dial your meter reading (*gli scatti*) or report breakdowns on telephone number 800 900 800. Newer meters have computerised automatic reading in which case you no longer have to read them as they communicate the reading directly to the electricity company.

You can also find more information on services provided on the website www.prontoenel.it. The cost of electricity in Italy is relatively high. There is a standing charge (*quota fissa*) for every two months and the consumption charge is based on the power rating of the property, the maximum being 6KW. Then there is a charge per Kilowatt hour (*scatto*). It is preferably to be on a 6KW power rating but changing your power rating from 3KW to 6KW can be costly. Out of 22 million electrical service contracts in Italy 18 million are for 3KW, including most apartments.

Power Supply. The electricity supply is limited in Italy to between 1.5-6 kW (the maximum) per house. This means that appliances with a high wattage (e.g. washing machine/dishwasher) cannot be running at the same time. The system will overload and there will be a power cut. In very rural areas where the lines are strung out for miles the power can be feeble or subject to wild fluctuations, which can be damaging to sensitive electronic equipment including televisions and that can be compounded by regular power cuts caused by storms which may affect the substation miles away from your home. If you rely on electricity for operating a computer, fax and other such equipment you need to seriously think about the installation of a back-up generator or solar power system as frequent power cuts can damage appliances not to mention leaving you without water if your water is supplied from a well by means of an electric pump.

Meters, Plugs, Fuses and Bulbs. Most meters are now installed outside the property for easy access for the meter reader.

Most Italian plugs have two or three round pins so if you are bringing electrical appliances from another country you need to purchase plug adaptors. The two-pin plug has no earth wire so large appliances using a high wattage must be plugged into earthed sockets.

When there is an overload in the electrical system, a circuit breaker is tripped. The fuse box is usually situated by an entrance. For this reason, it can be a good idea to keep a torch on or near the box. Before inspection and reconnecting one must make sure that all high power appliances are switched off.

All electric light bulbs in Italy are screw fitting. You can buy adaptors to change appliances such as lamps from bayonet to screw fittings.

Gas

Gas is widely used in northern Italy for central heating and cooking. Most cities and large towns are supplied by the major companies Italgas and Enel Gas (www. EnelGas.it) and smaller municipal companies; Milan has AEM Gas and Azienda Energetica Municipale. If you purchase a property with mains gas you should contact the gas company in order to have your meter read and get connected. Mains gas is costly. You receive a bill every two months and you can pay at the post office, bank or gas company offices or by direct debit (*domiciliazione*) from your bank account. Gas appliances have to be approved and installed by a registered GAS company. It is obligatory to have gas water heaters checked annually, as gas leaks can be fatal.

Unfortunately the gas network does not penetrate rural areas where many foreign residents buy homes. For inhabitants of these areas who wish to have central heating, the solution is a gas tank known in Italian as a *bombolone*. Gas tanks can be loaned from the larger gas companies for example Agip gas, Shell gas, and Liquigas, and installation is governed by strict regulations. For obvious reasons, the tank should not be immediately adjacent to the house or road, it must be at least 25m away. The tank can be sited underground and pipes laid to connect it to the house. The contract with the gas company supplying liquid gas will stipulate a minimum annual purchase usually in the region of €1,200. The size of your tank depends on your needs.

Bottled gas

The gas bottle (*bombola*) is commonly used in rural areas but can be used in towns and cities. Bottled gas is mostly used for cooking though it can also be used for portable gas fires. You pay a deposit on your first purchase of bottled gas and then you exchange your empty bottle for a full one. The bottles weigh 10 kg and 15 kg and a 10kg bottle costs about €20, plus a delivery charge if necessary. A bottle used just for cooking will last an average family six weeks. The bottled gas is sometimes kept outside with a connecting pipe to the cooker. If you choose this method you must buy propane gas and not butane as propane can withstand changes in temperature – butane is for internal use only. For those who do not wish to go to the bother or expense of arranging connection with mains gas, particularly if you are only using your Italian home for holidays, the *bombola* is a useful alternative to mains gas.

Water

Italy's notorious water shortage may not be acute by Saharan standards, but it can still be a possible inconvenience for some people thinking of setting up home in the south of Italy. In summer, the water supply is liable to be cut off during the day and resumed at night. The water supply is under the control of the local commune, eg CIGAF and there are conditions governing the various uses of this precious commodity. There is usually plenty of water in the North of Italy but in central and southern parts there may be only a meagre supply. For this reason it is essential if you live in a rural area especially in the south to have a storage tank (*cisterna*), which can be topped up when the water supply is on or filled by tanker, though this is expensive. For flat-dwellers in the main cities a 500-litre tank may be sufficient. In remote rural areas it may be necessary to store several months of water in huge underground tanks. Water shortages can be made worse whatever the region by the poor infrastructure; much water is lost because of old leaking mains water pipes. If water in your area is metered it may be rationed to a fixed number of litres per house, regardless of the number of occupants. This is likely to happen mostly in extremely dry areas in the South and Sicily.

Recycling Water. Due to the shortage of water in some areas, there are restrictions on watering the garden and a ban on swimming pools. However, if you are clued-up and possess a little ingenuity there are solutions. It is possible to recycle water used for washing and bathing for the garden by draining it into a separate tank (*serbatoio*).

Another method of recycling your domestic water, both white and grey is to install a water purifier (*depuratore*). This is a large tank, which is made up of sections. It is placed underground and in a position where the treated contents of the septic tank spill into it. This water passes through an aerated section. The aeration is done by means of an electric pump, programmed to work at least 16 hours a day. This pump passes oxygen into the water to feed the 'good' bacteria, which in turn eat the 'bad' bacteria. The filtered water collects in the last section and overflows into another tank; this water can be used for watering or irrigation and is especially beneficial for an orchard, or large lawns that you want to keep green. The total cost of a *depuratore* is €9,500 (about £6,270). This includes the tanks, pipes, pump and labour.

When is a Swimming Pool not a Swimming Pool? Answer, when it's a *vasca*. The way round the swimming pool ban is to build an artificial water basin (*vasca*) common in rural areas and ostensibly for domestic use when the mains water is cut off. The idea is that it fills up during the winter when rain is plentiful; it may also be fed by a spring or well. With a proper lining and some kind of filtering system to keep the water clean, a vasca could be used as a swimming pool, the less obviously the better.

Wells and Water Diviners. It is a good idea when you buy your house that if it states there is a well (*pozzo*), that you have it confirmed by an expert, that there is plenty of water and that it is not likely to dry up. Also make sure who owns the well and your rights to use it, e.g. that it cannot be stopped or indeed diverted or drained away by your neighbours. If you are lucky enough to have a well on your land, this can make your life easier. You may even wish to call in the services of a water-diviner (*rabdomante*) to detect where the water is and put markers down for future bore-holes. A *rabdomante* can usually determine the depth of the water, with a high degree of accuracy. If you buy a property with a well – you can take a sample to be tested by the local water authority to make sure it's safe to drink. In general water is hard in Italy and has a high calcium content. The water stains sinks and deposits settle in taps, kettles etc, which require cleaning with *anticalcare*. It is possible to install a water softener – this has many benefits and prevents furring of appliances and pipes.

Turning Off the Water. If you are moving into a new house or apartment it is a good idea to check where the stopcock is situated, so that in an emergency the supply can be turned off. If you are absent from the property during the winter it is a good *security* measure to turn off the water as burst pipes can cause untold damage, and if the water hasn't been turned off you are in default of your insurance conditions.

Telephone

Installing/Getting Connected. The Italian telephone service (*Telecom Italia*) was privatised in 1997. In 1998 deregulation meant competition was introduced. To get a new telephone line (*nuovo impianto*) installed in your home you can apply at Telecom Italia offices; there, you can fill in the application form. You need to bring your passport (and a photocopy) for identification purposes. You can also arrange this over the telephone, presumably your mobile or someone else's. Note that if you live in a remote rural area the cost of a telephone line, especially if your nearest connection point is miles away is likely to be prohibitive. If you manage to get connected the cost of installation will appear on your first bill.

Bills. Billing is in the form of an itemized bill *(bolletta in chiaro)*. Payments can be made by direct debit from your bank.

Directories and Yellow Pages. If you have a private phone – you are given a copy of the local telephone directory (*elenco*) www.paginebianche.it and a copy of the Yellow Pages (*pagine gialle*) www.paginegialle.it annually. There is also an *English Yellow Pages* (EYP), which can be bought. The EYP contains names, addresses, postcodes, telephone and fax numbers plus e-mail and website addresses. You can contact EYP, www.englishyellowpages.it. There is also the Into Italy information website (www.eypdaily.it).

Mobiles. The Italians have taken to mobiles (*telefonini*) and the number of providers is growing as is the quality and coverage of the services. For more information see *Media and Communications* in the *Daily Life* chapter.

REMOVALS

The amount of possessions that an expatriate will take with them to Italy is likely to vary considerably. Generally speaking, however, anyone moving to a new home in Italy for their retirement and families moving there on an expatriate employment contract, will want to export a large enough quantity of bulky possessions to require the service of a professional removal company with international expertise. There are a number of bureaucratic formalities to be dealt with before the shipping company can deliver your possessions. If you live outside the EU the first step before you leave for Italy is to submit a list of the items you wish to import into Italy to the nearest Italian Consulate (see Chapter *Residence and Entry Regulations* for addresses), who will officially stamp it. All nationalities must also apply for their *permesso di soggiorno* (permit to stay – see *Residence and Entry Regulations*) from the *questura* (police station) in Italy once you have arrived. Once the permit is issued you can then import your belongings.

The removal firm will require both the list stamped by the Consulate, the *permesso* and copies of documents relating to your ownership of property in Italy or proof of address. If you have not been resident in Italy long enough to have obtained the *permesso* you can obtain an attestation from the *commune* to the effect that you have purchased or leased accommodation in the area. This should allow the shipping company to import your belongings successfully.

However, the official requirements above may not always be essential as Jerry Fresia and his wife Conchitina discovered:

> **Jerry and Conchitina moved to Como from San Francisco**
> *We applied for a long stay visa* (residenza ellectiva) *and we did not have to submit a customs/shipping list. When we were researching information about shipping requirements, we came across several sites – shipping company sites that stated that you have to submit such a list to the consulate. They also stated that you have to apply for an Import Licence* (Nulla osta Ministero PP) *for stereos, radios, VCRs or TV once you arrive in Italy, but again, we did not do this. The Italian shipping company (sub-contractor of the American company we dealt with) requested a copy of the Inventory Statement. We believe you are supposed to submit the inventory list and bill of lading to Customs, but the Italian company did not ask for these because they already had them from the US Shippers (the company we signed a contract with). The bill of lading is a vital document that you must not lose as it provides proof of ownership of the container..*

Shipping personal belongings internationally is always best done by a professional and reputable company that has, most importantly, experience in dealing with the system of the country you are going to. When leaving Italy it is also important to make sure you use a company that is experienced in that process too, as there are procedures such as cancelling your residence permit to be undertaken so that you can export your possessions again.

General Import Conditions

The good news for those importing household goods into Italy is that there are no regulations about how long they must have been in your possession. However, a large selection of expensive, pristine equipment would undoubtedly arouse the avaricious instincts of the customs officers. It is advisable that any new items show a few obvious signs of wear and tear in order not to attract import duty and VAT – another way to lessen the interest of customs officials is to make sure that the items are not perfectly wrapped in their factory packaging.

The most important regulation regarding the import of personal possessions is that the items must be imported within six months of taking up residence in Italy. Excess Baggage Co lists current import regulations on their website: www. excessbaggage.co.uk.

If you decide to take a loaded van of furniture and other items for your home from one other European Union country into Italy, you should have no problems, especially if the country is inside the Schengen area. If you are driving from an EU country through Switzerland to get to Italy (which is not strictly necessary) and you are stopped by Swiss customs, you should inform the Swiss customs that you are in transit to another EU country. An employment contract, rental agreement or ownership document would undoubtedly help convince the Swiss officials of your legitimacy.

If you are going to drive your possessions from a non-EU country into Italy you should have your consul stamp and *permesso di soggiorno* in your possession at the point of entry. However, you should also ensure that you have the necessary paperwork required to transit through any country *en route*.

Removal Firms

There are a number of large firms that specialise in international removals and it makes sense to consult one of these. UK residents can obtain a list of such companies from BAR, the British Association of Removers (www.bar.co.uk; ☎020-8861 3331). Be sure to ask for a list of international movers as these are a subgroup of the association's members. BAR also provides handy hints for those contemplating removals overseas. You can also get a list of international house removals firms and an estimate at www.shippingandmoving.com and www.europeanremovals.com/.

Residents of other countries should consult the membership directories of the international associations listed below. Most of the organisations also maintain their directories online.

Household Goods Forwarders Association of America: www.hhgfaa.org
International Federation of International Movers (FIDI): www.fidi.com
Overseas Moving Network International: www.omnimoving.com

Useful Contacts - Removers

American Services Srl: Via Giacosa 3/5, 20153 Taccona di Muggio, Milan; ☎ +39 039 746 181; fax +39 039 746 429; ameriserv@tin.it. American owned moving and storage company operating throughout Italy. Main office in Milan and branch in Rome to handle S. of Italy.

Arrowpak: ☎ 0800 136 332; www.arrrowpak.co.uk. Full or part loads.

Andrew Wiffen: ☎ 07803-014955; e-mail andrewwiffen@btinternet.com. Offers a weekly service from the UK to Italy and will take full or part loads.

Baxter's International Removers: Brunel Road, off Rabans Lane, Aylesbury HP19 3SS; ☎01296-393335. Specializes in removals to Italy and Germany.

Interdean: Worldwide removals (UK 020 8961 4141; USA Headquarters , 55 Hunter Lane, Elmsford, New York 10523-1317; ☎ 914-347 6600; fax: 914-347 0129; Chicago 630-752 8990, fax 630-752 9087; Dallas 817-354 6683, fax 817-354 5570; Houston 281-469 7733, fax: 281-469 9426; Los Angeles 562-921 0939, fax 562-926 0918; Raleigh/Durham 919-969 1661, fax 919-969 1663; San Francisco 510-266 5660, fax 510-266 5665; www.interdean.com). Interdean have offices in a number of European countries (including Italy) and the Far East, which can be found via the website. They also offer relocation services.

Wright Move: ☎ 01983-884409; e-mail stuart@wrightmove.freeserve.co.uk; www.wrightmove.co.uk. Full or part loads.

IMPORTING A CAR

Whereas non-residents may freely drive back and forth between the UK and their Italian holiday home with British car registration documents and an EU or International Driving Licence, residents are obliged to either officially import their British registered vehicle or buy one in Italy. For drivers moving to Italy who are already resident in Europe (except UK and Irish residents who will have right hand drive cars), taking their own car with them is often a good idea. This is because you have to be a resident before you can buy an Italian car and therefore have to manage without private transport for a number of months, unless you can afford a rental car for that length of time. UK and Irish residents, who know far enough in advance that they are moving to Italy, may want to buy a left hand drive car in preparation for their relocation. Second hand left hand drive cars for sale in the UK can found online on the Exchange and Mart website (www.exchangeandmart.co.uk).

To import a car from Britain into Italy you have to send your Vehicle Registration Document (V5) to the Driver and Vehicle Licensing Agency (DVLA) and ask for a permanent export certificate (V561). Then you take this to the Italian consulate (with an Italian translation), your MOT (and an Italian translation and any other documents requested by the Consulate). Then, taking a UK registered car to Italy it will be necessary to ensure that the insurance cover purchased in the UK will be applicable for a long stay abroad. In the past, failing to notify the insurance company that the car will be used predominantly outside the UK for an extended period has been grounds to refuse an insurance claim. 12-month Europe-wide car insurance can be secured through *Stuart Collins & Co.*, 114 Walter Road, Swansea SA1 5QQ; ☎01792-655562; fax 01792-651126; e-mail mail@stuartcollins.com; www.stuartcollins.com.

To register a foreign vehicle in Italy it must first pass an Italian MOT. For some reason MOTs carried out in one EU country are not acceptable in another EU country. The Italian equivalent of an MOT is the *revisione*. From then on the process becomes the usual Italian, time-consuming rigmarole. No wonder most people are happy enough to call on the services of one of the specialist agencies (*agenzie pratiche auto*) that wade through the necessary procedures on your behalf. Once the car has passed an MOT, usually with some modifications such as realignment of headlights, it must be taken with all its car documents and a residence certificate, to a *notaio* who will apply for the car registration at the local (*Uffizio della Motorizzazione Civile e dei Trasporti in Concessione*) and register the vehicle with the local *Pubblico Registro Automobilistico*. The car will then be issued with a registration certificate (*carta di circolazione*). Licence plates (*targe*) are issued by the *Pubblico Registro Automobilistico*. Registration costs vary according to car size.

Following registration you become liable for car tax. Note that it is not necessary to display a car tax disk (*bollo auto)* on the windscreen. You will also need an insurance badge (*contrassegno*). Classic and vintage cars may qualify for reduced bollo rates but the rules are complicated; if the car has been modified for instance it may become ineligible for a discount. Classic car enthusiasts can check out the Classic car site www.passioneauto.it, which also lists Italian car clubs for different makes.

For further information about driving in Italy, the rules of the road, buying or selling a car and insurance see *Daily Life, Cars & Motoring*.

Useful addresses:

Automobile Association (AA): Import Section, Fanum House, Basingstoke Hants RG21 2EA; ☎01256-20123; www.automobileassociation.co.uk. Information is supplied only to members of the AA. Ask for information on the permanent importation of a vehicle into Italy. For membership details contact your nearest AA office.

Automobile Club d'Italia (ACI): Via Marsala 8, 00185 Rome; ☎06-49981; www.aci.it.

IMPORTING PETS

Many pet owners find the thought of leaving their pets behind when they move overseas heartbreaking. Children, especially, can find leaving the family pet or their own pets, behind a traumatic experience. However, it is a reasonably straightforward process to transport your dog, cat, ferret as well as other creatures, which are not endangered species, with you to your new home in Italy, providing that you take care to follow the regulations. To the pet-obsessed British it may seem that for many Italians their dog tends to be either a fashion accessory (unusual breeds are sought after), or a working animal, rather than an empathetic faithful companion. However, for many Italians their dog is as much a part of the family as their children and grandchildren.

Regulations now in force in most areas of Italy compel owners to have their dogs tattooed on the body as a means of checking their registration. An alternative to the tattoo is for the dog to have a tiny microchip inserted under the skin of the neck. The tattoo/microchip insertion can be done by a vet, or in some areas by the *Unita Sanitaria Locale.* Dog insurance against claims for damages is advisable for those with unpredictable animals and those whose canines have no traffic sense.

Rabies vaccinations have to be given yearly and a log-book will be provided by the vet for the purpose of recording these. Apart from rabies, which is reputedly prevalent in the far north of Italy, hazards further south are more likely to include encounters with porcupines and snakes. For animals (and human beings) it is advisable to keep a supply of venom antidote in the fridge, but make sure that it is regularly renewed before the expiry date has been reached.

UK Pet Passport Programme. UK resident pet owners who wish to take their pet back and forth between Italy and the UK should be aware that the Passport for Pets scheme only applies to cats, dogs and ferrets. There are also a limited number of entry points where an animal can be returned to the UK as part of the programme. Consult your veterinarian well in advance of departure from the UK as it can take up to six months to fulfil the requirements necessary for your pet to qualify for the scheme. Residents of Italy can take their cat or dog to the UK for a holiday without having to place them in quarantine if they have fulfilled the necessary requirements as outlined below.

In addition to having an up to date pet passport, the animal should also have a microchip inserted under the skin of their shoulder and be vaccinated against rabies. Though the animal does not have to undergo quarantine it can take a number of hours after arrival in the UK for the animal to be cleared through customs.

Current details about the scheme (which is subject to regular amendments), are posted on the website of the *Department For Environment, Food and Rural Affairs* (DEFRA) www.defra.gov.uk/animalh/quarantine/pets/. DEFRA also has a PETS helpline: 0870-241 1710 (or +44 20 7904 8057 from outside the UK) – open 8.30am to 5pm, Monday, Tues, Thursday and Friday and from 10am-5pm Wednesdays. Further information about the quarantine rules can be obtained from 020-7904 6224.

Importing Pets into Italy from the USA. Pets belonging to US residents who wish to take their pet back and forth between Italy and the USA are governed by the same EU regulations applicable to non-commercial movement of pet animals in EU states, as these also apply to some other third countries including the United States. It is obligatory to have a European Community veterinary certificate for each pet. This document has the same list of requirements as for pets coming from other EU countries. Information is available on the website of the Italian embassy (www.italyemb.org/animali.htm) and the US department of agriculture website (www.aphis.usda.gov/NCIE/iregs/animals/).

Exporting cats and dogs from Italy to the USA. Pets exported from Italy back to the USA need a certificate of good health from an Italian veterinary in order to get a pet export certificate from the local ASL (*Azienda, Sanitaria Locale*). Needless to say there are charges for these documents. Full, up-to-date instructions and timings can be found on the US Embassy in Italy's website under Foreign Agricultural Service at www.usembassy.it/agtrade/files/pets.htm.

Transporting Pets by Air. If the animal is to enter the country by air, it can often accompany passengers as excess baggage, though it is necessary to book cargo space in advance as airlines limit the number of animals per flight. Airlines can also advise on the current bureaucratic requirements for importing an animal, as they are responsible for checking the paperwork before accepting the animal on board their aircraft. Taking a dog or cat as excess baggage is often easier than sending the animal as air cargo independently from the owner as customs officials are less worried that the animal is being imported for commercial reasons.

Useful Contacts – Pets Travel

Airpets Oceanic: ☎0800 371554; +44 1753 685571' fax 01753-681655; e-mail info@airpets.com; www.airpets.com.

ECS Horse Transport: Hawthorn Stud, Banbury, Oxfordshire; ☎01608-

683911; Kevin@ecshorsetransport.com; www.ecshorsetransport.com. Horse transportation throughout Europe.

Independent Pet and Animal Transportation Association International Inc.: fax +1 903 769 2827; e-mail ipata@aol.com; www.iapata.com. A directory of members, as well as advice on transporting pets, is contained on this website.

Par Air Services: ☎01206-330332; fax 01206-331277; e-mail parair@btconnect. com; www.parair.co.uk.

D.J. Williams: Animal Transport, Littleacre Quarantine Centre, 50 Dunscombes Road, Turves, Nr Whittlesey Cambs PE7 2DS; ☎01733-840291; fax 01733-840348. International pet collection and delivery service, will deliver overland or arrange air transport. Will collect from your home and arrange all the necessary documentation. For those people whose pet is not covered by the PETS scheme, they also provide quarantine services.

Pet Travel Insurance

There are a number of companies offering this service including:
   www.mrigroup.com
   www.petplan.co.uk
   www.pinnacle.co.uk
   www.rapidinsure.co.uk

DAILY LIFE

- To cope successfully with life in Italy, the ability to speak the language is essential.
- The Italian state education system is generally good but standards are generally better in the more affluent north of the country: international schools are the best bet for the children of expatriates who do not intend to stay in Italy for too long.
- There are English-language papers and websites to help new arrivals settle down, and if they are homesick there is English-language TV on satellite .
- Buying a car in Italy is reasonably uncomplicated for the foreigner, but the public transport is good with cheap, reliable trains, more buses than any other country in Europe and well-used internal air services including some budget fare routes for both trains and planes.
- The Italian banking and postal systems, once the most inefficient in Europe have been modernized; internet banking has taken off in Italy and the post office can also be used for banking services.
- Tax in Italy is complicated, high, and widely evaded by the Italians.
- The state health service is mostly very creditable but regional variations in standards are noticeable. Private insurance is essential to cover the percentage not paid for by social security, or if you are not eligible to use the Italian NHS.
- Despite the evil reputation of the Mafia, there is generally less street crime (bar the main tourist cities), than in many other European countries.
- Italians are sociable, tending to stay with their families into adulthood and young people like hanging out in groups, rather than going out alone or in pairs.
- In Italy over-indulgence in food and drink (especially the latter) is frowned upon but spending extravagantly on your appearance is regarded with approval.

The mundane rituals of daily existence in your home country are liable to assume an alarming aspect when encountered in the context of a foreign country with different customs, culture and language. Buying a car, using public transport, opening a bank account can all become frustrating and bewildering tasks when you realise that you do not know whether your driving licence is valid in Italy, you have forgotten the word for season ticket and do not know the phrase for banker's draft in Italian.

This chapter deals with all of these issues, and many more everyday concerns. Its aim is to help familiarise you with Italian ways and lessen the headaches that arise with each new and initially daunting task. However, it cannot be overstressed that the key to coping successfully with life in Italy whether domestically, socially or professionally lies in the ability to speak and understand the language with some degree of fluency. Thus, the first section deals with ways of brushing up, or initiating, your knowledge of Italian, either before leaving home, or on arrival in Italy.

Please note that all information provided here is subject to regional variation and that the difference in procedures between the city and country areas of Italy may be particularly striking.

LEARNING THE LANGUAGE

If you don't speak Italian you are forced to rely on the expatriate community for your survival; few Italians speak English. Learning Italian can be a rewarding and therapeutic experience. Most Italians are flattered if you make an attempt to speak it. They will encourage you in your efforts; and it is a beautiful language to learn.

> **Roger Warwick stresses the importance of speaking the language**
> *I speak fluent Italian which is essential. I know foreigners who have lived in Italy for twenty years and can only mumble a few words in Italian which severely limits the possibilities of making friends with Italians as hardly any of them speak English well enough to have an interesting conversation.*

Standard Italian evolved from Tuscan, the language of Dante (*la lingua di Dante.*) It was forged by the poets Dante and Petrarch in the Middle Ages, and consolidated by writers like Alessandro Manzoni in the nineteenth century. Manzoni's novel *The Betrothed* (*I Promessi Sposi*), familiar to generations of Italian schoolchildren, was set on the shores of Lake Como, but instead of speaking the Comasco dialect the characters were made to speak in Tuscan. Manzoni washed his language in the river Arno 'rewriting' the book in 1840. In 1861 only 2.5% of Italians spoke standard Italian, in 1955 the figure was 34%, in 1988 it was 86%. By 1995, 93.1% Italians were speaking standard Italian, 48.7% were bilingual dialect Italian speakers and only 6.9% spoke in dialect alone. Television has accelerated the standardisation of the language, especially among young people, sometimes to the dismay of their elders. In Milan recently some old locals in a trattoria were moved to tears by a group of very young people at the next table speaking and singing songs in their old dialect. The youngsters came from Ticino in neighbouring Switzerland where the dialect still survived. Nowadays a teenager from Naples and a teenager from Como, whose grandparents would not have understood each other, speak the same standard Italian. This is the language for foreigners to learn.

Apart from the variations in Italian spoken around the country, some of the inhabitants of the border and outlying regions do not, in fact, use Italian at all. Various forms of French are spoken by a large percentage of the population in the Val d'Aosta and a strongly Germanic minority in the Trentino-Alto-Adige region uses German. The majority of the island population of Sardinia speaks a mixture of Italian, Latin, Punic and Spanish while in Calabria and Sicily, entire villages still speak Albanian and Greek.

Learning Italian Before You Go

Part-time Courses. Part-time courses are ideal for those with domestic or professional commitments and are cheaper than the language courses offered by commercial organisations such as Berlitz, Inlingua, etc. Local colleges of education and community or adult studies centres are the best option as they often run day and evening courses in a wide and amazing variety of subjects. The courses cater for a variety of standards, ranging from beginners who want to learn Italian for next year's holiday or for general interest, to those who wish to take an exam leading to a qualification at the end of the course. Italian cultural organisations also offer courses and sometimes lessons can be arranged through the Embassy in countries where there is no formal Italian cultural organisation.

Intensive Language Courses with International Organisations. One real advantage of an international organisation is that it offers language courses which, begun in your home country, can be completed on arrival in Italy. Each course is specifically tailored to the individual's own requirements as far as the language level and course intensity is concerned and the cost of the courses varies enormously depending on these factors. Further information is available from the addresses below:

Berlitz School of Languages: 2nd Floor, Lincoln House, 296-302 High Holbourn, London WC1V 7JH; ☎020-7611-9640; fax 020-7611 9656: Berlitz USA – 40 West 51st Street, New York City, NY 10020, USA; ☎212 765 1001; fax 212 307 5336; www.berlitz.com for international centres.

Linguarama: Quality Cobden Hotel, 166, Hagley Road, Birmingham B16 9NZ; tel/fax 0121-455 6677; www.inlingua.com; for information about US inlingua schools visit www.inlingua.com/usa.html.

Self-Study Courses. For those who prefer to combine reciting verb endings with cooking the dinner or repeating sentence formations while walking the dog, then self-study is the most suitable option and has the advantage of being portable to Italy where you can continue to learn while practising total immersion in the language amongst the locals. Various well-known organisations produce whole series of workbooks, CDs, audiocassettes and videos for learning a wide range of foreign languages. Unfortunately, the BBC no longer produces language courses for adults although the excellent (1982) series *Buongiorno Italia* (see below) is still available to buy and the BBC Education website provides interactive language tutorials online. The Italian bookshop (7 Cecil Court, London WC2 4EZ; ☎020-7240 1635; Italian@esb.co.uk) is a well-known stockist of Italian language books and courses. Grant and Cutler, the UK-based foreign language bookseller stocks a range of over 30 teach yourself courses for Italian (www.grantandcutler.com/catalogues/Italian/main/b04i103.htm). A very comprehensive reference list of course books, dictionaries, grammar books and and exam preparation books can be found at www.liv.ac.uk/ulc/independent%20learning/catalogue/ItalianCat2.htm and also at www.wannalearn.com/Academic_Subjects/World_Languages/Italian/. Sample self-study courses listed below are all available at grantandcultler.com.

Buongiorno Italia! Coursebook, £10.99 (plus three cassettes at £6.99 each). This combination of texts and recordings from the BBC focuses heavily on such aspects of everyday, conversational Italian as finding the way, shopping and understanding numbers and prices. The textbook, teacher's notes and cassettes can all be purchased individually.

Colloquial Italian: Routledge 1996, book £8.99 and cassettes (2) £11 arpprox each. And *Colloquial Italian 2* (2003), book £9.99 and two CDs approx £15.60 each. *Italianissimo*, also from the BBC, has courses ranging in price from £6.99, through to a full course at £42.99. Further details on all BBC courses can be obtained online at: www.bbcshop.com.

Hugo: Italian in three months: Italian: £5.99 (book); book/CD pack £25.

Immersionplus Italian: audio immersion course (2003), £20 approximately. Pack includes 3 CDs and a listening guide in English and Itallian.

Online bookstores such as www.amazon.com, www.amazon.co.uk and www.bn.com have a wide range of courses at discounted prices on their North American, European and other regional sites.

For those who want to maintain or improve their fluency in Italian *Acquerello Italiano* audio magazine is ideal for anyone interested in Italian language and culture. *Acquerello Italiano* is an hour-long programme on audiocassette with news, features and interviews from Italy. Rather than teaching you to order meals or book a hotel room, the programme is aimed at helping you expand and update your vocabulary. The cassette comes with a magazine that has transcripts, glossary and copious background explanatory notes. There are optional study supplements also available. For six editions annually the subscription is £69 (US$99), the study supplements are an additional £18 (US$30) from *Aquerello Italiano,* UK ☎0117-929 2318; fax 0117-929 2426; USA ☎1-800 824 0829; www.acquerello-italiano.com or www.champs-elysees.com).

Learning Italian in Italy

The most famous Italian language schools are at Perugia and Siena universities, at the British Institute in Florence and at the Scuola Leonardo da Vinci in Florence, Rome and Siena. But all major Italian cities have schools of Italian. A list of courses in Italy can be found at www.goto4me.com/pages/it/Italian-school.php and also at www.studying-italian-in-italy.tinusi.com and www.studyabroaditaly. org and www.italianlanguagecourse.com.

A typical university course in Italian e.g. at the University of Trento, costs 400 euros (about $520), for outsiders for 50 hours of lessons in total.

The first step in learning Italian is to understand that it is phonetic: the words are pronounced exactly as they are spelt. Once you have mastered the phonetic rules listed below, you can make yourself understood, immediately, by learning a few key phrases and idioms, of which a few examples are also listed.

To acquire the sound and the cadence of the language it is worth listening to Italian radio or TV. Quiz programmes are particularly educational in that they show words and their spelling on screen.

Useful addresses

An extensive list of language schools can be found on the websites mentioned above and at www.intoitaly.it.

Centro Lingua Italiana Calvino: Viale Fratelli Rosselli 74, 50123 Firenze; ☎055-288081, fax 055-288125; www.clicschool.it; info@clicschool.it. School open all year. Residential summer courses are organised in Calabria.

The Centro Linguistico Italiano Dante Alighieri: Piazza della Repubblica 5, 1-50123 Florence; ☎055-210 808; fax 055-287828; also Via B. Marliano 4, Rome; ☎06-8320184, fax 06-8604203; www.dantealighieri.com; e-mail study@clida.it.

CESA Languages Abroad: Western House, Malpas, Truro TR1 1SQ; ☎01872-225300; fax 01872-225400; www.cesalanguages.com. Organises language courses in Florence Venice, Rome and Siena.

Istituto Europeo: Piazza dell Pallottole 1 (Duomo), 50122 Firenze; ☎055-2381071; fax 055 289145; info@istitutoeuropeo.it. Language courses; also cultural, professional and music courses.

Istituto Italiano: Centro di Lingua e Cultura, Via Machiavelli 33, 00185 Rome; ☎06 704 52138, fax 0670085122; www.istitutoitaliano.com. Contact in the USA: Lingua Service Worldwide (75 Prospect Street, Suite 3, Huntingdon NY 11743; ☎1-800-394 5327 or 1-631-424 0777; www.linguaserviceworldwide. com/IsItalia.htm

It Schools is an online directory of Italian language schools in Italy and around the world: www.it-schools.com.

Italiaidea: Piazza della Cancelleria 85, 00186 Rome;   ☎06 683-7620; fax 06-6892997; www.italiaidea.com; e-mail.italiaidea.com.

Italian for You (Online Course): www.italianforyou.it.

Scuola Leonardo da Vinci: Schools in Rome, Florence and Siena;☎055 290 305; www.scualoaleonardo.com.

Essential Phonetics

The Italian alphabet is pronounced as follows: 'a' (ah), 'b' (bee), 'c' (tchee), 'd' (dee), 'e' (eh), 'f' (ehf-fey), 'g' (jee), 'h' (ak-ka), 'i' (ee), 'j' (ee loongo = *i lungo* or long i), 'k' (kahp-pah), 'l'(ell-ley), 'm' (em-mey), 'n' (en-ney), 'o' (oh), 'p' (pee), 'q' (koo), 'r' (ehr-rey), 's' (ess-sey), 't' (tee), 'u' (oo), 'v' (voo), ('w' is *doppio v* (dop-pyo voo), 'x' (eeks), 'y' (*ipsilon* = eepseelon), 'z' (zeta = dzeh-tah).

Vowels. must all be distinctly enunciated, never slurred or diphthongised as in English.

'a' sounds a in father	e.g. *padre* (pah-dray) = father
'e' has two sounds	open as in whey e.g. *pésca* = fishing,
	closed as in whet e.g. *pèsca* = peach
'i' sounds as in machine	e.g. *bambino* (bambeeno) = child
'o' has two sounds	open as in 'got' e.g. *uomo* (waw-mo) = man,
closed as in goat	e.g. *limone* (lee-moan-ey) = lemon
'u' sounds as in rule	e.g. *uno* (oo-noh) = one, except before vowels when it sounds like the unstressed u in quit e.g. *buono* (bwaw-noh) = good.

Diphthongs. In Italian, these are formed automatically by giving the full phonetic value to each successive vowel,

e.g. *Ciao!*	Chee-a-oh-(chow)	hi!
Vai!	va-ee-(vye)	go!

Consonants. Pronounced as they are in English but without any aspiration (except in demotic Tuscan – supposedly – from the Etruscan), and they are never swallowed or glottalised.

'*c*': has two sounds: before 'a, o, u' and 'h' like 'c' in car e.g. *caro* (kah-roh) = dear and *chiave* (kyah-vey) = key. Before 'e' and 'i', like ch in church e.g. *cena* (chey-na) = dinner.

'g' : has two sounds: before a, o, u and 'h' it is like 'g' in go, before 'e' and 'i' it is like 'j' in jump e.g. *gusto* (goose-toe) = taste, *gente* (jen-tey) = people, *ghetto* (get-toe) = ghetto.

'h': is never pronounced in Italian e.g. *ho* (oh) = I have.

'r': is *always* sounded with a distinct trill e.g. *carne*(carr-ney) = meat. This 'R' sound is more like the Scots 'R' than the West country or north American R. It can change the meaning of the word if you drop it e.g. *carne* = meat, *cane* (kah-ney) = dog.

's': has two sounds: 's' as in so, and 's' as in rose e.g. *presto* = quick and *rosa* (raw-zah) = rose.

'z': has two sounds: 'ts' as in hats, and 'dz' as in heads, e.g. *zio* (tsee-oh) = uncle, *zappa* (dzahp-pa) = hoe.

'ch': has the sound of 'k' as in kettle e.g. *bruschetta* (bruce-ket-ta) = toast..

'gh': has the sound of 'g' as in go e.g. *traghetto* (trag-et-toe) = ferry.00

'gl': has the sound of 'lli' in million e.g. *piglio* (pee-lli-oh) = take.

'gn': has the sound of 'ny' in canyon, e.g. *bagno* (ba-nyo) = bath ,

'ng': sounds like 'ngg' as in hunger e.g. *lungo* (loong-goh) = long.

'sc': has two sounds. Before a, o, and u it sounds like 'sc' in scar, before e and i it has the sound of 'sh' in she e.g. *scusa* (skoo-za) = excuse, *scena* (sheh-na) = scene.

DOUBLE CONSONANTS

Note: all double consonants in standard Italian are fully sounded:

e.g. the 'tt' *in brutto* (ugly) is pronounced as in hat-trick

the 'cc' in *pacco* (package) is pronounced as in book-case

the 'll' in *bella* (beautiful) is pronounced as in male lamb

and so on with all the consonants.

Note: the meaning can change if you fail to sound the double consonant e.g. *penna* = pen; *pena* = pain.

SOME USEFUL PHRASES AND IDIOMS

Buongiorno, buona sera, buona notte,	good day, good evening, good night.	Mi piace…	I like.
Come sta?	(formal) how are you?	Da morire	to die for.
Come stai?	(familiar) how are you?	Permesso? Posso?	May I?

Non c'è male	not too bad.	*Scusi*	excuse me.
Molto bene	very well.	*Complimenti!*	Congratulations!
Tutto bene	all well.	*Grazie*	thank you.
pronto!	hello! (on the phone) literally = ready!	*Prego*	don't mention it, you're welcome.
a domani	till tomorrow.	*Guardi!*	look!
Ciao!	hi! or bye! (informal)	*Guarda*	(familiar) look!
salve	formal version of ciao.	*Che bella!*	How beautiful!
arrivederci!	see you!	*Che brutta!*	How ugly!
ieri	yesterday.	*Certo!*	sure!
presto – tardi	early, late.	*Senta!*	hey listen!
quanto?, quando?	how much? when?	*ascóltami*	listen to me (familiar)
dove? qui	where? here.	*è vero?*	is it true?
non lo so	I don't know.	*mi raccommando*	I urge you.
non si sa mai	one never knows.	*dai!*	go on!
un giorno sì, un giorno no	every other day, literally one day yes, one day no.	*vai!*	go! come off it!
a che ora parte? arriva?	what time does it leave? arrive?	*via!*	away!
La strada, il pullman, il treno per Firenze	The road, the bus, the train to Florence.	*un sacco di soldi*	loads (literally, a sack) of money.
Che ore sono?	what time is it?	*Buone cose!*	all the best! (literally, good things).
Che ora è?	what time is it?	*Lasciamo perdere!*	forget it! (literally, let's lose it!).
Sono le tre	It is three o'clock.	*il mondo è paese*	the world is like a village.i.e. things are the same everywhere.
Come si chiama questo?	What's this called?	*Molto fumo e poco arrosto!*	(lit. a lot of smoke and not much roast; i.e. much ado about nothing.
Questo, quello	this, that.	*Buon lavoro!*	Enjoy your work!

Adesso, allora	now, then.	*Buona giornata!*	Have a nice day!
Ora	now.	*Buon proseguimento!*	Carry on, and all the best.
Quanto costa?	how much does it cost?	*Che diàmine! Per carità!*	What on earth...!For goodness sake![
Magari!	if only!		

GENDER IN THE ITALIAN LANGUAGE

A distinction is made in Italian between masculine and feminine – in the ending of nouns and adjectives – feminine – a, masculine – o, thus *Brava!* well done! (of a girl), *Bravo!* well done! (of a boy). Girls especially must remember to make adjectives agree with their gender: thus *sono contenta* not *sono contento* (I am happy) when they are talking about themselves. Exceptions: some words of Greek origin ending in -a are masculine such as: *il poeta, il problema*, etc.

It is a good idea to learn *by rote* the alphabet, the numerals, the days of the week, the months of the year, the colours, and so on. Study the dictionary or an Italian language textbook and *Buon divertimento!* (Enjoy yourself!).

Body Language

Italians are famous for their expressive body language and gestures (bunched fingers, the wagging forefinger etc.). These are an integral part of any language and can only be learnt by personal observation and mimicry. The degree of gesticulation, closeness and body contact increase the further south you go, as you move from Northern European to Mediterranean norms of tolerance.

Familiarity

Italian retains certain polite forms such as the distinction between *Lei* and *Tu* (= you in the singular), *Lei* literally means She. The plural is *Loro*, which literally means they or them. It is the equivalent of English waiter-speak. 'Would the gentlemen like a drink?' meaning 'Do you want a drink?' The third person is used to avoid the familiarity of speaking directly with the second person. *Darsi del Lei* – (to use the *Lei* form) means not be on first-name terms with, which is *darsi del Tu*. *Tu* is used with children, colleagues, work mates, fellow students, relations and patronisingly with servants. When in doubt use *Lei*, or wait for the native speaker to shift to *Tu*. Italians generally prefer to be reserved and courteous and do not have the same compulsion to be on first-name terms as some English-speaking people have.

ADDRESSING AND SIGNING LETTERS

The Envelope. On the envelope the polite form is: *Gentile Signore/Dottore Mario Rossi*, which is abbreviated to: *Gent.Sig./dott. Mario Rossi*.

Often abbreviated superlatives are used, such as: *Gentma dott.ssa Mario Bianchi* for *Gentilissima dottoressa Maria Bianchi*; (= very gentle) or *Preg.mo sig. Bruno Giordani* (= highly esteemed) for *Pregiatissimo signore Bruno Giordani;* or *Chiar. mo prof. Ezio Landi* for *Chiarissimo professore Ezio Landi, (Chiarissimo = very illustrious is only used for university professors).*

Then the address:

> *via Nazionale, 23*
> *53031 Buonconvento SI.*

NOTE

- Put the postcode before the town name (CAP = *Codice di avviamento postale*), followed by the abbreviation of the province (two letters in capitals).
- If it is confidential write, *riservata-personale; c/o* or *presso* is used for 'care of'.
- 'For whom it may concern' is *a chi di competenza*.
- The sender's address must be written on the back of the envelope: *Mittente:-* (= sender:-).
- In many business and personal letters polite titles can be ignored.

Beginning The Letter. You begin the letter with the recipient's address on the top and the date below it, either in the short form (03.04.05) or preferably in the full form (3 aprile 2005).

Then you start with:

Caro...(masc.), or *Cara...* (fem.)   Dear... (followed by name).

Carissimo... (masc), or *Carissima...*(fem.)   Dearest ... (followed by name).

or just bluntly *Oggetto...*   Subject...

or more politely: *Gentile Signor Rossi,...*

or more formally: *Egregio Signor Fabbri,*

Signing Off. You end the letter with: *Cari*, or *Cordiali saluti* (dear or warm greetings), or more familiarly with: *Baci* (kisses) or *abbracci* (hugs) which can be *cari* or *affettuosi*. Thus: *affettuosi saluti* (affectionate greetings).

Distinti saluti (respectful greetings) is a cold formal ending which is normally qualified by a polite preceding phrase such as: *'in attesa di un Vostro gradito riscontro'* (awaiting your kind reply). More formal and grovelling are the endings *con ossequio* and *con osservanza* (with deference, compliance), and finally, if you want to affirm your trustworthiness: *In fede* (in faith).

E-mail. Italian e-mail 'netiquette' follows the American example: Cut out all formality and get straight to the point as if you were speaking. *Oggetto:-* (= Subject....). The neutral greeting *salve* (hail!) and ending *saluti* are permissible. The use of capital letters means you are shouting.

ITALIAN FORMULA FOR SPELLING OUT NAMES ETC.

When Italians have to spell out names etc. the following alphabet mainly of town names is universally used. This alphabet is indispensable for foreigners and must be learnt.

a = Ancóna	b = Bari	c = Como
d = Domodóssola	e = Èmpoli	f = Firenze
g = Génova	h = Hotel	i = Ímola
j = Jesolo (ee-yeh-so-lo)	k =Kursaal	l = Livorno
m = Milano	n = Nàpoli	0 = Òtranto
p = Palermo	q = Quarto	r = Roma
s = Savona	t = Torino	u = Údine (oó-di-neh)
v = Venezia	w = Washington	x = (pronounced ee ks)
y = York (or Ipsilon)	z = Zara	

THE ITALIAN NATIONAL ANTHEM

Most Italians consider the national anthem *Fratelli d'Italia*, (Brothers of Italy) archaic and uninspiring. It was written by the youthful patriot Goffredo Mameli who died while defending the Roman Republic in 1849 and its sentiments are somewhat romantic and high flown for these days. Although meant as an interim anthem it was never replaced. A recent contender as a replacement anthem is reported to be the 'Chorus of the Hebrew Slaves' (*Va, pensiero, sull'ali dorate*) from Verdi's Nabucco.

Cultural Training Courses

Apart from being able to speak the language of the country you are going to, understanding why the host nationals behave the way they do in both a social and a business context can make the difference between loving the country and hating it. A number of organisations offer cultural awareness courses and these can be as valuable as language courses, though they are often expensive. Working through culture shock is an important an unavoidable aspect of living abroad and its importance cannot be underestimated and this book will help you through many of the practical aspects of culture shock.

In addition to the specific addresses below there are some useful Websites to consult. *Italian Cultural Institutes in the World* is an online directory of Italian associations categorised by region and country; www.italcult.net. There is also an online directory of Italian Cultural organisations, language schools, formal Italian course and Italian related events in the UK: ww.embitaly.org.uk/culture/mainpage.html. For an online directory of Italian institutions in the USA look at www.italyemb.org/ItalianInstitutions.htm.

Useful Addresses

Amerispan: 117, South 17th Street, STE 1401, Phipadelphia, PA; ☎215-751- 1100; fax 215-751 1986; www.amerispan.com; info@amerispan.com. Amerispan specializes in language immersion programmes, academic study abroad, volunteering/intern placements and other educational travel experiences including language and culture immersion programmes in Florence.

Dante Alighieri Society: is an Italian cultural society based in Siena, Italy, with branches around the world including the USA and Australia. Their main website (www.dantealighieri.com) provides information on the activities offered in Sienna and allows visitors to contact regional representatives of the Siena institution. The society organises year-round language courses and other events. Other branches around the world can be found at: http://orb.rhodes.edu/encyclop/culture/lit/Italian/da-s.htm.

Federazione Italiana Lavoratori Emigranti e Famiglie (FILEF): (96/98 Central Street, London EC1V 8AJ;   ☎020 -7608 0125; fax 020-7490 0938; e-mail fileggb@punto.u-net.com). Cultural organisation that runs Italian evening classes for all levels.

The Italian Cultural Institute: 39 Belgrave Square, London SW1X 8NX;   ☎020-7235 1461; fax 020-7235 4618; www.italcultur.org.uk. Runs courses at the Institute in London. Also, can advise on language courses throughout Italy. Helps undergraduates and postgraduates find out about courses at Italian universities.

Private schools/language services, which offer business Italian:

International House: 106 Piccadilly, London W1J 7NL;   ☎020 7518 6950; fax 020 7418 6951; main website – www.ihworld.com; USA branches – 2725 Congress Street #2M, San Diego, CA 92110, USA;   ☎1 (619) 299 2339; fax 1 (619) 299 0235; www.ih-usa.com. Has 120 schools in 30 countries.

Italiaidea: Via dei due Macelli, 47/1 floor, 00187 Rome; ☎06-69941314; www.italiaidea.com/business.htm. One month course based in Rome. 24, 1-hour lessons €310.

Italian in Business: www.italianbusiness.co.uk; ☎0845 127 9897; offers one-to-one and group classes in your place of business in London/Surrey.

Lingualearn: ;   ☎01273-597169; www.lingualearn.co.uk; info@lingualearn.

co.uk. Offers in-company language training either on site or distance learning using telephone, e-mail and web-based materials. Minimum 20-hour course.
Linguaviva: www.linguaviva.it; info@linguaviva.it. Offers business Italian courses in Italy, at schools in Florence, Milan and Syracuse.

Business Traveller and Cultural Briefing Courses:

Farnham Castle International Briefing and Conference Centre: Farnham Castle, Farnham, Surrey GU9 OAG; ☎01252-721194; fax 01252-711283; www. farnhamcastle.com. Programmes are aimed at corporate expatriates and business travellers so prices are high. Intercultural briefings and language course lasting from one to four days. Families can also attend the courses.

inlingua School of Languages, 28 Rotton Park Road, Edgbaston, Birmingham B16 9JL; ☎0121-454 0204; fax 0121-456 3264; www.inlingua.com; for information about US inlingua schools visit www.inlingua.com/usa.html. inlingua offer cultural awareness courses in addition to language courses.

Italian Societies

It is essential to delve into Italian culture before leaving for Italy if you want to avoid feeling culturally stranded on arrival in Italy. Various societies exist in the UK, USA and other countries that organise social events and discussion groups of an endlessly diverse nature which will serve to soften the culture shock. The Italian Cultural Institute (see above) is the main Italian government agency whose function it is to promote cultural relations between Britain and Italy. The Institute organises lectures, exhibitions and promotes concerts and has a library facility of approximately 21,000 books including subjects such as Italian literature, art, history, criticisms and essays. The library is open to the general public although only members are eligible to take the books out on loan. Anyone looking for a scholarship to study in Italy should contact the Italian Institute as all scholarships for study and research in Italy are awarded by the Italian Ministry of Foreign Affairs and other Italian institutions through them. Membership of the Institute is on an annual basis and entitles members to receive information on all of the cultural events that it arranges and gives free access to its facilities. There is a reduced annual membership for under 18's, full-time students, senior citizens and anyone with an address outside London.

Another potentially useful organisation is the British-Italian Society (Offices of Venice in Peril Fund, Hurlingham Studios, unit 4, Ranelagh Gardens, London SW6 3PA; e-mail jo.t@british-italian.org) which exists to foster relations and increase awareness between Britons and Italians.

Americans have strong links with Italy through emigration and America has a clutch of Italian American sights for forging closer contacts with the old country; try www.italiaamerica.org/

SCHOOLS AND EDUCATION

Reforms to the Italian education system in 2000 increased compulsory education from eight to ten years, and raised the school leaving age to 18 years. Children are legally required to attend school until this age. This reform was overdue to prevent many children in the south leaving school at age fourteen to try to find a job in order to contribute to their family's poor income, usually finding themselves more often than not joining the swelling ranks of the Mezzogiorno's 20% unemployed. Among other aims, the reforms are intended to render less traumatic the transition from primary to secondary school by unifying both these cycles into one large primary cycle. The second aim is the focus the education provided by upper secondary schools on preparing young men and women for entry into higher education or workplace. Reforms at university level are aimed at bringing comparability at degree level study throughout the European Union.

Regarding the quality of Italian schools, however, over the last ten or fifteen years, massive improvements have been implemented within the Italian state education system and Italy can now boast a system of education which equals most others in Europe. The system of education is administered centrally through the government, with the exception of elementary schools that are usually run by the local commune. As in other countries there is wide disparity in the quality of education available between the rich and poor sections of the country. In Italy this is a further wedge between the north and the south of the country – the standard of schools in the large northern cities like Turin, Genoa, Rome and Milan are much higher than those found in Molise, Calabria or Campania. Although state education is free in Italy, parents are responsible for buying their children's textbooks and stationery.

Private schools also exist, of which nearly all are Roman Catholic (although pupils are not required to be) and most are day schools only. Although private schools do not carry the same kind of status with which they are often associated in Britain and America, they do form an attractive option to those who can afford them, especially where the local state school is not of the best. Like many large cities of the world, some of the large cities of the Mezzogiorno, particularly in Naples, some state schools are facing serious and growing drug problems.

The decision as to whether to educate children within the Italian, British, American or International system of education (see the section, *International Schools* below) is one which must include such considerations as the age of the child, the length of time you are planning to live in Italy, how much you want your child to be bilingual and your financial situation. Remember also that the watershed age for learning a language with relative ease appears to be around eleven to twelve and after this it becomes more and more difficult to pick up the language quickly. There is also the problem that important exams are much closer and there is therefore less time for the child to catch up on the work they missed whilst learning the language.

The Structure of the Italian Education System

Asilo Nido. Pre-school from six months to three years. Can be public or private but the public ones are notoriously oversubscribed. Public places are awarded on a points system; basically the more disadvantaged you are the more likely you are to get a place for your offspring. For instance a poor widow with three children has a higher points rating than someone who is poor with one child. Better-off families tend to have to go for the private option which can cost as much as €500 per month.

Scuola dell'Infanzia. May also be called *scuola materna* this is an optional public pre-school education which is provided by the commune, and is usually much easier to get into than the *asilo nido*. It is for three to six-year-olds and is free. Italian women do, however, complain that the availability of pre-school care from a young age is limited. To a certain extent it seems that in Italy women have to choose between a career and parenthood.

Scuola di base: formerly *scuola elementare* (primary school), known as elementary or grade school in north America, begins at age six and continues for seven years (formerly it was for five) until children enter the next level at age thirteen. Lessons usually last for only four hours each day and this short time does not allow room for sports, music, drama, etc, which are largely regarded as not only extracurricular activities but outside school activities. The *scuola di base* is the easiest stage at which to integrate foreign children into the school system; the younger the better as far as becoming fluent in Italian is concerned. After passing some fairly straightforward exams, children pass on to the next stage, the *scuola media*.

Note that often in country areas but not so much in cities children may also go to primary school on Saturdays as many parents have to work in shops and post offices on Saturdays. The schools can decide independently to open Saturdays.

Scuola Secondaria: Secondary school, known as Middle School in north America, covers the ages thirteen to eighteen, the first two years being compulsory. The *liceo* and *istituto* into which students were traditionally divided into academic and technical streams are now in the process of replacement by an obligatory two-year period *(biennio)* of general studies which precedes a three-year *(triennio)* optional schooling period of specialized studies geared to better prepare students for the university or their future careers. To successfully complete the *scuola secondaria*, exams must be passed and an average of not less than sixty percent maintained throughout each school year. The *diploma di licenza media* is awarded to all those who successfully take the examination at the end of compulsory secondary schooling. At this point, the less academic tend to go on to one of the vocational *istituti tecnici to study anything from accounta*ncy to farming (if they do stay in the system), while the academically better students stay at school for a further two years, taking either the *liceo classico* or *liceo scientifico*. This involves a certain amount of specialisation, although not to the same extent as the UK A level system. At 18 or 19, ie in the final year of upper secondary education is the *esame di stato* of which the full title is *esame di stato conclusivo dei corsi di studio di istruzione secondaria superiore*. Formerly liceo students took the *maturità* (equivalent of the French baccalaureat), while *tecnici* students took a diploma which bestows the equivalent qualification of a British City and Guilds.

University: until recently, everyone who obtained either the *maturità or a tecnici* diploma was automatically entitled to go on to an Italian university. Consequently, universities became flooded with students and Italy had one of the highest percentages in Europe of the relevant age group attending university. Italy, however, has far fewer non-university higher education courses than France and Germany, which probably accounts for much of this high percentage. Though a high percentage of young people attended university many of them failed to graduate; in fact, only about one third of students enrolled for a university degree ever finished their courses.

Italian universities have been, and some argue still are, the victim of under-investment and a lack of courses and venues. Inevitably, there is an unofficial league table of the universities with graduates of some institutions being in a better position to get good jobs than graduates of others. Indeed, a survey found that some graduates were only marginally better off in the job stakes than holders of a high-school diploma. One fact that makes Italian universities exceptional, is the low cost of tuition fees in public universities; even the top ones are not allowed to charge above a thousand euros a year and if you are disadvantaged you may be exempt from paying fees altogether, or eligible for small scholarships. One of the much-needed reforms has forged closer links between business and universities, thus ensuring that academic products are competitive and relevant to the job market.

The picture is not, however, entirely bleak. Some of Italy's universities have a very good reputation and several are internationally renowned. For example, the private Bocconi University in Milan is excellent, particularly in the faculties of business studies and economics, with fierce competition for the few available places each year. Rome's *Libera Università degli Studi Sociali* (LUISS) has a similarly high reputation. Both of these universities are private and their tuition fees run into several thousand pounds each year, with only a few scholarships and other awards available.

The state universities vary in quality but among the most prestigious are:

Politecnico in Milan (famous for its engineering faculty).

Bologna University, which is the oldest in Europe and has a very high reputation in most subjects.

Pavia University, which excels particularly in medicine.

Orientale in Naples boasts the oldest oriental language school in Italy.

The method of university teaching in Italy is similar to that in the UK, i.e. it requires students to do much of their work independently and without a lot of supervision from faculty members; if anything it is even more remote and reliant on each individual's often faltering, self motivation. Lectures are frequently over-crowded, sometimes to the point that it is practically impossible to squeeze into the lecture halls. One peculiarity used to be that students could postpone exams indefinitely until they decided they were ready to take them, while no degree could be completed in less than four years and completion of a first degree could take up to six years. A large proportion of all courses rely on oral examinations. Italian universities are not residential and do not even organise accommodation for their students, so many students live at home and go to a local university.

University reforms introduced in 2001 are aimed at making Italian universities more international. They have also standardised the system of degree awards. The new first level degree *Diploma di Laurea* is more like a BA or BSc (it replaces the *Laurea* which took four to six years to complete). There is also a two-year specialization degree (*Laurea di Specializzazione)* which is the rough equivalent of a masters degree. A research doctorate *(Dottorato di Ricerca)* or other postgraduate degree takes a further one to two years to complete*).*

International Schools

International schools tend to be regarded as the best option for the children of expatriates who do not expect to remain in Italy in the long-term, or who want their children to have the option of attending university in their home country. Different schools within the category of International School offer UK, German, French, Japanese, Swedish, Spanish, and US curricula. Though international schools can be seen to isolate children from the communities in which they live, most International Schools admit students from many nationalities, including that of the host country, and students are given the chance to study the local language in a way suitable for non-native speakers. There are numerous schools in Italy that are possible options for expatriates, the majority of which are of high quality and offer a continuous style of education for transient expatriate children. They also offer easier access to UK and North American higher education and ensure that the level of English (or German, French or other language) of the expatriate child remains at native level.

The main English medium international schools are listed below, along with their address and phone number and the age range they cover. Schools whose classes are taught in other languages, as mentioned above, can be contacted via the appropriate embassies. The European Council of International Schools (21B Lavant Street, Petersfield, Hants GU32 3EL;   ☎0730-68244; www.ecis.org), International Schools Services – ISS (15 Roszel Road, PO Box 5910, Princeton, New Jersey, USA;   ☎609 452 0990; www.iss.edu) and the International Baccalaureate Organisation (www.ibo.org) maintain lists of English medium schools on their websites.

English medium schools in Milan:

The American School of Milan, Via Marx 14, 20090 Noverasco di Opera, Milano; ☎02 530 0001; fax 02 5760 6274; www.asmilan.org. Ages three 18.

International School of Milan: Via Caccialepori 22, 20148, Milan, Italy;   ☎02 487 08076; fax 02 487 03644; www.ism-ac.it. Ages three to 19.

Sir James Henderson British School of Milan: Via Pisano Dossi 16, 20134, Milan; ☎02 264 13332/13310; fax 02 264 13515). Ages three to 18.

Rome:

Ambrit School: Via Filippo Tajani 50, 00149 Rome;   ☎ 06 559 5301/5; fax 06 559 5309; www.ambrit-rome.com. Ages three to 14.

American Overseas School of Rome: Via Cassia 811, 00189, Rome, Italy;   ☎06 334381; fax 06 3326 2608; www.aosr.org. Ages three to 18.

Castelli International School: 13 Via Degli Scozzesi, 00046 Grottaferrata, Rome; tel/fax 06 943 15779. Ages five to 14 years. www/pcg.it/cis.

Greenwood Garden School: Via Vito Sinisi 5, Rome 00189 (tel/fax 6 3326-6703; greenwoodgarden@libero.it).

International Academy of Rome: Via di Grottarossa 295, 00189 Rome (☎ 06 3326 6071). Ages three to 14.

Kendale Primary International School: Via Gradoli 86, Tomba di Nerone, 00189 Rome (tel/fax 06 366 7608; www.diesis.com/kendale). Ages 3 to 10.

Marymount International School: Via di Villa Lauchli 180, 00191 Rome (☎06 362 9101; fax 06 3630 1738; www.marymountrome.com. Roman Catholic school. Ages three to 19.

New School: Via della Camiluccia 669, 00135 Rome;   ☎ 06 329 4269; fax 06 329 7546). Ages: three to 18 years.

Notre Dame International School: Via Aurelia 796, 00165 Rome (☎ 06 680 8801; fax 680 6051). Ages 10-18.

Rome International School: Viale Romania 32, Parioli (off Piazza Ungheria, Rome;   ☎ 06 844 82650; fax 06 844 82651. Ages three to 18 years.

Southlands English School: Via Teleclide 20, Casal Palocco, 00124 Rome;   ☎06 505 3922; fax 06 509 17192). Ages three to 14 years.

St Francis International School: Via S. Borgia 85, 00168 Rome;   ☎ 06 355

11023; fax 06 35072669; www.stfrancisinternationalschool.com. Ages three
to 14. American system.

St George's English School: Via Cassia KM 16, 00123 Rome; ☎ 06 3790141/23;
fax 06 3792490). Ages three to 18.

St Stephen's School: Via Aventina 3, 00153 Rome; ☎06 575 0605; fax 06 574
1941; www.ststephens-rome.com. Ages: 13 to 19.

Other Cities:

American International School of Florence: Via del Carota 23/35, 50012 Bagno a
Ripoli, Florence; ☎055 640033; fax 55 644226. Ages 2½ to 19.

American International School in Genoa: Via Quarto 13/C 16148 Genoa;
☎010 386528; fax 010 398700). Ages three to 14.

Anglo-Italian School Montessori Division: Viale Della Liberazione, Comando
NATO, 90125, Bagnoli, Naples; ☎081 721 2266; fax 081 570 6587.

European School: Via Montello 118, 21100 Varese; ☎0332 806111; fax 332
806202. Ages four to 18. Waiting list of 2 years and the school generally only
takes children of EU employees.

International School of Naples: Viale della Liberazione, 1 H.Q. AFSouth Post,
Bldg 'A', 80125 Bagnoli, Napoli; ☎081-721 20 37; fax 081-762 84 29.
Ages three to 18.

International School of Trieste: Via Conconello 16, Opicina, 34100 Trieste;
☎040 211452). Ages three to 18.

International School of Turin (American Cultural Association School of Turin):
Vicolo Tiziano 10, 10024 Moncalieri; ☎011 645967; fax 011 643298).
Ages three to eighteen.

International School of Modena: Via Silvio Pellico 9, Fiorano, 41042, Modena,
Italy; ☎0536 832904; fax 0536 911189.

United World College of the Adriatic: Via Trieste 29, 34013 Duino (Trieste);
☎040-3739111; fax 040-3739225. Takes boarding students aged 16 to study
for the pre-university IB diploma. Entry is exclusively by scholarship.

MEDIA AND COMMUNICATIONS

Newspapers

In common with the Spaniards, the Italians are not avid newspaper readers
compared with the British, and only 60% of Italian families buy a daily newspaper. There is no real equivalent of the well-established British tabloids and US
supermarket newspapers and only the down market papers, e.g. *Il Messaggero*
carry horoscopes, cartoons or fun features.

ITALIAN PAPERS

Newspaper	City	Political leaning
La Nazione	Florence	Socialist
Il Mattino	Naples	Christian Democrat
Il Messagero	Rome	Communist
Il Resto del Carlino	Bologna.	
L'Ora	Palermo	at the forefront of anti-Mafia movement in the media environs of Sicily.
Il Tempo	(Rome)	
La Gazzetta del Mezzogiorno	(Bari)	
La Nuova Sardegna	(Cagliari)	
Paese Sera	(Rome)	
Il Piccolo	(Trieste)	
La Nuova	Venezia (Venice)	

Of about 80 daily Italian newspapers only a handful are distributed throughout the country. The most popular Italian dailies are *Il Corriere della Sera (Milan)* and *La Repubblica* (Rome) – both of which boast a daily circulation of between five and six hundred thousand. *La Stampa* (Turin) follows with a much lower circulation. *Il Giornale* and *Il Messagero* trail in with fewer than two hundred thousand.

Il Corriere della Sera and *La Repubblica*, in particular, are constantly vying for circulation supremacy, mostly using *allegati* (enclosures) of books or DVDs. Books are themed: e.g. masterpieces of literature, several volume histories, touring guides etc. which are offered free with the paper, or artistically packaged and offered to readers at special prices. There are also regular inserts including a women's magazine and TV guide. However, *La Repubblica*, an unusually liberal publication, tends to create the most controversy and excitement, with its talent for political insight and cultural reporting. By contrast, the conservative *La Stampa* which belongs to Fiat tends to back whatever Fiat wants to back; historically this has been the Christian Democrats.

The two main financial dailies – *Il Sole/24 Ore* and *Italia Oggi*, – are extensive in their coverage, and of similar standard to t*he Financial Times* or *Wall Street Journal*. The three sports dailies are *Corriere dello Sport, Gazzetta dello Sport* and *Tuttosport*. The regional newspapers, which focus on national news but include several pages of local news and comment, are particularly popular and widely read in Italy.

There are no separate Sunday papers as such in Italy; instead all of the national dailies print on Sunday and then have a day off on Monday. The website www. italydaily.com is a useful link to the sites of the most important daily Italian newspapers both national and local and the academic website www.tcd.ie./ CLCS/Italian/Italianmedia.html gives a very useful rundown and description of Italy's newspapers and magazines and tells you where to access local newspapers online.

The English-language newspaper, *The International Herald Tribune* (6 bis rue des Graviers, 92521 Neuilly, Cedex Paris; ☎ +33-1 41 43 92 61; fax +33-1 41 43 92 10; subs@iht.com; www.iht.com), is published in Paris in conjunction with the *New York Times and Washington Post*. It is available in Italy at newsagents or by subscription in Italy from 800-780 040, in the UK from 0800-4 448 7827 and in America from 800-8822884 or e-mail subs@iht.com. Those on the job hunt in Rome should check the expat sites including *Rome Buddy, Expats in Italy and When in Rome,* which have jobs offered in their advertising sections.

Magazines

The Italian magazine market is swamped with publications that churn out the same themes, features and cover-spreads week after week. The main three publishing houses, Mondadori, RCS Mediagroup and Hachette Rusconi are in constant competition to control a saturated market. The better-quality magazines include *Panorama* (which supports the rightist government) *and L'Espresso*, both of which contain a good deal of serious and well-written news and arts coverage. At the other end of the spectrum are *La Gente, Oggi, Novella 2000, Eva Express* and the incredibly lurid *Stop,* which are pure gossip and scandal reading.

Italy also boasts some of the classiest women and men's fashion and home furnishing magazines in the world. The most popular of which are *Moda, Marie Claire, King* and *Vogue Italia*.

A list of Italian Magazines and their websites can be found at www.ciaoitaly. com/categories/magazine.htm

English Language Publications. Expatriate website *The Informer* (www. informer.it), was formerly a monthly newspaper but is now totally online in a format that contains a variety of both useful and interesting articles ranging from tax and money matters to general interest and is a mine of information highly recommended for expatriates in Italy. *The Informer* also has electronic newsletters and extensive archives of information available online to its subscribers who can sign up at www.informer.it. Also full of useful tips about how to survive daily life in Milan and northern Italy as a foreigner is *The Survival Guide to Milan, available from the The Informer* and *Easy Milano*, a bi-weekly publication with lots of adverts useful to expats. There is a fortnightly English-language paper published in Rome: *Wanted in Rome* (www.wantedinrome.com) sold on news-stands and in some bookshops, and the Metropolitan. English language magazines *Italy* (www.italymag.co.uk) and *Italia!* (www.Italia-magazine.com) are two lifestyle and property magazines There is also *The International Spectator* published by the *Istituto Affari Internatzionali* (www.iai.it/) which is a way of keeping up with international affairs online.

The English Yellow Pages (via Belisario 4/B, 00187 Rome; ☎ 06-4740861;

fax 06-4744516; www.intoitaly.it) updated annually, will be invaluable to any new arrival in Italy. The directory contains listings for English-speaking professionals, businesses, organisations and services in Rome, Florence, Bologna, Naples, Genoa and Milan and is available at international bookstores and from news-stands. The online version also has listings for Palermo and Catania. For a free listing, contact the above address. Free classified ads can also be posted on the website. Also from the same publisher is the *English White Pages*, an alphabetical directory of English-speakers living in Italy.

Two UK-published monthly glossy magazines which might be of interest to those living and working in Italy are *Italia!* (www.Italia-magazine.com) and *The Italian* (☎01273-786844) which both contain features on food and wine, property, holidays and Italian culture.

Books

The Italian publishing market tends to cater for the extreme ends of the reading public; at one extreme the intellectual highbrow of contemporary literature; at the other downmarket, gossip and romance for Barbara Cartland-imitation junkies. The Italian best-seller list reflects the refined intellectual tastes of the literary minority. Surprisingly, foreign authors such as Milan Kundera and Gabriel Garcià Marquez often sell better than Italy's home-grown talents such as Primo Levi, Leonardo Sciascia and Umberto Eco. The recent Italian trend of giving away books with newspapers or offering sets of books at vastly reduced prices if purchased by a newspaper reader (principally of *Corriere della Sera* or *La Repubblica*) has produced a phenomenal rise in book sales at newsagents which are now reckoned to be the number two outlet for book sales in Italy.

Expats usually have wide-ranging tastes, which include a large component of Anglophone literature, which was once catered for by the independent and often quirky, English-language bookshops of Italy's cosmopolitan cities. Such shops are being superseded by Amazon and other online purveyors of cut price books worldwide.

English-language bookshops:
Anglo American Bookshop: Via della Vite 102, Rome;   ☎06 6783890; www.aab.it.

Almost Corner Bookshop: Via del Moro 45, 00153 Rome;   ☎06 5836942.

American Milan Bookshop: Via Camperio 16; 20123 Milan;   ☎02-878920.

Lion Bookshop: Via dei Greci 33/36, 00187 Rome; 06 32650437; fax 06 32651382.

Paperback Exchange Bookshop: Via Fiesolana 3lr, 50122 Florence;   ☎055 2478154; fax 055 2478856. All fields, hardbacks and paperbacks, new and secondhand, academic/library supplies, bibliographic service, special order and mail order.

Online bookshops and DVD/video suppliers:

www.amazon.com

www.amazon.co.uk - (cheaper postage than Amazon.com for books sent to Italy)

www.bn.com – US company Barnes and Noble

www2.uk.bol.com (UK store of Bol)

www.choicesdirect.co.uk (supplies UK PAL video by mail order).

www.internetbookshop/it – one of Italy's largest online sources of books, DVDs and videos (in Italian)

www.unilibro.com Italy – Claims to be Italy's largest online bookstore with English version (also supplies CDs and DVDs)

Television

The Italians are telly-addicts and Italy has more terrestrial channels than any other country in the world with an output of programmes that tend to be of a uniform awfulness. This saturation of television space was the unsurprising response to the deregulation of the television board in 1976; before this time, there had only ever been one, black and white, state-run channel, heavily influenced and censored by church authorities. The great majority of these relatively new channels are crammed with rubbishy quiz shows and low quality sitcoms and soaps, while the three state-run channels, RAI 1, 2 and 3 manage to provide a higher quality programming and command higher viewing levels. However, the standard is evidently not high enough and viewing figures are falling for the state-run channels. The state channels (RAI 1, RAI 2, RAI 3) are now no longer as subject to political patronage as they once were. RAI 3 tends to show more cultural programmes than the others.

The important independent television channels are Italia 1, Canale 5 and Rete 4 that collectively account for about 45% of Italian viewing and are owned by Prime Minister Berlusconi's Mediaset empire. Although Rete 4 is thought to be more highbrow than the other two, none of them offer really serious news coverage although Canale 5 has been attempting to give greater emphasis to documentaries and news. La 7 (formerly Tele Montecarlo) is a new independent national channel which is gaining popularity due to its large cultural content. Satellite packagers include RAI Sat and Sky Italia. A full list of TV channels in Italy can be found at www.obs.coe.int/db/persky/it.html. Information in English on the Italian licence fee and how to pay it is at www.abbonamenti.rai.it/Ordinari/canone_eng.asp. The company Solsat (www.solsat.com; info@solsat.com; ☎+34 616 314 068) can provide its clients anywhere in Europe with a Sky digibox and a fully activated Sky Digital Viewing Card at the same time. Insat International (http:sky-cards.no-ip.com/sky/sky-tv-italy.html) supplies Sky Viewing Cards and digiboxes for expats living in Italy.

In recent years there has been something of a public crusade in Italy against the probable dangers of certain types of television on the psychophysical development of children and younger viewers. The result was a watershed of 10.30pm for X-rated movies and other violent/sexually explicit programming. Italy was also a pioneer of the so-called 'violence chip' a piece of technology designed to filter out violent programmes on television when children are watching.

When shipping personal belongings to Italy it is worth remembering that Italian TV and videos operate on the PAL-BG system. The UK operates PAL-I, the USA and Canada operates NTSC and France operates MESECAM. TVs of one system do not correctly work with another (you can get black and white instead of colour, or have no sound). However, multi-system TVs and videos that play all system types are freely available in Italy – in fact, many TVs and videos now sold in Europe are multi-system.

Expatriates can find watching local television channels not as relaxing as what they are used to due to the concentration required to follow a foreign language. Thanks to satellite technology it is now possible to receive a huge variety of international channels via satellite, including BBC World (free to air), BBC Prime (subscription only), CCNI (free to air), CNBC, The Disney Channel and other good quality English language channels throughout Europe. There are also many other channels available in the numerous European languages, plus the languages of the immigrant population – Arabic, Urdu, Hindi, etc. Italy also has interactive terrestrial digital TV from RAI with special decoders that were being distributed free by the government.

Video and DVD

For those unable to find enough substantial fare, at the right time of day, on Italian television and the available satellite and digital channels, there is always recourse to videos or DVDs.

Apart from *Amazon.com, Amazon.co.uk and Barnes and Noble* online, there are www.choicesdirect.co.uk and www.bbcshop.com who supply UK standard videos in English. Expats are well recommended to buy a multi-system video player so they can watch videos they collect around the world during their travels (see Television above for explanation). DVD players, however, offer the advantage that each DVD disc gives the viewer the chance to choose the language they hear – i.e. original language or a number of dubbed languages. With this capability, expats no longer have to search out the obscure shops that sell imported videos in their original language, or order them from outside the country and can instead buy DVDs in their local shops.

DVDs, like videos, come in different formats. There are, however, only two

– American and European. They will, of course, not work on a player intended solely for the other format – so you have to buy a dual format player to ensure you can play American DVDs brought over to Italy. Blockbuster Video now operates rental stores in the larger cities and offers some videos in their original language. As most DVDs come with original soundtrack available, buying a DVD player can give you a much wider choice of films to rent.

Radio

The Italian radio network was deregulated in 1976, the same year as television, with the result that the airwaves are crammed with a diverse range of obscure stations; over two and a half thousand of them. However, the three main radio channels are Radio 1, 2, and 3. The first two feature light music and entertainment while Radio 3 is similar to the UK equivalent, broadcasting serious discussion programmes and classical music. Finally there are Radio 1 and 2 rock stations which, although technically part of RAI, are on separate wavelengths. The accumulated audience for rock stations is immense (12½ million listeners). The total audience for radio nation-wide is estimated at 35 million. However, there are so many stations that this audience is hopelessly fragmented and some local stations are estimated to have no more than a few dozen listeners.

As with television, the main radio channels are all under the wing of a powerful sponsor who consequently has a substantial influence over the station's output.

BBC World Service. The final issue of the monthly publication *BBC On Air* was in December 2004. For details of schedules, advice and information about BBC World Service radio (www.worldservice@bbc.co.uk) and BBC Prime (bbcprime@bbc.co.uk) and BBC World Television (bbcworld@bbc.co.uk) you now have to go to the BBC World Service website. You can also sign up for a monthly e-mail update of the BBC World Service Network, highlighting BBC World Service radio programmes.

Voice of America For details of Voice of America programmes, contact VOA, Washington, D.C. 20547;   ☎1-202 619 2358. Details of programmes and frequencies are also online at www.voa.gov.

The Post Office

The Italian postal system, *Poste Italiane* (www.poste.it) been considerably modernized since 1998 and the state-owned service even makes a profit (compare this with the UK's ailing service) and also has over 13,000 outlets. Improvements have included the automation of all outlets/counters, removing security screens, improving disabled access and retraining of staff to be more customer-focused.

Selected post office outlets sell books, mobile phone accessories and have internet access. Mail deliveries are getting quicker and overnight delivery is traceable, though evidently not reliable enough to negate the demand for courier services for important letters and packages. Subpostmasters (about 1,000 of them) still provide just a basic postal delivery service in very rural areas).

Stamps can be bought from the post office (*ufficio postale*) and also tobacconists (*tabaccherie*). Post office opening times vary depending on location but they are open Monday to Friday (some open at 8am) until 2pm (some until later 6.30/7pm) and until lunchtime on Saturdays. You can get precise information on post offices' opening times from your municipal website.

There are various postal services for letters and parcels; some internal some both internal and international. Domestic post under 3 kg can be sent *posta celere*, which is supposed to take one day, or priority (*posta prioritaria* – almost guaranteed next day delivery for post less than 2 kg), or ordinary (*ordinaria* – probable delivery within three or four days). With registered post (*posta raccomandata*) the post office supply a confirmation of receipt of your letter at its destination. *Posta assicurata* insures the contents of a letter, within Italy. The overseas service is also slow and mail can take a week or more to arrive at a European or North American destination but there are a variety of services to accelerate delivery including EMS corriere espresso internazionale and Quick Pack Europe; further details at www.poste.it/postali/prodottiestero/a_index. shtml.

Parcel Post. Parcel post can only be insured. For parcels there is *Pacco celere1* – takes a day, less than 30 kg within Italy; *Pacco celere3* – takes 3 days, less than 30 kg within Italy.

International mail. Can be sent by airmail or surface mail – surface mail from any country can take many weeks and Italy is no exception to this rule.

Poste Restante. For those who have no fixed address, the post restante (*fermoposta*) service is useful; just write the addressee's name, then *fermoposta* and the place name on the envelope; the addressee can then pick up his or her mail from the post office after providing a passport as identification. In large cities it is always better to address poste restante mail to the main post office.

Telegraph. The state-run Italcable operates a telegraph service abroad by cable or radio; both internal and overseas messages can be sent over the phone.

Other services offered by the post office. In addition to the regular postal services, post offices offer financial services, as do post offices in other parts of Europe. Services offered include probably the cheapest Italian personal banking.

An account *(conto bancoposto),* costs about 69 euros a year. Financial services include mortgages, personal loans, debit and credit cards, tax refund payments (for the Revenue service), foreign currency exchange, moneygrams, savings schemes and bill payment services for most bills you are likely to receive (gas, electricity, telephone, rent, etc.). Non-residents opening a post office bank account will get a chequebook and credit card and use of ATMs. Note: the conto bancoposto is not very efficient for money transfers; for these you need international banking services.

Telephones

The Italian telephone giant Telecom Italia was privatised in 1997 in order to comply with the market liberalisation directives of the EU. Since the early 1990s the phone Italian phone system has been almost totally modernised and fibre optic cables installed throughout the country – except in the usual remote rural districts that always seem to be left somewhere in the past.

American users will find having to pay as you go for local calls different to the system prevalent in many US locations. Local and long distance calls do not vary much in price, though the time of day affects the cost of a call – out of business hours is cheaper than during them. International calls within Europe are cheaper in the evenings. As peak rates and off-peak rates and their applicability vary it is worth checking with Telecom Italia to find the best time to make your calls to America or the UK.

The cheap rate for evening calls in Italy doesn't come into effect until 6.30pm, which means it is quite usual to make long distance calls late into the night. However, there are deals that provide discounts on the numbers you call most often, including your Internet connection number.

Phone users need to dial the complete number of the person they wish to contact, including the area code, even for local calls. This system is common in Europe and possibly heralds the introduction of a seamless European phone system sometime in the future. When dialing Italy from abroad (except to mobile phones) it is necessary to dial the Italian country code (39) and then the complete phone number, including the zero of the area code.

Expatriates *(extracommunitari)* who use international phones more than most for keeping in touch with friends around the world have long used call-back services and other alternative phone services. These are advertised in international newspapers and magazines *(International Herald Tribune, Time, Newsweek)* and expatriate websites can also be very informative on the best deals which can be a great cost saver.

The telephone market has changed dramatically in the last five years: Telecom Italia provides only the line (which costs about €14 monthly plus VAT). Telephone services are provided by several companies of which Telecom Italia is one along with Tele2 (Swedish), Tiscali, Libero and Albacom. Fast internet companies, fibre optics such as Fastweb allow users to replace Telecom Italia completely (in large towns) and pay monthly subscriptions and make free calls.

LOCAL TELEPHONE CODES

Alassio	0182	Naples	081
Aosta	0165	Palermo	091
Bologna	051	Pesaro	0731
Bolzano	0471	Pisa	050
Cagliari	070	Riccione	054
Cattolica	0541	Rimini	0541
Como	031	Rome	06
Cortina d'Ampezzo	0436	San Remo	0184
		Siena	0577
Diano Marina	0183	Sorrento	081
Florence	055	Taormina	0942
Genoa	010	Trento	0461
Grado	0431	Trieste	040
La Spezia	0187	Turin	011
Lido di Jesolo	0421	Venice	041
Lignano	0431	Verona	05
Milan	02	Viareggio	0584

Emergency & Useful Numbers

Ambulance	118
Breakdown Services	116
Carabinieri	112 or 113
Coastguard emergency	1530
Fire	115
Forest Service (fires/environmental emergencies)	1515
International Directory Enquiries	170
Enquiries for Europe & the Mediterranean	176
Police	113
Telephone faults/engineers	182

The latest innovation in reducing telephone costs is the utilisation of the internet for international phone calls. Services such as www.Net2Phone.com allow internet users whose computer is equipped with a microphone and sound card (most computers produced within the last two years allow a microphone/headphone set to be plugged into their soundcard) to log on to their local internet Service Provider (ISP) and call a standard phone, via the internet, in most countries around the world. The cost of the call is then limited to the cost of being online. Also check out IsCard.com (www.iscard.com) an online, prepaid rechargeable calling card, which can be used in over 50 countries.

Some phone users even avoid *Telecom Italia* completely by making long distance calls through France Telecom, or Deutsche Telecom or Sprint etc. To do this you need a hardware gadget than allows you to connect direct with the provider. You need to contact a private telecommunications broker to do this (see below) or look in the telephone yellow pages of your city under *telefonia e telecommunicazioni*. The attraction of this is lessening with the increase in quality of internet-to-telephone services.

Public telephones. Public telephones take phone cards that are available from tobacconists, news-stands, Lotto windows, machines at telephone offices, stations and airports. The Lotto company Lottomatica, sells cheap cards for calling Europe and North America. Coin operated phones have been phased out in favour of card phones. Note that the sign frequently seen on public telephones, *guasto*, is Italian for 'out of order'.

Italian international phone cards offer the cheapest rates for telephoning home, especially to the USA, from a public telephone (or mobile). They have an access number and a code printed on the back which gives you access to amazingly cheap calling rates. These international cards are usually sold in the same outlets as the regular phone cards and from other places such as travel websites. The company www.1ˢᵗ4phonecards.com sells their cards online.

Mobiles: The mobile phone (*telefonino*) has become the vital accessory without which no self-respecting Italian would dare to be seen. The usage rate in Italy is heading for 100% and is consequently one of the highest in the world; but not as high as Luxembourg (which has 120 mobile phone subscriptions per 100 inhabitants!). Italian children are nearly as bad as their parents with over 60% of nine and ten-year-olds owning their own phone. In common with other European countries, Italy auctioned off mobile phone licences and there are several mobile networks: H3G. TIM, Wind and Vodafone Omnitel which between them offer a bewildering range of price structures and payment options depending on the type of service required, the amount of time you spend on the phone per month, what time of day you phone and how often you want to phone abroad. The area of coverage also varies between providers.

When choosing a mobile phone it is important to check that the provider covers the areas where you live, work and visit. Telecom Italia Mobile (TIM) is the mobile telephone subsidiary of *Telecom Italia* and has the widest coverage for those who travel extensively. Roaming agreements, where you can use the phone outside Italy, are another useful option for frequent travellers but can work out very expensive as you have to connect to the local network abroad and pay charges in addition to paying your home country network provider. Normally, you have to contact your home network provider to get a PIN that will give you access to your voice mail while you are abroad. For roaming, you can get a pay monthly contract and you pay an additional small charge, which reduces the cost of calls while roaming.

You can avoid roaming charges completely by buying a foreign SIM card. To do this you have to unlock your mobile (there may be a charge for this on some networks) and when you buy the foreign SIM card you will get a new telephone number with it. Swapping SIM cards is useful for anyone making frequent visits to the same country. You can buy SIM cards at any tobacconist or other outlets in Italy but note that you are required to provide passport identification when buying a SIM card in Italy. If you want to get an Italian SIM card before you go, you can do so online at www.0044.co.uk who ask for a faxed copy of your passport and charge £25 for an Italian SIM card.

If you are living and working in Italy for a longer period you will probably consider getting an Italian mobile. If your Italian is not up to it, take someone along to translate for you so that you can get the best deal for your needs.

All mobile phone numbers begin with a 3.

International Calls to and from Italy: To telephone the UK from Italy dial 00, wait for the continuous tone and then dial 44 and continue immediately with the UK number, omitting the first number of the UK code. For example, to ring Vacation Work Publications from Italy you would dial: 00-44-1865 241978.

To telephone the US from Italy the country code is 1 followed by the ten digit number, including the area code, e.g. 00-1 123 456 7890.

To telephone Italy from the UK dial 00 39 and then the Italian number. The first zero of the provincial code must be included. For example to ring a Rome number of 06-123456 you would actually dial 00-3906-123456. From the US it is necessary to dial the international access code of your service provider (usually 011), followed by 39-06-123456. The table Local Telephone Codes above contains a list of some of the most important provincial codes:

The Internet

Italy was one of the slowest European countries to jump on the internet bandwagon when Telecom Italia Net (TIN) launched public access to the net in 1994. Since then, Italy has caught up with internet technology and many municipalities e.g. Rome, Florence and lately, smaller places now have their own websites where they provide information in English for expatriates.

The internet is a great resource for expatriates and email is an easy, cheap and reliable way to keep in touch with friends and relatives around the world. There are a number of free access (you pay for the phone call) ISPs in Italy including, www.tiscali.it, www.libero.it, www.tele2.it and www.virgilio.it, which give away CDs in store to attract new clients. Once you have a CD, insert it in your modem-equipped computer and follow the instructions. Within a few minutes you should have internet access – assuming *Telecom Italia* have installed your telephone line. As in other countries, heavy users may find it more cost-effective to pay for a subscription service as there are special deals available. If you need broadband, Italy's main providers are FastWeb (only in large towns), Tele2, Libero and Tiscali. Alice which is part of Telecom Italia is the most expensive and Albacom is more of a business provider.

Expatriates should be aware that different phone systems around the world are wired differently. Modem sockets have four connectors, different Modems are wired to use either the inside pair or the outside pair. If your modem worked before you arrived in Italy but not after arrival, try changing the connector cable to one that is wired differently. Remember to keep the cable for when you go home again. Remember, that for dial-up modems using Windows, that the computer has to be set up to recognise the Italian dialing tone.

For expats who move frequently it can be worth having an email address that you can take with you each time. Hotmail (www.hotmail.com), Yahoo! (www.yahoo.com), iMail (www.imail.com) and Altavista (www.altavista.com), to name the most popular, offer free email service that you can access online, or have forwarded to your current local email address that comes free from your ISP. When you move you can access your email from an internet café until you are set up at home, or just change the forwarding address of the email to your new ISP email and not have to tell everyone you have ever given your email address to that the address has changed.

Other Italian Search Engines

www.excite.it
www.godado.it
www.google.it
www.iltrovatore.it
www.lycos.it
www.msn.it
www.supereva.it
www.virgilio.it

CARS & MOTORING

Buying a Car

Expats moving permanently to Italy have the choice of importing their own cars to Italy (see Importing a Car, in the section: *Setting Up Home*), or buying a new one after arrival in Italy. All of the main European makes, and their spare parts, are available in Italy. American cars have not been so popular in Europe as, for many years, US manufacturers did not apply for European certification of their cars, which is expensive, to enable them to be sold through dealerships. Imported American cars are also more expensive to maintain and run as they frequently have large engines that consume quantities of expensive European petrol. If need be, the local ACI office can direct you to the nearest car dealer of whatever make of car you are interested in, though dealerships should be relatively easy to find through the personal recommendations of colleagues. To buy a car with an Italian registration plate, you must be an Italian resident. If you do buy a car in Italy then you will be liable to pay ownership transfer fees (*passaggio di proprietà*), which cost about €440 (£270, US$514). When considering buying a car, it is worth bearing in mind that hiring a car in Italy is very expensive compared to UK and North American rates. It currently costs around £200 a week to rent a medium-sized car with unlimited mileage. However, there are an increasing number of budget rental agencies that are offering more competitive rates, especially for long-term rentals.

There are second-hand car deals at most car dealers. Most of the cars have been part-exchanged for newer models and come with a year's guarantee (a legal requirement). There is considerable bureaucracy and expense involved in buying a second-hand car. Firstly, you have to pay ownership fees (*passagio di proprietà*), you then have to wait a minimum of two weeks for the arrival of the car log-book (*libretto di circolazione*). As it is an offence to drive without having the log-book (commonly called the *libretto*) to hand, you must obtain interim documents (*foglio sostitutivo*) which expire after three months though you should have received your log-book within that time. Additional irritations used to include reminders to pay fines incurred by the previous owner – though this happens far less frequently than it used to as a result of the computerisation of records.

There is also the problem of persuading dealers to give expatriates hire purchase agreements.

One US expatriate couple had the following experience when trying to buy a car

The dealer seemed reluctant to sell us a car at first, even though my husband's colleague, who also speaks English, was friends with the owner and accompanied us. They told us that there is more paperwork for them to fill out because we are foreigners. They were also concerned with the fact that we are here on a temporary basis. My husband's employer had to call the dealer to put in a good word for us. We were only able to finance the car for 18 months, I think because we told them we were going to be here for 2-3 years. The whole process took several weeks, but we did manage to buy the car we wanted in the end. We were advised to buy either

> *German or Italian made cars because they are the easiest to resell, diesels are also popular.*

When selling a car, the popular motor magazine, *Porta Portese* is invaluable if you are living in Rome. Otherwise you can buy and sell cars online at www. secondamano.it or through the classified adverts of free newspapers. You can check all the models on the market and the current used prices in the magazine *Al Volante* which costs one euro and includes pictures of all makes and models sold in Italy. Alternatively, simply stick a 'for sale' sign (*vendesi*) in the car window. Alternatively, you may prefer to sell your car to a garage in part-exchange for a new one. A general proxy (*procura*) must first be obtained through a notary, empowering the garage to sell the car on your behalf. The buyer then pays ownership transfer fees (see above). At least in this version of second-hand car dealing, the legwork generally has to be done by the garage.

Car Tax. A tax stamp (*bollo*) must be purchased for your car and is obtainable from the ACI and renewable at the post office. The tax is dependent on the power rating and size of the engine. The tax is paid on a regional basis and cost depends on region though variations are not huge.

Driving Licences

EU drivers' licences are a standard pink and holders of these may drive their home registered car in Italy with no alteration to their licence at all. However, holders of the old UK green coloured driving licences must first obtain a translation, available free of charge from the Italian State Tourist Office (1 Princes Street, London W1R 8AY; ☎020-7408 1254), or update them for the new style. Owners of Italian-registered cars should theoretically have an Italian-registered licence, this involves converting your EU driving licence to an Italian one. To do this a certificate confirming that you have never been convicted for a driving offence in the country of issue is required – such certificates are available from the nearest Embassy or Consulate. In practice, however, many expatriates avoid doing this and carry an international driving licence instead.

Non-EU drivers licence holders are in a slightly different situation and the usefulness of their drivers licence depends on where it was issued. Some countries have reciprocal agreements with Italy to recognise each other's driving licences, others do not. Further information can be obtained from your embassy. If your country does have a reciprocal agreement with Italy (America does not) you can apply to exchange your current licence for an Italian one. The Italian licence replaces your previous one – it is not in addition to it.

If your country does not have a reciprocal agreement with Italy you will need to take a two-part driving test, in Italian. The first part is a written test and the second part (after passing the written test) is the road test. The written test is a multiple choice, which is difficult for non-Italian speakers. Foreigners usually opt for an oral test, which is in Italian, but examiners are a bit more lenient to foreigners with broken Italian. Taking driving lessons for the oral test is a great way to learn the necessary vocabulary for the exam. Exams must be taken at a driving school, who will also apply for the licence for you after you have passed the tests.

It is possible to drive in Italy for a year, on an International driver's licence, though you must always carry your national licence to show at the same time. International licences can be obtained from your national drivers association (e.g. the AA in the UK, or your state organisation in the US). However, international licences can also be obtained via the internet from sites such as: IDL International (www.idl-international.com) who can supply five year licences.

All Nationalities will find that though it is not essential it is definitely advisable to carry an international green card for your car and remember that it is a legal requirement to carry your driving licence *(patente)*, all of your car documents *(libretto)* and passport with you while you are driving. You may be required to present any or all of the papers if you are stopped by the police and can be fined for failing to do so.

An EU-approved driving test has recently been introduced to Italy, replacing the previous Italian test which involved as much paperwork about mechanics and road safety as actual driving. Driving schools *(scuola guida)* are widely available, and listed in the *Yellow Pages*.

Insurance

Italian car insurance covers the car and passengers, not the driver, and is nearly always third party. Full, comprehensive cover *(kasko)* is available, at a price, upon consultation with the insurance company. Note that insurance is rather more expensive than in other EU countries. Unfortunately, Italian insurance companies are both notoriously slow and mean in honouring claims and be prepared for a hard battle and an even longer wait before a cheque is actually signed, delivered, and in your bank account. Often drivers do not report minor accidents because it puts up the cost of insurance. Instead, they just come to an agreement, particularly if they both live in the same town to have the person at fault pay the damage costs directly to the repair shop. For less serious accidents where the person at fault admits liability and signs a friendly agreement form *(costatazione amichevole)*, which is carried in all Italian cars. With this, you can speed things up as it is a simple procedure for your insurance company can ask the other party's insurance company to repay them.

Royal International Insurance (Royal & Sun Alliance, Via F.lli Gracchi, 30/32, 20092 Cinisello Balsamo – (Mi);   ☎02-660791; fax 02-66011760; www.royal.it.), also sell motor insurance through direct marketing in Italy. Copeland Insurance (230 Portland Road, London SE25 4SL;   ☎020-8656 8435; fax 020-8655 1271; www. andrewcopeland.co.uk) can also provide insurance in Italy in certain circumstances and AXA insurance (www.axa-italia.it) is widespread throughout Italy and a list of regional insurers there can be found on their website under 'Carlink'.

Roads

Driving in Italy can be a costly business. The tolls (*pedaggi)* on Italian motorways *(autostrade)* are expensive at about €0.50-€0.60 per ten kilometres. As you drive on to an *autostrada* you collect a toll ticket, which you pay on exit. Alternatively buy a 'Viacard' from tollbooths (must be paid for in cash) and usable at both manned and automatic tollbooths. You can also use your credit card in automatic toll booths. *Strade Statali* (SS) are the equivalent of British A roads. *Autostrade* and *strade statali* are main roads and are numbered, while smaller roads such as *strade provinciali* and *secondarie* are not. For drivers new to roads outside the UK and North America, it is as well to realise as soon as possible that the law of the jungle applies to the Italian roads. It takes courage and an ability to learn to drive like an Italian to survive on Italian roads and only the fittest and most adept will survive without at least a couple of minor prangs as proof of having negotiated the Italian road system. Information in English about the *autostrade* network, including maps, tolls, service stations and rescue services can be found at www. autostrada.it (in Italian).

In Europe it is customary to give way to cars entering traffic from the right – even if it is a small side road they are coming from. Not all drivers approaching you from the right will slow down to make sure you will give way. Unless the road joining the one you are on has a solid white line across it where the two roads meet, you do not have right of way. As road rules become harmonised across Europe, drivers are confused by the new rules as much as foreigners getting used to the alternative way of doing things. One of the biggest changes in Europe has been who has right of way at roundabouts. Though it is supposedly the person on the roundabout, this was not the case until recently in Italy and some other European countries. Therefore, it is important to take great care whilst driving in Italy as everyone gets used to the new traffic rules. More information about driving in Italy can be found on the Slow Travel website (www.slowtrav.com/italy/driving/introduction.htm.

Italian petrol (*Benzina*) is cheaper than that in the UK, but more expensive than US residents are used to. Petrol is unleaded comes in two octane ratings, 95 and 98, and cars are set-up to take only one of these. *Gasolio* (diesel) is popular in Europe because it is much cheaper than unleaded petrol and is as widely available as unleaded petrol. LPG (Liquified Petroleum Gas), known as GPL in Italy, is becoming increasingly popular because of its lower price and environmental cleanliness. Only those petrol stations displaying the GPL symbol sell GPL. Petrol stations along the *autostrade* are open 24 hours while those on secondary roads usually open between 7am and 12.30pm and then from 2.30 to 7pm or 7.30pm and close on Sundays.

24 hour self-service petrol stations are now nearly everywhere. In most cases standard garages will have one or more pumps, alongside traditional pumps, that are entirely self-service. The self-service stations require you to insert a credit or debit card into a slot on the pump, then enter your PIN number, as in a cash point machine (ATM), before petrol can be pumped. The machine authorises the transaction and charges your card for amount of petrol received. Petrol brands include Agip, Api, Erg, Esso, Q8, Shell and Tamoil.

Accidents

Italy has one of the highest road accident rates in the whole of the EU. This, despite traffic law enforcement by the *Vigili Urbani* (traffic police) which seems inadequate to handle the frenetic style of driving for which Italians are known. However, although the accident rate is astronomical (approximately 250,000 injured each year), the death rate is mercifully lower (estimated at 5,000 deaths each year) – probably because the Italians introduced the points system which means you lose your licence if you get 20 penalty points on your licence and have to take your driving test again. This also means much higher motor insurance premiums. Italy has one of the highest densities of cars in the world; higher than both the UK and the USA which may also be a factor in the high accident figures.

Part of the insurance documentation that is required to be carried in every car is an insurance claim form *(costatazione amichevole)* that has space for the parties involved to sketch the accident scene as well as other questions that need to be answered. If the two parties have differing views on what happened, ensure that you sketch your version on your form. Also call the police to review the scene and if you are correct they should support you in their official report. As with all accidents, never admit liability or your insurance company has good grounds not to pay up, which leaves you financially liable. Both parties are required to sign the accident claim forms.

If you have an accident it is mandatory to stop. If you see an accident happen, even though you are not involved, you are required to stop and help. After an accident you are expected to take the names and addresses of witnesses and their car details if applicable. Always inform your insurance company of any accident you have whether or not you file a claim – the small print of most European insurance policies requires you to do so (unless the accident is a fender bender) and failure to do so can invalidate your insurance.

The red triangle that it is 'recommended' you carry in your car becomes mandatory to have after an accident, as you are required to place the triangle 50 metres (approximately 60 yards) behind the accident to warn approaching drivers and wear a fluorescent tabard or jacket whenever you get out of the car. You can be fined by the police for non-compliance.

INSTRUCTIONS/INFORMATION ROAD SIGNS

Accendere i fari in galleria	Switch on headlights in tunnel
Attenzione	caution
Caduta massi	fallen rocks
Casello a ....metri	toll in ....metres
Curve	bends
Dare precedenza	give way
Deviazione	detour
Divieto di accesso	no entry
Divieto di sorpasso	no overtaking
Divieto di sosta	no stopping
Divieto di transito	no right of way
Lavori in corso	roadworks
Passaggio a livello	level crossing
Pedoni	pedestrians
Rallentare	slow
Senso unico	one way
Sosta autorizzata	parking permitted
Strada chiusa	road closed
Strada ghiacciata	icy road
Tenere la destra	keep to the right
Transito Interrotto	no through road
Uscita camion	truck exit
Veicoli al passo	dead slow

Breakdowns

The Italian Automobile Club, *Automobile Club d'Italia*, is the Italian equivalent of the RAC and the AA. The head office of the ACI is at Via Marsala 8, 00185 Rome (☎06-49981; fax 06-4457748 – General Secretariat; 06-49982426 – Presidency; 06-49982469 – Tourism Department; www.acit.it).

The emergency 24-hour phone number is Rome 06-4477 with multilingual staff providing round the clock assistance.

If your car comes to an unprompted and definitive halt, then dial 116 (ACI breakdown Service) from anywhere in Italy, from either a telephone box or a mobile phone.

On motorways, you can also use SOS phones that are placed every 2km along the road and connected with the motorways radio centres – road assistance can be provided either by the ACI 116 or by a local operator. The service is permanently available on all roads throughout Italy. In all emergencies (personal injury and all kinds of accidents or mishaps) dial 113 (police), 112 (Carabinieri) or 115 (Fire Brigade). Note that it is now the law to wear a reflective safety vest to walk to an emergency telephone to summon assistance for a breakdown or accident.

Breakdown service comprises transportation of the car from the place of breakdown to the nearest ACI garage or, in major cities, the roadside repair of the vehicle if possible. Road Assistance provided by the ACI is free of charge only for tourists with an AIT or FIA Assistance booklet, otherwise the service for all motor vehicles up to 2.5 tons is chargeable. An annual subscription can be purchased from the ACI that covers breakdown service either within Italy only, or throughout Europe, depending on the fee paid.

Driving Regulations

In theory, the Italian speed limits are as follows: 130 kph (80 mph) on the *autostrada, 90 kph (55 mph) on highroads (le strade statali)* and 50 kph (30 mph) in all built-up areas. Since 1 January 2003, some three-lane autostradas have been given a higher speed limit of 150 kph (93mph). Although the police have become a lot more enthusiastic over the last few years, they are notoriously slack at enforcing driving regulations. Nonetheless, be warned that if you are caught then hefty fines (in the region of €150 to €250) are usually made on the spot.

It has only been compulsory for motorbike riders to wear helmets since 1986 (it is still legal to ride a moped without a helmet if you are over 18). Wearing seatbelts became law in 1986 and only as a result of EU directives and Italy planning to introduce drink drive legislation. Italian drink drive regulations a limit of no more than 0.04% milligrams of alcohol per litre of blood, and the police can perform random testing without having to have due cause.

From August 2004 it has been obligatory to drive with headlights on during the day on Italian motorways (*autostrade*) and also on dual carriageways (*superstrade)* and all out of town roads e.g. ringroads (*tangenziale)* and slip roads (*raccordo*). Motorcycles have to drive on dipped headlights during the day at all times.

Italian road signs are standardised by European norms, which helps UK expatriates – though North Americans should have no trouble working out what most of them mean either. Note that circular signs are used to announce restrictions (or the end of them), rectangular green ones are used on the *autostradas* and rectangular blue ones on the secondary roads.

TRANSPORT

Railways

The Italian railway system, *Ferrovie dello Stato* (FS) runs one of the cheapest railway services in Western Europe. This is more remarkable than you might think, considering the substantial reforms that were made to services during the last two decades, which resulted in a greater network of inter-city lines and a generally modern, fast and reasonably reliable service. Unlike the UK and North America, branch lines reach the most remote areas, with connecting buses that will get you to the most obscure spots. Despite the heavy subsidies handed out to the rail network, the railways still run up a huge deficit.

STATION SIGNS AND PHRASES

Al Binari/Ai Treni	to the platforms/trains
Arrivi/Partenze	arrivals/departures
Biglietteria	ticket office
Deposito Bagagli	left luggage
Entrata/Uscita	entrance/exit
Orario	timetable
Sala d'Attesa	waiting room
Vietato l'Ingresso	no entry
Andata/Andata e ritorno Firenze	single/return to Florence
Il primo/l'ultimo/il prossimo treno	the first/last/next train
A che binario?	which platform?
C'è un posto?	Is there a seat?
È questo posto libero?	Is this seat taken?
Dove siamo?	Where are we?

Tickets and timetables. There are usually long queues for tickets at main stations. You can find automatic ticket machines, but these are usually a problem for newcomers, though you can ask someone to help you (*Può aiutarmi per favore? Voglio un biglietto por ....*). Also, it is compulsory to validate all tickets by inserting them in the yellow machines on the platforms, which clip and stamp them. Failure to punch your ticket can make you liable for an on the spot fine. Self-punching of railway tickets is a common practice on European railways, though the machines are not always yellow.

There is a complete national pocket timetable (*Il Pozzorario*), which can be bought at stations and newspaper kiosks. It has useful maps, and tables to work out costings. Travelling by train in Italy is by far preferable to the localised and sluggish bus system. The FS website is www.fs-on-line.com and you can avoid queueing by getting regional train information and booking tickets online at www.trenitalia.com. For internal and international travel information Thomas Cook produces a European railway timetable (in English) that includes many Italian services and there is a European Rail Timetable, Independent Travellers' edition which carries additional information including bus and travel, embassies, rail passes and more. Discounted prices on the above books are available from www.Amazon.co.uk in the UK, or www.railpass.com/eurail/cooks.htm in North America. Very cheap international tickets (*tariffe speciali*) are sold under the tag 'Smart Price' on the trenitalia website (www.trenitalia.com) and include from €15 Italy to Nice (Riviera trains), Italy to Paris from €25 (Artesia trains) and Italy to Austria from €29 (Allegro trains). These are usually overnight trains and the prices quoted are just for seats; sleeping compartments are extra. The Italian superfast trains are the Pendolini (leaning trains) now exported to many other countries. Confusingly, high speed services in Italy are called Eurostar Italia.

The *rapido and IC* (Inter-city) trains are invariably the fastest and most expensive internal trains, stopping only at the major cities. For these a supplement (*supplemento rapido*) is required according to mileage. Remember that the best prices are for tickets bought in advance, as tickets bought on the train are subject to a surcharge. Reductions of around 50% are available to children under 12 and people over 65. The Milan to Rome *rapido* train takes under four hours, with an onward link to Naples. You can also get a Eurostar train from to Milan to Rome (650kn) at very cheap fares if you go at night. Using the Channel Tunnel from the UK the trip to Paris takes three hours; from there you get a Paris to Milan connection.

The *espresso and diretto* trains are the next fastest, and more reasonably priced, stopping at most large towns. Lastly, and to be avoided wherever possible (unless you are hoping to enjoy the leisurely pace of Italian rural life) are the painfully slow *locale* trains which seem to stop at every small village and country backwater imaginable.

There are national discount cards for train travel apart from the passes aimed at tourists travelling around Italy or through it. Cartaverde is for anyone 26 years and under, lasts a year, costs €21 and entitles the holder to 20% reduction on fares.

There has been a no smoking policy on all Italian national trains since 12 December 2004.

Eurostar and European train tickets including Italy (railpasses and tailor-made travel to and within Italy from the UK can be booked through www.railbookers.com. A list of Trenitalia agents in the UK can be found at www.trenitalia.com/home/en/international_travel/agenzie/uk.htm and they include Railchoice (☎0870 165 7300; fax 020-8659 7466; sales@railchoice.co.uk); visits can be made by appointment only to their office address at 15 Colman House, Paris Square, High Street, London SE20 7EX. In North America tickets can be bought through Wandrian Inc (☎617-5073488; fax 617-5073488; miche@wandrian.com, or CTS USA (☎212-7601287; fax 212-7600022;

cmcwintal@ctstravelusa.com, or Touritalia (☎312-6645757; fax 312-6640088; italy@touritalia.com).

Buses

Italian cities are dotted with bright orange town buses weaving chaotically through the traffic as Italian motorists resolutely refuse to acknowledge the function of bus lanes. Italy has more buses than any other European country but no national bus company. This means a proliferation of companies, some providing local and others long distance services known as *urbano* (town) and *extraurbano*. (inter-town) respectively. Some companies e.g. www.saj.it run both local and national networks. Bus tickets are fairly inexpensive (though more expensive than train tickets) and are not obtainable on town buses or trams but from tobacconists (*tabaccherie*) which have the black 'T' sign displayed, from ticket offices at the bus termini (*capolinea*) and from some news-stands, tobacconists, lotto window etc. Tickets should be cancelled at the ticket machine once you are on the bus. Tickets can be bought on inter-city buses, after hours.

There are a number of ticket types, including single tickets (*corsa semplice*), morning or afternoon tickets also known as half-day tickets (*biglietti orari)* and season tickets (*abbonamenti*) of varying length. A season ticket can include use of bus, tram and subway routes (*intera rete*) if necessary. Each city has its own day/several week or month passes for local transport details of which you can usually find on the municipal website.

Buses in the provincial areas of Italy can be a nightmare and bus services are often severely reduced at the weekends. Provincial bus journeys are long and slow and often timetables can be erratic. Tickets can be bought on the bus and most of them will stop for you if you flag them down along the road and look desperate, though tickets can be bought in advance and used as necessary. Although travelling by train is preferable, especially between large cities, the buses and coaches are a reasonable alternative for shorter trips and are a useful alternative during a train strike.

International services from Italy include Eurolines (www.eurolines.it) and Stam. Information on bus systems throughout Italy can be found at viaggiare. cerca.com/automezzi_pubblici/centro.html.

The Metro

Both Rome and Milan have metros. Milan has three lines and an underground mainline trainline. The Rome metro (*Metropolitina*) consists of two lines, which exist principally to ferry commuters in and out of the centre to the suburbs. A new line with over 30 stations is being built through the city centre to the north and is due to be opened in 2006. The metro is less crowded and less hot than the buses, so it can be worth catching the metro if you're travelling around the city; there are stations at the Colosseum, the Spanish Steps and the Piazza Barberini. A transport map (available from the *Piazza dei Cinquecento* information booth) is invaluable when attempting to negotiate your way through the metro system. Books of five or ten tickets can be bought in advance from *edicole (news-stands) and tabaccherie* (tobacconists), otherwise a standard single ticket fare is €1.

In Milan, stations are marked MM and tickets can be bought from places where the black and yellow sign *Biglietti ATM* is displayed. Tickets are also available from stations. A single ticket gives integrated access to other city transport above ground, but only allows one metro trip.

A plan to built a five mile train tunnel under Venice from the airport on the mainland via the island of Murano to the terminus at the Arsenale east of St. Mark's is due to start in 2006.

Taxis

Italian taxis are either a cheerful canary yellow in colour (like the New York cabs), or white and are more expensive than London cabs. This is partly due to the list of hefty surcharges that are imposed for countless extras including excess luggage, night trips and rides to the airport. Often the meter becomes irrelevant for longer journeys (e.g. 50km to an airport), and it is advisable to negotiate a price in advance rather than recklessly jumping in the cab and finding the price outlandish later.

Air

The Italians indulge in internal flights far more than the British, though not as much as North Americans. This is partly due to the distances that separate Italy's most important cities, principally Milan and Rome (flight time about 50 minutes). Alitalia and a clutch of lower cost and charter airlines fly to most of the major cities throughout mainland Italy, Sardinia and the smaller islands. Internal flights used to be pretty expensive but the last seven years have seen the development of no frills airlines businesses in Italy operating on both the domestic routes, and also inter-Europe. National airline Alitalia has some discounts: passengers aged 12 to 25 qualify for a 35% discount over normal fares, as do students. There are also reductions of 50% for group family travel, 30% for night travel, and children up to two years of age only have to pay 10% of the adult fare while children aged two to twelve pay half fare. The other large Italian carrier, Meridiana (www.meridiana.it; ☎020 7839 2222), owned by the Aga Khan, is transmuting into a lower cost airline with regular special offers, and discounts for advance booking. Fares from about £50 on domestic routes. Also flies inter-Europe. A website claiming to find the cheapest fares from anywhere to anywhere is www.lowcost.com.

Italy's small airlines, which sprang up following the opening up of the skies to the free market include:

Air One: www.air-one.it, regional Italian network.
Air Dolomiti: www.airdolomiti.it, regional Italian network.
Alisarda: flies between main Italian cities and Sardinia.
Alpi Eagles: www.alpieagles.com, regional Italian network.
Azzurra Air: www.azzurraair.it. Rome to Bergamo.
Ryanair: www.ryanair.com. Rome to Alghero, Venice & Verona.
Transavia: www.transavia.com. Amsterdam to Genoa & Venice.

Milan has two airports, Malpensa and Linate, which are 46km and 8km respectively from the city centre. Airport buses run between Linate and the Garibaldi Central Station, a journey of about 30/40 minutes. Malpensa can be reached by a train that takes 40 minutes from the city centre. Note that most low cost airlines fly to Bergamo (45 minutes from Milan) for Milan but there is a frequent bus service which operates from the central bus station in Milan.

Rome also has two airports: Leonardo da Vinci/Fiumicino, 32 km west of the city for scheduled flights, and Ciampino airport for charter flights. Buses run every quarter of an hour between Fiumicino and the Termini Station of Via Giolitti; a journey of about an hour. There are also trains, which take about half an hour to reach Ostiense station.

It is possible to arrange personal transport to and from the airport, which is well worth the cost when arriving in a new country for the first time. Allegro Italiano offer a private car service, with English speaking driver, and bookings can be made online at: www.allegroitaliano.com/bus.htm. A useful web page for everything to do with air travel in Italy is viaggiare.cerca.com/in_aereo/.

Ferries

There are regular ferry connections between the mainland of Italy and the islands. Large car ferries run from the ports of Genova, Civitavecchia and Naples to Sardinia and Sicily. There are also ferry connections from the mainland to the smaller Tremiti, Bay of Naples and Pontine islands. The ferries also make international trips from the mainland to Malta, Corsica, Spain, Greece, Turkey, Tunisia, Egypt and Israel. Fares are reasonable although you may have to book well in advance, especially over the holiday season in the summer months. In the winter the number of crossings is greatly reduced. In Italy the tourism office and travel agents can provide information, which can also be found on the website: www.traghettionline.net or www.fun.informare.it which is a comprehensive guide to all Italian ferries, with timetables and booking online. Alternatively to the websites of the individual ferry operators.

BANKS AND FINANCE

The Banking System

Before becoming involved in the Italian banking system it is advisable to become acquainted with its peculiarities. From the tenth to the fourteenth centuries parts of Italy, mainly Venice and Lombardy, were responsible for some of the most innovative banking practices in Europe. The Italians virtually brought banking to England (hence Lombard Street in London) and then the rest of the world. Italian banking services are no longer the model for all of Europe; indeed they are frequently held to be one of the least efficient. Having said that, a progressive overhaul of Italian banking has been set in motion and there have been many improvements; there are now 37,000 ATMs in Italy and internet banking has taken off in a big way.

In recent years there have been a number of mergers and acquisitions among Italian banks thus reducing the number of smaller banks. There were 970 different banks in Italy in the 1990s; the number now is 785, including a number of foreign banks that operate local branches (*filiali di banche estere or FBEs*). In the past the phenomenon of the single-outlet bank meant that customers found it virtually impossible to obtain cash outside the town where their account was held as other banks were certain to refuse to cash the cheques of other banks. Now there is Bancomat, the network of automatic cash dispensers, which dispense cash to clients of other banks. Expatriates can also use ATMs to withdraw cash from their accounts held outside Italy, as long as both the machine and their card carry a matching pair of symbols such as Cirrus, Maestro, Visa, MasterCard or Plus. Depending on the account accessed and the issuing bank, the charges levied on the transaction can vary significantly and it is worth checking with your bank before utilising this service.

About 10% of the banking system is controlled directly or indirectly by the state and local government compared with about 70% in 1992. The two remaining state enterprises are the Cassa Despositi e Prestiti, CDP which is the bank used by local authorities, and the Banco Posta, the post office banking division. Despite mergers and consolidation the banking system is still recognized as having too many branches; the number has actually increased by over 500 to about 30,500. For comparison, the UK with a similar population has about 12,500 branches.

The frustration of dealing with Italian banks is not usually as stressful as that experienced in close encounters with the state bureaucracy. However, the most simple transaction can still take a preposterous amount of time and queuing is a random affair in Italy, necessitating an opportunistic approach to any window that may become vacant. According to a poll in *Corriere della Sera* a couple of years ago, nearly 60% of Italians found going to the bank stressful. This might explain why there has been an extremely rapid rise in electronic banking which reached six million online accounts in 2004 (up by one million from the previous year). Credit cards are also extremely popular in Italy, which has the third largest credit card market in Europe with over 47 million cards in circulation in 2004. Italians prefer the pay-later type where the account is paid off each month to avoid interest charges.

Until recently it was extremely difficult to get a personal loan from an Italian bank and, as in other European countries, issuing a cheque for which there are insufficient funds, is illegal.

The governing body of Italian banks is the Banca d'Italia (Via Nazionale 91, 00184 Rome; www.bancaditalia.it). Two of the biggest banks are the Banca Intesa and Capitalia.

Expatriates may find that some Italian banks are more helpful than others or they can use the foreign banks with subsidiaries in Italy: National Westminster and HSBC both have branches in Italy. Barclays Bank only provides banking services to larger multinational clients and not to individual clients.

Opening an Account

Anyone who is considering living and working in Italy on a long-term basis will need an Italian bank account. Accounts are available for foreigners with non-resident and resident status, though anyone working in Italy will need to wait for their *residenza* (residence permit) before being able to open their residents' account. The only option if you are not yet in possession of this is to enlist the assistance of an influential Italian who may be able to persuade a bank manager to let you have a residents' account pending the arrival of the paperwork. Alternatively, if the institution you currently bank with has a branch in Italy near where you will be living or working, you can ask for a letter of introduction that may smooth and quicken the process of opening an account. HSBC banks are particularly popular with expatriates because of the number of countries where HSBC operate and the process of referrals that they operate between their various branches. If you can not open an Italian bank account before receiving your *residenza* you will have to manage with Eurocheques, cash and credit cards until you receive the piece of paper in question – see above for advice on obtaining cash from your accounts outside Italy.

Once an Italian bank account has been set up the customer receives a *libretto di assegni* (cheque book) and he or she will be able to cash cheques (*incassare un assegno*) at their branch. When paying for goods and services by cheque a *carta di garanzia* (cheque guarantee card) is obligatory. For larger purchases a bank draft (*assegno circolare*) is normally required.

Using an Italian Bank Account

The majority of expatriates do not normally choose to transfer all their assets into their Italian bank account. There are sound reasons for this related to the higher bank charges in Italy, and Italian tax considerations. The consensus seems to be that you should maintain an account outside of the country (either 'at home' or 'offshore somewhere') and transfer money as needed to Italy. Credit and/or debit cards linked to accounts outside the country can be used to make purchases in Italy. If UK citizens do maintain accounts in the UK it is essential to inform the British tax authorities and the bank that they are resident abroad in order to prevent double taxation.

When calculating the amount of funds needed in your Italian account you should err on the generous side as there are various ways you can be caught out. For example there are charges levied per cheque written and the gas and electricity companies may automatically adjust your standing orders after the bi-annual meter readings (see the *Setting Up Home* chapter, under 'Utilities'). Banks do pay a small amount of interest, usually two or three per cent, on current accounts in credit, but this is cancelled out by bank charges. If one is unfortunate enough to issue a bouncing cheque (*un assegno a vuoto*), albeit by accident, it can lead to legal problems, being disbarred from holding any bank account and even to having your name gazetted in the local press so doing this should be avoided at all costs. On the other hand pre-arranged overdrafts are usually possible.

Transferring Funds from Abroad into Italy

For retirees and expatriates paid in their home country, transferring funds to Italy is necessary on a regular basis. By using the same bank at each end of the transfer the process can be speeded up, which is a good reason for using a larger bank. However, nowadays the system has been greatly improved and Swift transfers that go directly to your local branch rather than via the head office of the bank in Milan, Rome, etc. are one of the best ways to transfer money. Online banking services from banks such as Citibank and HSBC allow customers to submit transfer instructions such as this 24 hours a day through their computer and can be very convenient for expatriates with internet access. Other banks have telephone banking service which can be just as convenient, though the cost of international phone calls to deal with them, especially when the lines are busy and you get put on hold, can be much higher.

Lastly, if the bank cards issued by your bank outside Italy carry the Maestro symbol and your Italian bank accepts Maestro payments, you can draw out money into your Italian bank account whilst sitting in the manager's office. Both the issuing bank and Italian bank can limit the amount of cash you can draw down at any one time. The issuing bank will place a limit on how much you can charge to your card in a specified time period and the Italian bank can have what is known as a floor limit, which limits how much they are allowed to accept via a single Maestro payment.

With these options in mind, it behoves the prospective foreign resident to base the selection of an Italian bank account and bank on what services are available, not just the charges levied and the nearness of the branch to your place of work or residence.

Choosing a Bank

Despite the problems within the Italian banking system in general, some banks do enjoy a better reputation than others in their dealings with foreigners. These include: *Istituto Bancario San Paolo* based in Turin, with 500 branches nationwide, and *Creditwest*, which is the product of a joint venture between the Italian bank *Credito Italiano* and the UK bank National Westminster. *Creditwest* has about 30 branches in the Milan, Rome and Naples areas many of which employ staff familiar with the banking needs of expatriates. Some of the smaller, privately-owned banks may also be worthy of closer acquaintance: in particular, *Credito Emiliano* (Milan, Rome and central Italy), has a policy of encouraging clients from the foreign community.

Useful Addresses

American Express Bank:, Piazza San Babila 3, 20122 Milan;   ☎02 77901; fax 02 76002308.

Banca Nazionale dell'Agricultura (BNA): Direzione Centrale, Via Salaria 231, 00199 Rome.

Banca Nazione di Lavoro: Direzione Generale, Via Vittorio Veneto 119, 00187 Rome.

Chase Manhattan Bank: Via M. Mercati 39, 00197 Rome;   ☎06 844 361; fax 06 844 36220. Piazza Meda 1, 20121 Milan;   ☎02 88951; 02 88952229.

Citibank: Via Bruxelles 61, 00198 Rome;   ☎06 854 561. Foro Bonaparte 16, 20121 Milan;   ☎02 85421.

Credito Emiliano: Via Emilia San Pietro 4, 42100 Reggio Emilia;   ☎0555 5821; fax 0522 *Creditwest:* Via Santa Margarita 7, Milan;   ☎02-8813.

Credito Romagnola: Via Zamboni 20, 40126 Bologna.

Istituto Bancario San Paolo di Torino: Via della Stamperia 64, 00187 Rome;   ☎06 85751; 06 857 52400. Piazza San Carlo 156, Turin;   ☎011-5551. 433969; www.credem.it.

Istituto Monte dei Paschi di Siena: U.S.I.E. Sett. Serv. V.le Toselli 60, Siena.

National Westminster Bank: Via Turati 18 20121 Milan;   ☎02 6251; fax 02

6572869.

Unicredit Banca per la Casa: Via Orefici 10, (zona centro), Milan; ☎02 8545651; fax 02 85456508; www.bancaperlacasa.it. National mutual credit bank that bought out the mortgage business of Abbey National Bank Italy in December 2003.

More banks are listed in the *Regional Employment Guide* section in the chapter on *Employment* later in the book.

Offshore Banking

One of the financial advantages of being an expatriate is that you can invest money offshore in tax havens such as the Isle of Man, the Channel Islands and Gibraltar, thus accruing tax-free interest on your savings. Many such facilities are as flexible as UK high street banking and range from current accounts to long-term, high interest earning deposits. Mortgage facilities are also available. Many of the banks that provide offshore facilities have reassuringly familiar names and include a number of building societies that have moved into this field since demutualising.

Useful Addresses

Abbey National: PO BOX 824, 237 Main Street, Gibraltar; ☎ 010 350 76090; www.abbeynationaloffshore.com.

Alliance & Leicester International Ltd.: P.O.B. 226, 10-12 Prospect Hill, Douglas, Isle of Man IM99 1RY; ☎01624 663566; fax 01624 617286.

Barclays International Personal Banking: PO Box 784, Victoria Road, Georgetown, Jersey JE4 8ZS, Channel Islands; ☎ 01534 880 550; fax 01534 505 077; www.internationalbanking.barclays.com.

Brewin Dolphin Bell Lawrie Ltd. Stockbrokers: 5 Giltspur Street, London EC1A 9BD; ☎020-7246 1028; fax 020-7246 1093.

Bristol & West International: P.O.B. 611, High Street, St Peter Port, Guernsey, Channel Islands GY1 4NY; ☎01481-720609; fax 01481-711658; www.bristol-west.co.uk/bwi/.

Halifax International (Jersey Ltd): P.O.B. 664, Halifax House, 31-33 New Street, St. Helier, Jersey; ☎01534 59840; fax 01534 59280.

HSBC Bank International: P.O. Box 615, 28/34 Hill Street, St. Helier, Jersey JE4 5YD, Channel Islands; ☎01534 616111; fax 01534 616222; www1.offshore.hsbc.co.je.

Lloyds TSB Offshore Centre: P.O. Box 12, Douglas, Isle of Man, IM99 1SS; ☎01624 638104; fax 01624 638181; www.lloydstsb-offshore.com.

Nationwide Internationals Ltd: 45-51, Athol Street, Douglas, Isle of Man; ☎01624 663494.

Woolwich Guernsey Limited: P.O. Box 341, Le Marchant House, Le Truchot, St. Peter Port, Guernsey GY1 3UW; ☎01481 715735; fax 01481 715722.

ITALIAN TAXES

There are numerous taxes in Italy and so only the main ones that expatriates are likely to be liable for, are covered below. There have been drastic tax cuts during the Berlusconi term. Indeed, the pivotal pledge of Berlusconi's electoral campaign was to reduce taxation and he has kept his word. The latest reforms for 2005 have wiped €6 billion off the government's fiscal revenues including a lowering of the top tax rate from 45% to 43% (less than a decade ago the top rate was over 60%). The generous tax cuts will have to be paid for by correspondingly huge public spending cuts, which in turn means higher local taxes from 2006. Fiscally speaking therefore, Berlusconi's promises are a double-edged sword for residents of Italy.

The Italian tax year runs from January 1ˢᵗ. As the tax regulations change frequently you need to get regular updates, often obtainable from international tax service providers' websites eg www.deloitte.com/tax and from the Ministry of Finance website (www.finanze.it) under *riforma fiscale* (tax reform). Information is available in English on the internet to help employees understand what taxes their employer is deducting, though self-employed expatriates are well advised to employ an accountant with experience of working with expatriates of their nationality. The website for professional accountants is www.consrag.it (Consiglio Nazionale dei Ragionieri Commercialista ed Economisti d'Impresa). If you look down the left hand menu and click on 'dialogonline' and then the box on the right hand side that says 'studi online; cerca il commercialista a te più vicino' you will get a map on which you can select your region and a list of accountants' names and addresses will pop up. *The Informer*, an English language website (www.informer.it) for expatriates in Italy is a goldmine of advice on tax issues and goes into much more detail than is possible here. The main taxes expatriates will encounter are:

Imposta sul redditi (IRE). Formerly known as IRPEF, this is personal income tax levied in a format most people are used to, i.e. it is a progressive tax that increases with the amount you earn. The threshold before you are liable for tax is €7,500. US citizens in particular are likely to consider the rates very high. However, Italians get a lot in return for their taxes in the form of pensions, health care and other social security benefits and the rates are not the highest in the EU and have been coming down steadily since Berlusconi took power. Tax rates begin at 23% and go up to 43% for high earners (over €100,000 per annum). Employees have the taxes deducted at source every month by their employer based on an estimate of the year's tax – any necessary adjustment will be made early in the following year. The tax form for the employees regime is known as the 730. Self-employed workers operate under a complicated system whereby some taxes are paid at source and some in arrears – expert advice from an accountant is recommended.

If you are self-employed, or if your situation is at all complicated you will have complete a tax return known as a *Modello Unico*. You should only declare income earned in Italy. For more information on taxation for the self-employed, see *Aspects of Employment* in the *Employment chapter*.

Imposta regionale sulle attività produttive (IRAP). This is a direct tax that is charged on a regional basis, on business activities no matter how small. The rate is decided by the region in which the business is located. It is a tax on services and goods produced, on the difference between the value realised after specified production costs (except labour costs) have been deducted. The basic rate of IRAP is around 4.25% (there is a reduced rate for agriculture). In 1998 and 1999 IRAP was levied directly into the National Treasury; after that it began to be a regionally payable tax, so local rates can vary quite widely. Increases of no more than 1% a year are permitted.

At the time of press there was an Italian court case being brought against IRAP by the Banca Popolare di Cremona (case C-475/03) in the European Court of Justice. The plaintiff, taxpayers and no doubt the Italian financial ministry is awaiting with bated breath a final ruling on whether IRAP contravenes Article 33 of the Sixth VAT Directive of the European Union which prohibits a member state from levying any taxes that would interfere with the paying of VAT. The case hinges on whether IRAP is sufficiently similar to VAT to contravene the Directive. The case has huge implications because payers of this tax in Italy could claim refunds going back several years.

Imposta sul reditti delle persone giuridiche (IRPEG). This is a corporate tax levied on S.r.l. and S.p.A. type companies; not generally applicable to self-employed workers.

Imposta sul valore aggiunta (IVA). This is known as VAT (value added tax) in the UK and is levied on all sales, whether retail or wholesale, and even by consultants and other businesses who do not sell an actual product. There are three rates of 4%, 10% and 20%, the standard rate being 20%. Most foodstuffs are taxed at 10%. For other goods including most clothing, shoes, records, cassettes and certain alcoholic goods the rate is 20%.

Social security contributions. Whilst these are not really a tax, they amount to approximately 10% of income – information on the benefits obtained in exchange for the contributions is included in the *Social Security* and *Unemployment* section of this chapter.

When trying to estimate your tax bill it should be borne in mind that a number of allowances are available that can be deducted from the taxable income and therefore reduce the amount of tax payable. Therefore, a married employee with a dependant spouse and two children in full-time education will pay much less tax than a single, childless employee. Housing allowances, education allowances, overseas living allowances and many of the other benefits that expatriates may enjoy are all counted as part of the income and their value will be taxed and added to the tax liability.

Personal allowances as listed below are allowed to reduce tax liability:

IRE (INCOME TAX) RATES FOR 2005		
Income in euros from	up to	Tax rate
0	26,000	23%
26,001	33,500	33%
33,501	100,000	39%
100,001	amount over	43%

- Allowance for a dependant spouse (i.e. not legally and effectively separated)
- An allowance for each dependant child older than 3 years
- Allowance for each dependant child under 3 years
- Other allowances, up to a maximum of 19%, including medical expenses, life assurance, mortgage interest on property in Italy and limited university tuition fees can also be claimed in certain circumstances.

Apart from the main taxes listed above there are a multitude of other taxes payable by residents, including expatriates: these include:

- Rubbish disposal (*nettezza urbana*),
- Water rates (*acquedotto comunale*).
- Car (or other motorised vehicle) tax.
- TV licence fee.
- Property tax.

(Note that the first two listed above are based on the floor area of the property. House owners with their own independent water supply such as a well or spring are exempt from water rates).

Tax evasion in Italy is a popular topic of conversation and supposedly occurs on a massive scale. Though Italians reputedly do it all the time, expatriates should consider the implications of doing it themselves and getting caught – being put in an Italian prison, deportation, the financial burden of playing catch-up with the tax authorities. It has been estimated by the tax inspectors' organization, *Il Servizio Centrale degli Ispettori Tributari*, that 83% of the self-employed category declare an annual income of less than £4,000. The reason such modesty does not attract the attention of the *Guardia di Finanza, a.k.a. i Finanzieri*, (the tax police) is that they are often in on the fraud at the highest levels. It is probably a mark of their schizophrenia that from time to time, *i Finanzieri* feel obliged to indulge in advertising campaigns to remind the public and themselves that they are there to root out the culprits, and not to co-operate with them. However, despite the enormity of the problem facing them, the Finance Ministry has been making some attempt to catch tax evaders, especially as far as high income earners are concerned. The *i Finanzieri* have proved more effective than their detractors might have expected in pursuit of offenders. Foreigners become taxable as residents if they are working in Italy for 183 days or longer and technically all their worldwide income is taxable.

Deciding to pay one's taxes gives rise to its own set of problems, particularly if one is in business or self-employed, as the system is constantly being amended. Unfortunately, new taxes are often brought in without the old ones being cancelled. This induces a permanent state of chaos in the tax system so that it is extremely difficult to ascertain which taxes one is actually liable for. However, it is undoubtedly better to pay some taxes rather than none at all. It is probably unwise to proceed without the services of an accountant (*commercialista*) preferably obtained through personal recommendation.

To combat tax evasion that the authorities decide to investigate, but that they can not actually prove, they have devised a cunning, if arbitrary, scheme for assessment based on perceivable assets. For instance, yachts, expensive cars, estates and household staff are all deemed to represent, according to their size and quantity, a specific amount of income. Since Italians are born showoffs, there is little chance that they will resort to driving around in battered Lancia's in order to conceal their assets and lower the likelihood of being hit with a perceived wealth tax bill

There are other peculiarities regarding the Italian tax system: unlike Britain where the tax office will chase you to fill in a tax form, in Italy it is up to the individual to present him or herself at the *Intendenza di Finanza* (local tax office) to fill in a standard tax form and be given a *codice fiscale (tax number)*. A *codice fiscale* is needed in order to work, and for various transactions such as property and car purchase, rentals and bill payments.

Owing to the fact that Italian personal taxation rates can be rather high at the top income levels it is advisable not to have all one's assets in Italy if one can avoid it. The alternatives, as already mentioned, are to maintain offshore accounts or investments. Owing to the complexity of taxation it is strongly recommended that you take independent, expert financial advice before moving to Italy as well as after arrival. A list of such advisors in the UK can be obtained from the Financial Services Authority (25 The North Colonnade, Canary Wharf, London E14 5HS; ☎020-7676 1000; www.fsa.gov.uk).

You will almost certainly need to consult a *commercialista* to work out how the new tax regulations apply to your particular circumstances.

In addition to IRAP there is an additional regional tax ICI (*Imposta Comunale sugli Immobili)* or property tax which is levied by the local borough or commune and is calculated on the rateable value *(valore catastale)*. The regions themselves decide the amount of additional local tax that needs to be levied as a subsection of IRAP. It is payable in two instalments (which you can normally do at the post office) and is due in June and December.

The estimated amount of both income and business taxes are payable in two tranches in May and November. There are big fines for non-payment and under estimation of the amount due. Late payment is also penalised with fines.

Useful Addresses

Further information and advice can be obtained from:
British Chamber of Commerce in Italy: www.britchamitaly.com.
American Chamber of Commerce in Italy: www.amcham.it.
Penta Consulting: www.geocities.com/WallStreet/4019/Italy.html; e-mail spedire@hotmail.com. Business & Fiscal Advisor Firm
Invest in Italy, Investor Advisor; http://investinitaly.com.
Studio di Consulenza Aziendale, Conti Costanzo Priori Palladino & Associati, Largo Augusto, 3 – 20122 Milano, Italy; ☎02 796141; fax 02 796142; info@scaonline.it; www.scaonline.it. Accountants.

EXPATS AND HOME COUNTRY TAX

UK Citizens and Residents

Uk citizens and expat residents who leave part way through the tax year (the UK tax year runs from April 5 to April 4) may be able to reclaim part of the tax already paid. For salaried employees UK taxes are deducted at source and the estimated amount of tax payable on a full year's income is deducted in equal amounts from each salary payment throughout the year. Departure part way through the year means that a larger percentage of the earned income is deductible and therefore less tax is due. Application forms for a tax refund are available from tax offices and should be returned to the office responsible for your tax file. Declaring non-residency status can also reduce, or eliminate, tax liability on rental income from property and interest on savings in the UK.

Specialist expat tax advice firms can provide individual advice, particularly useful high-income expatriates and those with property and savings in the UK.

These include the Fry Group, Crescent House, Crescent Road, Worthing, West Sussex BN11 1RN (☎01903-231545; fax 01903-200868; www.wtfry.co.uk). They also have offices in Hong Kong and Singapore.

The situation is reasonably straightforward if you are moving permanently abroad. You should inform the UK Inspector of Taxes at the office you usually deal with of your departure and they will send you a P85 form to complete. The UK tax office will usually require certain proof that you are leaving the UK, and hence their jurisdiction, for good. Evidence of having sold a house in the UK and having rented or bought one in Italy is normally sufficient. You can continue to own property in the UK without being considered resident, but you will have to pay UK taxes on any income from the property.

If you are leaving your UK company to work for an Italian one then the P45 form given you by your UK employer and evidence of employment in Italy should be sufficient. You may be eligible for a tax refund in respect of the period up to your departure in which case it will be necessary to complete an income tax return for income and gains from the previous 5th April to your departure date. It may be advisable to seek professional advice when completing your P85; this form is used to determine your residence status and hence your UK tax liability. You should not fill it in if you are only going abroad for a short time. Once the Inland Revenue are satisfied that you are no longer resident or domiciled in the UK, they will close your file and not expect any more UK income tax to be paid.

If you are moving abroad temporarily, then other conditions apply. You are not liable for UK taxes if you work for a foreign employer on a full-time contract and remain abroad for a whole tax year (6 April to 5 April) as long as you spend less than 183 days in a year, or 91 days a year averaged out over a four-year period, in the UK. If you are considered a UK resident and have earned money working abroad then taxes paid abroad are not deductible. If you spend one part of a year working abroad and the rest in the UK you may still be considered non-resident for the part spend abroad, the so-called split tax year concession; this only applies to someone abroad for a lengthy period of time.

Italy has a double taxation agreement with the UK, which makes it possible to offset tax paid in one country against tax paid in another. While the rules are complex, essentially, so long as you work for an Italian employer and are paid in Italy then you should not have to pay UK taxes, as long as you meet residency conditions outlined above. For further information see the Inland Revenue publications IR20 *Residents and non-residents, Liability to tax in the United Kingdom* which can be found on the website www.inlandrevenue.gov. uk. Booklets IR138, IR139 and IR140 are also worth reading; these can be obtained from your tax office or from *The Centre for Non-Residents (CNR) Newcastle:* Longbenton, Newcastle-upon-Tyne NE98 1ZZ; ☎0845 915 4811 ; from outside the UK: +44 191 2254811; fax 0845 9157800; from outside the

UK: +44 191 2257800; www.inlandrevenue.gov.uk/cnr.

US Expatriates

The US Internal Revenue Service (IRS) expects US citizens and resident aliens living abroad to file tax returns every year. Such persons will continue to be liable for US taxes on worldwide income until they have become permanent residents of another country and severed their ties with the USA. If you earn less than a certain amount abroad in one tax year then you do not need to file a tax return. The amount varies depending on whether you are a single person, pensioner, married person head of household etc.

Fortunately, the USA has a double taxation agreement with Italy so you should not have to pay taxes twice on the same income. In order to benefit from the double taxation agreement you need to fulfil one of two residence tests: either you have been a bona fide resident of another country for an entire tax year, which is the same as the calendar year in the case of the USA, or you have been physically present in another country for 330 days during a period of 12 months which can begin at any time of the year. Once you qualify under the bona fide residence or physical presence tests then any further time you spend working abroad can also be used to diminish your tax liability.

As regards foreign income, the main deduction for US citizens is the 'Foreign Earned Income Exclusion', by which you do not pay US taxes on the first $160,000 (married couple allowance; half that for a single person) of money earned abroad. Investment income, capital gains etc. are unearned income. If you earn in excess of the limit taxes paid on income in Italy can still be used to reduce your liability for US taxes either in the form of an exclusion or a credit, depending on which is more advantageous. The same will apply to Italian taxes paid on US income.

The rules for US taxpayers abroad are explained very clearly in the IRS booklet: *Tax Guide for US Citizens and Resident Aliens Abroad,* known as Publication 54, which can be downloaded from the internet on www.irs.gov. The US tax return has to be sent to the IRS, Philadelphia, PA 19255-0207; ☎215-516-2000.

There are penalties for not filing tax returns and late filing, just as there are for US residents. US embassies can provide tax forms for their citizens, though many expatriates utilise the services of specialist expatriate tax consultants, especially if they are high earners resident in countries that levy low tax rates (which does not include Italy). Yahoo! has a limited directory of expatriate accountancy firmsathttp://dir.yahoo.com/Business_and_Economy/Shopping_and_Services/Financial_Services/Taxes/Expatriate/. Expatriate magazines and websites aimed at US expatriates also carry adverts for firms offering such services.

Canadian Expatriates

Canadians moving overseas for an extended period of time need to inform their tax authority that they will be non-resident. This means Canadians can avoid having to pay tax on income earned outside of Canada during their time abroad, among other benefits. Expert advice should be taken on how non-resident status affects investment regulations and other aspects of financial planning. Information and advice should be sought from specialists in expatriate financial advice, two such firms are listed below:

The Expatriate Group Inc., Suite 280, 926 5th Ane SW, Calgary, Alberta, Canada T2P ON7; ☎ 403 232 8561; fax 403 294 1222; expatriate@expat.ca; www.expat.ca.

Canadian Relocation and Expatriate Taxation and Resource Center, Braemar Place, Suite 330, 1201 – 5th Street S.W., Calgary, Alberta, Canada T2R 0Y6, ☎403 531 2200; fax (403) 263 1826; www.expatax.com; peter@expatax.com.

The Yahoo! directory listed in the section for US expatriates above has a subsection for Canadian firms. Some US firms in the directory also offer services for Canadian expatriates through Canadian affiliate offices.

HEALTH CARE, INSURANCE AND HOSPITALS

It would perhaps be a salutory lesson for those who are accustomed to bash the British National Health Service to be sent for treatment in an Italian National Health Service (Servizio Sanitario Nazionale or SSN) hospital in Sicily for instance. They would be guaranteed never to complain again. In common with other systems under state control in Italy, the state medical system costs the government (i.e. the taxpayer) a fortune (100 billion euros), eats up 8% of GDP (more than in Britain, France or Germany and employs 1,280,000 people (4.2 of the national labour force) and still at some hospitals, particularly those run by religious foundations, no meals or bed linen are provided; relatives have to see to these and other daily non-medical needs of hospitalised family members.

Italy has a glut of doctors and produces more medics than any other European country. Some of these, however, are theoretical graduates who will never end up practising medicine. For those that do, practical experience is usually gained by becoming the acolyte of a consultant (*primario*) and following the great man or woman on their ward rounds. Despite the erratic standard of Italian medical training, there are many excellent and compassionate doctors, especially (but not exclusively), in private clinics. Italy has a clutch of world-renowned specialists including a Nobel prize winner (Daniel Bovet) and a singing heart surgeon with a string of hit records as well as medical successes under his gown (Enzo Jannacci). Simultaneously with some of the best doctors in Europe, Italy possesses some of the worst hospitals (for a rich nation), with long waiting lists for treatment, haphazard in-hospital care, and inadequate facilities. That said, state hospitals in the north of Italy are much better run than those in the south which also has its good ones, but not very many. Italian residents may prefer not to chance their luck in the state system unless their local state hospital has a good reputation. Both nationals and expatriates, often take out private health insurance (see below) to cover themselves in case they need basic care, let alone long-term, expensive hospitalisation. Note that a list of local national health centres and hospitals is available from your local health authority (*Unita Sanitarie Locali*) in Italy; also most local embassies or consulates should be able to provide a list of English-speaking (private) doctors in your region. You can also search for a practitioner via the website of the Italian doctors and dentists association, FNEMCeO, the *Federazione Nazionale degli Ordini dei Medici Chirurghi e degli Odontoiatri* (www.fnomceo.it), but these will not be English-speaking.

When purchasing private healthcare it is essential to read the small print to ensure that the coverage is as complete as possible and covers all your possible future requirements – exclusions can be extensive. Paul Wolf of Innovative Benefits Solutions (www.ibencon.com) says, 'There are no bargains out there, you get what you pay for'.

The E111/European Health Insurance Card (EHIC)

In the initial moving period, or on holiday visits, or while on a speculative visit to Italy to look for work you will not be covered by the Italian social security system, and in such cases you can take out private travel insurance. However, it is also possible to obtain free, or mainly free treatment under a reciprocal agreement, which exists between EU countries. To qualify for such treatment you need form E111. The E111 is valid until the 31 December 2005. From January 1 2006 an EHIC (European Health Insurance Card) will replace the E111 (and gradually the other E-forms including the E128, E110 and E119). The EHIC will be valid for two years and is renewable on the proviso that the applicant still makes their home country National Insurance contributions.

The application form for the E111/EHIC is available from post offices, doctors' surgeries, travel agents etc. or you can download it at the Department of Health Website (www.dh.gov.uk). Irish citizens can download the new application form for the EHIC at www.oasis.gov.ie/moving_country/moving_abroad/e111.html. Note that, as with any journey abroad, it is a good idea to take out travel insurance, which includes health benefits.

Although the E111/EHIC covers emergency hospital treatment while abroad it does not include the cost for prescribed medicines, specialist examinations, X-rays, laboratory tests and physiotherapy or dental treatment. Consequently, private insurance should still be taken out for the required period, as this will provide financial protection against medical treatment costs which are not regarded as emergencies and which are not covered by the E111/EHIC.

UK National Insurance Contributions

If you start paying into the Italian social security system you become eligible for their benefits. However, if you are planning to return the UK it is advisable to keep up your UK contributions in if you want to retain your entitlement to a UK state pension and other benefits. Class 1 contributions are for those in full-time employment with a British-based employer, but there are alternatives if your employer is not paying: class 2 (self-employed) and class 3 (voluntary) contributions. Many UK tax advisors advise that you should pay UK NICs if you possibly can for future benefits available. Further details from DWP (Pension Service, International Pension Centre, Medical Benefits Section, Tyneview Road, Whitley Park, Whitley road, Newcastle-upon-Tune NE98 1BA; ☎ 0191-218 7547). Your local Jobcentre Plus office, or the website www.jobcentreplus.gov.uk also have useful information and contact details for those looking for official advice and information. Financial consultants such as KPMG (020-7311 1000; 8 Salisbury Square, London EC4; www.kpmg.co.uk) can advise expatriate employees.

Using the Health Service

Anyone who makes social security payments in the EU, who receives an EU state pension, is unemployed, or under the age of 18 is entitled to medical treatment in the Italian state health service free of charge. These include free hospital accommodation and medical treatment and up to 90% of the cost of prescription medicines; a contribution (*il ticket*) of 10% is required from the patient. Social security payments, which account for approximately 8% of a worker's gross income, are deducted from the employee's gross salary by the employer.

Foreigners working for foreign firms will almost certainly be insured for treatment under a private medical scheme and thus will be spared the lottery of public health care in an Italian state hospital (*ospedale*). If you are not insured by your employer the cost of purchasing your own private coverage can be well worth it if you ever need hospital treatment. The numerous private hospitals in Italy are often run by the church and being both hygienic and efficient prove pleasant contrast to the worst of the state-run hospitals.

Any foreigner who has become a resident and who wishes to receive treatment under the Italian state system is obliged to register with and obtain a national health number from the ASL (*Azienda Sanitaria Locale*) of their district. You will need to produce your *permesso di soggiorno* or the more permanent *certificato di residenza* and a letter from your employer confirming your employment. Self-employed or freelance workers should first register with the Istituto Nazionale della Previdenza Sociale (INPS), the national social security institute in Piazza Augusto Imperatore 32, Rome (www.inps.it), where they will be given the necessary documentation to take to the local ASL office together with their *permesso di soggiorno/certificato di residenza*. ASL addresses can be found in the *Tuttocittà*, a supplement that comes with Italian telephone directories, or alternatively in the local newspaper. If you are non working, non-EU with elective residence visa (i.e. non-working visa), there is an annual fee of about €400 a year. Once you are registered with the ASL, the next step is to register with *un medico mutualistico* (general practitioner). The system of free treatment is known as *la mutua*. Outpatients are normally treated at a *studio medico* or *ambulatorio* (surgery). A private clinic is *una clinica private*.

If you find yourself in an Italian state hospital it is essential that your relatives know where you are and that someone visits you regularly to ensure that you have adequate personal care. There are wide variations in these areas and it depends where you are as to whether you are in a 'good' hospital or not. Delays in diagnosis are common and some hospitals have appalling standards of hygiene.

Some of the better hospitals are in Rome: the *Salvator Mundi*, the *Fatebenefratelli* (Via Cassia 600) and the Roman American Hospital. In Milan there is the *Ospedale Maggiore di Milano Policlinico* (via Francesco Sforza 32). Local advice should always be taken from other expats as certain doctors and hospitals will be better set up to meet the needs of expatriates.

Emergencies

If you are involved in or at the site of a serious accident then get to the nearest phone box and dial 118; you can also dial 113 for police and be put you through to the emergency services; ask for an *ambulanza* (ambulance). Less serious injuries should be treated at the casualty (*Pronto Soccorso*) ward at the nearest hospital. Alternatively, most major railway stations and airports have first-aid stations with qualified doctors on hand – many of these first aid stations are reputed to be very effective.

In the event of minor ailments, aches and pains it may well be worth avoiding the chaos of the state hospitals and applying directly to your local chemist (*farmacia*). Chemists are generally extremely well qualified in Italy, and will probably be able to prescribe something for you. The *farmacia* are usually open all night in larger towns and cities and if the one you end up at is closed, there should be a list displayed on the door that lists which chemists in the area are open that night.

Sickness and Invalidity Benefit

Any EU citizen who is moving to Italy permanently and who claims sickness or invalidity benefit in their home country is entitled to continue claiming this benefit once in Italy. Strictly speaking, to claim either benefit, you must be physically incapable of all work, however, the interpretation of the words 'physically incapable' is frequently stretched just a little beyond literal truth. If the claimant has been paying National Insurance contributions in the UK for two tax years (this may be less depending on his or her level of income) then he or she is eligible to claim weekly sickness benefit. After receiving sickness benefit for 28 weeks, you are entitled to invalidity benefit.

Anyone currently receiving either form of benefit should inform their Jobcentre Plus/social security office that they are moving to Italy. If you are abroad contact the The Pension Service of the DWP (☎ 0191 21 87777; fax 0191 21 83836; e-mail TVP-IPC-Customer-Care@thepensionservice.gsi.gov. uk). They can ensure that a monthly sterling cheque is sent either to your new address or direct to your bank account. The only conditions involved are that all claimants submit themselves to a medical examination, either in Italy or the UK, on request.

US Citizens. The United States has a totalisation agreement with Italy regarding social security payments and sickness benefits for Americans living and working in Italy so that they do not end up paying for two social security systems. The agreement also covers pensions. For more details go to www.ssa.gov/international/ Agreement_Pamphlets/italy.html.

Italian sickness benefit. Benefits for workers (*operai*) and salaried staff (*impiegati*) in commerce and industry is paid partly by the employer and partly by the state national sickness fund (INPS). Salaried staff get 100 per cent of their salary (at the employer's cost) for up to six months. For manual workers the amount is dependent on their labour contract and the length of service

Private Medical Insurance

In contrast with the lack of organisation in the public sector, the private sector of the health service is amazingly well organised. However, it is also expensive; charges at private hospitals and clinics are a minimum of £150 (US$191) per day for a room, so private health insurance is a must.

Those who are going to Italy seeking work, or who spend a few weeks or months a year there, will require private medical insurance to cover the balance of the cost not covered by the E111/EHIC (see above). If you already hold private health insurance you will find that most companies will switch this for European cover once you are in Italy. With the increase of British and foreign insurance companies offering this kind of cover, it is worth shopping around as cover and costs vary. You can get a quote online for travel or expatriate medical insurance at www. worldtrips.com (☎709-200-6334; e-mail contact@cambridgeserver.com).

Of course, if you are employed in Italy, you and your family may be able to join (or be provided with) a health insurance scheme (*il mutuo*) through your employer, which tops up the state health service.

Private health insurance can be arranged through organisations such as BUPA, AXA/PPP or Expacare, all of which offer international health insurance schemes. The cost, coverage and conditions of private health schemes vary enormously and the small print should be checked carefully. The annual premiums on the policies will vary according to age group of the insured and some will include dependent children at reduced rates, or even for free (though their premiums may be higher to start with).

The policies can offer a full refund for medical treatment undertaken in hospital up to pre-set limit. Some also provide cover for out-patient treatment, and visits to a general practitioner and the dentist, also with pre-set limits. The premiums can be paid monthly, quarterly or annually by direct debit, credit card or cheque – though it should always be borne in mind than failure to make a stage payment invalidates the coverage. Optional extras that can significantly add to the cost of coverage, include:

- Nursing at home
- Pregnancy and childbirth (natural and caesarian).
- Stress counselling.
- Disability compensation
- Cover during travel outside of the country where you live.
- Emergency evacuation and repatriation.

Self-employed expatriates are liable to INPS contributions as a percentage of their annual taxable income. However, if you wish to join the Italian National Health scheme, you are required to pay nearly 8% of your taxable income, quite apart from what it may cost to keep your non-Italian pension rights going. It is very doubtful if the benefits achieved by such a contribution in Italy outweigh the disadvantages of possible unnecessary involvement in the Italian tax system and the answer is almost certainly recourse to a private health insurance policy, some of which will even pay GP and dental charges.

Useful Addresses – Private Healthcare Insurers

Amariz Ltd.: 1, Harley Place, Bristol BS8 3JT; ☎0117-974 5770; fax 0117-974 5780; e-mail amariz@lineone.net; www.amariz.co.uk..

AXA PPP Healthcare: head office Phillips House, Crescent Road, Tunbridge Wells, Kent TN1 2PL; ☎ *01892-612 080;* www.axappphealthcare.co.uk..

British United Provident Association (BUPA): (Russell House, Russell Mews, Brighton BN1 2NR; ☎01273-208181; e-mail info@bupaintl.com; www. bupa-int.com). BUPA International offers a range of worldwide schemes for individuals and companies of three or more employees based outside the UK for six or more months.

Centers for Disease Control and Prevention: 1600 Clifton Road, Atlanta, GA 30333, USA; ☎404-639-3534/800 311 3435; www.cdc.gov/. General travel health advice.

Community Insurance Agency Inc.:, 425 Huehl Road, Suite #22a Northbrook, IL 60062; USA ☎ 847-897-5120; fax 847-897-5130; e-mail info@ciainsagency. com; ☎1 800-344-9540 (toll free). International health coverage agency.

Exeter Friendly Society: Lakeside House, Emperor Way, Exeter, Devon; ☎01392-353535; fax 01392-353590; e-mail sales@exeterfriendly.co.uk; www. exeterfriendly.co.uk.

Expacare: Columbia Centre, Market Street, Bracknell, Berkshire, RG12 1JG; ☎01344-381650; fax 01344-381690; e-mail: info@expacare.com or visit www.expacare.net. Specialists in expatriate healthcare offering high quality health insurance cover for individuals and their families, including group cover for five or more employees. Cover is available for expatriates of all nationalities worldwide.

Goodhealth Worldwide (Europe): 5 Lloyds Avenue, London; ☎0870-442 7376; e-mail enquiries@goodhealth.co.uk.

Healthcare International: UK Administration, 84 Brook Street, London W1K 5EH; ☎020-7665 1627; fax 020-7665 1628; e-mail enquiries@healthcareinternatio nal.com; www.healthcareinternational.com.

HIFAC Health Insurance: ☎0871 424 0022; www.insurancewide.com. Provides access to all the top private medical insurance providers.

Taurus Insurance Services Ltd.: Suite 323, 2nd Floor, Block 3, Eurotowers, Gibraltar; ☎+350 52776; fax +350 51352; e-mail sales@taurusinsuranceservices.com; www.taurusinsuranceservices.com. Health, travel and accident insurance providers to the expatriate community.

Worldwide Assistance: 1825K Street NW- Suite 1000, Washington, DC 20006, USA; ☎1-800-777-8710; fax +1 202 331-1528; e-mail info@worldassistance. com; www.worldassistance.com. Affiliate to Europ-Assistance, the world's largest assistance organisation with doctors, air ambulances, agents and vehicle rescue services.

SOCIAL SECURITY AND UNEMPLOYMENT

Social Security

The Italian welfare state (*lo stato assistenziale*), and social security system (*il sistema di previdenza sociale*), is generally regarded as being disastrously wasteful but there were massive cutbacks in the system in order to meet economic criteria for joining the euro. However, as in many European countries there are serious reservations among the Italian populace about cutting back too much of the social welfare system – one of the more popular of the Berlusconi election pledges was his promise to increase the minimum level of pension payments. The Italian system provides an array of old age and disability pensions, sickness and unemployment benefits and health and medical services. However, these services are lacking in facilities, finances, are sometimes corrupt, always ridden with bureaucracy and mostly inefficient.

If you have a regular job with an Italian firm you will be paying INPS contributions, the equivalent of National Insurance in the UK. The rate of contribution is on average about 45%, of which around 9% is paid by the worker and 30% - 37% by the employer. Self-employed contributions are 10% - 13%

For UK citizens it is possible to keep up National Insurance contributions (the equivalent of Italian social security) in the UK on a voluntary basis after moving to Italy. This can be quite a canny move for anyone who is not working, but who hasn't yet reached official retirement age, as you will be eligible to claim a UK pension throughout your time in Italy. However, continuing UK National Insurance contributions will be unnecessary for those who intend to work in Italy as EU regulations ensure that social security contributions made in one member state are counted as a contribution period in the contributor's own country's social security system for the purpose of determining their future benefits from that system.

Unemployment Benefit

Considering Italy's inclusion in the group of the world's seven most industrialised nations, the country has a high unemployment rate. The unemployment figures peaked at 14.2% in 1985 and now stand at around 9% which is roughly the same as France. Unsurprisingly, unemployment is higher in the poor *Mezzogiorno* which, although only comprising a total of 36% of the Italian population, accounts for about half of the total number of unemployed. On the other hand, unemployment is less than half the national average in the prosperous north. However, Italy's thriving black economy (which contributes, by some estimates, up to 27% of GNP) provides thousands of jobs for those officially out of work and undermines the representational value of these statistics. Moreover, many of Italy's unemployed refuse to do certain jobs, such as street sweeping, washing dishes, making pizzas; leaving such menial chores to the millions of illegal immigrants who scrape a living off the country's black economy. Particularly in the south the Italian practice of taking second or third jobs (*il secondo/terzo lavoro*), is a frequently-used means of topping up the often low incomes (as compared to other European countries), which exist in Italy.

Any worker who registers as being unemployed within 45 days of losing their job is entitled to unemployment benefit (*sussidio di disoccupazione*), administered by the provincial employment office, SCICA. *Family allowances, ANF (assegni per il nucleo famigliari)* also exist which cover offspring up to the age of 26 who are still in full-time education. Income support (*reddito minimo di inserimento*) is also paid in some instances. State support for the long-term unemployed is minimal.

For any EU national who is unemployed and contemplating a tentative work-finding trip to Italy, unemployment benefit can be transferred to Italy for thirteen weeks while you look for employment there. Benefits can be claimed at the UK rate throughout this period. This arrangement only exists in the European Economic Area that is made up of the EU plus Iceland, Liechtenstein and Norway.

If you are British and thinking of going to Italy to look for work, it is worth knowing that you can continue to receive UK unemployment benefit at UK rates for three months in Italy. This is only applicable if you have already been unemployed for a month in the UK. It is essential to apply as soon as you can, as entitlement to transfer benefit expires within three months of becoming unemployed. You will need to have paid full Class 1 contributions during the two tax years previous to the one you are claiming in. You should contact your usual benefit office who will in turn contact the Centre for non Residents of the Inland Revenue (Longbenton, Newcastle-upon-Tyne NE98 1ZZ; ☎0845 9154811 helpline). They will issue a form E303, the document needed to claim benefit in another EU country. In order to receive the medical care you are entitled to under Italian regulations for unemployed people you should also ask for the form E119 at the same time. For general information about benefits and social security in EU countries, ask for forms SA29 and JSAL22, either from your Jobcentre or from the Pensions and Overseas Benefits Directorate, Department for Work and Pensions, Tyneview Park, Whitley Rd., Benton, Newcastle-upon-Tyne NE98 1BA.

LOCAL GOVERNMENT

Running parallel to central government in Italy are three tiers of local government listed in order of ascending importance: *il comune* (the town council), *la provincia* (province) and the twenty *regioni* (regions); the latter comprising the country's largest administrative units. Of the twenty regions, only five have evolved any kind of semi-autonomous powers; Sicily, Sardinia, Trentino-Alto Adige, Friuli-Venezia-Giulia and Valle d'Aosta. The devolution of power in these regions was necessitated by both geographical factors and ethnic history. There are 106 *province* and 8,100 *comuni*.

For example, Trentino-Alto Adige was only annexed to Italy after World War I and has a strong German-speaking contingent with pro-Austrian sympathies. It remains an uncomfortable Italian annexe with a strong move towards political and administrative independence which has included violence in the past. The five regions are known as *regioni a statuo speciale* and they differ from the other fifteen regions in that their assemblies resemble mini-parliaments which enjoy varying economic and administrative powers – similar to the Scottish Parliament and Welsh Assembly in the UK and Federal Parliaments in Germany and Switzerland.

All five autonomous regions have total control over their education systems, although legislation passed in 1970 provides, theoretically, for limited powers of autonomy in the assemblies of the remaining fifteen regions. In practice, however, central government remains very much the dominant force in these areas. Additionally, 14 cities have a special constitutional status as *città metropolitane* (metropolitan city areas) including Milan, Naples, Tome, Genoa and Turin which gives them a great deal of power over local spending and allows them to charge small additional taxes.

Each of Italy's 106 provinces has a two-letter sign, which forms part of the postcode and is also evident on official documents like driving licences and identity cards. The bureaucratic function of the *provincia* (provinces) is to represent the national government at local level, but this is merely one of the two tiers of local government. A good deal of the provincial budget goes into sponsoring usually costly cultural and other prestige projects, which are deemed to increase international awareness of their existence and tourist potential, as well as spending on schools and roads. Finally, the *comunes*, elected once every five years (as are all other tiers of government), deal with all matters of local administration – local taxes, administration of social security services, housing, roads and transport etc. The *comunes* are headed by the *sindaco* (mayor) who is assisted by *gli assessori* (the councillors). An excellent website www.perjol.net/Italia/italkom.html gives you not only a list of all the regions, provinces and the provinces' capital towns and links to all their official websites representing a mine of information about local matters in Italy (in Italian).

CRIME AND THE POLICE

Overview

Most European countries have experienced a high increase in crime over the last two decades, and Italy is no exception. However, whereas in Britain the increase has been in theft and malicious offences against property, particularly cars, in Italy nearly three-quarters of all crime is drug-related. The three areas with the highest crime rates are *Latium, Puglia and Campania*. The last two in particular have shown a spectacularly rising crime rate based on the statistics for reported crimes of theft and robbery in recent years.

Organised violent crime in Italy is infamous and needs little introduction. There are Mafia black spots where murder is a regular occurrence and there are vicious kidnappings where traditionally, the perpetrators have the charming custom of sending the odd ear or finger of the victim to the family as an *aide-mémoire* to pay the ransom are not uncommon, but most expatriates will never knowingly come face to face with Mafia crimes. In fact, although kidnapping regularly occurs, predominantly in Calabria or Sardina, instances have fallen to one every few years (in the 60s and 70s, it was up to sixty a year). An Italian law forbids victims' families to mediate privately with kidnappers and allows magistrates to freeze the family's assets in order, it is argued, to discourage kidnapping. Apart from Mafia violence, which is on the increase in well-recognised areas, there is less violent crime, i.e. muggings and street violence in general, than in many other Western countries. This may be connected to the fact that drunkenness, which proves the catalyst to much crime in the UK, is very rare in Italy. Indeed the Italians look with consternation upon the hooliganism of drink-inflamed British football supporters. Also little-known in Italy are the type of crazed gunmen found in North America, who blast away a few dozen complete strangers in an orgy of gunfire. Private arsenals, except for hunting rifles, are a rarity (except of course amongst the Mafia). Until recently, serial killings and crimes against children were a rarity in Italy, but sadly these types of crime are on the increase – or they are being reported more frequently as in other countries.

A new crime wave that has erupted in the last few years is connected with the influx of refugees and immigrants from Albania – the Albanian Mafia are reputed to be more ruthless than the indigenous groups. Most large towns have a contingent of Albanian Mafia along with Romanians and Serbs. According to local police chiefs the Albanian criminal element is much more aggressive and ruthless than other foreign criminals and they are simply murdering the Italian, African and Arab competition out of the way.

According to the UK government's travel advice, major crime is not a problem in Italy but petty crime (*microcriminalità)* is, and the Italian Government tells its citizens that petty theft is rife in big cities and tourist sites (mainly Rome, Naples and Florence), on trains and buses, in museums and autostrade filling stations and in campsites; thieves and pickpockets operate on foot or moped. Danger spots are: Naples city centre and station area, Rome's public transport services connecting the station with the Vatican, and Palermo in Sicily. Gangs of juvenile pickpockets, called *slavi* or slavs, from former Yugoslavia, have always been a problem at places like Rome's Termini station.

Petty crime has been eliminated in central Bari for example by patrolling Carabinieri, and they are also working on central Naples. In danger areas the only way to be sure of not being robbed is to adopt draconian measures:

- ✪ refrain from wearing jewellery and watches.
- ✪ don't carry cameras or videocameras.
- ✪ keep car doors locked while driving in cities.
- ✪ don't carry large sums of cash.
- ✪ keep credit cards and cheque books separate and secure.

By contrast, some rural areas, however, in places like Umbria, Tuscany, the Marches, Emilia Romagna, Piemonte, Friuli, Molise, where the old local cultures prevail, are nearly crime free. You are told that the only crimes there are committed by outsiders. In places like Buonconvento (Tuscany) you can confidently predict, still, that a wallet lost in the street will be handed in to the local police station (the Carabinieri) with its money intact.

Organised Crime

Organised crime in Italy is a veritable state within a state. Based in the South its tentacles spread throughout Italy – and abroad. It is nicknamed the octopus – *la piovra*. The *Mafia* or *Cosa Nostra* in Sicily is bigger, more calculating, and structured than the more chaotic and opportunistic outfits in the toe and heel and ankle of Italy: the *Camorra* in Campania, the *Ndrangheta* in Calabria and the *Sacra Corona Unita* in Puglia. Brave magistrates and policemen have struggled to quell the phenomenon. General della Chiesa of the police *carabinieri* was assassinated by the *Mafia* in 1982 and Giovanni Falcone and Paolo Borsellino ten years later, these latter two heroic magistrates now commemorated in the name of Palermo's international airport.

Despite the best efforts of the police and judiciary, crime unfortunately continues to pay. It yields billions of euros in protection money, and from drugs and cigarettes. Add to that millions of euros from kidnappings, prostitution, loan-sharking, illegal immigration, building scams, markets, the commercialisation of Padre Pio – any lucrative field is fair game. The clans or *cosche* and their bosses or godfathers (*padrini*) have armies of young men at their bidding, arsenals of weaponry and sophisticated computer technology. They wield political power and gain collusion from local borough councils right up to the Senate in Rome. They command blocks of votes on their home turf, which have been crucial to the electoral success of *La Casa delle Libertà*, prime minister Berlusconi's ruling coalition. The mafia have moved upwards into white collar crime – laundering money through banks and running legitimate businesses with the proceeds. Murder and the conspiracy of silence (*omertà*) are the means by which they retain power and respect; excellent cadavers (*cadaveri eccellenti)* the name given to their illustrious victims. Young boys of exceptional criminal daring and cunning are talent-spotted and recruited, and women have a powerful educational role inculcating the Mafia ethos into their boys. Note that these extremes of mafia influence and power are mostly restricted to some parts of Calabria, Sicily and Naples (Campania).

The state minimises the problem although spending massively to contain it: 50 million euros a year for the protection of witnesses alone. It is beginning to achieve some results. In 2001 over 360 mafia fugitives were captured and 2,600 suspects prosecuted. In 2002 the state attacked the mafia's financial empire, confiscating villas, offices and a factory near Palermo worth 500 million euros, belonging to the bosses Buscemi and Catalano, which judges ruled were part of the Mafia's illegally gained wealth. Numerous bosses are in prison, including the infamous Totò Riina. It even looks as though the net might finally be closing around the superboss Bernardo Provenzano. Early in 2005 police uncovered a plot to murder the chief prosecutor of Palermo and the assistant prosecutor in Rome and arrested 46 suspects alleged to have helped Provenzano evade the law. He has so far spent 41 years as a *latitante* (fugitive) avoiding justice, while running a lucrative criminal empire. How the police will know they have arrested the right man is anyone's guess as he is now over 70 years old and the only likenesses available are from 1963.

Foreign visitors can console themselves that they are not the targets of organised crime, and they can be blissfully unaware of its existence. The local population of the supposedly crime-ridden south, in a survey by Demos for the *Repubblica* newspaper, were more than three times more worried by unemployment (48.2%) than by crime (14%). (In the industrial North-East the figures were 8.6% for unemployment and 20.5% for crime.) The spate of confessions by repentant mafia members (*pentiti)* starting with Tommaso Busceta in 1984, who spilt the beans with perfect recall on the arcanest areas of *mafioso* activities, could have been the turning of the tide – or a change in tack; the mafia mind is always two steps ahead of its adversaries. It remains to be seen whether heartfelt appeals by glamorous – and repentant – Camorra and Mafia bosses to young boys not to go into crime, combined with the new strategic educational reforms aimed specifically at 15-18 year old males, will succeed in reducing the twin evils of unemployment and organised crime.

The infiltration of Albanian criminals throughout Italy has been an alarming result of the Balkan troubles of the 1990s. Ruthless operators, compared with whom the homegrown *mafiosi* are gentlemen, Albanians have been carving out territories throughout Italy involving drugs, cigarettes, prostitution, carjacking, burglaries. Italian businessmen driving top of the range German cars have been mugged at autostrada filling stations and their cars made to vanish without trace, presumably to the Balkans. In peaceful country areas villas have been ransacked at leisure and antique furniture taken away in pantechnicons.

The so-called white slave trade – mainly prostitutes from the former Yugoslavia and USSR – is run by Albanian pimps and competes for territory with a black slave trade. 60,000 prostitutes mostly from the Benin region of Nigeria ply the leafy lanes of il Bel Paese, masterminded from Africa. Shocked by this phenomenon the Italian government has set up a free charter flight service to fly the girls home where charitable homes have been set up to take care of them. It has been proposed to re-open state supervised brothels – abolished by a woman senator called Merlin in 1947. Italians seem to be fairly laid back about, and tolerant of, the trade, although sixty Nigerian girls were found murdered in 2001.

The Police

It is unfortunately the case in Italy that the police have a dismal record in beating crime – around three-quarters of all crimes committed in Italy go unsolved. This is mainly because the bulk of crime occurs in the far south and Sicily – in other words Mafia territory. Italy has four main, separate police forces, for historical reasons. Liaison between the forces has historically been extremely bad with the result that when representatives of two different ones are called out to the same incident, unseemly scuffles are liable to break out amongst the policemen from the different forces! The situtation has improved in recent years with more cooperation taking place. Most usefully, there is a division of territory allowing the police to be the main operators in towns and the carabinieri everywhere else including rural areas. Owing to the singular ineffectiveness of the police in combating organised crime in cities such as Naples and Reggio Calabria, the provision of private security forces has become a booming industry. Often bizarrely uniformed, the private security men are nevertheless a more effective deterrent against underworld-inspired violence than the regular police are. To be fair, the lack of effectiveness is often due to the difficulty of finding witnesses brave enough to testify. The official police forces are:

I Carabinieri: the militarily-associated carabinieri are the largest force, numbering nearly 86,000. They have been striving in recent years to shake off their thick image, and they are generally personable and helpful. This one-time bastion of masculinity was thrown open to women recruits in 2000 (as was the army proper). *Carabinieri* are recognisable by their dark blue uniforms (designed by Giorgio Armani) with red stripe and matching peaked cap. Accessories include white belts with matching cartridge holder and holster. They may also carry machine guns (e.g. when looking for kidnappers in the Calabrian Mountains). *Carabinieri* squad cars are also dark blue, but with a white stripe. Their dress uniform features an ostrich-feather decorated bicorn hat, white gloves, sword and cloak. *Caribinieri* police stations are known as *la caserna* or *la stazione dei carabinieri.* The *carabinieri* are responsible for stopping motorists in contravention of traffic regulations and administering on-the-spot fines.

La Polizia di Stato: there are a few thousand fewer Polizia than Carabinieri and around 5% of the force is comprised of women. Their uniforms are lighter blue than the *Carabinieri* and have a deep pink stripe. They also have a riot squad section (formerly known as the *celere,* for their green uniforms). *La Polizia* have a reputation for uncouthness and being rather trigger-happy. Their plain-clothes section is often mistaken for armed robbers. A police station is *una questura*.

La Guardia di Finanza/I Finanzieri: These are the customs police who can trace their origins back to the eighteenth century. Their force level is half that of the *Carabinieri*. They wear light grey uniforms and dark green berets with a yellow badge. Their poor reputation reached its trough when their former head, Generale Raffaele Giudice, was jailed for corruption on a multi-billion dollar scale, but has marginally improved since. When leaving an Italian bar or restaurant it is obligatory to carry your till receipts for 100 metres after leaving the premises in case *i Finanzeri* wish to inspect it, as a check on whether restaurant owners are fiddling their VAT.

I Vigili Urbani: These are the local municipal police forces. They are normally dressed in navy blue, with white jackets and a matching helmet. Of all Italian police they are the least professional. Like the *carabinieri*, they can stop and fine motorists. They are responsible for checking residence permits, investigating planning infringements and other local matters. In Rome their on-going feud with the *Polizia* provides regular street entertainment for local citizens.

There are additional police groups in Italy including the coast guard, prison police (*polizia penitenziaria*), the forest police (*corpo forestale dello stato*) and commercial security guards such as the armed ones in combat gear that patrol the Rome metro. Note that outside towns and cities it is generally the *carabinieri* who will come if you call out the police, whereas in towns you will get I vigili urbani. The police emergency numbers are 112 or 113. Theft being one of the most common crimes in Italy, the chances are that sooner or later you will require the police to make out a stolen goods report (*la denuncia*). If they are unwilling to do this you will have to insist as you need a *denuncia* for insurance purposes. It is best to go to a *comando dei carabinieri,* or *questura*, in person.

If you are unfortunate enough to be accosted by any type of police, be warned that they expect you to be awe-struck. If you show any signs of unwillingness to co-operate, they will make your life difficult. Remember that they have the authority to arrest you should you go so far as to insult a state official.

Under state laws the police have powers to detain suspected criminals for twenty-four hours without informing a magistrate. Suspects may also be interrogated without a lawyer being present. Owing to the congestion and inefficiency of the Italian judicial system it is legally possible for someone waiting to be brought to trial, to remain in police custody for an inordinate length of time.

RELIGION

As the home of the historic administrative centre (the Vatican), as well as the focal point of world Catholicism, Italy has a unique religious heritage that has permeated almost every aspect of Italian culture. Although the Vatican ceased to be a political power in the eighteenth century, its spiritual influence, backed up by the Papal road show, is still capable of producing profound awe amongst the Catholic populations of underdeveloped countries worldwide. The Vatican is also a member of the United Nations, which belies its claim to have no interest in politics. In Italy itself, however, there exist extreme attitudes of both devotion and profanity to *Cattolicesimo* (Catholicism). The traditional areas of fervour are the poor regions of the south and the area around Venice, while from Emilia Romagna to Umbria has a reputation for sacerdotal antipathy; there is even a pasta named *strangolapreti* (priest-stranglers).

The Vatican has often caused controversy in Italy by not limiting itself to religious pronouncements, which has not done its reputation much good. For instance it had a long-running feud with the Italian government on the basis that it regarded parliament as ideologically unsound and all its members were therefore ineligible for Communion. This state of affairs was finally remedied by the Lateran pact of 1929 that secularised the Italian state. The Vatican showed equal implacability towards members of the former Italian Communist Party and anyone of that persuasion was excommunicated, despite the fact that many of them were fervent Catholics. During the liberal seventies, the Catholic church came in for some sacrilegious lampooning, the most notorious example of which is probably the scene in Frederico Fellini's film *Roma*, in which flashing fairy lights are incorporated in the sacred vestments during a glitzy clerical fashion parade.

In contemporary times, Pope John Paul II who died in 2005, was one of the few non-Italian popes. He caused outrage in many quarters for his ultra-conservative dictats on current issues of concern, and many people believe this conservatism has led directly to devastating effects on some countries. For instance, the Papal commendation of large families while on visits to the faithful in Africa shows his blinkered disregard for what is the main problem facing that continent along with AIDS, namely an ecological crisis exacerbated by poverty often caused by overpopulation. Meanwhile, back on home ground, the majority of Italian Catholics have reacted to papal dictums with common sense. Despite a religious ban on 'non-natural' birth control and abortion on demand, Italy has one of the lowest birth-rates in the world, whilst also having one of the most prosperous condom industries. Coincidentally, Italy also has one of the lowest teenage pregnancy rates and abortion has been legal since 1981.

Away from the developed areas of Italy, religion moves in mysterious ways. Although generally more devout than their metropolitan countrymen, the country people mingle Catholicism with older beliefs inherited from pagan times.

Even amongst the highly educated, occult consulting is very popular, fortune-telling, witchcraft, and sooth-saying are services apparently indispensable to the 10 million plus Italians a year who are willing to pay for them.

English Speaking Churches and Services

Aviano: US Air Force Base Chapel; ☎ *04 1520 0571.*

Bologna: ☎ *05 198 2891.*

St Mark's Church: Via Maggio 18, 50125 Florence;   ☎ 05 5294 4764 (also fax); www.stmarks.it; e-mail Lawrence.maclean@virgilio.it). Founded in 1877 and considered a minor masterpiece of the Pre-Raphaelite movement. Located on the ground floor of the 15th century Palazzo Machiavelli at the above address on the south bank of the Arno. Sunday sung Eucharist followed by drinks in the ballroom of the Palazzo Machiavelli is a good way to meet people and if necessary network for jobs. The notice-board in the church foyer is 'full of job and house offers for anglophones'. Rev. Lawrence MacLean.

Città della Pieve (near Perugia): Anglican worship. St John the Baptist, Via Beato Giacomo Villa, in the Umbrian hills. For details contact Peter Hurd (☎057 829 9260).

American Church of the Anglican Communion in Florence; fax 055-294417.

Church of the Holy Ghost: Piazza Marsala 3, 16122 Genoa;   ☎010-889 268.

All Saints' Church, Via Solferino 17, 20121 Milan;   ☎02-655 2258; e-mail frnigel@boxingkangaroo.org.uk; www.allsaints.it. Rev. Nigel Gibson.

Methodist Church (Evangelica Metodista): Via Porro Lambertenghi 38, Milan; ☎02-6072631. English-speaking service.

Christ Church: Via S. Pasquala a Chaiai 15b, 80121 Naples;   ☎081-411842; fax 081 409 789; vicar@Christchurch.it. Also serves Bari, Capri and Sorrento.

Church of the Holy Cross: Via Mariano Stabile 118b, 90139 Palermo;   ☎091-334 831; e-mail holycrosspalermo@libero.it. Rev. Ronald Rogers.

At University Church: Perugia; occasional services   ☎057 829 9260. Peter Hurd.

Anglican Church of All Saints: Via del Babuino 153, 00187 Rome;   ☎06-3600 1881; e-maio j.boardman@allsaintsrome.org. Reverend Jonathan Boardman.

St Andrews Church of Scotland: Via XX Settembre 7, 00187 Rome;   ☎06-4827627. Reverend John Ross.

Roman Catholic Church: San Silvestro in Capite, Piazza San Silvestro, 00187 Rome;   ☎06-6785609. Father Larry Gould.

Methodist Church: Via Banco di San Spirito 3, 00186 Rome;   ☎06-6868314.

St Peter's Siena: Anglican in Via Garibaldi, Siena. Same chaplain as St Marks, Florence.

St George: Campo San Vio, 253 Dorsoduro, 30123 Venice; ;   ☎041 520 0571. Rev John-Henry Bowden.

www.Europe.Anglican.org/directory/webdir2.html: webpage that provides a comprehensive list of Anglican places and times of worship in Italy.

SOCIAL LIFE

B usiness and social life are intertwined in Italy so that anyone who is considering living and working there will almost certainly find themselves socialising with Italians. The first indispensable step in creating a social life that encompasses expatriates and host nationals is to acquire knowledge of the Italian language (see *Daily Life*, Learning the Language). Without a good grasp of Italian, an expatriate could miss much of the exciting and pleasurable aspects of living and working in a foreign country and it would be a shame not to get the full benefit of a period spent in Italy.

Every country's population (including your own) has idiosyncrasies and expatriates in Italy will no doubt find Italian social customs at times perplexing, though mostly enjoyable. Occasionally, there will be instances of total mutual incomprehension, but learning the language will go a long way towards helping an expatriate through the maze of Italian social etiquette (and also in allowing them to apologise for their latest *faux pas*).

The Italians

As already explained in the *General Introduction*, it can be misleading to talk about Italians, since they are clearly less homogeneous than many other European nations; although being part of the EU has probably made them feel more of a nation than hitherto. In any case stereotyping a nationality can lead to problems (and objections), but there are undeniably some traits which are recognisably Italian. For instance, the importance of the family. The closeness of Italian families means that Italians generally, have a support system from birth. Not only will *mamma e papa* indulge their children's every whim and support them financially *ad infinitum* if possible, but a network of relatives will aid and abet their progress in life. This type of string pulling was practically invented, in Europe, by the Italians whose word for nephew is *nipote*, hence nepotism. *Mammismo*, is generally recognised as another typically Italian trait, whereby mothers do everything for their sons. More than half of all Italian men live at home with one or more parents until their mid-thirties. For foreigners, particularly women, becoming romantically involved with Italians usually means taking on an exhausting number of responsibilities across the family network; far more than one would expect from a similar relationship in the UK or North America.

Another manifestation of the Italian group-oriented social life is the urge to cluster, which is particularly noticeable amongst teenagers, *ragazzi*. This phenomenon is known as *stare insieme* (hanging out) and youngsters usually congregate on streets in groups with no discernible objective other than to operate as a mutual admiration society – rather than to cause trouble as they can do in other countries.

Italians will often show warmth towards a new acquaintance, much like outgoing North Americans. This is unlike northern Europeans who, with their traditional Anglo-Saxon reserve wait until they know someone better before getting really enthusiastic towards them. This willingness to communicate on the part of Italians is a great ice-breaker on social occasions, particularly if you are feeling inhibited about speaking Italian. Being born gesticulators, Italians are very receptive to sign language, which is a gift to foreigners wishing to illustrate their shaky Italian with hand mime.

Other fairly uniform Italian traits are an obsession with personal cleanliness and *la bella figura*, (cutting a good figure), which usually includes leading them to dress beyond their means. Italians also pride themselves on their *xenofilia*, an approval of foreigners – though this is wearing thin with the recent influx of legal and illegal immigrants from Albania.

Manners and Customs

The Italian concept of individualism can appear to be incredibly selfish and anti-social to some non-Italians. Loyalty and consideration are reserved for the family or those of one's immediate, intimate circle. This contrasts with the northern European idea of having a responsibility to society at large. Thus litter-dropping in Italy is considerably less frowned upon than in the UK, Switzerland and Scandinavia, since to Italians it is always someone else's (usually the hated state's) problem. In matters of friendship, it is customary for Italians, especially young people and families to go out in a group; one-to-one friendships are less common, although older Italians may disagree. This is changing however, and as usual, there are differing attitudes between the north and south of Italy.

Shaking hands is considered paramount at meetings and social occasions. Social kissing is also reasonably prevalent as in most Mediterranean countries, though the practicalities do vary from country to country. In Italy men and women kiss both their own, and the opposite sex on social occasions; two kisses, one on each cheek, not three as in Russia or France. If you do not feel comfortable with kissing then just shake hands – though holding back from a kiss can make you appear stand-offish and arrogant. On social occasions it is considered good manners to take presents. Generous to a fault themselves, Italians resent meanness in others, so expensive presents are called for, such as quality whisky or champagne, generous bouquets, handmade chocolates or other sweet delicacies.

In Britain it is common to go drinking with your friends, increasingly to the point of excess, as a way of letting off steam. North American attitudes towards alcohol are almost the opposite extreme; lunchtime drinking and hard liquor often being frowned upon. Italians, however, enjoy social drinking but they regard drunkenness as totally unacceptable behaviour. Whilst you may see heroin addicts by the dozen shooting up in public in certain areas of the larger Italian cities, you almost never see a drunkard. Italians release pressure by shouting and gesticulating, which is probably healthier than bottling it up British fashion before indulging in a fit of temper or road rage and cheaper than going to therapy US-style.

Making Friends

Undoubtedly, one of the most rewarding aspects of living and working in a foreign country is meeting host country nationals, making local friends and forming long-lasting friendships. Making friends in a foreign country can take longer than at home, because cultural differences and the language barrier constitute formidable impediments, which means greater effort is required than at home to get to know the locals. Making the time to cultivate host nation friends can be extremely worthwhile, as, once their hearts are won, Italians can be loyal and generous friends. However, despite Italian enthusiasm on first acquaintance, it can take a long time before the Italian mask of formality drops and you are considered part of the family. As already mentioned, there is a formal and an informal version of address, *lei* and *tu*. It should be noted that lei is considered even more formal than the French *vous*, and thus slipping into *tu* without being invited to can cause offence. Likewise *ciao* (hello/goodbye) should never be used with *lei*, use *buon giorno/buona sera* (good morning/afternoon) and *arrivederci/arrivederla* for goodbyes.

Despite the joys of having host national friends, most expatriates find it necessary to have friends of their own nationality. Being able to pass sarcastic comments, make jokes and generally let off steam without the fear of being misunderstood and causing offence is an important aspect of life abroad. A selective list of expatriate social clubs is included later in this chapter.

Georgina Gordon-Ham visited expatriate clubs in Rome
Here in Rome there are clubs for the British, Canadian and Americans. Actually they tend to be mixed nationality as there are a lot of Italian husbands. It's not so easy for a newcomer to socialise with Italians who although open and welcoming are reserved. Playing sports is another good way to socialise. Also, there are two types of foreign communities, those en passage who are here for two or three years and those who live here permanently.

Homosexuality While the narcissistic habits of the Italian male may suggest otherwise, homosexuality in Italy keeps mainly in the closet. It is frowned upon, largely due to the oppression of the Catholic Church and the tradition of machismo in Italian society. The national left-wing gay and lesbian organisation, *Arcigay* (information on www.gay.it), based in Bologna, campaigns against hypocrisy (the Vatican staff includes several homosexual noblemen) and the persecution, which is inflicted on Italian gays. But attitudes are changing slowly. Until recently,In the south of Italy you risked being murdered by your own family or the Mafia if you were not heterosexual. Now Puglia has an openly gay, communist President Nicky Vendola. Rome has a few clubs where gays can meet. The only pink magazine is *Babilonia*. Information on gay life in Italy can be found on websites such as www. gay.it and www.gay.com.

Entertainment and Culture

As already mentioned, entertainment in Italy is always pursued in groups. The idea of eating out or going to a film alone would be strange to Italians, with their group mentality. Single expatriates should therefore get into the habit of collecting telephone numbers at social functions and ringing round, however slight the acquaintance, to see who might be interested in joining them when they fancy a night out.

Municipal websites and tourist offices are a possible source of information on entertainment and cultural events, as are the national newspapers *La Repubblica* and *Corriere della Sera*, both of which publish listings in their weekly magazines.

Italy has a *patrimonio culturale* (cultural heritage) second to none and many outsiders believe the Italian government could do more to conserve it. Like Greece and Turkey Italy has so much heritage lying around and there are so many unscrupulous collectors willing to buy it, it is almost impossible to protect it comprehensively. However, there is no doubting Italian pride in their Classical and Renaissance art and architecture. Italy does not lack exponents in the performing arts either, perhaps most notably in the field of opera, which had a heyday in the nineteenth century, thanks to amongst others, Verdi, Donizetti and Puccini. Likewise, the Italian cinematic tradition, together with the French, is universally accepted as one of the greatest – among modern Italian films worth seeking out are *Il Postino, La Vita è Bella* and *Cinema Paradisio*.

In common with many other European countries, and increasingly so the further south you go, culture in Italy has a general appeal. This contrasts with the elitist reputation of the arts for which Britain in particular is notorious. This may come as a pleasant surprise to foreign residents who can fall back on the arts, especially cinema, as a topic of conversation with Italians of all backgrounds.

Nightlife: Italian city nightlife may not compare with the bright lights of New York, Barcelona or London in terms of quantity, but the *ragazzi* can do their heads in at the huge discos, especially in Emilia, Turin and Milan, which are also some of the venues for rave parties. Elsewhere, as already mentioned the *ragazzi* make do with 'hanging out' in groups which is less effort than making the logistical arrangements necessary for any positive action. Italian teenagers are however, avid consumers of *il fast food*, which hit Italy in the form of American hamburger joints in the late eighties and early nineties. For other Italians, bars with outdoor tables are the main form of nightlife, not that the Italians are great drinkers (see above), but they enjoy the company and the gossip. For those who like music with their whisky, retro jazz and other live music clubs exist in most cities. Also popular are video bars showing non-stop rock videos.

Opera and Classical Music: surprisingly, for a country so closely linked to opera, the season is short – running only from December to May. There are around a dozen important opera houses the best known of which are: *La Scala* (Milan), *Teatro dell'Opera* (Rome), *Teatro Communale* (Florence) and *San Carlo* (Naples). Venice's *La Fenice* was destroyed by fire in 1996 (not for the first time in its long career which began with a fire in 1792). Eight years and 60 million euros later it reopened in November 2004 in all its renowned glory complete with chandeliers, gold leaf and red plush. Less flamboyantly, most provincial towns have an opera season showing productions of a varying standard from reasonable to good.

Despite a venerable musical tradition, there are few Italian musicians of international renown (pianist Maurizio Pollini and several opera greats being the exceptions), and the best symphony orchestras are usually attached to opera houses. Compared with other European countries including Britain and with the big orchestras in North America, the standards of other Italian orchestras are not always high. However, Italy has three outstanding conductors on the international circuit: Riccardo Muti, Claudio Abbado and Carlo Maria Giulini.

A calendar of music festivals in Italy together with links to individual festival sites can be found at www.initaly.com/regions/music.htm.

Cinema: Italian cinema provides rich ground for the enthusiast. Over the years Italian audiences have become very discriminating and Italian films have a reputation for being stylish and sophisticated. Unfortunately for the foreign resident whose Italian is not up to following dialogue, films from the English-speaking world are customarily dubbed into Italian. Cinema listings are given in every newspaper and cinema categories are *Prima Visione* (new release and smart cinema), *Seconda Visione* (older cinema and re-run films) and *Cinema d'Essai* (classical world cinema with original soundtrack). Some cities have *Cinema all'aperto* (open air movies) during the summer. The *Pasquino* cinema (Vicolo del Piede 19, 00153 Rome) in Rome may be worth a visit for nearby expats weary of long Italian-speaking days as it shows a good selection of films in English.

Dedicated film freaks might like to take advantage of AIACE (Italian Cinema-goers' Association) membership, which entitles patrons to discounted tickets on weekdays (not Fridays). Details can be obtained from local cinemas. There are English cinemas also in Milan, Turin, Florence and other major cities.

Main Art and Arts Festivals. *Venice Film Festival:* The Venice Film Festival is held annually, during the first two weeks of September and is one of the big three, the others being Cannes and Berlin. It is however smaller, and therefore less commercially influential, than the other two. The Festival programme is available from the tourist office a few weeks in advance. Festival premieres are held in the *Palazzo del Cinema* and the *Astra* cinemas, and the public can queue for tickets on the day of the performance.

Venice Biennale: The Venice Biennale is a prestigious international exhibition of contemporary art first held in 1895. Now held in even-numbered years from June to September, it has a permanent site in the *Giardini Pubblici*, where exhibits from over forty countries are housed in separate pavilions.

Spoleto Festival dei Duo Mondi: The Spoleto Festival of the Two Worlds is Italy's main international festival of the performing arts including classical music and ballet, held in and around the walled mediaeval town of Spoleto (Umbria), during two months in summer. Further details from the Italian Tourist Office.

Panatenee Pompeiane: The Pompeii music festival is held in the dramatic surroundings of those famous ruins during the last week of August.

Verona Music Festival: One of the oldest Italian annual music and opera festivals, held in the spectacular surroundings of the Roman Arena di Verona from June to August. Further information from the Verona tourist offices: APT, Via Dietro Anfiteatro 6/13;   ☏045 800 5151; www.arena.it.

Sport

The concept of sports like squash and golf as fashionable recreation activities has yet to seize Italy with quite the same force as it has northern Europe and North America. The exception to this is probably cycling, of Tour de France type, which is a popular recreation, especially in the north.

Football, which is played by virtually every man and boy (even the Vatican sports a team), is almost as important as the Church and it is not uncommon for there to be lighting strikes when one of the big clubs or the national team is playing an important game during working hours. The introduction of football to Italy occurred at the turn of the last century, courtesy of British industrialists who imported factory sports clubs as part of their workers' welfare ethos. Sports generally were slow to evolve until Mussolini built many large stadia in the twenties and thirties, thus promoting a cult of the physique which hearkened back to the games of Classical Rome.

In 1960 Rome played host to the Olympic Games which led to the building of Nervi's Palazzo and Palazzeto dello Sport di Roma. However, as in the UK, Italy's would be champions are seriously hampered by a lack of sports provision in the school curriculum. However, unlike the UK, children who want to participate in sports will find plenty of opportunities to do so in their own leisure time. Italy has generous sponsors and a strong cultural bias to enjoy certain sports socially or individually which means that Italy always makes a good showing in international sports (skiing and cycling for instance). The health and fitness boom of the 1980s has also left its mark on Italy and tennis clubs and gymnasia have mushroomed. However, there is always the sneaking suspicion that the attraction of such places for Italians who are too stylish for their own good, is that they provide a place to hang out and show off their designer sports gear first, and their toned bodies second.

Cycling: The Italians, especially in the north, have taken to *il ciclismo* (cycling) in much the same way as the French. The Italian version of the *Tour de France* is the *Giro d'Italia*. The majority of the recreational ciclisti can be spotted at weekends, crouched over Bianchi or Campagnolo (Campy) racing bikes in the Po Valley.

Football: To the foreigner Italian football *il calcio* is perhaps best known for its 1982 World Cup win and ability to buy the hottest foreign players for mind-boggling sums and then find they have feet of clay. Maradona livened up Napoli for a while before his cocaine habit led to his being sent back to Argentina, while Lazio (Rome) are probably regretting the day they ever signed up the auto-destructive 'Gazza'. Most of the top league teams (known as *Serie A*) are in the north where big cities have two teams each: Turin has Juventus and Torino, Milan has Internazionale and AC Milan and Rome has Roma and Lazio. The fans (*i tifosi*) are noisy and boisterous but need only their Latin blood rather than an alcohol transfusion to galvanise them.

Until 1996 Italian football clubs were non-profit organisations. Now that the Italian government has allowed them to raise profits, which they desperately need to improve facilities, some have been doing so on the financial markets and others are doing so via the stock exchange. With huge profits to be made from football products and with Italians keener than most to buy them, any club that believes it can make a profit (which many have not done previously) by converting to a business and then listing on the stock exchange is likely to do so at the earliest opportunity. A stipulation of the stock exchange, however, is that any company has to show three consecutive years of profit in order to qualify for stock market flotation.

Tickets for matches can be obtained from local stadia or team headquarters, well before the game and are standing (*in tribuna), non numerato* or *numerato.*

Motor Racing: After football, motor racing is Italy's second national sport – speed and Italians go together. Throughout motoring history the Italians have produced some of the world's most thoroughbred sports cars: Bugatti, Ferrari and Alfa Romea to name a few. Originally, only Italian aristocrats could afford such cars and the sport of motor racing. However, out of these illustrious beginnings such classic races as the *Mille Miglia and the Targa Florio*, which takes place in Sicily, were born. The best known Italian racing circuit is probably Monza, just outside Milan. San Marino also hosts a Grand Prix circuit .

English-Language Clubs

At any age, socialising in a foreign country requires a certain amount of innovative thinking to locate people with similar interests who you can communicate with. Expats on a short-term posting will find many clubs and societies aimed at them – i.e. those suffering from culture shock, struggling to learn Italian and trying to explore as much of Italy as is humanly possible in the few short years they will be living there. Such clubs can be great sources of information, friends and cultural sanctuary, where expats can meet and put the stresses and strains of expatriate life into perspective.

For retired people and other non-working expatriates, who are at liberty to follow their own interests at their own speed, whenever they are inclined, few countries compare to Italy in the available range historical and artistic related pursuits (see *Hobbies* section in the *Retirement* chapter). However, despite there being plenty of options for activities and hobbies, expatriate clubs and associations of permanent foreign residents spring up to fulfill the expatriate's need to mix and socialise with people in the same position as themselves and who speak the same language. Italian life may be a dream come true amongst olive groves, vineyards and beautiful Tuscan scenery populated by welcoming and friendly locals, but the reality is that on occasions, there are feelings of frustration and isolation. Those considering a permanent move to, or retirement in Italy should seriously consider where and how they are going to maintain an active social life with locals and other foreigners.

Whether you decide to revive a long-neglected passion for Scottish dancing, cultivate a dormant theatrical talent, learn to play bridge, or even if you simply wish to share some of your time and experiences with other expatriates over an espresso or a stronger beverage, then the list provided below should be a good starting point in your search for an English medium social life. Other social reference points include International Schools, Churches and Chambers of Commerce. These have been listed elsewhere in this book, or they are easily found through telephone directories and expatriate websites (www.expatexchange.com, www.expatnetwork.com, etc.). The Federation of American

Women's Clubs Overseas has seven branches in Italy (see below for details). The British, Canadian, Australia and American embassies and consulates should be able to provide the address of the various expatriate clubs for their nationals in the area they cover. The organization *American Citizens Abroad*, (www.aca.ch; e-mail acage@aca.ch) has local affiliates in Rome, Sorrento, Palermo and there is a list of Anglophone clubs and groups in Italy at www.euroexpats.com/index.php?italy_clubs_and_groups and at www.newcomersclub.com/it.html.

Useful addresses – English-speaking clubs

Bari: *The International Women's Club of Bari*, Via Petrarca 2, I-70010 Adelfia; ☎08 04592672.Florence, Genoa, Milan, Palermo, Rome, Turin and Vercelli.

Bologna: *The International Women's Forum* for international women who speak English: www.iwfbologna.org.

Cagliari: *Associazione Italia Inghilterra:* Via Machiavelli 97, 09100 Cagliari, Sardinia; ☎070-402835; fax 070-402966.

Florence: *British Institute Library and Cultural Centre*, Palazzo Lanfredini, Lungarno Guicciardini 9, I-50125 Florence; 055 2677 8270; www.britishinstitute.it.

English Language Library of Florence, voiale redi 49, 50155 Florence; 055 8998089; www.ellf.it.

American International League of Florence, Casella Postale No 33, Via Fratelli Orsi, 50012 Bagno a Riploi; ailo@ailoflorence.org; www.ailoflorence.org.

Genoa: *New-comers' Club:* meets at the Hotel Astor ☎Via delle Palme 16, Nervi, Genoa).

American International Women's Club of Genoa, Via Ribloi 6/7, 16145 Genoa; ☎010 316 179; info@aiwcgenoa.fawco.org.

Italo-Britannica Centre for Cambridge Language Courses and Examinations. Also houses the British Library (13,000 books in English). Same address as the British Consulate (Piazza della Vittoria 15, ☎010-564833). The cultural centre also has other activities.

The Anglican Church: (Piazza Marsala, Genoa).

Milan: *Benvenuto Club for English-speaking ladies of any nationality:* Meet every second Tuesday of the month 10am-3pm at the Circolo A. Volta, Via Giusti 16, 20154 Milan; ☎025468719; benvenutopresident@yahoo.co.uk.

Naples: *American Women's Club of Naples,* ☎ 081 575 0040.

Palermo: *Americans Abroad Palermo*, Via Vaccarini 1, 90146 Palermo; ☎0348 510 4196.

Rome: *The American Women's Association*, c/o Savoy Hotel, via Ludivisi 15, I-00187 Rome; ☎06 4825268; fax 06 482 5268; www.awar.org.

The Commonwealth Club.: ☎06-58330919.

The Luncheon Club of Rome: ☎06-50913274.

Professional Women's Association: ☎06 20404613; www.pwa-milan.org.
Rome Labour Party: tel 06-6384227.
United Nations Women's Guild: ☎06-57056503.
Turin: *Esprit Club*. Contact Peter Allen (☎011-8111623).
American International Women's Club, refer to www.fawco.org for information.
Umbria: *English Speakers Club*, Harry and Margaret Urquhart, San Lorenzo di
    Rabatta 1M, 06070 Cenerate; ☎075 690693.
Varese: *Bienvenuto Club of Varese:*, ☎0332-949815.

Food & Drink

Many myths surround the Italians, and their eating habits are no less liable to
exaggeration or misconception than other aspects of their lives. Admittedly,
whether the pasta is cooked *al dente* (just right) or *una colla* (sticky and
overcooked) is a subject treated with an almost religious reverence. However,
despite the world-famous ice creams, pizzas and pasta dishes, the Italians boast
one of the lowest incidences of heart disease in Europe (and consume less ice
cream than most of their European neighbours). The basis of Italian eating tends
towards quality, not quantity, and as with all matters of Italian life, is subject to
the rigorous demands of *la bella figura* (cutting a fine figure). Just as the majority
of Italians looks upon drunkenness as a disgusting and unnecessary foreign fetish,
obesity is similarly unacceptable, unless accompanied by a corresponding amount
of Pavarotti-like charisma. Even so, it is noticeable these days that the increasing
problem of obesity in western children includes Italy where a recent article in
Corriera della Sera claimed that one in three Italian children is now overweight.

Although every Italian region proclaims the excellence of its own cooking, the
region of Emilia-Romagna is thought by some to boast the finest and richest
of Italian cuisine. However, Tuscany is renowned for its high-quality meat
and Genoa for its herb-based dishes while the food of the south is the most
spicy. The three main meals of the Italian day are treated with varying degrees
of importance. Breakfast, *(colazione)* is usually a frugal offering of croissant
(cornetto) or biscuits *(biscotti)*; although cereals are gaining popularity in the
Italian market. Lunch *(pranzo)* is treated as the main meal of the day in the
southern regions although home-cooked food is increasingly being superseded
by convenience food. Finally, dinner *(cena)*, as in the majority of Mediterranean
countries, is eaten late in the evening, usually between 8pm and 10pm, especially
during the summer months.

Eating Out. Traditional Italian restaurants are signalled by the *ristorante trattoria*
or *pizzeria* signs. Sparse or unpretentious decor is common and does not reflect
on the quality of the food or service. When eating out with Italians you should
offer to split the bill *alla romana* – dividing it by the number of those present.

However, if you have been invited out to dinner, your host or hostess will probably insist on paying the entire bill. As far as giving tips is concerned, service was traditionally added at the customer's discretion, usually at around 10%-15%. These days though, a 10% charge is generally included in the total bill, as is a cover charge per person. The easiest way to tell if service is included is by looking at the bill (*il conto*), it will have *servizio* and *coperto* for service and cover charges respectively.

Slow Food. Italy, more than France which has surrendered to Disney and Macdonalds, is still holding out as a counter culture to the Americanization of Everything. Americans are attracted in Italy by what they miss out on in America, such as fresh produce that has a taste, culinary artisans at work, life in the piazza, and slow food. Slow Food began in Italy and has grown into an international movement (whose symbol is a snail), which now includes Slow Travel. Slow Food is lobbying against genetically modified organisms, and is pro organic food. Also, through its publishing company (*Slow Food Editore*) it produces a range of books which deal, in encyclopaedic fashion, with all the food traditions of Italy, historical and regional. If you want to join the Slow Food Association, buy their publications, or find out where you can eat and drink slow food in your area contact the Slow Food International Office (Via Mendicità 8, 12042 Bra (CN) Italy; ☎(0)172 419611; fax (0)1792 414498; e-mail info@slowfood.it, www. slowfood.com).

Thus, far from fulfilling the image of a nation of pasta-stuffing, wine-guzzling Pavarotti prototypes, the reality of Italian eating habits is far more discerning and infinitely healthier. Italians are still providing a role model for every aspiring *buongustaio* (food and drink connoisseur) the national gastronomic motto seems to be, enjoy, but not to excess. In Italy, Macdonalds is in retreat.

Drinking. As mentioned above, the Italians are not great drinkers and being drunk (*ubriaco*) carries a special disapproval amongst the majority of Italians, which would be thought curious amongst the beer-swilling section of the British pub population. Though drinking wine from a young age is an accepted part of the culture, unlike in the USA. Alcohol sales have flagged in Italy, as mineral water (*acqua minerale*) sales escalate nationwide. Italy is now second only to France in annual consumption of mineral water and is ahead of Germany and Belgium. Another beverage that has taken off in Italy is beer. According to the Italian Statistics Institute, ISTAT, the majority of men and a significant percentage of women now choose beer above wine. This may be a result (or a cause) of the mushrooming of English-style pubs in the larger cites (there are scores in Rome alone). The new pubs appeal mainly to the twenty-something party crowd of cosmopolitan Europeans that can be found in most major commercial cities of Europe. In contrast to the increase in beer sales, the annual consumption of wine is dropping to such a level that the wine marketing board is now advertising it in order to encourage sales. If you prefer wine-bars then look for the signs *cantina or enoteca* above the door.

Wine. Most of Italy is wine country and there is no time to do justice to the many varieties here. Suffice it to say that some areas have gone in for professional production and export while others have kept their traditions and best wines a secret from the outside world. The northwest (Piemonte) is famous for its vermouths and spumantes and purplish wines and barolo and barbera grapes. The north-east, particularly the part under Austrian influence, has gone in for mass production. Probably the best known wines abroad are those from central Italy, especially the Chianti wines from the Tuscan hills between Florence and Siena. Southern Italy has the Neapolitan wines of Ischia, Capri and red and white wines from the area around Mount Vesuvius. Sicily's best-known wine is probably the sweet and treacly Marsala.

WINE LABEL GLOSSARY

DOCG – *Denominazione di Origine Controllata Guarantita*: the highest quality, similar to France's *appellation contrôleé*.
DOC – *Denominazione di Origine Controllata*: the second highest quality.
DS – *Denominazione Semplice* – the equivalent of the French vin de table.
Messo in bottiglia del produttore all'origine: estate-bottled.
Classico: from the central, i.e. best area of the region.
Imbottigliato nello stabilimento della ditta: bottled on the premises of the firm.
Riserva: wine that has been aged for a statutory period.
Wine Colours: Bianco (white), *Rosso* (red), *Rosato* (pink), *Chiaretto* (very light red), *Nero* (very dark red).
Secco: dry.
Amaro: bitter or very dry.
Amabile/Abboccato: medium sweet.
Dolce: very sweet.
Spumante: bubbly.
Frizzante: slightly fizzy.
Vin/Vino santo: sweet dessert wine made from dried grapes.
Stravecchio: very old, mellow.
Vino liquoroso: fortified wine.

SHOPPING

Non-food Shopping

Italy excels in design and manufacturing. It produces exquisite objects of desire for discerning consumers, and Milan is the style capital of the world. No wonder that Americans, from the home of the shopping mall, flock to Italy for a very superior fix of retail therapy. Busloads of Japanese are also disgorged

daily at the Prada factory outlet in Levane (Arezzo). Whether it is shoes in
Vigevano, handbags in Naples, painted crockery at Deruta, glass at Murano,
jewellery in Arezzo or Ferrari cars in Maranello, Italy tempts the consumer with
the best quality products that the globe can offer. Every large town has at least
one shopping centre *(centro commerciale)*, which is up to the best European
or American standards of quality and design. The *Ipercoop* Co-op chain now
dominates the scene. It is a mutual co-operative society which sells everything
from white goods (made in Pordenone), to bread baked fresh on the spot in
wood-fired ovens. Preference is given to local products and goods sourced in
Italy under strict ecological control. *Superal, Conad, Esselunga, Upim, Standa,
Despar* are names of other chains, and *Auchan* from France has partnered *La
Rinascente* of Milan to carve a large niche in the north.

The Small Shops. Back in the ancient city centres the local townsfolk (*borghesia*)
maintain a tradition of dazzling small shops and boutiques which are more alluring
than anything in Bond Street or Fifth Avenue: *Fendi, Furla, Valentino, Gucci,
Versace*, big names or no names – Via Montenapoleone in Milan, Via Condotti
in Rome, Via Tornabuoni in Florence, the Rialto in Venice, the covered arcades
of Bologna – all cities have shopping streets (*corsi*) which attract discreet hordes
of opulent shoppers and gourmets. At the lower end of the social scale weekly or
permanent street markets under awnings supply the needs of locals and tourists
alike in towns and cities throughout Italy.

THE COUNTERFEIT INDUSTRY

Alongside the production of genuine articles, there is a huge sweatshop counterfeit
industry producing cut-price designer-label goods and pirate CD's etc. seemingly
identical with the original, which are sold in the markets, or in the streets by platoons of
'*vu cumprà*' Senagalese pedlars, who respond to ferocious haggling in any language,
'*Vu cumprà?*', their nickname, means 'Wanna buy?'

Everyday Shopping

At a daily level, shops for basic needs, *negozi di prima necessità* – are to be found
in every village or town quarter *rione*.

○ **Food shops** (*alimentari*) are an area in which Italians thrive throughout
the world. A slicing machine will dominate the counter for salamis, hams
and cold cuts. Most produce and wine will be seasonal, and rolls, *panini*
or sandwiches can be ordered expressly, put on the scales, and paid for by
weight.

○ **Papershop** (*edicola*) sells papers, magazines, stationery.

○ **Tobacconist** (*il tabacchaio,* or *la tabaccheria* is marked with a big T sign which stands for *tabacchi* (tobaccos) which is what the English also call the shop. Tobacco is no longer a state monopoly but only T-licensed shops can sell it through some complicated distribution deal with the Italian Federation of Tobacconists. As a state monopoly outlet the *tabacchaio/tabaccheria/tabacchi* is also the still the place for postage stamps, official forms, bus tickets and historically also salt (but not any longer).

○ **Chemist's shop** (*farmacia*) dispenses medical advice as well as medicines, but does not handle photographic products.

○ **Houseware shop** (*casalinghi*) sells anything for the house from electric blankets to dustpans.

○ **Gift shop** (*articoli da regalo*) sells souvenirs, crockery, cutlery etc, beautifully packaged.

○ **The draper** (*merceria*) or haberdashery is fast disappearing from the scene.

○ **A laundry** is a *lavanderia.*

○ **A dry cleaner** is a *lavanderia a secco.*

○ **A barber** is a *barbiere* where the men talk.

○ **A hairdresser** is a *parruchiera* where the women talk.

○ **A butcher** is a *macelleria* which supplies locally sourced meat.

○ **A fishmonger** is a *pescheria*, for fresh fish from the coast,

○ **A upholsterer** is a *tappezzeria* for cushions and curtains,

○ **A picture framer** is a *cornicaio*,

○ **A bookshop** is a *libreria*

○ **A shoe shop** is a *calzoleria*

○ **A bakery** is a *panificio* where you can order cakes and bread at all hours,

○ **A perfume shop** is a *profumeria*,

○ Other shops are tailor *sartoria*, paints and DIY *mesticheria* (Tuscany), delicatessen *pizzicheria*.

Most shops are open from 8.30am to 7.30pm and close for three hours or more at 1pm for lunch. They are closed by law for one day in the week.

Sarah Rasmer found that the shopping hours took some getting used to
Business hours are improving, but can still be frustrating. Many government offices are only open for a few hours in the mornings. It is always a good idea to call ahead to check business hours. Banks are open from 8:30-12:30 or 1pm and again between 3 and 4pm. Most shops are open from 9am through tp 12:30 or 1:00 pm, and open again from 3:30 or 4 to 7pm (4:30 or 5-7:30/8pm in summer). Each city designates one morning or afternoon a week that the shops close. Small, family run businesses close for funerals and vacations; they will leave a note on their door to notify their customers.

> Most businesses close for at least a couple of weeks in August. Many shops are opening on Sunday afternoons; and some do not close for lunch. All Tabacchi shops, which sell various items like stamps and prepaid phone cards in addition to cigarettes, remain open for lunch.

Most villages have a weekly vegetable stall *fruttivendolo* and fish van *pescivendolo*.

Bargains. One way to have your cake and eat it, in this case have designer clothes but not pay the outrageous prices, is to buy from factory outlets. Expat groups and websites are good places to find out about the best places to shop, as is the website, www.made-in-italy.com, which is a good source of information about shopping in general as well as factory outlets. Also worth a look is www.italydaily.it/Italian_life/Shopping/luglio/outlets.shtml and www.dolcevita.com/outlets/outlets.html. The following publications are guides to bargain shopping in Italy and worth looking at: the best-selling bargain finder which details over 1,200 outlets *Lo Scoprioccasioni,* (5th edition 2004) is now published in English (ISBN 88-86132-13-1) at €16,50 (www.scoprioccasioni.it/eng_chi_siamo.html by Editoriale Shopping Italia S.r.l. They also arrange day shopping trips in Milan, Venice, Florence etc. (info@scoprioccasion.it; tel/fax 0344 86176). In addition, the annual outlet guide *La Guida agli Spacci* by Marina Martorana lists over 2000 outlets 2004/05 edition €12 from Italy's online bookstore www.unilibro.com; also try www.guidaspacci.it.

SHOPPING GLOSSARY

abbligliamenti	clothes
agenzia di viaggi	travel agency
calzoleria/calzatura	shoeshop/footwear
calzolaio	cobbler/shoe repairer
cartoleria	stationery/bookshop
confezione	clothes
drogheria	grocer
ferramenta	hardware
fioraio	florist
fotocopisteria/typografia	photocopying/printing
frutta e verdura/fruttivendolo/	fruit and vegetables/greengrocer
giocattoli	toys
gioielleria	jeweller
ipermercato	hypermarket
latteria	dairy
lavaggio a secco	dry cleaning
oreficeria	jeweller (lit. goldsmith)
orologiaio/orologeria	watchmaker/repairer
ottico	optician
panificio/panetteria/panettiere	breadshop/bakery/baker
pasticceria	cake/pastry shop

pastificio	fresh pasta
pelleteria	leather goods
rosticceria	shop selling cooked food to take away
salumeria	delicatessen
sarto/sarta	tailor/dress-maker
surgelati	frozen food

Each city has one morning or afternoon a week when the shops close – in Ferrara for example, the shops close on Thursday afternoons. Many shops, though, are opening on Sunday afternoons and some do not close for lunch. Small, family run businesses will also close for funerals and vacations and they will leave a note on their door to notify their customers about the length of the closure. Most businesses close for at least a couple of weeks for a summer vacation in August. All *tabacchi* shops, which sell various items like stamps and prepaid phone cards in addition to cigarettes, remain open for lunch. There are fruit and vegetable shops in most neighbourhoods in the city where the shopkeeper will pick out the produce for you, so it is best to find one you like, and frequent it, as they give the best selection to regular customers.

Pasta is the universal diet of all Italians. In the north *polenta* (a porridge made from maize meal) and rice are traditional, although these days polenta is eaten only on special occasions or as a dish provided in rural restaurants. This is mainly because preparation is too time-consuming for modern Italians. Pasta is however common as a basic constituent of main daily meals. Italian meat is patchy in quality as it often is in countries that suffer from a lack of rain and green grass. Pork and famous pork products, like *prosciutto crudo* from the north, are excellent but much of the veal (*vitello*) is imported. Beef (*vitellone*) is considered best when it comes from Tuscany. In the mountainous regions of the south, prime lamb (*agnello*) is produced. Italians also eat farmed rabbits and fowl, and traditionally, a variety of small birds (including skylarks *allodole,* blackbirds *merli,* sparrows *passeri* and thrushes *tordi*) that will have little attraction for British and North American diners. These small songbirds are usually trapped with nets and sold skewered. This last activity is highly illegal but nonetheless is carried out by poachers while the Forest Service and environmental volunteers try to prevent it. It makes one wonder whether Marco Polo took the dish with him to China, or brought it back to Italy. After grilling, each bird constitutes a small and bony mouthful. Meat is purchased from a *macelleria* and poultry from a *polleria*.

One of the other main dietary constituents, cheese, comes in many delicious specialities, a number of which (e.g. Parmesan, Gorgonzola and Mozzarella) will already be familiar to most expatriates. Parmesan increases in price with age, the most expensive being *stravecchione* (very old) and no self-respecting Italian would dream of buying it ready grated. Sheeps milk cheeses (*pecorino*) are specialities of Sardinia and the Tuscany region. If you are in doubt about what cheese to buy a good cheese monger (*formaggiaio*) will always let you taste before buying.

If there are some consumables that you have grown up with and for which there is no Italian substitute (Marmite, digestive biscuits, Bird's custard, Maple Syrup, etc.), or the substitute is just not the same then there are a few specialist shops that stock these and other familiar items. Another good reason to join an expatriate club is to find the best place to buy your favourite imported food items. The availability of these items can be variable and when you see a rare item it is often a good idea to buy it on the spot, because it probably will not be there next week.

The online shop, www.expatshopping.co.uk, will deliver many of the delicacies that expatriate desire, though they do have a minimum quantity, so a joint order with friends can share the burden of postage.

METRICATION

CONVERSION CHART

LENGTH (NB 12inches 1 foot, 10 mm 1 cm, 100 cm 1 metre)

inches	1	2	3	4	5	6	9	12		
cm	2.5	5	7.5	10	12.5	15.2	23	30		

cm	1	2	3	5	10	20	25	50	75	100
inches	0.4	0.8	1.2	2	4	8	10	20	30	39

WEIGHT (NB 14lb = 1 stone, 2240 lb = 1 ton, 1,000 kg = 1 metric tonne)

lb	1	2	3	5	10	14	44	100	2246	
kg	0.45	0.9	1.4	2.3	4.5	6.4	20	45	1016	

kg	1	2	3	5	10	25	50	100	1000	
lb	2.2	4.4	6.6	11	22	55	110	220	2204	

DISTANCE

mile	1	5	10	20	30	40	50	75	100	150
km	1.6	8	16	32	48	64	80	120	161	241

km	1	5	10	20	30	40	50	100	150	200
mile	0.6	3.1	6.2	12	19	25	31	62	93	124

VOLUME

1 litre = 0.2 UK gallons   1 UK gallon = 4.5 litres
1 litre = 0.26 US gallons   1 US gallon = 3.8 litres

CLOTHES

UK	8	10	12	14	16	18	20
Europe	36	38	40	42	44	46	48
USA	6	8	10	12	14	18	

SHOES

UK	3	4	5	6	7	8	9	10	11
Europe	36	37	38	39	40	41/42	43	44	45
USA	2.5	3.3	4.5	5.5	6.5	7.5	8.5	9.5	10.5

Italy uses the metric system in all respects: the standards of measurement are recognisable to English speakers. Temperature is always measured in celsius.

In the long run it is much easier to learn and think in metric rather than to always try to convert from metric to imperial. To facilitate this process a metric conversion table (including clothes and shoe size conversions is) given below.

In all cases measurements are quoted as a decimal and not a fraction; for example, on road signs, 'Napoli 12.7 km'.

TIME

The 24-hour clock system is used for all times in Italy. For example, shop opening hours are given as 09.00 à 17.30 (9am to 5.30pm) or train times as 20.20 (8.20pm) or 00.15 (12.15am).

Italy follows Central European Time (CET) which is Greenwich Mean Time (GMT) +2 hours in summertime. Summer time lasts from the last Sunday in March at 1am to the last Sunday in October at 1am, when clocks are advanced one hour. Consequently Italy is one hour ahead of the UK, whether the UK is operating to Greenwich Mean Time (GMT) or British Summer Time (BST).

PUBLIC HOLIDAYS

Note that on Italian national holidays (*feste*) offices, shops, banks, post offices and schools are all closed. Whether museums, parks, etc, are closed will vary from region to region:

PUBLIC HOLIDAYS

1 January (New Year's Day; *Capodanno*)
6 January (Epiphany; *La Befana*)
Easter Monday (*Pasquetta*)
25 April (Liberation Day; *Anniversario della Liberazione*)
1 May (Labour Day; *primo maggio*)
15 August *(Assumption; Ferragosto)*
1 November (All Saints'; *Ognissanti*)
8 December (Immaculate Conception; *L'Immacolata Concezione*)
25 December (Christmas Day; *Natale*)
*26 December (*Boxing Day; *Santo Stefano*)
The festival days listed below are held to honour each specific city's own patron saint. Shops and offices usually remain open on these days although it is as well to check with the local tourist board for specific information.
25 April (Venice, St Mark)
24 June (Turin, Genoa and Florence; St John the Baptist)
29 June (Tome, St Peter)
23-25 July (Caltagirone in Sicily, St James)

26 July (island of Ischia in the Bay of Naples, St Anne)
19 September (Naples, St Gennaro)
4 October (Bologna, St Petronius)
6 December (Bari, St Nicholas)
7 December (Milan, St Ambrose)

RETIREMENT

CHAPTER SUMMARY

- A modest pension that is just enough to survive on in the UK would probably not be enough to live on in Italy.
- Italy offers those who can bear the higher costs of living abroad an enviable quality of life in terms of climate, history, culture and pace of life.
- Those considering retiring to Italy are advised to try it out gradually and become acclimatized for several longish periods that should ideally include both the cold of winter and the heat of summer, before making a final decision to retire there.
- To obtain the *permesso di soggiorno* (residence permit) you will need to be able to prove that you have sufficient funds to live on.
- Those entitled to a British pension can arrange to collect it in Italy: it will be subject to Italian tax.
- EU nationals resident in Italy are entitled to use the Italian state healthcare system, but this is not as comprehensive as the UK National Health Service. Although the standard of doctors is usually very high, the standard of state hospitals varies; those in the north being mostly better than those in the South of Italy.

Anyone considering Italy as a country to retire to, will probably have taken into account that Italy really is unique and replete with frescos, fragments of ancient civilizations, culture and *bella figura* (personal aestheticism). It is definitely Italian, with little allowance made for the needs of foreigners who want to have what they had at home, with a bit more sun. So, if you are after an abundant supply of fish and chips, English beer and imported foodstuffs, or lots of people who speak English, try Spain! Many retirees in Italy also retain homes in their country of origin, splitting their time between the two countries each year. The bulk of the estimated 30,000 retired expatriates in Italy are Britons, who have planted themselves in the beautiful country spots of Tuscany and Umbria, where living and property costs continue their upward spiral. These areas are well away from the industrial centres of Milan and Turin and also the services associated with large centres of population. Despite being remote and rural, it is worth remembering that in the northern regions of Piedmont, Lombardy, Veneto, etc., the cost of living is considerably higher than that in the UK, other European countries and North America. Living abroad also brings additional costs, not just bigger versions of what you are used to – international telephone costs, medical insurance, travel to and from your home country, administration costs and internal travel to regularise your status. Survival, therefore, on a modest pension that just about allows you to live in your current country would be difficult in Italy, if not impossible. There is also a noticeable lack of welfare and after-care services for the elderly throughout Italy, which is especially true in rural areas.

However, potential retirees will almost certainly find the excellent climate and the easy-going nature of the people, the progressive upgrading of the infrastructure and the lively expatriate community, combined with an ambition to make the most of Italian art and culture are sufficient to justify retirement in Italy. Additionally, away from Umbria and Tuscany or the Italian Riviera (Liguria), property bargains are still to be found in some of the less-discovered regions of Le Marche and Puglia and even further south.

THE DECISION TO RETIRE ABROAD

Most importantly, anyone considering retiring to Italy must be able to afford the move financially. No less vital is being aware of the stresses involved in moving to another country and the ultimate effect lack of proximity to friends and family will have on your wellbeing.

Also essential before moving to a new country under your own auspices is the willingness to upgrade language skills, in this case Italian (see *The Italian Language* in the *Daily Life* chapter). Trying to negotiate the bureaucracy in any foreign country without being able to understand the language is bound to make things problematic. You may be able initially to manage with amateur interpreters but eventually you will have to make friends in the language of the country that has adopted you in your retirement.

As many decisions to move abroad grow out of a love of the country discovered through past holidays of only a few weeks at a time it can be a good idea to have an extended stay in the country before making the final decision to complete a permanent move. A six-month stay, perhaps through a home swap or a long-term rental (see *Setting up Home*) that should ideally include the winter period or the heat of summer, is the minimum time you should allow yourself to clarify the reality of retiring abroad. Ideally the stay should be in the area in which you are most interested, so that you can get to know it really well and do your research before buying property and moving there. If you have yet to decide which region to move to, a succession of more long-term stays in various areas would also be possible.

> **George and Wendy Scott bought a farmhouse in Le Marche after staying in the region and making friends with the locals**
> *In the summer of last year we were visiting Le Marche (Ascoli Piceno region) and staying in an agriturismo which we found in Karen Brown's* Charming Italian Bed & Breakfast *book. As a consequence of establishing warm friendships with a number of talented people running the enterprise, the natural beauty of the countryside and the attractive old hilltop towns, we decided to search for a suitable property for purchase and redevelopment. We chose one in a dilapidated state but with stunning views, and it was a bonus to find that it came with 12 acres of land partly covered in olive trees. We chose a local geometra because he lives in the small town where we are registered in the local commune and he is one of the friends we made during our stay. This is a long term project and we hope that we will eventually recoup some of the costs by taking the overspill from the agriturismo where we originally based ourselves.*

Some people precede their move to Italy with long holidays spent there over a number of years and which may mean they already own a property in Italy. If funds are not a problem, purchasing a second home in Italy and sharing time between it and your home country residence can ease the transition until you decide where you want to settle permanently, or allow you to have the best of both worlds if the decision is too hard to make.

Residence Requirements

Anyone intending to retire to Italy must first obtain a permit to stay (*permesso di soggiorno*) from the local police station (*questura*) three months after arrival in Italy. The *permesso di soggiorno* will be renewed after a five year period and annually thereafter on condition that proof of funds are presented in the form a bank letter or statement to the sum of approximately £12,000 (US$17,000) each year. The basic regulations regarding permanent residence both before and after leaving your home country can be found in the *Residence and Entry Regulations* chapter. Additional documents required from retirees by the *questura* in Italy include proof of retirement or old age pension, indicating the amount received monthly and proof from a bank in Italy that you have opened an account with them. Non-EU nationals must also prove that they have private health insurance; whereas EU nationals can register for state health care. However, note that it is now possible for non-EU nationals also to use national health care assistance for a nominal fee, but this happens on a regional basis (Lombardy is one region where it may be possible) and is by no means standard practice.

CHOOSING AND BUYING A RETIREMENT HOME

The main and very obvious points to make regarding buying a retirement property in Italy is to choose something within your financial scope, which is suitable for year-round living for many years to come. You will need to keep a firm grasp on reality when it comes to house prices, the lowest prices are often for derelict, isolated farmhouses in need of major or total renovation. This may be perfect as a project for someone with plenty of enthusiasm, energy and financial backing and with strong hermitic tendencies, but inappropriate for someone retiring to Italy to make new friends and indulge in all the possibilities of what Italy has to offer. To get the most out of what the Americans call, 'the third age', you need a comfortable, but not necessarily palatial Italian home to do it from. The other extreme is to find yourself tempted by something beyond what you can really afford, which may then become a financial liability. Further information regarding property prices throughout Italy and a list of agents can be found in the *Setting up Home* chapter.

Most people will have to budget carefully the expenses involved in moving abroad and will need to take into consideration the running and upkeep costs of the property in question. For instance, the *palazzi* (blocks of flats containing several different apartments) where maintenance and renovation costs are paid for on a communal basis may work out more expensive than you think, and you may not have a choice as to when renovation is done and needs to be paid for. A budget should allow for these maintenance costs, which are continuous and an inescapable if you are to keep a home in reasonable repair.

Proximity to health services and other facilities is also an important consideration for anyone reliant on public transport.

Once you have decided where you want to establish your home for retiring to, you will need to follow all of the procedures regarding property purchase that are described in full in *Setting Up Home*.

HOBBIES

Once you have settled into your new home, and obtained all the permits and documents you need to reside legally in Italy, thoughts of socialising will become pre-eminent as will the pursuit of hobbies and interests. Italy offers a host of possibilities in this area, which is one reason why so many people retire to the country.

Horticulture. Keen gardeners will find that Italy offers a variety of gardening climates and the Italians themselves are renowned as horticulturists and Italian-type villa gardens are copied all over the warmer parts of the western world. You can derive hours of pleasure not only from growing exotic plants in different growing conditions, but also learning the Italian names for the common garden and wild plants: *giglio* (lily), *papavero* (poppy) and *violaciocca gialla* (wallflower) to name but three. If vegetables are your interest you can get an idea of the varieties grown in Italy from the website for Seeds from Italy (www.growitalian.com) and you can order seeds via the online, illustrated catalogue of Franchi Sementi (www.franchisementi.it), one of Italy's two biggest seed companies. A list of seed producers all over Italy, and their postal and email addresses can be found at www.sementi.it/acrobat/orto.pdf.

Remember that although it is legal to take seeds into Italy, it is against the law to import plants and bulbs without a phyto-sanitary certificate issued DEFRA. An inspector will have to see the plants in question and an inspection can be arranged with a local office through DEFRA, Plant Health Division (Room 340 Foss House, Kings Pool, 1-2 Peasholme Green, York YO1 7PX; ☎01904-455174; fax 01904-455163; www.defra.gov.uk/planth/phnews/service.htm; e-mail planthealth.info@defra.gsi.gov.uk). One potential problem for the keen gardener in Italy is the water shortage that affects most of the country. There are solutions for drought areas, such as recycling water used in the kitchen and for bathing to the garden and also using well water if your property has a source.

Once you have grown your vegetables you will want to know how to and what to cook them with so you can go on Italian cookery courses in Italy or buy Italian cookbooks: www.italianculinary.it and www.italianculinary.it/cookbooks1.htm.

Sports. For those with sporting inclinations, activities abound both strenuous and gentle. Cycling (*ciclismo*) is a particularly popular national sport but if this is too energetic and you would rather be a spectator, there is plenty on offer from rugby and football to motor racing. For further details on sport see the *Daily Life* section.

Heritage. Lovers of old properties, ancestral homes and formal gardens will find Italy an endless source of marvels. The Italian equivalent of the National Trust in the UK and historical associations in the US, the FAI (Foundation for the Italian Environment) organises trips to the many places of interest which form Italy's almost inexhaustible architectural heritage. Although thirty years old and with a membership of 60,000 (compared to the National Trust's two million), interest in the FAI is still growing. Joining a local FAI branch is a good way to meet English-speaking, educated retired Italians with interests in common. The annual membership cost is minimal and entitles members to free entry to all FAI properties and a regular newsletter, as well as the outings mentioned above.

Study. Studying is another way of enhancing retirement. The most obvious subjects are those connected with Italy itself, the language and culture. Over 40 American universities and colleges run programmes in Italy. The US Embassy in Rome's website (www.usembassy.it) maintains a full list of them, which is accessible on their website. For something more ambitious you can enrol with the UK based Open University through their office in Milan (OU Representative, The Open University, CP1141, 20101 Milan Milan; ☎02-813 8048; fax 02-813 8048; e-mail jpollard@open.ac.uk). The Open University offers over 150 courses which can lead to a degree and many others that lead to diplomas and certificates. Studying for pleasure does not have to result in an academic qualification however and there are numerous organisations in Italy and around the world that offer courses, both in traditional classrooms, via correspondence or online through the internet. To find out more on the internet, key in 'lifelong learning' into Google or other search engine and see what a huge choice comes up.

Useful Addresses – Continuing Education

CineHollywood Srl: via P. Reginaldo Guiliani 8, Milan 20125; ☎02 661 04935; fax 02 661 03899; e-mail info@cinehollywood.com. Distributor in Italy of learning materials from the Open University's courses (books, videos, software, audio cassettes).

Edupoint.com a California-based online (www.edupoint.com) marketplace for continuing education providing centralised access to thousands of learning opportunities worldwide.

Useful Contacts – History, Culture and National Parks

Gruppi Archaeologici d'Italia: Via Degli Scipioni 30/A, 00192 Rome; fax 06-39734449; www.gruppiarcheologici.org. Season tickets and subscription to the magazine *Archaeologica Ritrovata.*. Details of archaeological volunteer work on the site above, and you can find your nearest gruppo archeolgoico at www.gruppiarcheologici.org/sedigai/sedilocali.htm.

Culturalia: www.culturalia.info/italiano/home.html. Magazine for cultural tourism in Italy available on subscription from abbonamenti@aculturali.info or distributed free to '*luoghi della cultura*' (cultural sites and places connected with culture).

Federazione Italiana Degli Amici Dei Musei (FIDAM): c/o Carla Giuducci Bonannivia Aurelio Nicolodi 2, 50137 Florence; fax 055 262 5702. Friends of Italian Museums Federation; www.fionline.it

Fondo per l'Ambiente (FAI): www.fondoambiente.it/English/How-to-sup/ volunteer/index.htm and www.fondoambiente.it/English/. Italian foundation that acquires properties (from castles and abbeys to miniature theatres and kiosks) of architectural, artistic, cultural or environmental significance and opens them to the public. Annual membership fee for members. Also takes on volunteers for events at its properties.

L'Istituto Italiano dei Castelli: www.castit.it. National Secretariat, Via G A Borghese 14, 20154 Milano; tel/fax 02 347 237; e-mail segreteria,castit@tin. it. For the historical, archaeological and artistic study of castles and fortified monuments and their restoration and re-animation. Magazine: *Giornate Nazionali dei Castelli.* Regional branches with contacts given on website.

Italia Nostra: www.italianostra.org. Created in 1955 to raise public awareness of the need to conserve the urban historical treasures and to promote environmental concern in the countryside. Also, to arrange the donation of art collections etc. to the State, in lieu of tax, and promote the public acquisition of historic buildings. Ordinary membership €31 per year.

Parks Italy: Italy has a wealth of natural as well as cultural assets and many stunning national parks to visit and walk in. Website www.parks.it has a fund of information on itineraries and opening times and is the organisation that covers all parks from national ones to protected marine areas. Membership and parks magazine (*Parchi*) costs €28 annually. It is also possible to find out about volunteer work in parks from the website.

Touring Club Italy (TCI): www.touringclub.it/international_TCI/0_join. asp. Founded in 1894 as a cycling touring club. Exists to promote all kinds of tourism. Membership €25 (2005). Members get discounts including on TCI books including *Italy*, which has nearly 1000 descriptions of towns and landmarks, 120 maps and plans of cities and historic sites and discount on entry to museums, historic buildings and sites.

Entertainment

If you are one of those for whom life without television would be unthinkable, even if only to keep up with world outside your country retreat, BBC Prime, BBC World, CNN International and Sky TV are available in Italy and provide the best of British and American entertainment and news services. Choices Direct, Amazon.co.uk and Amazon.com can also supply English language videos and DVDs, by mail order, to Italy too – see the *Daily Life* section earlier in the book for further details.

Alternatively, there is BBC Radio and Voice of America. Most countries operate an Overseas Service for their own nationals too, but the BBC World Service, relayed by satellite and broadcast on FM in many parts of Italy, is still in a class of its own. British newspapers are expensive abroad, tend to arrive late and are obtainable only in the large towns – though many are now available online (as is the BBC news) and some also offer weekly editions for overseas readers that summarise the daily editions. Listening to the World Service is therefore the easiest and cheapest way to keep in touch with home, especially if you are not on the internet. By day, reception is best on higher frequencies (15-21 mHz) but at night the lower frequencies (around 6-7 mHz) are preferable while early in the morning and evening, the middle bands of 9-11 MHZ provide the best quality reception. The BBC broadcasts continuously over a 24-hour period, 365 days a year. Programmes and frequency charts can be found on the internet at www.bbc.co.uk/worldservice or e-mail www.worldservice@bbc.co.uk. This site lists all overseas radio programmes as well as listings for BBC Prime and BBC World (see above and below) and much additional information such as a wavelength guide, useful tips on reception, suitable radios to buy and similar matters.

BBC World is a 24-hour international news and information free to air television channel which can be received in Italy. A monthly programme guide is given in *BBC On Air* (see above).

For a list of some English-speaking clubs in individual cities, see *Social Life* in the *Daily Life* chapter.

FINANCIAL CONSIDERATIONS

Pensions

Italy is well-known for having one of the highest European rates of expenditure on social security in general, and pensions in particular. 70% of social protection expenditure goes on pensions (compared with 49% in France and 52% in the UK). In 1998 and 2004 the government, after many months of consultations introduced radical changes. These included making pension requirements in the public sector the same as for the private sector i.e. employees in both sectors will have to pay contributions for the same number of years (40) in order to claim a full pension. The changes are being phased in gradually until parity is achieved in 2008. Italy will probably still come out well on top over the UK as regards pension entitlements; for one thing, the basic state pension is indexed to the cost of living. This parity of the public and private systems will end the extremely high number of state workers claiming substantial pensions after 'retiring early' at the age of 50. During the phasing in of the parity reforms between 2004 and 2008, workers may opt to work for longer than the legal pensionable age and obtain a so-called super-bonus.

One of the reasons that pensions (*pensione di vecchiaia*) were so high was because they were on a sliding scale, rises of 2% of each individual's earnings for every year in which contributions were made. For instance, someone who had worked for 30 years received an Italian pension of 60% of their earnings in the five years prior to retirement; after working in Italy for 15 years, a worker could earn 30% of his or her salary in pension. By contrast, British workers have only been eligible for a full UK pension after approximately 40-45 years of work and this represents only approximately 18% of average earnings. Moreover, the employee's contribution in Italy used to be less than 2% of earnings (it is now 8.89%), compared with 9% in the UK. The minimum contribution period to result in entitlement to an Italian pension is now five years (but was formerly as little as three months). From 2008, 40 years of contributions will be required to receive a full old-age pension. Until 2007 the retirement age for women and men is 57 to 60. From 2008 it will be 65 for men and 60 for women with 40 years of contributions, regardless of employment age. Once a worker has paid contributions for the minimum period, there is an absolute right to receive the pension wherever he or she lives in the EU. The pension is paid by the country in which it was earned at the appropriate pension age. If someone has not worked abroad for the minimum period to entitle them to any pension, then another rule comes into effect and calculates what is called a pro rata pension. This is the theoretical pension they would have earned if they had worked abroad for a longer period, which is then scaled down in proportion to the actual time spent working there.

Pension challenges for the future in Italy include the highest rate of old-age dependency in the EU. It is hoped that by reducing the generosity of the basic old-age pension by raising the necessary number of contribution years and by encouraging the development of private contribution programmes, financial disaster will be averted. However, the low unemployment rate amongst women in Italy is likely to cause them in particular, financial hardship in the future.

UK Citizens. UK citizens and those entitled to a UK pension or benefits who are living in Italy and want to receive their pension or benefits in that country should apply to The International Pension Centre (IPC), Newcastle-upon-Tyne NE98 1BA (☎0191-218 7777; fax 0191-218 7293; www.thepensionservice.gov.uk) who will send out a form which should then be taken to the nearest social security office (*Istituto Nazionale di Previdenza Sociale INPS*) in Italy. The INPS will then make the necessary arrangements for your pension/benefits to be transferred to Italy. If you became entitled to a UK pension before leaving for Italy, this can either be paid to you in Italy or in the UK.

If you reach retirement age after taking up residence in Italy, you can arrange to have your UK pension paid into your Italian (or a UK) bank account each month. Anyone who moves to Italy before reaching retirement age should continue to pay voluntary National Insurance contributions in the UK in order to qualify for a British state pension. Depending on which country you have paid the majority of contributions in, you are eligible to draw the pension in either country. Note that pensions are not frozen at the level they reached on arrival in Italy and instead the pension will rise in accordance with any increases that take effect in the UK. Retired expatriates in most other non-EU countries (with the exception of Mauritius, the USA and Switzerland) are not so lucky as pensions in these cases are frozen at the level levied in the year the expatriate left the UK to retire abroad. Leaflet SA29 available from the International Pension Centre and post offices in the UK, provides details on EU pension and social security legislation.

It would be advisable to inform the Inland Revenue office with which you last dealt about your plans; they will supply leaflet IR138 *Living or Retiring Abroad? A guide to UK tax on your UK income and pension* or you can contact the Inland Revenue's specialist office for non-residents (Inland Revenue, Centre for Non-Residents, Longbenton, Newcastle-upon-Tyne, NE98 1ZZ; ☎0845 9154811; fax 0845 9157800; from outside the UK: 0191-225 4811; fax 0191-225 7800; fax 0115-974 1919; www.inlandrevenue.gov.uk/cnr/osc.htm).

Italy itself also offers invalidity pensions (*pensione di invalidità*), which are widely abused in the south of the country where able-bodied workers are certified as being unable to work in order to decrease the unemployment statistics. There is also something called *la pensione di anzianità* (a long-service pension) to which someone is entitled after thirty-five to forty years of work. As recently as 1998 the government brought in new regulations to abolish a scandalous variant on this system, awarding pensions to certain state employees, such as teachers, after only ten years' service (allowing 30-year-olds to retire and get another job on the quiet). Political parties also found the generous pension system invaluable for bribing the electorate when it came to voting time.

The *Instituto Nazionale di Previdenza Sociale* (INPS) effectively dominates the Italian pensions system though there also exist several pension funds linked to certain state industries (water, gas, the railways, etc.). Private pension plans, of which there was a dismal shortage of choice only a few years ago, are likely to prove a booming sector for the newly wealthy Italians in the north, who will eventually start looking to invest their money rather than spend it.

If you are employed by a UK company but working in Italy you should check how long you are able to contribute to the UK company's pensions scheme; normally, employees are able to remain with the UK scheme for at least three years, and with the approval of the Inland Revenue, for longer. However, UK citizens who leave the UK and cease to earn an income in the UK, are often not allowed to contribute to traditional UK-based pension schemes. To continue saving for the future they need to invest in US-style funds-information and advice should be sought from professional financial advisers, preferable ones who are registered in the UK and not ones who phone you up out of the blue. You can also look on the internet. Paley.com carries details of websites pertaining to pension transfers abroad of occupational pensions that are frozen in the UK.

Finally, if you are subject to tax in Italy it is worth checking whether your employer's pension contributions are taxable there. Previously, as a UK taxpayer you would not be taxed on your employer's contributions. Also take advice from an independent financial adviser as to whether it is best for you to continue with a personal pension scheme in the UK and for how long, and what other conditions and/or restrictions apply to the scheme once you are resident in Italy.

Other Pension Entitlements: The European Commission has recently put forward proposals for a pension directive. Current differences in pension provision between member states are seen as barriers to the total freedom of movement of employees within the European Community. The proposals now under discussion are intended to remove the obstacles and to encourage pension provision by employers. These are to include freedom to manage pension funds within the EU, freedom of cross-border investment and cross-border membership of pension fund schemes. The last clause is the one that is causing the most controversy, as it allows for the creation of pan-European funds, and the final outcome is still being awaited.

Note that it is always worth checking on your entitlements to a foreign state pension if you have worked abroad for any length of time. For instance, a British expatriate discovered that she was entitled to a pension of approximately £50 a week and more than £20,000 in payments backdated to her 55th birthday as she had contributed to the Italian state pension scheme for about ten years while working in Rome.

Advice regarding, and administration of, offshore pension funds is available through Bacon and Woodrow Pension Trustees Ltd (Albert House, South Esplanade, St Peter Port, Guernsey GY1 3BY, Channel Islands; ☎ 01481-728432; fax 01481-724082; www.bwcigroup.com) as well as many of the Offshore Banks in Jersey, Guernsey and the Isle of Man. The UK tax authorities have tightened up the rules on offshore investments, especially trust funds that were popular with expatriates, and it is always worth seeking up to date professional advice before making decisions on investment activity.

Finance

Anyone considering retiring to Italy should take specialist financial advice regarding their own personal situation. Most people in a position to retire overseas have an amount of capital to invest, or will have once they sell their UK home and it is essential to take good advice on how and where this may best be done. Moreover, those who intend to maintain connections with both the UK and Italy will need advice on how their taxation affairs can be arranged to their best advantage. However, there is no reason why one should not continue with bank accounts or investments already established in the UK and in most cases interest will be paid on deposits paid without deduction of tax where one is non-resident, providing the correct paperwork is completed at the bank.

Taxation

Inheritance tax was abolished in Italy on October 25th 2001, and became effective immediately. Gifts and legacies to relatives no longer attract inheritance tax, though some taxes relating to the transfer of ownership still apply. For non-relatives, large legacies (more than €180,760/£125,000,$235.921 approx) will attract some taxes such as Property Registration Tax (*Imposta di Registro*). Transfers of all inheritances/gifts still remains complex and legal advice should be sought to avoid conflict between Italian and UK/US/Canadian law and ensure that the correct paperwork is filed punctually after the death, as late filing can attract large fines.

UK pensions paid to British expatriates are subject to Italian tax unless the pensioner is exempted by a double taxation agreement, or he or she is a former public service employee who worked abroad (in which case the pension is taxable in the UK, although sometimes not liable to any tax at all). The double taxation agreement only taxes pensions in Italy if you are resident there. If your pension is going to be liable for UK income tax or Italian tax, it may be better to elect to take a tax-free lump sum pension option, thereby reducing the level of pension liable to tax. A recent survey found that a UK couple who retire to Italy on a pension of £20,000 with no other income would take home significantly less than they would have in France, Germany and Switzerland, but more than they would have done in any Scandinavian country.

Non-EU retirees resident in Italy should take specialist tax advice to avoid paying tax in both the country where their income is generated, and Italy.

Offshore Banking

Retired people with a lump sum of money to be invested, or put into a long-term deposit account, will find it well worth looking at the tax-free interest bearing accounts that financial institutions offer through offshore banking centres such as Gibraltar, the Isle of Man and the Channel Islands. There is usually a minimum amount of money required to open a deposit account; usually a few thousand pounds. The deposit account interest rates work on the basis that the more inaccessible one's money, the higher the rate of interest paid. Interest can be paid monthly or annually, although the account holder will receive slightly less overall on the monthly payments because of the number of transaction charges involved. The monthly payments, however, offer a steady income flow and seem an invariably more popular option with retirees. A list of banks which offer offshore banking facilities is given in the *Banking* section of the *Daily Life* chapter.

SOCIAL SECURITY AND HEALTH

EU pensioners who are resident in Italy on a permanent basis are entitled to free or subsidised healthcare under the Italian national health care system (*servizio sanitario nazionale*). Fee benefits include hospital and emergency treatment and routine visits to the GP. Dentists are included but generally most people go to a private dentist; only the very poor go to state dentists, whereas both rich and poor use the health service as in the UK. Those who are retired or who are otherwise eligible for UK social security should apply in Britain as far in advance of departure as possible to the Department of Work and Pensions Overseas Branch (address provided above) for form E121, and on arrival in Italy should register with their nearest government health centre (*Azienda Sanitaria Locale ASL*).

The Italian national health service provides particularly poor outpatient and after-care treatment and facilities. Social security covers all the cost of hospitalization but there is a contribution required (10-15%) for medicines and tests. Those on a very low income are exempt from all charges. Those who have worked in Italy and paid into a private top-up scheme, as most people do, have the bulk of this contribution covered, but those who are retired and move to Italy may not.

A list of English-speaking doctors is available from British and US Consulates and Embassies, though these lists will, however, often only list private doctors and medical facilities.

For details of private health care plan organisations, see *Private Medical Insurance* in the *Daily Life* chapter.

WILLS

The easiest and most effective policy regarding the disposal of his or her estate for foreign citizens resident in Italy is to make a will that follows the law of their own country. If a will involves the dispersal of property both within and without Italy, it is advisable to consult a lawyer (*avvocato*) with experience of both your own country's and the Italian legal systems to avoid legal complications later on. In this case, you may find that it is simplest to make two wills, which deal with non-Italian and Italian assets separately, rather than trying to combine the two. If you wish, you can make an Italian-style will, but unless you have taken Italian nationality during your time in Italy, this will be executed in accordance with the law of your home country. Non-Italian wills also avoid the Italian system of *Legittima*, common to most Western European countries, which gives those directly related to the deceased an absolute right to a share in the estate, regardless of the wishes of the deceased as expressed in the will. Remember that to validate an Italian will you will need to obtain a certificate of law from your consulate, which will state that the will is being made under the terms of your own country's law and includes a provision for the free disposition of property. Any good lawyer will be able to organise this for you. An especially useful website, particularly for Americans, is www.italianlaw.net which has a mass of useful information about wills and inheritance for property and assets owned in Italy by American citizens.

Useful Addresses in the UK

Claudio del Giudice: Avvocato and Solicitor, Rivington House, 82 Great Eastern Street, London EC2A 3JF; ☎020 7613 2788; e-mail delgiudice@clara.co.uk; www.delgiudice.clara.net.

The International Property Law Centre: Unit 2, Waterside Park, Livingstone Road, Hessle, HU13 OEG; please contact Ugo Tanda, Italian Avvocato, on ☎0870-800 4591 (e-mail ugot@maxgold.com); or Stefano Lucatello, Italian Solicitor on ☎0870-800 4565 (e-mail Stefano@maxgold.com); fax 0870-800 4567; general e-mail internationalproperty@maxgold.com; www.internationalpropertylaw.com.

John Howell & Co: The Old Glassworks, 22 Endell Street, Covent Garden, London WC2H 9AD; ☎020-7420 0400; fax 020-7836 3626; e-mail info@europelaw.com; www.europelaw.com.

Death

Dying abroad complicates matters slightly, in that one's near relations are not often on the spot to deal with the formalities surrounding burial or cremation. It is therefore advisable to make your wishes concerning the matter i.e. what form of burial is desired and where, known in advance and preferably also written down in a will. Note that burials in Italy must take place within 48 hours of death.

All deaths must be registered with the local *municipio* (town hall) within 24 hours. The attending doctor issues a death certificate, though you will need an international death certificate if a body is to be transported back home. You can also register the death overseas of a foreign national with their respective embassy or consulate and get a death certificate from their own country so that the death can be registered in the home country as well as in Italy. Even though this is not obligatory, there could be advantages to doing this, which may not be apparent at the time. The embassy or consulate will charge for registering a death and issuing a certificate of death. The British Embassy also offers bereavement advice and can provide a list of Italian undertakers (www.britishembassy.gov.uk). Cremation, particularly in the north of Italy, is fairly common, although practically every Italian comune has its own cemetery in which all residents are entitled to be buried free of charge. There are also British cemeteries in large cities like the one at Staglieno in Genoa.

The British Embassy warns that sending a coffin back to the UK by air is an expensive business – to North America it is of course, even more expensive. Freight charges depend on weight but the minimum cost is about £2,000; prolonged storage will also add to your costs. The body will have to be picked up once it arrives home, and some Italian funeral directors have contacts in other countries, who will see to it that the body is safely delivered to its final destination. It is advisable to get a few quotations from Italian undertakers who offer such a service. An alternative is to have just your ashes returned home, which is much cheaper. Courier companies should be able to handle this if a friend or relative cannot do it.

Section 2

Working in Italy

EMPLOYMENT

BUSINESS AND INDUSTRY REPORT

REGIONAL EMPLOYMENT GUIDE

TEMPORARY WORK

STARTING A BUSINESS

EMPLOYMENT

CHAPTER SUMMARY

○ The official national unemployment rate is about 9% the lowest it has been for some years.

○ Unemployment remains lowest in the north and highest in the south.

○ The European Union has a system under which professional qualifications obtained in one member country can be recognised in another.

○ Sources of information about jobs include the pan-European job information network EURES, professional organisations, online job resources and Chambers of Commerce in Italy.

○ Possibilities for temporary work in Italy include working on a farm or as an au pair, teaching English, and in the summer and winter tourist industries.

○ Each industry in Italy has its own national minimum wage. Overtime is paid at 130%-150% of the normal rate, but in some fields of work it has been banned by the unions.

○ All employees receive an extra month's salary in December.

○ **The economy.** Although privatization has advanced in recent years there remains a large state interest in a variety of industries.

  ○ Small and medium-sized businesses (SMEs) have traditionally pre-dominated in Italian industry.

○ **Industry.** The main industries offering prospects for permanent work include aerospace, agriculture, the automotive industry, chemicals, clothing and textiles, electrical household appliances, high technology, iron and steel, the IT sector, machine tools, mining and oil and gas.

  ○ The different industries are not evenly spread around the country so some research into what takes place where is necessary.

THE EMPLOYMENT SCENE

If you are keen to live and work in Italy, as an increasing number of Europeans and North Americans are, but you are neither being sent to Italy by your current employer nor retiring, then you will have to find employment yourself. The prospects for finding a job are better now than they have been as unemployment rates in Italy, traditionally slightly higher than in most of the EU have decreased. Recent years have provided minimal market growth but it has been constant, and the unemployment rate has dropped from 11.4% to 8.6% according to the OECD and official figures released by the National Statistics Bureau, www.istat.it.

According to the same statistics, the Italian employment rate grew by 3.3% in 2004 mainly due to the rise of employees working on temporary contracts. North-eastern areas have been particularly dynamic. The manufacturing sector of Emilia Romagna, Abruzzo, and Molise show greater increases in employment. However, these are mainly throughout the services sector, which is also in a state of expansion in the rest of the country as well. The employment downside of Italy is the great differences in the unemployment rates between the Northern, Central, and Southern areas with the south having an unemployment rate four times higher than in the north: Unemployment is about 5% in northern regions, 8% in the Central regions, and 20% or more in the remaining areas. Nevertheless, there is the prospect of a constant growth in overall employment in all the regions.

RECOGNITION OF DIPLOMAS, CERTIFICATES AND DEGREES

It can be difficult to have your diplomas, certificates, and any other special qualifications, fully recognised in Italy as there are significant differences between training courses and diplomas from country to country. EU job seekers have an advantage in that they can make full use of their training and skills in another EU country thanks to the *European Union Professional Qualifications Directives* below.

If you are a doctor, a general nurse, a dentist, a midwife, a veterinary surgeon, a pharmacist or an architect (professions for which qualifications have been co-ordinated at EU level), your national qualifications are, in principle, recognised automatically, allowing you to practice in any other EU country. If your profession is not regulated in the country in which you wish to work, no recognition of your qualifications is necessary. You are entitled to go and work in that country without any formalities linked to your training or qualifications.

For nationals of non-EU countries procedures vary. It is advisable that you check with the Italian embassy before starting the process of looking for a job. In order for non-EU nationals to get a work permit an employer must sponsor them and they will be required to prove they have special skills, not available in Italy at that moment. Graduates in the ICT sector are currently one such specialist in demand.

For most professionals working in Italy requires fluency in Italian. This applies even to EFL teachers in Italian state schools.

EC Professional Qualifications Directives

European Union Professional Qualifications Directives The EC Directive on the mutual recognition of professional qualifications (89/48/EEC) was notified to Member States in January 1989. This Directive (usually referred to as the first diploma directive), dealt with professional qualifications awarded after at least three years of higher education (e.g. doctors, dentists, pharmacists, architects, accountants, lawyers etc.). The second diploma directive (92/51/EEC) dealt with all qualifications that take less than three years to obtain. The second directive includes: qualifications achieved after post-secondary level education involving course of 1-3 years (defined as diplomas); awards made on completion of a course following a minimum school leaving age qualification (defined as certificates); and work experience. This means that NVQs and SVQs and their equivalents are recognised by the EU. The member states implemented the second diploma directive in 1994. This mutual recognition of qualifications may in some instances be subject to certain conditions such as proficiency in the language of the state where the professional intends to practice and length of experience. A copy of the First Directive is contained in the booklet, *The Single Market, Europe Open for Professionals, EC Professional Qualifications Directive* which can be downloaded as a pdf at www.dti.gov.uk/Europe/openpdf. Prospective job seekers are also advised to consult the association relevant to their profession for the exact conditions for acceptance in Italy.

Although some professionals such as doctors and dentists have been able to practice in any EU state for a decade, it has not been the case for other professions who want to practice in the EU area, but outside their home country.

Comparing Qualifications between Italy and the UK

NARIC (Professional Qualifications). UK National Academic Recognition Information Centre (NARIC, Oriel House, Oriel Road, Cheltenham, Glos GL50 1XP; ☎0870 9904088; fax 0870 990 1560; e-mail info@naric.org.uk; www.naric.org.uk) provides information on the comparability of overseas professional qualifications in each EU country. There is a charge for this. You can also do this in Italy where the NARIC is based in Rome (NARIC, CIMEA (Centro di

Informazione sulla Mobilita e le Equivalenze Accademiche), Viale XXI Aprile 36, 00162 Rome; ☎+39 06 86 32 12 81; fax +39 06 86 32 28 45; e-mail cimea@fondazionerui.it; www.cimea.it). Also: General Directives for Professional Recognition, Dipartimento Coordinamento Politiche Communitarie, via del Tritone 142, 00187 Rome.

Certificates of Experience and Vocational Qualifications. If you have experience but no skills, you can apply for a European Certificate of Experience. These are handled by the Certificates of Experience Team in the UK, which is part of the Department for Education and Skills. Their role is to implement Directive 99/42/EEC (the so-called third directive) concerning the mutual recognition of experience gained in a profession in EU member countries. A certificate costs £105 and takes 15 days to process. Contact: DfES, Certificates of Experience Team, DfES, Qualifications for Work Division, Room E3B, Moorfoot, Sheffield S1 4PQ; ☎0114-259 4237; www.dfes.gov.uk/europeopen. You can download an application form for a Certificate of Experience at application.coe@dfes.gsi. gov.uk A considerable amount of information on professional bodies and EC Directives can be found on the EU website www.citizens.eu.int.
Residents of other EU countries should contact the nearest Chamber of Commerce to ask about the issuance of certificates in the country where they are resident.

In Italy you can contact OFPL (Direttore Generale, Ufficio Centrale OFPL, Ministero del Lavoro, Via Castelfidardo 43, 00185 Rome).

Other Contacts for Recognition of Foreign Professionals in Italy

CONSOB (Commissione Nazionale Societa e Borsa): Via GB Martini 3, 00198 Rome; ☎06 84 771; Milan office: Via Broletto 7, 20121; ☎02 72 42 01; fax 02 89 010696; www.consob it (has English version). Professionals: promoters of financial transactions.

Dipartimento del Turismo: Ufficio 11/C, c/o Presidenza del Consiglio dei Ministri, Via della Ferratella in Laterano, 51, 00184 Rome; ☎06-677991. Contact Dott. Antonio Sereno (+39 06 77 32 553). All tourist professions including guides and sports instructors.

Ministero della Giustizia: Direzione Generale Affari Civile e Libere Professioni, Ufficio VII, Via Arenula 71, 00186 Rome; ☎06-68851; fax 06-6889 7350. Accountancy professions agronomists, biologists, chemists, engineers, forestry experts, geologists, journalists, lawyers, psychologists, social workers, surveyors etc.

Ministero delle attivita produttive: Direzione Generale Commercio, Assicurazioni e Servizi – Div. IV. Via Sallustiana 53, 00187 Rome; ☎06 47051; 06 42 13 62 54. Industrial patents, trade brokers and technical experts.

Ministero del Lavoro e della Previdenza Sociale, Ufficio Centrale Orientamento e

Formazione Professionale Lavoratori: Div I, Vicolo d'Aste 12, 00159 Rome; ☎06 43 58 88 86. Professional profiles based on vocational qualifications.

Ministero dell'Istruzione, Universita e Ricerca (MIUR), Dipartimento per lo Sviluppo dell'Istruzione, Direzione Generale Ordinamenti Scolastici: Ufficio IX, Viale Trastavere 76, 00153 Rome; ☎06-5849 2345. Teachers in state schools and in higher artistic institutes such as music conservatoires and fine arts academies.

Ministero della Salute, Direzione Generale Risorse Umane e Professioni Sanitarie – Uffici IV and V: Viale dell'Industria 20, 00144 Rome; ☎06 59941. Medical and dental professions of all types and medical and dental technicians and veterinarians.

RESIDENCE AND WORK REGULATIONS

Unfortunately, Italy's enthusiasm for the EU has not diminished the need for time-consuming bureaucratic procedures required of even EU nationals who wish to work in Italy. If you arrive in Italy with the intention of working, you must apply at the *questura* (police station) for a *ricevuta di Segnalazione di Soggiorno*, which allows you to stay for up to three months looking for work. Upon production of this document and a letter from an employer, you must go to the labour office or the commune for a *libretto di lavoro*, a form of work authorization, which strictly should not be necessary for EU nationals. However, anyone wishing to work in Italy should be prepared to apply for a *libretto di lavoro* as well as a stay permit (*Permesso di Soggiorno*) if intending to stay and work for longer than three months. You only need a *libretto di lavoro* if you are an employee. Self employed people do not need one. One English woman, who was offered a job EFL teaching in Bari, reported that she had to visit three different government offices about eight times in total. Her health card arrived about six months after the wheels were set in motion.

Note that au pairs, and academics employed by Italian universities are exempt from obtaining the *libretto di lavoro*. Full information on entry regulations to Italy are given in the chapter *Residence and Entry Regulations*. You can find useful advice and information about working in Italy from various job websites include www.career-plus.com/life/gnit-1.htm as well as from the Italian police (www.poliziadistato.it). Embassies cannot help with finding a job in Italy but they can give advice on visas and provide contacts such as translators (for English documents): British Embassy (Via XX Settembre 80a, Porta Pia, I-00187 Rome; ☎06-482 5551/5441; fax 06-487 3324). The US Embassy (via Vittorio Venetto 119/A, 00187 Roma Italy; ☎06-4674 1) also provides similar information for its nationals.

SOURCES OF JOBS

THE MEDIA
National Newspapers and Directories

The combined effects of the Single Market and the implementation of the EC Professional Qualifications Directives (see above) have not exactly triggered a flood of trans-continental job recruitment, but mobility has certainly increased and become practicable for an increasing number of EU nationals. UK newspapers carry a growing number of job advertisements from other member states including Italy. Many British newspapers including, *The Times, The Financial Times* and the *Guardian* carry regular job adverts from other European countries. Every Thursday, the Appointments section in *The Times* provides a comprehensive list of opportunities throughout the market place both in Britain and overseas. The *Times Educational Supplement* (published Fridays) and the Education pages of the Tuesday edition of the *Guardian*, carry prolific advertisements for teaching English abroad. The *Guardian* also has a Europe supplement on Fridays, which includes a job section. In America, the *Wall Street Journal, Washington Post* and other leading newspapers also carry international job listings.

One of the biggest changes in recent times is in the way we look for new jobs by using the internet. It is possible to do much of your initial research, trawl dozens of sites including the ones for the above newspapers for suitable jobs, post your CV and send an initial application from your computer. Alternatively, a wide range of casual jobs including secretarial, agricultural, tourism and domestic work, are advertised in the annual directory *Summer Jobs Abroad*, while *Teaching English Abroad* lists schools worldwide which employ English language teachers each year and *Working in Ski Resorts Europe & North America* includes all the main Italian resorts and tells you how and where to get jobs in them. These publications are available directly from Vacation Work (9 Park End Street, Oxford OX1 1HJ; ☎01865 241978; fax 01865 790885; www.vacationwork.co.uk) as well as bookshops and online booksellers.

International and European Newspapers and Magazines

A number of international English-language newspapers, drawing on journalistic input from around the world, are available in most countries with a sizeable expatriate population. These publications circulate editions across national boundaries and usually carry a modest amount of job advertising. The volume of adverts carried is rising, though the number of such publications has consolidated in recent years. Presently, the newspapers to consult include the *The International Herald Tribune, The Weekly Telegraph* and *The Weekly Guardian* and *Wall Street*

Journal Europe.

In addition to the above newspapers, magazines such as *Time, Newsweek, Asiaweek* and *The Economist* are distributed internationally and include adverts for senior employees in various countries, including Italy. International subscriptions are available, though they are expensive. Individual copies can usually be purchased from major bookstores in cities with a sizeable expatriate population. Bookstores at international airports and also main railway stations in large cities where expatriates are resident, often stock English language publications such as those listed above.

There are specialist expatriate magazines such as *Nexus* (Expat Network Ltd., Rose House, 109a South End, Croydon CR0 1BG; ☎020-8760 0469; fax 020-8760 0469; nexus@expatnetwork.com; www.expatnetwork.com), which carry international job adverts and also allow members to include their CV in the members' database.

When living outside the UK and North America, the newspapers and magazines listed in both the National and International sections above can often be found in the libraries of *The British Council* (www.britishcouncil. org) and cross cultural associations such as the *American Chamber of Commerce* (AmCham) and the *Franco-American Association*, as applicable to the country you are in.

As well as employers advertising in the International and European newspapers, individuals can also place their own adverts for any kind of job, although bilingual secretaries and assistants, marketing managers and other professionally qualified people seeking to relocate abroad are in the greatest demand. Obviously, advertising rates vary but will be several US$ per line, per insertion. For details contact the classified advertising departments of the newspapers at the addresses listed below.

The Financial Times: 1 Southwark Bridge, London SE1 9HL; ☎020-7873-3000. *The Financial Times* is printed in English in the UK, Germany, France, the USA and Japan and distributed worldwide. International appointments appear on Thursdays in all editions.

The Guardian Weekly: 164 Deansgate, Manchester M60 2RR; 020-7713 4111; fax 020-7831 5712. The condensed weekly version of the British daily newspaper.

International Herald Tribune: 63 Long Acre, London WC2E 9JH; ☎020-7836 4802; Appears daily: the IHT international recruitment section appears on Thursdays.

Wall Street Journal: The International Press Centre, 76 Shoe Lane, London EC4; ☎020-7334 0008; online news and subscriptions from www.wsj. com. European edition published in Brussels: Wall Street Journal Europe, Bld. Brand Whitlock 87, 1200 Bruxelles; ☎+32 27411211; www.europe. wsj.com. US subscriptions 1-800-369-2834. The recruitment section which covers appointments and business opportunities worldwide and appears on Tuesdays.

For information on the Italian press, see below and the *Daily Life* chapter, *Media* section. Some Italian newspapers can be obtained in major city newsagents in the UK on the day of publication. Alternatively, try major city reference libraries.

Italian Publications and Newspapers

Italian publications worth looking at include the annual *The Career Book,* which usually comes out in October and is published by the newspaper *Il Sole 24 Ore* for its subscribers, or you can buy it for €9.50 (2005) from Redazione Il Sole 24 Ore, Via Lomazzo 52, 20154 Milan; fax 02-3103426; or 02 341062; www. careerbooklavoro.somedia.it or from the website www.carriera24.ilsole24ore. com. Also worth checking is the weekly Friday jobs bulletin *Corriere Lavoro www. corriere.it/lavoro,* of the newspaper *Corriere della Sera* as well as that newspaper's Friday jobs pages. Another useful source of jobs and news about the Italian job market is the monthly magazine published on and offline, *Bolletino del Lavoro* (www.bolletinodellavoro) which has listings of jobs in Italy.

Advertising in Newspapers

An advertisement in an Italian newspaper may produce an offer of employment. Smyth International (Archgate Business Centre, 825 Hard Road, London N12 8UB; 020-8446 6400; fax 020-8446 6402; www.smyth-international.com) deals with *La Stampa* (Turin daily), and other provincial newspapers. The Milan paper *Il Giornale* is published at Via Gaetano Negri 4, 20123 Milan. You can also advertise directly in Italian newspapers through their websites. It may also be worth advertising your skills and services in the monthly English-language website *The Informer* which has a classified section. Adverts can be placed online and subscriptions to the members' section of *The Informer* website is €49 per year. The Italian American Heritage Foundation website also has extensive links to Italian newspaper websites at: www.iahfsj.org/links.htm.

Professional and Trade Publications

Professional journals and magazines are another possible source of job vacancies abroad, from British companies wishing to set up offices elsewhere in Europe and foreign firms advertising for staff, e.g. *The Architects' Journal, The Architectural Review, Accountancy, Administrator, Brewing & Distilling International* and *The Bookseller* to name but a few. Anyone in the air transport industry should consult *Flight International* while those employed in the catering trade could try *Caterer and Hotel Keeper* and agricultural workers *Farmers Weekly.* Although published in the UK, some of these magazines are considered world authorities in their field and have a correspondingly wide international readership.

An exhaustive list of trade magazines can be found in media directories such as *Benn's Media* available in major reference libraries. More limited lists can be found in writers directories such as *The Writers Market* (US), *Writers' and Artists' Yearbook* (UK) and *The Writers Handbook* (UK), which are available in major reference libraries and bookstores.

PROFESSIONAL ASSOCIATIONS

Professional associations are a useful point of contact for their members with regard to practising elsewhere in the world. Most professional organisations have links with their counterparts around the world and can often provide generic contact details, if not personal contact. During the negotiations involved in finalising the EU mutual recognition of qualifications directives, most professional associations negotiated with their counterparts in other member states and can therefore be much more helpful in providing contacts.

Details of all UK professional associations may be found in the directory *Trade Associations and Professional Bodies of the UK*, available at most UK reference libraries. It is also worth trying to contact the Italian equivalent of UK professional associations – the UK body should be able to provide the address. Alternatively you can consult your trade union for information, as they may have links, however tenuous, with their counterpart organisation in Italy. A list of addresses of the more mainstream professional organisations is given below.

Contact details of US and Canadian professional organisations can be found in a similar fashion – through local libraries and chambers of commerce. Additionally, most professional organisations in North America and the UK have an internet presence and a growing number of Italian ones do too. A simple search using Google, Yahoo! or other search engine will generally produce the required results. A comprehensive directory of UK trade associations can be found at www.martex.co.uk/taf. Their US counterparts can be found in the Yahoo!directory:http://dir.yahoo.com/Business_and_Economy/Organizations/Trade_Associations/.

Useful Addresses – UK Professional Associations

Architects Registration Board: 8 Weymouth Street, London W1W 5BU; ☎020-7580 5861; 020-7436 5269; e-mail: info@arb.org.uk www.arb.org.uk.

Association of Professional Music

Therapists: Administrator, 61 Church Hill Road, East Barnet, Herts. EN4 8DY; ☎01458-834919; e-mail apmtoffice@aol.com.

Biochemical Society: 59 Portland Place, London W1B 1QW; www.

biochemistry.org.

British Computer Society: 1 Sandford Street, Swindon SN1 1HJ; ☎01793-417424; e-mail bcshq@hq.bcs.org.uk.

British Medical Association: BMA House, Tavistock Square, London WC1H 9JP; ☎switchboard 020-387 4499; fax for international department: 020-7383 6644; e-mail international info@bma.org.uk; www.bma.org.uk. The BMA's International Department gives extensive help and advice to its members wishing to work elsewhere in Europe, and general advice to incoming doctors from other countries.

British Dietetic Association: 5th Floor, Charles House, 148/9 Great Charles Street, Queensway, Birmingham B3 3HT; ☎0121-200 8010; e-mail: info@bda.uk.com.

Chartered Institute of Bankers: 4-9 Burgate Lane, Canterbury, Kent CT1 2XJ; ☎01227-762600; e-mail institute@cib.org.uk.

Chartered Institute of Building: Englemere, Kings Ride, Ascot, Berkshire SL5 7TB; ☎01344-630700; fax 01344-630777; e-mail reception@ciob.org.uk www.ciob.org.uk.

Chartered Institute of Housing: Octavia House, Westwood Business Park, Westward Way, Coventry CV4 8JP. The CIH may be able to help individual members further by putting them in touch with key people/organisations in the EU.

Chartered Institute of Library and Information Professionals, 7 Ridgmount Street, London WC1E 7AE; ☎020-7255 0500; fax 020-7255 0501; e-mail info@cilip.org.uk; www.cilip.org.uk.

Chartered Institute of Marketing (CIM): Moor Hall, Cookham, Maidenhead, Berks SL6 9QH; ☎01628-427500; fax 01628 427499; www.cim.co.uk.

College of Radiographers: 207 Providence Square, Mill Street, London SE1 2EW; ☎020-7740 7200.

Faculty of Advocates: Parliament House, 11 Parliament Square, Edinburgh EH1 1RF; ☎0131-226 5071; www.advocates.org.uk. The Scottish lawyers association does not have a formal information service which helps members to find jobs abroad but it does maintain close links with other European Bars.

General Council of the Bar: 3 Bedford Row, London WC1R 4DB; 020-7242 0082.

General Dental Council: 37 Wimpole Street, London W1G 8DQ; ☎020-7887 3800; fax 020-7224 3294; e-mail information@gdc-uk.org www.gdc-uk.org.

General Optical Council: 41 Harley Street, London W1G 8DJ; ☎020-7580 3898; fax 020-7436 3525; e-mail: goc@optical.org.

Institute of Actuaries: Napier House, 4 Worcester Street, Oxford OX1 2AW; 01865-268200; fax 01865-268211; e-mail institute@actuaries.org.uk.

Institute of Biology: 20-22 Queensberry Place, London SW7 2DZ; ☎020-7581 8333; fax 020-7823 9409; www.iob.org. Can give members advice/contacts in Europe.

Institute of Cast Metal Engineers: Bordesley Hall, The Holloway, Alvechurch, Birmingham B48 7QA; ☎01527-596100; fax 01527-596102; e-mail: info@icme.org.uk.

Institute of Chartered Accountants in England & Wales: Chartered Accounts' Hall, P O Box 433, Moorgate Place, London EC2P 2BJ; ☎+44 (0)20 7920 8100; fax +44 (0)20 7920 0547; e-mail: international.affairs@icaew.co.uk; www.icaew.co.uk. The Brussels Office ☎+322 230 3272; fax +322 230 2851 is able to offer members advice on working within the EU.

Institute of Chartered Foresters: 7A St. Colme Street, Edinburgh EH3 6AA; ☎0131-225 2705; fax 0131-220 6128.

Institute of Chartered Shipbrokers: 3 St. Helen's Place, London EC3A 6EJ; ☎020-7628 5559; www.ics.org.uk.

Institution of Civil Engineers: 1 Great George Street, Westminster, London SW1P 3AA; ☎020-7222 7722; www.ice.org.uk. Also has an international recruitment agency: Thomas Telford Recruitment Consultancy (020-7665 2438).

Institute of Marine Engineers: 80 Coleman Street, London EC2R 5BJ; ☎020-7382 2600; www.imarest.org. Provides its members with contacts and information through its network of branches throughout Europe.

Institution of Materials, Minerals and Mining: 1 Carlton House Terrace, London SW1Y 5DB; ☎0207-451 7300; www.iom3.org.

The Institution of Electrical Engineers: Savoy Place, London WC2R OBL; ☎020-7240 1871; fax 020-7240 7735; e-mail postmaster@iee.org. Helps members who wish to travel or work abroad with details of the IEE contacts in their new location.

Institution of Gas Engineers & Managers: Charnwood Wing, Ashby road, Loughborough, Leics. LE11 3GH; ☎01509-282728; www.igem.org.uk.

Pharmaceutical Society of Northern Ireland: 73 University Street, Belfast BT7 1HL; ☎028-90326927; fax 028-90439919; e-mail: chief.executive@psni.org.uk.

The Registrar and Chief Executive, United Kingdom Central Council for Nursing, Midwifery and Health Visiting: 23 Portland Place, London W1B 1PZ; ☎020-7637 7181; fax 020-7436 2924; www.ukcc.org.uk.

Royal Aeronautical Society: 4 Hamilton Place, London W1J 7BQ; fax only 020-7499 6230; www.raes-hfg.com.

Royal College of Speech and Language Therapy: ☎020-7378 1200.

Royal College of Veterinary Surgeons: Belgravia House, 62-64 Horseferry Road, London SW1P 2AF; ☎020-7222 2001; fax 020-7222 2004; e-mail: admin@rcvs.org.uk www.rcvs.org.uk.

Royal Pharmaceutical Society of Great Britain: 1 Lambeth High Street, London SE1 7JN; ☎020-7735 9141; fax 020-7735 7629; www.rpsgb.org.uk.

Royal Town Planning Institute: 41 Botolph Lane, London EC3R 8DL; 020-7929 9494; fax 020-7929 9490; e-mail: online@rtpi.org.uk.

EMPLOYMENT ORGANISATIONS

EURES. the European employment services (EURES) is a computerised, pan-European job information network accessible through Jobcentres that have a specially trained Euroadvisor. The idea is that you contact the Euroadvisor nearest you in your own country and with their help use the EURES system (which has computer links with job organisations in the countries of the European Economic Area – the EU plus Iceland and Norway), to track down a suitable vacancy in another country. EURES can be used free by employers. Details on the EURES service can be obtained from the International Jobsearch Advice Team, Jobcentre Plus Regional Office, 6th Floor Whitehall II, Whitehall Quay, Leeds, LS1 4HR; ☎0113 307 8090; fax 0113-307 8213, or from the EURES website: http://europa.eu.int/jobs.eures where search criteria can be refined to specific categories and professions as well as regions of Italy.

Note that Jobcentre Plus vacancies including ones for overseas are also advertised on the internet at www.jobcentreplus.gov.uk. There are thousands of vacancies of all types registered on EURES, from unskilled to executive and professional posts and a proportion of these will be in Italy. Jobseekers can also search the EURES system online at: www.europa.eu.int/jobs/eures.

EURES CV-search (www.eurescv-search.com) allows jobseekers in the European Economic Area to enter CVs into a database that employers can search. At the present time the system is only set up for those looking for work in the IT, Hotels and Restaurant, Healthcare and Air Travel sectors. Italy has 22 Euroadvisors (*euroconsiglieri*) who mainly help Italians wanting to work abroad.

UK Employment Agencies. Contact details of employment agency members of the national organisation, the Recruitment and Employment Confederation (36-38 Mortimer Street, London W1N 7RB; www.rec.uk.com) can be ordered for £3.75 by ringing 0800 320588. The agencies listed deal mainly with specific sectors e.g. electronics, secretarial, accountancy etc., and will only recruit qualified and experienced staff. Alternatively, hundreds of recruitment agencies can be located through the *CEPEC Recruitment Guide*, which is available in reference libraries or from CEPEC Publications (Kent House, 41 East Street, Bromley, Kent BR1 1QQ) for a fee, plus postage and packing. The *Recruitment Guide* lists agencies which arrange jobs, predominantly for graduates and professionals, within the UK and sometimes abroad.

Recruitment agencies also advertise specific vacancies in the newspapers mentioned above and contacting them about other vacancies they have on their books can also be productive.

Italian Employment Agencies. The state-run *Centri per L'Impiego* (good for simple, unskilled work) have lost their monopoly in employment and recruitment and private agencies have proliferated. A complete list of authorised Italian agencies can be found at www.minlavoro.it, the Italian *Ministero del Welfare* website and some a listed below. For those interested in temporary employment, there are also agencies listed in the Italian *Yellow Pages*. It should be borne in mind, however, that there is little point in applying for most of the jobs you will find listed in the resources mentioned above if you are not proficient in Italian.

CESOP. *CESOP Communication* (Via San Felice 13 - Galleria Buriani, 40122 Bologna BO, Italy; ☎051 272441; fax 051 272265; t.joel@recruitaly.it) operate www.recruitaly.it, a website providing comprehensive information on the working world in Italy, and a window for Italian companies interested in recruiting staff from abroad. The site allows a direct approach to recent graduates interested in working in Italy, helping companies that have difficulties in finding qualified personnel in Italy, especially in the ICT sector.

ONLINE JOB RESOURCES

Online recruitment agencies are becoming increasingly common and many traditional recruitment agencies now have a web presence where their vacancy lists can be accessed and CVs submitted for consideration. A search using the main search engines such as Yahoo, Google and Lycos or meta engines such as www.mamma.com and www.dogpile.com will generate many such agencies. There are agencies that recruit for the whole of Europe and also some that specialise in Italy, e.g. www.monster.it, where you will find thousands of job offers (Italian version available only).

Alternatively, www.recruitaly.it gives access to job postings in English and provides further information on living and working in Italy and the site *Jobs in Italy* also provides useful links and resources, as does the website www.payaway. co.uk which lists agencies offering work in most areas covered in the *Temporary Work* section below, i.e. Agriculture, Au Pair and Tourism. Finally, *Job Partners* provide a recruitment service for employers around the world and local contact details can be found via their website, www.jobpartners.com.

Other Useful Websites for Jobs

www.adecco.it (temporary jobs agency)
www.alispa.it (temporary work agency)
www.assioma.org (IT specialist)
www.bestjob.it (portal of teleworking opportunities)
www.cambiolavoro.com (prepares and sends CVs to headhunters)
www.cercolavoro.com (claims to have over 30,000 job offers)

www.cliccalavoro.it (also has a newsletter about the job market)
www.corriere.it/lavoro/index.jhtml (newspaper jobs listings)
www.coopquadrifoglio.it (all kinds of jobs)
www.easyjob.it (temporary jobs agency)
www.eurointerim.it (temporary jobs agency)
www.eurometis.it (agency recruiting for banks, industry, IT etc)
www.ideallavoro.it (temporary jobs agency for service sector)
www.infojobs.it (claims 30,000 firms advertise on the website)
www.intoitaly.it (English-speaking jobs)
www.italialavoro.it (informative official Ministry of Welfare portal)
www.jobonline.it (useful general job site with newsletter)
www.jobsintourism.it/job/ (Italian tourist industry jobs)
www.manpower.it (temporary jobs agency)
www.maw.it (temporary work)
www.jobpilot.it (part of the worldwide Monster jobs network)
www.kangaroo.it (jobs in the IT sector)
www.lavoroeweb.com (very useful portal to everything to do with work)
www.lavoro.tiscali.it (Italian jobs portal)
www.temporary.it (temporary work agency)

TELEWORKING

The Società Italiana Telelavoro or SIT, the Italian teleworking organisation, was founded a decade ago when working from home using modern technology emerged as a feasible alternative employment opportunity. The advantages are that it is both flexible and cheap for the employee and the employer as it cut out commuting costs and employer overheads. There is now quite a large selection of employment that can be categorised as teleworking and not all of it involves tele-sales or computer software development. Possibilities include graphic designing, journalism, proof-reading, accounting, research, telephone interviewing, financial consulting, market analysing, translating, English tutoring and more. SIT supplies consultancy services to companies that wish to start this type of employment. A useful website for teleworkers is www.assotelema.it of the Associazione Italiana per la Divulgazione e l'Utilizzo della Telematica fra I cittadini.

CHAMBERS OF COMMERCE

The main function of the Italian chambers of commerce (*Camera di Commercio Industria*) is to promote business and trade in their area, but they may well do a sideline in providing information on potential employees to interested companies. The Italian Chamber of Commerce for Great Britain is based at 1 Princes Street, London W1R 8AY, UK; ☎020-7495 8191; fax 020-7495 8194;

info@italchamind.org.uk; www.italchamind.org.uk and you can access the Italian addresses and contact details of Italian companies on their website.

Anyone setting up in business or self-employment in Italy has to register with the local chamber of commerce on arrival; there are local and regional chambers of commerce in virtually every town and city. Their main task is to provide enthusiastic support for local industries and companies and, on request, will provide details of these and a list of government incentives for new industry (see the section, *Government Incentives*, in the *Starting a Business* chapter). The British Chamber of Commerce and Industry in Milan (Via Dante 12; ☎02-877798; fax 02-86461885; e-mail bcci@britchamitaly.com) actually does this. For a fee (up to €62) they will lodge your CV on their files for possible employers to see for up to a year; you can also place a classified advertisement both in their monthly newsletter and online. For more details and an online application form or download at www.britchamitaly.com/index.asp?Page=jobs. The BCCI also hold information on member companies and though you have to pay them for the printed version of their directory, all the information is online at their website, www.britchamitaly.com. This site also advertises job vacancies for bilingual staff.

British Chambers of Commerce in Italy.

Bergamo; Mr Arnold Attard (Hon. Area Secretary for Bergamo), c/o British E.L.T., Via Taramelli, 52 - 24121 Bergamo, Italy; tel/fax 035 249150.

Bologna; Mr Roger Warwick (Honorary Regional Secretary for Emilia Romagna), c/o Pyramid Int.Srl., Viale Masini, 20 - 40126 Bologna, Italy; ☎051 254568; fax 051 254948; e-mail pyramid@interim.it.

Brescia; Ms Julia A. Jones; C.S. International, Via Magenta 15, 25125 Moniga del Garda, Brescia, Italy; tel/fax 0365 504988; e-mail info@csinternational.191. it.

Florence; Maria Grazia Antoci, Via Giotto 37, 50121, Firenze, Italy; ☎055 601830; fax 055 6540332; e-mail mgantoci@inwind.it.

Gorizia; Mr D. Katan, Via F. Filzi 14, 34132 Trieste, Italy; ☎040 6762322 or ☎040 6762385; fax 040 6762301.

Naples; Roy Boardman, St. Peter's ELC, Riviera di Chiaia 124, 80100 Napoli, Italy; ☎081 683468; fax 081 682721; e-mail st.peterselc@mbox.netway.it.

Novara; Area Secretary for Novara Andrea Sacchi, Piazza Bertarelli 1, 20122 Milano; ☎02 83241513; fax 02 86996120; e-mail acsacchi@virgilio.it.

Padova ; Ms Christine King, c/o Unicredit Banca per la Casa, Via Altinate 8, 35121 Padova, Italy; ☎0498 761380; fax 0498 761381; c_king@ubcasa. unicredit.it.

Pordenone; Mrs Susan Clarke (Hon. Regional Secretary for Friuli Venezia Giulia), c/o Overseas Language Consultancy, Corso Vittorio Emanuele 54, 3170 Pordenone, Italy; tel/fax 0434 29089.

Rome; Honorary Regional Secretary for Lazio Luca Tantalo, Via Germanico 168, 00192 Roma, Italy; ☎06 32609190; fax 06 36004651; lucatantalo@st udiotantalofornari.it.

Taranto; Ms Stefania Lo Cascio, Worldwide Trusts Consultants Srl, Via Nitti 45/a, 74100 Taranto, Italy; ☎0348 3851033 or ☎099 4590880; fax 099 4590809; staff@trustsitaly.com.

Trieste; Prof. John Dodds, Università di Trieste, Via F. Filzi 14, 34132 Trieste, Italy; ☎040 5582322; fax. 040 6762301; dodds@sslmit.univ.trieste.it.

Turin; Mrs Jocelyn Holmes (Hon. Regional Secretary for Piemonte), c/o Musci & Holmes Architetti, Via Genola 3, 10141 Turin, Italy; tel/fax 011 331216; e-mail mharchitects@dada.it.

Udine; Mr C. J. Taylor, Via del Torso 41/8, 33100 Udine, Italy; tel/fax 0432 600397.

Venezia; Mr Ivor Neil Coward, Lexicon Translations SAS, Via Caneve 77, 30173 Mestre, Italy; ☎0422 780505 or 041 5348005; fax 0422 782821 or 0415349720; lexivor@tin.it.

Verona; Hon. Regional Secretary for Veneto, Vittorio Biondaro, Via Roma 4/b, 37147 San Bonifacio, Verona, Italy; tel/fax 045 7611230; fax 045 7611381.

Vicenza: Area Secretary Diego Creazzo, Finlean Vicenza Srl. Via del Progresso 2, 36100 Vicenza; ☎04 449 64833; fax 04 44964815; e-mail creazzo@profingroup.it.

The American Chamber of Commerce is at via Cantu, 20123 Milano, Italy; ☎0286 90661; fax 028057737; amcham@amcham.it; www.amcham.it/English/ home.asp. Their website lists job vacancies for those with Italian-US experience and Italian language skills. The American Chamber of Commerce also offers a business advisory service to its members. The membership directory of the American Chamber of Commerce is only available to their members.

APPLICATION PROCEDURE

To avoid disappointment it is as well to accept that even if your speculative letter of employment successfully negotiates the Italian postal system and lands on the desk of the right person, your application is still only at the very earliest stages in the job finding process. Remember that the Italians are notoriously bad at answering letters and faxes and that each application will have to be backed up with copious amounts of persistence and patience, if not goodwill. However, after accepting these drawbacks as inherent in postal applications, proceed with the utmost enthusiasm and determination. The *Directory of Employers* later in this chapter is a good source from which to base a speculative job hunt list. If your Italian is not up to scratch, or you prefer to make sure it is perfect, then a translator may be called for. In the UK the Institute of Linguists (Saxon House,

48 Southwark Street, London SE1 1UN; ☎020-7940 3100; 020-7940 3101; www.iol.org.uk) provides a good service of freelance translating, putting callers and visitors to their website in touch with translators who will provide a fluent translation for a fee of approximately £100 per thousand words. Translators can also be found online, for example, www.angloitalian.com. The *inlingua School of Languages* also offer translation services from their schools in the UK and North America and contact details can be found on their websites (www.inlingua.com and www.inlingua.com/usa.html).

Keep your letters formal, clear and polite and to the point; a flood of personal history will not be greeted appreciatively. Always send a CV /résumé with your application, whether the letter is speculative or in response to an advertised vacancy. For advice on how to compile and write your CV you can look on the internet e.g. www.createyourcv.co.uk or www.handsoncv.co.uk or the international job site www.glo-jobs.com or refer to the publications *The Right Way to Write Your Own CV*, John Clarke (www.right-way.co.uk) and *CVs and Written Applications*, Judy Skeats (Cassell Illustrated). Agencies which prepare CVs for a fee can be found under the heading *Employment Agencies* in the local *Yellow Pages* or online. It would be best to have someone familiar with the Italian employment market, who is also fluent in Italian, prepare your CV to ensure it will be suitable for submitting to Italian employers. After the CV has been written, any abbreviations, etc. which may confuse a foreign reader should be modified. Do not send any original certificates or documents with an enquiry or application as it is extremely unlikely that you will ever see them again.

If you are offered an interview, remember that first impressions and appearances are always important. Whatever the number of interviewers, you will usually find that the meeting is formal as a casual approach to interviews is an Americanism not yet in vogue with most Italian or European employers. As for dress, try to look smart, as the Italians invariably are. However, it is probably wisest to err on the side of conservatism in your dress, rather than attempting, and more often than not failing, to beat the Italians at their own game (i.e. the notorious *bella figura*, which involves looking one's best at all times). Remember that handshaking is popular throughout Italy with both men and women and that it is polite to shake hands both on arrival and departure. As with any job interview in any country, it is best to find out as much background information as possible about the company and the position for which you have applied in advance of the interview. An interest based on knowledge and hard facts is bound to impress a potential employer.

TEMPORARY WORK

The growth in Italian employment is a consequence of the introduction of more flexible working arrangements which are directly linked dip in the unemployment rate. The progressive diffusion of atypical contracts (part-time, seasonal, work training, temporary, etc.) has boosted employment. The role of flexible work contracts is especially important in the tertiary sector starting from the services industry and professional services.

Non-EU nationals will have a greater problem finding temporary work as the employer may be taking the risk of employing someone illegally. Most of the information below is therefore only applicable to EU citizens – except the EFL teaching and au-pair sections. Some language schools and state schools specifically want North American teachers to teach American-English and many North Americans find teaching jobs every year in Italy. Overseas Teachers Digest (www.overseasdigest.com) provides information for Americans looking to teach abroad and provides numerous links to possible employers. Non-EU citizens can become au-pairs and enter Italy on a cultural or educational visa as long as they attend language classes whilst in the country; further information is in the relevant section below.

AGRICULTURE

Casual labouring jobs in Italy are harder to come by than in some other Mediterranean countries. This is because farmers and vineyard owners traditionally employ migrant workers from North Africa, Albania etc. who are prepared to work for a pittance throughout the duration of grape (*vendemmia*) or other harvests, each year. The enlargement of the EU in 2004 has meant that opportunities for such jobs are dwindling further still unless you have local contacts or can charm your way in using your fluent Italian. Some people do manage to get jobs by approaching the cooperative depot where all the farmers from an area deliver their harvest for central processing. The areas for grape picking most worth trying are the north west of the country, for example in the vineyards lying south east of Turin in Piedmont, in the north-east in Alto Adige and to the east and west of Verona. The harvest takes place in September and October. There are other possibilities for fruit picking earlier in the year, but again there will be stiff competition for the limited number of jobs available. Strawberries are picked in the region of Emilia Romagna in June and apples from late August in the Alto Adige region and in the Valtellina, which lies between the north of Lake Como and Tirano. Jobs are also available picking grapes and tobacco leaves in Tuscany in September each year.

The Val di Non apple harvest around Cles in the river valley of the Adige, north of Trento, is a mecca for migrant workers and is a veritable cultural melting pot of Italians, East Europeans, Africans, South Americans, et al, and picking begins around 20-25th September for about four to five weeks. Women normally get the sorting jobs and the men earn slightly more picking. The object seems to be to get the harvest gathered in record time, so expect to work ten hours a day with no days off. If lunch and accommodation are provided there is a standard deduction and most farmers eat lunch with their pickers. And yes, Italian workers do sing operatic arias in the orchards while they work.

The International organisation WWOOF (World Wide Opportunities on Organic Farms) has a national organisation in Italy: WWOOF Italia, c/o Bridget Matthews, Via Casavecchia 109, 57022 Castagneto Carducci, Livorno, Italy (wwoofitalia@oliveoil.net; www.wwoof.org/italy). Membership costs €25, €13 of which is for compulsory insurance. It is very important that you are a member of WWOOF, which is an officially registered organization in Italy, otherwise you risk getting yourself deported and the farmer a huge fine as this kind of work is very strictly regulated in Italy. Further details of WWOOF International can be obtained from WWOOF in your own country. In the UK send a s.a.e. to WWOOF UK, PO Box 2675, Lewes, East Sussex BN7 1RB. Membership benefits include a bi-monthly newsletter with adverts for helpers in the UK and abroad. You can also buy a *Green Holiday Guide* to Italy (German language only) for €13/£6/US$12 from the European Centre for Eco Agro Tourism (Postbox 10899, 1001 EW Amsterdam, Netherlands; fax: 31-20 463 0594; www.pz.nl/eceat). However, this list is aimed at promoting *agriturismo* (i.e. paying stays on farms) and it is merely a suggestion that you can use it for contacts who might let you work and learn about organic farming in return for keep.

For those with a professional interest in farming, the International Farm Experience Programme (YFC Centre, National Agricultural Centre, Kenilworth, Warwickshire CV8 2LG, UK) arranges courses combining language tuition and work experience on farms for five months beginning in February and July. Five weeks at a language school are followed by four months on a farm. Free board and lodging throughout the language course and wages at local rates while on the farm are provided. Applicants must be aged 18-26 and have at least two years of practical farming experience. Travel costs and insurance are subsidised.

The Italian organisation SCICA – Sezione Circondariale per L'Impiego et il Collocamento (Via Maccani 76 38100 Trento; ☎0461-826433 & 826434) organises agricultural jobs and training placements in the Alps.

AU PAIR

There is always a demand for au pairs (known as *alla pari* or *le babysitter* in Italian), and also for qualified nannies. The rules for EU citizens who are au pairing are slightly confused in that they are not in general eligible for a *libretto di lavoro* (see *Residence and Entry Regulations*) but must apply for a stay permit (*permesso di soggiorno*) if they are staying for longer than three months. They must also register at the local registry office (*Ufficio Anagrafe*). Au Pairs from the EU who are staying a short time (i.e. the summer) need not apply for a *permesso di soggiorno* to open a post office bank account which you can do with a *domicilio* (address where you are staying in Italy). Non-EU or EEA nationals are not eligible for a *permesso di soggiorno* and must therefore arrive in Italy with an exchange or cultural visa.

The Almondbury Aupair & Nanny Agency (Damian Kirkwood; tel/fax +44 (0)1288 359 159; fax/ans: +44 (0)207 681 2508; in the USA (419) 844-8497; Damian@aupair-agency.com; www.aupair-agency.com) who arrange au-pair placements in numerous countries say that for an au-pair that comes from outside of the EU, the following documentation is needed to obtain a long stay visa:

○ A certificate of enrolment (plus receipt of payment) at any Italian School or College where the au-pair-to-be will be attending a course of Italian language. This school or College must be legally acknowledged (*legalmente riconosciuto*) and the above mentioned certificate must be stamped by the local police. The visa will be issued for the length of time of the enrolment in school.

○ A return air ticket.

○ Travel assistance insurance and medical insurance.

○ A written statement of support signed by the host family which must be stamped by the local police.

○ A written agreement between the au-pair-to-be and the host family (which should specify the duration of stay, salary, study benefits, etc.). The above must be stamped by the *Ufficio Provinciale del Lavoro*, together with a permit issued by the local police. In some areas it is sufficient to just have this stamped by the local police.

The au pair visa is granted for study purposes and the age guidelines are 18-30. In general, the conditions of work for an au pair among the affluent Italian middle classes who take them are reasonably good. They get board, lodging and pocket money of €80-€90 per week. Mothers' helps will work longer hours a week and get more money. Au pairs are expected to devote a certain amount of time to their hosts' offspring (not usually more than 4-6 hours per day), to attend a part-time language course at the local school and to be an active member in the family's social milieu. In Italy particularly, au pairs tend to be embraced into the bosom of the host family and to the uninitiated this can be an overpowering and bewildering experience. Most people seem to adapt to the Italians' demonstrative and vociferous ways and whatever else this arrangement may involve, it is unlikely that you will ever feel alienated or lonely in the midst of Italian family life. As the Italians who can afford au pairs tend also to be the ones who can afford luxury holiday villas on the coast, keep your fingers crossed for a trip to the seaside in the holiday month of August and one to the Italian Alps in the skiing season.

The majority of European au pair agencies deal with Italy and so you should have no trouble arranging a job there. Watch out for a wide variation in registration fees from about £15 to register to search a data base up to £150 to arrange a job through an agency (though some charge a third of that). Au pairs who are EU nationals have to visit the local police station (*Questura*) after three months accompanied by a member of the host family who will need to sign that he or she is willing to take responsibility for you. Proof may also be required that you are actually attending a language course. Au pairs are then granted a three-month extension, which must be renewed for a further three months on its expiry. The publication, *The Au Pair and Nanny's Guide to Working Abroad* is an invaluable source for those looking for an au pair job abroad and is available from Vacation Work in Oxford (☎01865-241978; www.vacationwork.co.uk).

North American au-pair agencies who arrange placements in Italy can be found in the list below. Non-EU citizens must obtain a visa before arriving in Italy and a good agency will be able to advise how to obtain this.

Useful Addresses

Useful Website
International Association of Au Pair Agencies (www.iapa.org): Lists their member agencies online.

Great Au Pair (www.greataupair.com): Lists 16,000 jobs in 140 countries including Italy.

Aupairconnect.com: matching-up site for au pairs and host families worldwide.

Agencies in Italy
A.R.C.E: (Attivitá Relazioni Culturali con l'Estero), via XX Settembre 20/124, 16121 Genova, Italy; ☎010-583092; fax 010-58309; e-mail info@arceaupair. it; www.arceaupair.it.

Au Pair International: Via S. Stefano 32, 40125 Bologna, Italy; ☎051-267575; fax 051-236594; info@au-pair-international.com; www.au-pair-international. com. Summer placements.

Au Pairs Recruitment: via Gaeta 22, 10133 Turin; ☎329-211 6277; e-mail annaparavia@paravia.it.

Euroma: Viale B Buozzi 19AA.int3, 00197 Rome; ☎06 806 92 130; e-mail info@euroma.info; www.euroma.info. Charges fee.

Europlacements Italy: Via Felica Cavalotti 15, 20122 Milan; ☎02 760 18 357; e-mail europlacements@studioventimiglia.com; www.europlacements.com.

Live in/out childcarers in Milan and throughout Italy. Also nursery assistants (EMT qualified only). No fees charged.

Intermediate: Via Bramante 13, 00153 Rome; ☎06-5747444; fax 06-57300574; www.intermediateonline.com.

Jolly Italian: Via Giovanni XXIII 20, 36050 Monteviale (VI); tel/fax 04 44552426; www.goldnet.it/jolly.

Mix Culture Roma: Via Nazionale 204, 00184 Rome; ☎06-4788 2289; web. tiscali.it/mixcultureroma/aupaireng.htm.

Agencies in the UK

Abbey Au Pairs: 8 Boulnois Avenue, Parkstone, Poole, Dorset BN14 9NX; tel/fax 01202-732922.

Academy Au Pair & Nanny Agency: 42 Milsted Road, Rainham, Kent ME8 6SU; tel/fax 01634-310808; www.academyagency.co.uk.

Angels International Au Pair Agency: 17 Crane Road, Twickenham, Middlesex TW2 6RX; ☎020-8893 4400; www.aupair1.com.

Anglo Pair Agency: 40 Wavertree Road, Streatham Hill, London SW2 3SP; ☎020-8674 3605; fax 020-8674 1264; www.anglo.pair@btinternet.com.

A-One Au-Pairs & Nannies: Top Floor, Union House, Union Street, Andover, Hampshire, SP10 1PA; ☎01264-332500; fax 01264-362050; www. aupairsetc.co.uk.

The Au Pair Agency: 231 Hale Lane, Edgware, Middlesex HA8 9QF; ☎020-8958 1750; fax 020-8958 5261; www.aupairagency.com.

English-Italian Agency; 69 Woodside, Wimbledon SW9 7AF; ☎020-8946 5728; partner agency in Italy.

Agencies in North America

Accord Cultural Exchange: 750 La Playa, San Francisco, CA 94121, USA; ☎415-386 6203; fax 415-386 0240; www.cognitext.com.

Au Pair in Europe: PO Box 68056, Blakely Postal Outlet, Hamilton, Ontario, Canada L8M 3M7; ☎905-545 6305; 905-544 4121; www.princeent.com/aupair/.

InterExchange Inc., Au Pair USA Programme, 13th Floor, 161 Sixth Avenue, New York, NY 10013, USA; ☎212-924 0446; fax 212-924 0575; www. interexchange.org.

Le Monde Au Pair: 7 rue de la Commune Ouest, Bureau 204, Montréal, Québec H2Y 2C5, Canada; ☎514-281 3045; fax 514-281 1525; e-mail au pair@generation.net.

Scotia Personnel Ltd: 6045 Chery Street, Halifax, Nova Scotia B3H 2K4, Canada; ☎902-422 1455; fax 902-423 6840; www.scotia-personnel-ltd.com.

World Wide Au Pair & Nanny, 2886 Davison St, Oceanside, NY 11672, USA; tel/fax 516-764 7528; www.worldwideaupair.com.

TEACHING ENGLISH AS A FOREIGN LANGUAGE

Italy is one of a number of European countries that has a steady demand for Teachers of English as a foreign language: this demand has increased greatly over the last five years as the popularity of the internet has increased. There are hundreds of language schools in Italy as any *pagine gialle* (yellow pages) will confirm, and between them they employ thousands of teachers, most of them on short-term contracts; longer term work is much harder to get. Moreover, it is not just the inhabitants of the large and sophisticated cities of Rome, Florence and Milan who long to learn English. Small towns in Sicily and Sardinia, in the Dolomites and along the Adriatic all have more than their fair share of private language schools and thus offer a variety of teaching opportunities. As you might surmise from the above range and distribution of schools, there is some variation of standards. At the elite end there are the schools which are AISLI (Associazione Italiana Scuole di Lingua Inglese) members; AISLI, c/o Cambridge Centre of English in Modena, Via Campanella 16, 41100 Modena; aisli@aisli.it; www.aisli.it. AISLI has very strict regulations and its schools are ultra-respectable. However, it would be a mistake to assume AISLI represents all the best schools; for instance neither the British Institute in Florence, nor International House in Rome is a member.

However, just because there are hundreds of schools does not mean jobs are always easy to come by. In some popular places supply outstrips demand and it can be difficult to get anything other than very short-term contracts and freelance work as the cost to employers of full-time employees is prohibitive. The best way of finding private teaching jobs on the spot is to head for any of the 31 university towns and put up notices that you are offering conversation lessons. Since all Italian university students have to take some type of English course, many are eager to be taught by a native speaker. For other teaching work, it is worth looking in English language papers such as the expat Italian websites like *Romebuddy*, *The Informer*, the Italian newspapers, *Messaggero in Rome* or *La Pulce* in Florence, or *Easy Milano* in Milan for adverts. For speculative applications you will find a list of language schools listed under *Scuole di Lingue* in the Italian Yellow Pages; the best time to apply to these schools is September/October time or just after Christmas. Do keep in mind, however, that your chances are much improved if you have some kind of TEFL qualification, either the Cambridge CELTA or Trinity TESOL certificates or a shorter TEFL training course. Below are listed some addresses for training courses in the UK, the US and Italy.

If you do not have any teaching qualifications it is still possible to talk your way into a job, bearing in mind, however, that competition tends to be keenest in Rome, Florence and Venice, so non-qualified job-seekers would be advised to avoid the major cities. However, reports suggest that the number of schools willing to employ unqualified teachers is declining so private conversation lessons are probably a better bet. As mentioned above, the publication, *Teaching English*

Abroad (Vacation Work, £12.95) is an invaluable source of reference for anyone considering teaching in Italy. Also, try the *Education section of the Guardian* on Tuesdays and the *Times Educational Supplement* on Fridays both of which are regular sources of TEFL jobs. The weekly *Times Educational Supplement*, better known as the TES, has weekly job listings including overseas appointments, which it also posts online along with useful articles at: www.tes.co.uk.

In the US the equivalent is the bi-monthly TIE (The International Educator) that includes both TEFL and regular teaching vacancies at (mostly American) schools around the world. TIE vacancies are posted online, but can be viewed by subscribers only. Subscriptions giving immediate access can be bought online at: www.tieonline.com.

One of the most comprehensive resources for EFL teachers is *Dave's ESL Café* (www.eslcafe.com), which provides extensive listings and information. Other online job sites include www.tesolmax.com, www.tefl.net, www.eslworldwide. com (38 institutions with vacancies in Italy at the time of writing), www.joyjobs. com (subscription costs $40), www.iteachnet.com and www.intlschools-k12. com. The *European Council of International Schools* (www.ecis.org), *International Schools Services* (www.iss.edu) and *Search Associates* (www.search-associates. com & www.search-associates.co.uk) who specialise in teacher placement at International Schools (see below) will also have a very few EFL vacancies in their job listings. The website www.wwteach.com has extensive information, advice and links for those considering going abroad to teach, all provided by an experienced international teacher.

The standard teaching wage in Italy is not high and EFL teachers should not expect to receive subsidised or free accommodation, though some help may be given in finding somewhere to live.

TEFL Schools in Italy:

A.C.L.E.: via Roma, 54, 18038 San Remo (Liguria); tel/fax 0184-506070; info@acle.org; www.acle. org. Requires teachers for summer camps.

Anderson House: Via Bergamo 25, 24035 Curno (Bergamo). ☎(035) 46 30 74. Fax: (035) 437 5698. E-mail: info@andersonhouse.it. Website: www.andersonhouse.it. degree plus CELTA (min. grade B) or DELTA and min. 2 years experience. Min. age 25. Couples with car a bonus. Contracts from October to May/June (8/9 months) or from January for 5 months. All contracts renewable.

Benedict School: C. so Alberto Pio 68, 41012 Carpi (MO). ☎(059) 695921. Fax: (059) 622 1007. E-mail: info@benedict-carpi. it. Website: www.benedict-carpi. it. TEFL (CELTA or equivalent certification). Mid-September until mid-July. 80% of work is with companies; 20% with private students. Assist non-EU and EU teachers with permits.

Benedict School: Via Salara 36, 48100 Ravenna. ☎(0544) 38199. Fax: (0544) 38399. E-mail: benedict@linknet.it. Website: www. romagna.com/benedict. University degree plus CELTA or equivalent required. Minimum 2 years experience. Minimum 6 month contracts, renewable.

Benedict School: Via Crispi 32, 1-80122 Napoli. ☎(081) 662 672. Fax: (081) 803 338. E-mail: benedictschool@librero.it. Website: www.benedictschool.it. 8-9 month contracts and 2 year contracts available. Minimum CELTA plus degree and 1 year of teaching experience.

British Institute: Viale Duca D'Aosta 19, 21052 Busto Arsizio (VA). ☎(0331) 627479. Fax: (0331) 634280. E-mail: britba@tin.it. TEFL, TESOL or CELTA certificate plus 1 year's experience and valid driving licence. October-June contracts.

British School Vicenza: Viale Roma 8, 36100 Vicenza. ☎(0444) 542190. Fax: (0444) 323444. E-mail: elsa@protec.it. Other schools: British Centre, Piazza Lamarmora 12, 10015 Ivrea. ☎(0125) 641618. Fax: (0125) 40242; British Centre, Via Tripoli 27, 15100 Alessandria. Tel/fax: (0131) 263475. degree, Cert TEFL and 1-2 years experience plus good Italian. Mid-September to mid-June. 25 h.p.w. Mainly evening work (to 10pm).

British Srl: Via XX Settembre 12, 16121 Genoa. ☎(010) 593591/562621. Fax: (010) 562621. E-mail: britishsrl@libero. it. BA plus CELTA and minimum experience. Italian useful. Contracts between mid-September and mid-June. Most pupils aged 16-40.

Byron Language Development: Via Sicilia 125, 00187 Rome. ☎(06) 4201 4436. Fax: (06) 482 8556. E-mail: info@byronschool.it. Website: www.byronschool.it. TEFL qualification, degree and 2 years' experience minimum. Freelance contracts of flexible length. To work either morning and afternoon or afternoon and evening.

Caledonian Communications: Viale Vigliani 55, 20148 Milan. ☎(02) 4802 0486/1086. Fax: (02) 4819 4706. E-mail: info@caledonian.it. Website: www.caledonian.it. Degree (preferably in a business subject) followed by TEFL qualification. Contracts 4-12 months, renewable.

Cambridge Insitute: Viale Cappuccini 45, 66034 Lanciano (CH). ☎(0872) 710291 or 727175. Fax: (0872) 724390. E-mail: cambridgeinstitute@tin.it. Website: www.cambridgeinstitute.it. One year contracts. Institute also a *Liceo Linguistico* or high school.

The Cambridge School: Via Rosmini 6, 37123 Verona. ☎(045) 800 3154. Fax: (045) 801 4900. E-mail: info@cambridgeschool.it. Website: www.cambridgeschool.it. Member of AISLI. CELTA (or similar), degree and preferably two years' experience. 9-month contracts.

Centro Linguistico British Institutes: Corso Umberto I, 17 - 62012 Civitanova Marche (MC). Tel/fax:

(0733) 816197. Also: Via Carducci 21, 62100 Macerata. Tel/fax: (0733) 231364. Also: Corso Matteotti 283, 62017 Porto Recanati (MC). Tel/fax (071) 979 9211. E-mail: jobs@centrolinguistico.it.   BA essential (MA preferred) and TEFL Certificate or Diploma. 8-month contracts from October.

CLM-Bell: Via Pozzo 30, 1-38100 Trento. ☎(0461) 981733. Fax: (0461) 981687. E-mail: clm-bell@clm-bell.it. Website: www.clm-bell.it. minimum 2 years experience with CELTA/DELTA qualification. 9-month contracts.

Darby School of Languages: Via Mosca 51, Villino 15, 00142 Rome. ☎06-51962205; Fax: 06-51965012. E-mail: darbyschool@tin.it. TEFL Cert. Freelance teachers.

English Academy snc: Via Carlo Zucchi 64, 41100 Modena. Tel/fax: (059) 33 4737. E-mail: callan@englishacademy.it. Website: www.englishacademy.it. No special teaching certification necessary because teachers are trained in the Callan Method. All lessons last 50 minutes; small groups of mainly adults (max. 6 per group).

The English Institute: Piazza Garibaldi 60, 80142 Naples. ☎(081) 287002. Fax: (081) 5548745. Website: www.sadra.it. TEFL Certificate. 10-month contracts.

Eurostreet Institute of Training: Via Losana 17, 13900 Biella (BI). ☎(015) 351269. Fax: (015) 352844. E-mail: info@eurostreet.it. Website: www.eurostreet.it.   University graduate. 1 year contracts.

GIGA: Via Roccaromana 6, Catania, 95124 Sicily. ☎(095) 721 2243. Fax: (095) 32 00 33. E-mail: info@gigact.com. Website: www. gigact.com.   Privately   owned language school and translation agency. EU passport or work permit required. Contract for a year from late September.

Ilk Ancona Scuola di Lingue: Scalo Vittorio Emanuele II, 1, 60121 Ancona. ☎(071) 206610. Fax: (071) 207 0169. E-mail: info@iik.it. Website: www.iik.it. Minimum 3 years' teaching experience and TEFL/TESOL Certificate. Generally from September to the end of June.

Interlingue School of Languages: Via Ennio Quirino Visconti 20, 00193 Roma. ☎(06) 321 5740/321 0317. Fax: (06) 323 5709. E-mail: info@interlingue-it.com. Website: www.interlingue-it.com. Minimum TEFL certificate, university degree, some teaching experience 9-month contracts.

International House (Campobasso): Via Zurlo 5, 86100 Campobasso. Tel/fax: (0874) 63240/481321. E-mail: mary@ihcampobasso.it.   CELTA qualification and experience essential teaching children and teenagers essential. Contracts for 2, 4 and 6 weeks from end of June to August. Recruitment through International House London or direct.

International House (Palermo): Via Gaetano Daita 29, 90139 Palermo. ☎(091) 584954. Fax: (091) 323965. E-mail: ihpa1@ihpalermo.it. Website: www.ihpalermo.it. Mailing address: Via Q Sella 70,

90139 Palermo. Degree and CELTA (minimum grade 'B'). School interested in career teachers only. 9-month contracts.

International School: Via Garibaldi 4, 07026 Olbia, Sardinia. Tel/fax: (0789) 21578. E-mail: xischool@tin. it. University degree plus CELTA or equivalent. Qualified primary/secondary teachers preferred. All teachers subject to *Contratto Nazionale* between October 1st and May 31st.

Intflex Srl: Via F lli Cairoli 9 (Isolago), 23900 Lecco. ☎(0341) 369383. Fax: (0341) 366138. E-mail: info@intflex.com. Website: www. intflex.com. TEFL or TESOL diploma. October to May.

Keep Talking: Via Roma 60, 33100 Udine. ☎(0432) 5015256. Tel/fax: (0432) 228216. E-mail: info@keeptalking.it. Website: www. keeptalking.it. University degree and CELTA or equivalent required plus minimum 1 year of experience. 9-month contracts (*contratto a progetto*).

Living Languages School: Via Magna Grecia 2, 89100 Reggio Calabria. Tel/fax: (0965) 330926. Also: via Madonna, 21 Gallico, 89100 Reggio Calabria. Tel/fax: (0965) 373794. E-mail: info@livinglanguages.it. Website: www.livinglanguages.it. TEFL, CELTA. 9-month renewable contracts. British contract.

London School International House: Via Emilia 34, 90114 Palermo. ☎(091) 670 4746. Tel/fax: (091) 526937. E-mail: london@londonschool. it. Website: www.londonschool.

it. Minimum CELTA. Experience desirable, especially of teaching Young Learners. 8-month contracts.

Lord Byron College: Via Sparano 102, 70121 Bari. ☎(080) 523 2686. Fax: (080) 524 1349. E-mail: info@lordbyroncollege.com. Website: www.lordbyroncollege. com. Authorised by Italian Ministry of Education and member of EAQUALS (European Association for Quality Language Services). Degree, TEFL qualification, at least one year's teaching experience and knowledge of a foreign language. 8-9 month contracts or 5-month contracts from January.

*Master Education Group:*Division of Linguaviva, Via C. De Cristoforis 15, 20124 Milan. ☎(02) 659 6401. Fax: (02) 2900 2395. E-mail: info@linguaviva.net or job@linguaviva.net. Website: www. linguaviva.net. minimum CELTA or equivalent, degree and some experience. Contract September to June/July.

*New School:*Via de Ambrosis 21, 15067 Novi Ligure (AL). ☎(0143) 2987. Fax: (0143) 767678. E-mail: new.school@libarnanet.it. TEFL Diploma/degree plus 1 year's experience. Recruit via www.tefl. com. 9-month contracts.

New School Ovada: Piazza Mazzini, 59, Ovada. Tel/fax: (0143) 821 081. E-mail: new.school@libarnanet.it. TEFL Diploma/degree plus 1 year's experience. 9 months, renewable.

*Oxford Institute:*10/12 Via Adriatica 10/12, 73100 Lecce. Tel/fax: (0832)

390312. CELTA plus 2 years' experience. 9-month contracts October to June.

Oxford International Centre: Via Fontivegge 55, 06124 Perugia. ☎(075) 500 3673. Fax: (075) 500 3678. E-mail: oxfordschool@tin.it. Degree plus any of the certificates for ELT (Tefl, CELTA, etc.). Experience preferred. 8-months minimum. Recruitment via internet. Telephone interview possible.

Oxford School of English Srl: Administrative Office, Via S. Pertini 14, 30035 Mirano, Venice. ☎(041) 570 23 55. Fax: (041) 570 2390. E-mail: oxforditalia@tin.it. Website: www.oxforditalia.it. Degree, TEFL and knowledge of Italian needed. 9-months or longer contracts.

Quagi Language Centre: Via Manzoni, C. Santa, 91100 Trapani, Sicily. Tel/fax: (0923) 557748. E-mail: quagi@quagi.com or quagi@quagi.org. Website: www.quagi.org (website under construction). Normally 8 months October to the end of May but 4-month contracts also offered (September-December).

Regency School: Via Arcivescovado 7, 10121 Torino. ☎(011) 562 7456. Fax: (011) 541845. E-mail: regency@tin.it or regency.international@regency.it. Web-site: www.regency.it. university degree essential plus CELTA or equivalent or DELTA or equivalent. Full-time and part-time contracts.

Scuola di Lingue Europe/Miles Scuola de Lingua: Via Zuppani 5, Belluno 32100. ☎(0437) 948182. Fax: (0437) 948182. E-mail: cristina.gavaz@libero.it or scuolaeuropa@hotmail.com. Website: www.mileseuropa.com. TEFL certificate (grade B) and degree minimum. Some TEFL experience preferred. Contracts run from October to May.

Step by Step English School: C.so G. Ferraris 135, 10128 Torino. Tel/fax: (011) 581 7635. E-mail: info@gostepbystep.it. Website: www.gostepbystep.it. university. Degree (BA or higher) plus TEFL Certificate and some teaching experience. Contracts for a school year.

Summer Camps: Via Roma 54, San Remo, 18038. Tel/fax: (0184) 506070. See entry for A.C.L.E. above.

The United College: Ronco a Via Von Platen 16/18, 96100 Siracusa. Tel/fax: (0931) 22000. E-mail: united.college@tin.it. degree plus Certificate (Cambridge or TESOL). Mid-September to mid-June. Recruitment is through www.tefl.com.

The Victoria Company: Via XXIV Maggio 55, 60035 Jesi (AN). Tel/fax: (0731) 648328. E-mail: info@thevictoriacompany.it. Website: www.thevictoriacompany.it. TEFL/CELTA, minimum 1 year's experience. 8-month contracts.

Wall Street Institute (Bergamo): Via Brigata Lupi 6, 24122 Bergamo. ☎(035) 224531/235442. Fax: (035) 238759. E-mail: eroberts@wallstreet.it. Qualified teachers with EFL experience.

Business English preferred. One-week teacher training course at the the beginning of the academic year.

Wall Street Institute (Ferrara): Via Zandonai 4, 44100 Ferrara. ☎(0532) 977703. Fax: (0532) 907446. E-mail: reception@wallstreetferrara.it. Website: www.wallstreetferrara.it. CELTA or other TEFL qualification; teaching experience (minimum 1 year) and knowledge of Italian needed. Driving licence may be needed. 10-month-contracts (September-June). Mostly adults.

Windsor School of English: Via Saluzzo 9, 10064 Pinerolo (TO). Tel/fax: (0121) 795555. Mobile: (348) 3914 155. E-mail: windsor@vds.it. Minimum CTEFL. 9-10 months. Flat provided.

OTHER SCHOOLS TO TRY (CITIES AND TOWNS IN ALPHABETICAL ORDER)

Note that these schools have been taken from various sources, such as the *Yellow Pages* and the internet.

Anglo American School, Piazza S Giovanni in Monte 9, 40124 Bologna (www.angloamericanschool.tin.it)

English Language Institute, Via Marconi 29, 40122 Bologna (051-236527)

Modern English Study Centre, Via Borgonuovo 14, 40125 Bologna (fax 051-225314)

british institute, Viale Duca D'Aosta 19, 21052 Busto Arsizio (VA). (Tel/fax: 0331-634280; britba@tin.it).

Victoria Language Centre, Viale G. Fassi 28, 41012 Carpi (Modena) (059-652545/fax 059-652499; victoria@carpi.nettuno.it)

Oxford School of Languages, Via Garibaldi 108, 06034 Foligno (0742-357430).

The Training Company, Via XX Settembre 34111, 16124 Genova (010-540964; www.thetrainingcompany.org). Affiliated to Teachers in Italy agency mentioned earlier in chapter.

British School of Gorizia, Corso Italia 17, 34170 Gorizia (0481-33300; gorizia@british-fvg.net). AISLI member

British School Of Monfalcone, Via Duca d'Aosta 16, Monfalcone, Gorizia, FVG. ☎(0481) 33300. Fax: (0481) 412228. E-mail: monfalcone@british-FVG.net.

Accademia Britannica International House, Via Bruxelles 61, 04100 Latina. (0773-624917; fax: 0773-608450; ih-latina@panservice.it; www.Internationalhouseitaly.com)

British Institutes, Via Leopardi 8, 20123 Milan (02-4390041; www.britishinstitutes.org). Website gives email addresses of British Institutes throughout Italy.

International House (Tradint), Via Jannozzi 6, San Donato Milanese (02-527 91 24; sandonato.milan@internationalhouse.com). 15 teachers for suburban locations around Milan.

Into English, Via Cadorna 5, 20037 Paderno Dugnano (MI) (02-990 43 215). 15 minutes north of Milan. Must be available for interview in

Milan.

Regent Italia s.r.l., Via Fabio Filzi 27, 20124 Milan (02-670 70516/fax 02-670 73625; regent@galactica.it). Summer, year-long and part-time contracts available.

Wall Street Institute (Milan), Corso Buenos Aires 79, 20124 Milan (02-670 3108). 45 teachers.

British Language Centre, Via Cumbo Borgia 8, Milazzo (Tel/fax: 090-928 1645; helenscorer@virgilio.it)

Cambridge Centre of English, Via Campanella 16, 41100 Modena (059-241004; fax 059-224238; norris@tin.it; www.cambridgecentre.com). 8 experienced teachers from the UK.

British School of Monza, Via Zucchi 38, 20052 Monza (MI) (039-389803; fax 039-230 2047; info@britishmonza.com). 5 teachers.

Shenker Institute, Via Cavalotti 17, 20052 Monza (039-386861; fax 039-388905; infomonza@englishlanguageinstitute.it; www.shenker.it).

American Studies Center, 36 V. D'Isernia, 80122 Naples (081-660562; info@americanstudiescenter.it)

British Language School, 73 V. Diaz Armando, 80555 Portici (NA) (081-480240)

International House Pisa, Via Risorgimento 9, 56126 Pisa (050-44040; ihpisa@alet.it). AISLI member

English School, Via Degli Arconti 25, 89127 Reggio Calabria. (Tel/fax: 0965-899535)

International School of Languages, Via Argine destro Annunziata, 13,

89121 Reggio Calabria (0965-20024).

Centro Linguistico Rimini, C. D'Augusto 144, 47900 Rimini (0541-56487)

The British Institutes, Via Aurelia 137, Rome (06-393 75 966; britishroma@euol.it). 70 per year (including part-time teachers).

Intrnational Language School, Via Tibullo 10, 00193 Rome (06-68 30 77 96). 20 teachers.

Prolingua, Via Angelo Ranucci 5, 00165 Rome (06-39367721; fax 06-393 67723; info@prolingua.it; www.linguapro.com). 15 native speaker teachers on initial 3 month contracts.

Interlanguage Point, Corso Vittorio Emanuele 14, 84100 Salerno. (089-275 3581; fax: 089-275 3581; interlanguagepoint@hotmail.com).

The English Centre, Via P. Paoli 34, 07100 Sassari (079-23 21 54; fax 079-23 21 80; theenglishcentre@tin.it or info@theenglishcentreonline.com). 8 British teachers with Cambridge Cert. plus 2 years' experience, mainly recruited through Saxoncourt in London.

International House (Seregno), Accademia Britannica Srl, Via Gozzano 4/6, 20038 Seregno (MI) (0362-230970; ih_seregno@worldonline.it). AISLI school that employs 10 British teachers.

English School, Viale Roosevelt 14, 67039 Sulmona (AQ). Tel/fax: (0864) 55606. E-mail mdicio@arc.it.

CLM-Bell, Centro di Lingue Moderne/

Bell Educational Trust, Via Pozzo 30, 38100 Trento (0461-981733; fax 0461-981687; clm-bell@clm-bell.it; www.clm-bell.it). Branches in Riva del Garda, etc.

Berla B.N.F. de Neil, Ursula & Forte Lucia S.N.C., Vicolo Biscaro 1, 31100 Treviso (tel/fax 0422-544242)

Globe School Valdagno, Via Cabianchina 5, 36073 Corredo V. no Vicenza. ☎(0445) 430800. E-mail: info@globeschool.com. Website: www.globeschool.com (under construction).

TEFL Training in the UK:

In addition to the addresses below many technical colleges and universities offer TEFL courses on a part-time or full-time basis; further information can be found from the colleges themselves.

Bell Teacher Training Institute: 1 Redcross Lane, Cambridge CB2 2QX; ☎01223-212333. Four weeks (130 hours). Also part-time courses (Tues and Thurs evenings) October to June. Six full time courses per year. Can advise on host families.

Berlitz (UK) Ltd: 296-302 High Holborn, London WC1 7JH; ☎020-7611 9640; fax 020-7611 9656. Does not run TEFL courses but compulsory method training for its own method lasting one to two weeks. This can be taken in the country in which the employee is successfully interviewed rather than in the country where they will be working.

inlingua Training Courses: Rodney Lodge, Rodney Road, Cheltenham, Glos GL50 1JF; ☎01242-250493; fax 01242-253181; e-mail training@inlingua-cheltenham.co.uk. Five weeks Trinity Certificate in Cheltenham.

International House: 106 Piccadilly, London W1 9FL; ☎020-75186999; www.ihlondon.com. Cambridge Certificate offered throughout the year.

TEFL Training in the US:

Cy-Fair College, 9191 Barker Cypress Drive, Cypress, TX 77433. ☎281-290 3986. Fax: 281-290-5283. E-mail: albarea@nhmccd.edu. Alternative site for North Harris College (see below). Full-time course 3 times a year, usually February, July and November US$1,736. Accommodation can be arranged on request at a cost of about US$400 per month.

College Of Lake County, 19531 W Washington Street, Greyslake, Illinois 60030. ☎847-543 2565. Fax: 847 543 3565. E-mail: jacath@clcillinois.edu. Website: www.clcillinois.edu.

Denver Bridge Linguatec Ltd, Bridge Linguatec International, 915 S Colorado Boulevard, Denver, Colorado. ☎800-724-4210. Fax: 303-777 7246. E-mail: tefl@bridgelinguatec.com. Website: www.bridgelinguatec.com. US$2,595.

Embassy CES, The Center for English Studies, 330 Seventh Avenue, New York, NY 10001. ☎212-629-7300. Fax: 212-736-

7950 or 212-497-8330. E-mail: lpainter@studygroupintl.com. Website: www.embassyces.com. 7 or 8 full-time courses per year. $2,545. Accommodation in student residences and bed and breakfasts. Job counselling given.

Intercultural Communications College, 1601 Kapiolani Boulevard, Suite 1000, Honolulu, HI 96814. ☎808-946 2445. Fax: 808-946 2231. E-mail: info@icchawaii.edu. Website: www.icchawaii.edu. Full-time 4-week courses run 4 times each year, beginning April, May, July and September. Fees US$2100 all inclusive. Help provided to find accommodation at an average cost of US$900-1200 per month.

International House San Francisco, 49 Powell Street, Suite 200, 2nd Floor, San Francisco, CA 94102. ☎415-989-4473. Fax: 415-989-4440. E-mail: cheyns@ih-sanfrancisco.com. Website: www.ih-usa.com. Full-time 4-week course. Half board homestay accommodation $200 per week. Application through Portland IH (see next entry).

International House – Teacher Training Usa, 200 SW Market Street, Suite 111, Portland, OR 97201. ☎503-224-1960. Fax: 503-224-2041. E-mail: teachertraining@ih-portland. com. Website: www.ih-usa.com. Also in Los Angeles: 530 Wilshire Blvd., Santa Monica, CA 90401. ☎310-394-8618. Fax: 310-394-2708. Full-time 4-week CELTA courses run 8-11 times a year. Approx $2,350. Half-board homestay accommodation can be arranged

or apartments available in Portland or Santa Monica. Help with job placement worldwide. Applications for all IH locations in the US should be sent to the Portland centre. 3 new courses planned in the San Francisco area for 2005. Contac the Portland office for further details.

North Harris College, Center for International Education and Languages, 2700 W.W. Thorne Drive, Houston, TX 77073. ☎281-618-5606. Fax: 281-618-5633. E-mail: edesouza@nhmccd.edu. Website: http://celta.nheducatesu. com. Full-time 3 times a year starting in March, June and October $1,736. Accommodation can be arranged on request at a cost of about $400 a month.

St Giles Language Teaching Center, One Hallidie Plaza, Suite 350, San Francisco, CA 94102. ☎415-788-3552. Fax: 415-788-1923. E-mail: training@stgiles-usa.com. Website: www.stgiles-usa.com. Offer year round Cambridge CELTA courses as well as intensive and semi-intensive Cambridge DELTA courses. CELTA course fee US$2,790. Postgraduate credit recommendation of six hours towards an MA TESOL degree and lifelong job assistance. Approved by the Cambridge University Local Examinations Syndicate and the California Bureau of Private Postsecondary Vocational Education and the Commission on English Language Programmes Accreditation (CEA).

School For International Training, Kipling Road, PO Box 676,

Brattleboro, Vermont 05302. ☎802-258-3310. Fax: 802-258-3316. E-mail: tesolcert@sit.edu. Website: www.sit.edu/tesolcert. SIT TESOL Certificate course can be co-validated by UCLES as CELTA. $2,500. (See entry below in *Training Courses Abroad*).

TEFL Training in Italy

Taking a course in Italy allows non-EU citizens to build up contacts in Italy that may lead to a job; some addresses are listed below. Courses cost about €1,500 and run throughout the year. Many EFL websites listed in this section will also provide links to EFL training course providers. There are also online TEFL courses such as the one at: www.teacher-training.net and www.onlinetefl.com.

British Council Milan, Via Manzoni 38, 20121 Milan. ☎02-772221. Fax: 02-781119. E-mail: simon. creasey@britishcouncil.it. Website: www.britishcouncil.it. Price on application. Help with employment in and around Milan offered.

British Council Naples, Via Morghen 36, 80129 Naples. ☎081-578 8247. Fax: 081-578 2046. E-mail: Annamaria.Vorraro@britishcouncil. it. Website: www.britishcouncil.it. Full-time CELTA course run every June, 8.30am-5pm Monday to Friday. Also 2-week CELTYL course also in June. €1,800 for CELTA (including pre-course pack) and €900 for CELTYL. Exam fees extra (approximately €130). Applications must be received before mid-March.

Accommodation available.

The Cambridge School, Via Rosmini 6, 37123 Verona. ☎45-800 3154. Fax: 45-801 4900. E-mail: info@cambridgeschool.it. Website: www.cambridgeschool.it. Full-time and part-time courses. Help can be given with accommodation (hotel, hostel, family, apartments). Help given with finding placements for graduates.

International House Milan. E-mail: info@teachertraining.it. Website: www.teachertraining.it. Full-time and part-time courses run all year round.

International House – Rome, Viale Manzoni 22, 00185 Rome. ☎06-704 76 894. Fax: 06-704 97 842. E-mail: info@ihromamz.it. Website: www.ihromamz.it. Full-time (June, July, September, February) and semi-intensive twice a week for 3 months (October to December and March to May). €1,410. Accommodation provided if necessary for €450 per month. Also run CELTYL and DELTA courses.

International House Palermo, Via Quintino Sella, 70, 90139 Palermo. ☎091-584954. Fax: 091-323965. E-mail: wood@ihpalermo.it. Full-time course for 4 weeks, 9.30am to 6.30pm, Monday to Friday. Run in September every year. Fees are £1,490 including RSA fee. Self-catering accommodation in individual flats is available at an avery age cost of €350-€400 per month (including bills).Applicants will be expected to attend an interview before being accepted on the course.

TEACHING IN PRIMARY AND SECONDARY (K-12) SCHOOLS

One effect of so many foreigners living in Italy is the large number of International and National Curriculum schools dotted around the country providing an education for the children of expatriate families. The schools offer a variety of curricula including English, American, International and various other national educational systems including French, German, Japanese and Swiss. They will recruit staff experienced in teaching their national curriculum, which means that American schools will sponsor experienced US teachers to work in Italy.

These schools employ experienced and qualified teachers in all the subjects and specialisms required for good private schools. Methods of recruitment vary from school to school; direct application works for some while others recruit through job fairs and recruitment agencies. The main international schools in Italy can be found in the directories on the websites of the European Council of International Schools (www.ecis.org), International Schools Services (www.iss.edu), the International Baccalaureate Organisation (www.ibo.org) and the Council of Independent British Schools in the European Community (www.cobisec.org).

Many schools will recruit their teachers both at job fairs in Europe and North America and through adverts in the education press. The main recruitment fairs are organised by the European Council of International Schools (www.ecis.org), International Schools Services (www.iss.edu), Search Associates (www.search-associates.com) and Carney Sandoe & Associates (www.carneysandoe.com). Also worth trying is www.teachitaly.com.

In addition to the vacancies listed on the websites of the organisations mentioned above, the *Times Educational Supplement* (www.tes.co.uk) and *The International Educator* (www.tieonline), contain advertisements for teaching vacancies around the world.

Useful Addresses – Jobs in Schools

Educational Staffing Program: MP.O.Box 5910, Princeton, NJ 08543 (☎609 452 0990; fax 609 452 2690; www.iss.edu). Recruits both teachers and administrative staff for US and British schools in Italy. Applicants should have a minimum BA degree and two years' of relevant experience. Produces a publication, the *ISS Directory of Overseas Schools.*

Europlacements: Pvia Cavalotti 15, MM San Babila, Milano; (☎02 760 18357; fax 02 763 96711; recruitment agency for teachers and childcare professionals.

Fullbright English Teaching Assistantships: US Student Programs Division, Institute of International Education, 809 United Nations Plaza, New York,

NY 10017-3580, USA (☎212-984 5330; www.iie.org). Competitive program for college graduates organizes assistantships in Italy.

International Schools Services: 15 Roszel Road, POB 5910, Princeton, NJ 08543-5910 USA (☎609-452 2690; www.iss.edu). Does the hiring for about two hundred overseas schools, including two in Rome. Relevant experience and two year minimum availability expected.

TOURISM

Italy's buzzing tourist industry is a major source of employment providing jobs for six to seven per cent of the population. It is often difficult for foreigners to gain access to this source of work since even the so-called menial jobs available in major resorts in other European countries have a readily available pool of impeccably turned out, well-trained, multi-lingual locals. This can be rather frustrating if you have set your heart on working in, and gaining an insider's knowledge of Florence, Venice, Rome, Pisa, etc. An alternative is to work for a foreign tour company. Even this is problematic owing to restrictions on the employment of non-Italians in the industry. Some companies have exploited a legal loophole and called themselves art and cultural associations in order to employ non-Italians. The main tourist areas apart from the cities are the coastal resorts of Rimini and Pescara (on the Adriatic), Portofino and San Remo on the Italian Riviera, the island of Capri, Sorrento and Amalfi (south of Naples) and the Costa Smeralda of Sardinia. If you don't mind being inland the popular resorts of Italy's lakes, Garda, Maggiore and Como, are a possibility. However, finding any kind of work in tourism is going to be difficult. Your chances might improve if you speak Italian, or if one of your languages is German as most Italian tourist spots are very popular with German holiday makers. If you speak Italian then you can use Italian temporary work agencies like Sinterim (www.sinterim.it). The magazine *Job in Tourism* (www.jobintourism) appears both on and offline and is a source of thousands of job offers throughout the Italian tourist industry in hotels, cruise lines and tourist holiday villages.

Competition for tourist jobs is now overwhelming with thousands of job seekers from eastern European countries that joined the EU in 2004 now flooding the market. Literally the only way to get a job is to go to your preferred resort before the season is underway (or halfway through the season as there is a fast turnover amongst these jobs) and use your face and personality (and possibly your CV in Italian) to win a job. For non-EU citizens, it is virtually impossible to get a job as the Ispettorato del Lavoro (illegal work watchdog) tend to make frequent visits to the resorts and tourist areas and hotel owners do not want to take the risk of employing a non-EU person without the proper working visa.

If your knowledge of Italian or German fails to get you a job with a local employer, your skill may be more valued as a campsite courier with one of the major British camping holiday organisers such as Canvas Holidays – though this will only really be an option for Brits. You can also try Italian-run campsites The two main campsites in Rome (the Tiber and the Flaminio) take on English help before the season begins in the early summer of each year and more campsites can be found at www.camping.it. If you have a background in the hotel trade or childcare you could try the Forte Village Resort (www.fortevillageresort.com) in southern Sardinia, which caters largely for families. What about trying for a job with one of the 20 Italian holiday villages run by Club Valtur (www.valtur. it) the Italian Club Med, which has a large staff (up to 150 per resort) to run the on-site restaurants, bars and shops and organize sports, drama and other activities. The website www.assistentituristici.it is a portal to all kinds of work with Italian tour operators and has is a list of over 40 tour operators and links to their sites.

Most major British tour operators have programmes to Italy, and if you want to work in the winter they offer summer staff first pick of winter sports jobs. Italian-owned tour operator Citalia accepts Italian-speaking staff in the UK, as do the tour operators listed below. The Association of British Travel Agents (ABTA) website (www.abtanet.com) contains contact details for their members.

Tour managers taking groups to Italy should have a recognised qualification and carry a copy of their certificate translated into Italian and certified by the local Italian consulate. Tour managers without this documentation have been unceremoniously hauled off coaches and landed with steep fines.

Prospects for Work

There are tourism jobs to suit everyone, from meet and greet staff working at the major airports and ports, tour guides for coach tours of culture vultures, ski reps for school groups, reps looking after young groups holidaying on the Adriatic and older groups taking in the Italian lakes and cities, incentive tour managers at glamorous resorts like the Costa Smeralda in Sardinia and so on. Areas of the country hitherto unexplored to British tourists are being opened up by the new no-frills airline routes, e.g. Ryanair flies to Pescara, Trieste, Ancona and Bari, though so far these mainly appeal to independent travellers rather than package tourists.

British coach operators need tour guides to take groups around Italy, either by coach from Britain or flying to an airport in Switzerland or Italy, picking up their coach and then touring. The UK is the main marketplace for obtaining jobs with coach companies touring Italy. American students come over in large numbers each year to visit Italy, and many of the companies handling their travel have their European offices in London. British coach companies offer every kind of tour to Italy, from the cheap and cheerful based on one or two centres, to upmarket tours around the cultural high spots.

Most of the potential work opportunities are found in the northern half of the country, between the alpine borders and Rome. The south is poorer with high unemployment and is not as easy to visit as the north with its excellent communications with the rest of Europe. The relatively low unemployment in the Veneto region (which includes Venice, Padua and Verona) makes it a better bet than some of the other tourist regions of Italy such as the Adriatic coastal resorts of Rimini and Pescara and the Italian Riviera (Portofino, San Remo, etc.), though it may be worth trying resorts on Lake Maggiore like Stresa and Cannero. Michael Cullen worked in three hotels around Como and Bellagio and found 'a nice friendly and warm atmosphere, despite the heat and long hours'. High unemployment together with a huge population of migrant workers from poor countries in the south of Italy means that it is probably not worth trying the resorts south of Naples, viz. Capri, Sorrento and Amalfi. Even in flourishing resorts like Rimini, there seems to be nearly enough locals and Italian students to fill most of the jobs. As Stephen Venner observed, 'Although prospects appeared to be good in Rimini, café and hotel owners were unwilling to take on foreigners because of the paperwork.'

Although less well known than the seaside resorts of other Mediterranean countries, there may be seaside possibilities for foreign job-seekers, especially in the resorts near Venice, as a local resident Lara Giavi confirms. She is familiar with two holiday regions: the Lake Garda resorts like Desenzano, Malcesine, Sirmione and Riva del Garda; and the seaside resorts near Venice like Lido di Jesolo (which she says is a great resort for young people), Bibione, Lignano, Caorle and Chioggia, all of which are more popular with German and Austrian tourists than Britons so a knowledge of German would be a good selling point. Large hotels usually recruit their staff in southern Italy and then move them en masse from the sea to the mountains in the autumn. Relatively few students and others find work serving pizzas or cleaning hotel rooms in Italy compared to other European countries, but Lara thinks that there are opportunities for foreigners in catering, bars and hotels in Italy, though she admits that a knowledge of Italian is necessary in most cases, apart from the job of *donna ai piani* (chambermaid). One campsite that caters to British holiday makers is Union Lido (Il Parco delle Vacanze, 30013 Cavallino, Venezia; 04-257 5111) which has a 'Job Centre' icon on its English-language website www.unionlido. it.

The Blu Hotels chain has hotels and holiday villages in Lake Garda, Sardinia, Umbria, Abruzzo, Tuscany, Rome, Palinuro and Calabria (as well as Austria); the head office is at Via Porto Portese 22, 25010 San Felice di Benaco (Brescia); 0365-441100. The website – www.bluhotels.it – carries information (in Italian) on applying to work for the group. Another group of three hotels on Lago d'Orta has in the past hired kitchen and waiting staff (www.lagodortahotels. com).

Once you get a toehold in an Italian community you will find that a friendly network of contacts and possible employers will develop. Without contacts, it is virtually impossible to find work. Arriving in Diano Marina on the Ligurian coast to look for work, Bernie Lynes went to church on her first Sunday. The local grapevine decided she was a 'nice' girl, and she was soon offered a job with a tour operator whose rep had fallen sick.

Charter yachts may need experienced sailors as crew. Harbour masters along the Adriatic coast, Italian Riviera and in Sardinia can tell you if there are yachts looking for crew.

British and Italian Tour Operators

If you can stand the pace, are young, footloose and fancy-free, there are jobs as shuttle hosts and hostesses taking groups by coach to Italy. Try *Cosmos* or any of the major coach companies. If you are less young, a more sedate pace might be preferable, working on Inghams and Saga mountains and lakes tours where the temperatures are cooler.

Contiki's coach tours for an 18-35 clientele spend some time in Italy, and staff are needed for their stopovers (e.g. Florence, Venice, Rome). Without knowing much about the company or the job she was applying for, Carolyn Edwards was interviewed by Contiki (Wells House, 15 Elmfield Road, Bromley, Kent BR1 1LS; www.contiki.com/jobs.asp) and in her first season was employed as a general assistant at their Florence stopover site (a haunted villa). The job involved everything from cleaning toilets to delivering the welcome spiel. Carolyn soon discovered that she loved standing in front of 53 people talking about the local sites.

The major camping tour operators like Eurocamp and Italian Life Holidays trading under Camping Life (see Introduction and Directory of Tour Operators) employ courier/reps and children's reps on their Italian sites, for which an ability to speak some Italian is a basic requirement. Many of these sites are on the Adriatic coast between Cattolica and Rimini. Jobseekers who turn up at the gates on the off-chance of work might find some employment though at local casual rates without commission and perhaps without accommodation. Catherine Dawes enjoyed working for a UK camping tour operator near Albenga on the Italian Riviera – 'a fairly uninspiring part of Italy' – even more than she did her previous summer's work on a French campsite. In her view the Italians seem more relaxed than the French, especially under high season pressure, and would always go out of their way to help her when she was trying to translate tourists' problems to the mechanic or the doctor.

G & D Gruppo Vacanze (Via del Portonaccio 1, 47100 Forlì; 0543 26199;

www.gedgruppovacanze.com) run holiday camps for which they need European young people to work as counsellors and instructors of sports, dancing, music and theatre. Pay starts at €430 per month in addition to free board and accommodation. Try also Anderson srl (Via Tevere 44, 00198 Rome; fax 06-884 4664; animazione@andersonclub.it) who hire about 100 young people for their holiday villages and tour operations.

The Alitalia Group actively recruits candidates who need not speak Italian but must have other relevant qualifications. Applications should be sent to Alitalia's Recruitment Department, Viale Alessandro Marchetti 111, 00148 Rome (www.alitalia.it/en/know/humanres/working/working. htm).

Useful Contacts – Tour Operators

Aeroviaggi: ☎02 436048; www.aeroviaggiclub.it. Club and holiday village holidays in Sicily and Sardinia.

Carefree Italy, Allied Dunbar House, East Park, Crawley, West Sussex RH10 6AJ (01293 552277; italy@carefreetravelgroup.com)

Ciao Travel Ltd, 76 New Bond St, London W1S 1RX UK (www.ciaotravel. co.uk).

Club Vacanze: www.clubvacanze.it; e-mail CV and work request to clubvacanze. infojob@clubvacanze.it. Camping villages and tourist resorts.

Eden Viaggi: via degli Abeti, 24, 61100 Pesaro (PU); www.edenviaggi.it; e-mail edenviaggi@edenviaggi.it or risorseumane@edenviaggi.it. Italian seaside holidays including Sardinia.

Eurotravel: ☎0165 773111; www.eurotravel.it; e-mail info@eurotravel.it. All kinds of tourism including coach tours and the Val d'Aosta.

ICT (Independent Coach Travel), Studios 20-21, Colmans Wharf, 45 Morris Road, London E14 6PA (020-7538 4627; info@ictsqt.co.uk).

Italiatour, 71 Lower Rd, Kenley, Surrey CR8 5NH (0870 733 3000; www. italiatours.co.uk). Part of the Alitalia group.

Magic of Italy, now part of TUI, Greater London House, Hampstead Road, London NW1 7SD (020-7506 8598).

Sunvil Holidays, Upper Square, Old Isleworth, Middlesex TW7 7BJ (020-8758 4722; discovery@sunvil.co.uk).

Teorema Tour: ☎02 5502951; www.teorema.it. Holidays in Calabria, Sardinia and Sicily.

Viaggi del Ventaglio: ☎02/46754484; www.ventaglio.com. Holiday clubs and villages.

USEFUL ITALIAN JOB CHANNELS FOR EU NATIONALS

EU nationals can try using official channels to find work at the beginning of the season (mid-May), i.e. the *Ufficio di Collocamento* and the local *Associazione Albergatori* (hotels association) which should know of vacancies among its members. Try to track down local hotel associations or hotel chains, for example the following along the Adriatic:

Alberghi Consorziatai, 61032 Fano (0721-827376)
Associazione Albergatori di Rimini, Viale Baldini 14, 47037 Rimini (fax 0541-56519)
Associazione Pesarese Albergatori, 61100 Pesaro (0721-67959)
Associazione Balneare Azienda Turismo – 0733-811600
Associazione Bagnini di Numana e Sirolo, 60026 Numana Ancona (0721-827376).

Special Interest Tours. Anyone with a degree in history, history of art, archaeology or any subject related to Italian culture may be able to find work with special interest firms like Exodus, Explore or Inntravel (Nr. Castle Howard, York YO60 7JU; www.inntravel.co.uk) who run exclusive walking tours throughout Italy from the Amalfi coast to the Dolomites including of course the Tuscan hills. Groups often go to Rome and the Vatican on pilgrimages; your local church may have some leads. Two companies which specialise in pilgrimages to Rome (and elsewhere) are Tangney Tours (Pilgrim House, 3 Station Court, Borough Green, Kent TN15 8AF; 01732 886666; info@tangney-tours.com) and Mancunia Travel (International House, 82-84 Deansgate, Manchester M3 2ER; 0161-834 4030; info@mancunia.com).

Operators that sometimes require tour leaders with specialist knowledge and tour guides to look after their groups include:

ATG Footloose (see entry). Wild flowers, mushroom hunting, walking and cycling.

Arblaster & Clarke Wine Tours Ltd, Farnham Road, West Liss, Hants. GU33 6JQ (01730 893344; www.winetours.co.uk/ac-careers.html). Wine tours of Tuscany, Umbria, Piedmont and Veneto.

Voyages Jules Verne, 21 Dorset Square, London NW1 6QG (020-7616 1000; www.vjv.co.uk). Art and culture tours.

Winter Resorts

Opportunities exist on the spot in the winter resorts of the Alps, Dolomites and Apennines. Many of the jobs are part-time and not very well paid, but provide time for skiing and in many cases a free pass to the ski-lifts for the season. Sauze d'Oulx and Courmayeur seem to be the best resorts for job hunting. Although Cortina is probably the most famous, it has a high percentage of year-round workers, and is über-sophisticated and expensive. Sauze d'Oulx is particularly recommended because it hosts so many British holidaymakers that every bar and shop in the resort likes to hire an English- speaker. Remember that places like this will be dead before the season. If you are job-hunting in November, choose a weekend rather than a weekday to catch some businesses open. It doesn't always work of course. Susanna Macmillan gave up her job hunt in the Italian Alps after two weeks when she had to admit that her non-existent Italian and just passable French were not getting her anywhere.

PGL Ski Holidays offer reps' jobs and instructor positions to BASI-qualified skiers, whose airfare to the resort is provided and whose salary is between £100 and £150 per week. As in other alpine resorts there are also jobs for chalet staff, though not as many as in neighbouring countries due to the very strict regulations which govern chalets in Italy. Other British ski companies employing staff in the Italian Alps include Equity Total Travel (www.equity. co.uk) and Interski (www.interski.co.uk); the latter is a school groups organizer that employs up to 250 instructors for Courmayeur, Aosta/Pila and La Thuile. Also try Crystal (www.shgjobs.co.uk) which employs winter and summer resort staff in the Italian Alps.

Dog sledding is the fastest growing team sport in the Alps, with good facilities in the Trentino region. Resorts such as Madonna Di Camiglio and Passo Di Tonale have excellent dog kennels and facilities, with several teams in each resort. One of the top sledders is Armen Khatchikian who runs the Scuola Italiana Sleddog Progres (Località Case Sparse 10, 25056 Ponte di Legno (BS); info@scuolaitalianasleddog.it) and who always has two or three assistants for the season. These kennels are very small and cannot handle many enquiries from jobseekers, so if you are serious about working with the dogs, track down other kennels through the local tourist office.

JOBS GLOSSARY	
aiutocuochi/aiuto-cucina	assistant chef/kitchen assistant
baristi	bar persons
camerieri/e di sala	waiters/resses
cameriere di piano	chambermaids
commessi/e	shop assistants
cuochi	chefs
lavapiatti	washer-upper
portieri	porters

VOLUNTARY WORK

In Italy, as elsewhere there are many volunteering opportunities, mostly during the summer months, to work on various and diverse projects including those based around heritage, conservation and communities. It is not uncommon for voluntary projects to request some form of payment from volunteers to cover administration, food, accommodation and other costs. If you prefer, on principle or from lack of funds, to have your basic daily needs provided for in return for your help, there are also organisations that provide free board and lodging to volunteers. Sources of voluntary work include *The International Directory of Voluntary Work* (£11.95), which is obtainable from www.vacationwork.co.uk. The book *Green Volunteers* (€16/£10.99) covers opportunities in the field of nature conservation; it is available worldwide from www.greenvol.com or in the UK from www.vacationwork.co.uk.

Abruzzo National Park: Viale Tito Livio 12, 00136 Rome; ☎06-3540 3331; fax 06-3540 3253; info@parcoabruzzo.it; www.parcoabruzzo.it. Volunteers carry out work protecting flora and fauna in an outpost of the Abruzzo National Park. Further details available from park offices: Pescasseroli (☎0863-91955) and Villetta Barrea (☎0864-89102; fax 0864-89132); or e-mail pna.international@flashnet.it.

Agape Centro Ecumenico: 10060 Prali, Turin, Italy ; ☎01 2180 7514; e-mail office@agapecentroecumenico.org; www.agapecentroecumenico.org. Domestic and maintenance work in return for free board and lodging.Ecumenical conference centre in the Italian Alps that takes on about 15 volunteers in the summer to help the permanent staff run the centre at the busiest time of year. 6-7 hours a day, 6 days a week. Applicants should be at least 18 years old and be available to work for a minimum of one month. Knowledge of Italian an advantage.

Archeoclub d'Italia: National Office, Via Nomentana 263, 00161 Rome; ☎06-44202250/39; fax 06-44202493; info@archeoclubitalia.it; www.archeoclubitalia.it. Can provide information about archaeological work camps.

Centro Camuno di Studi Preistorici: Via G Marconi 7, 25044 Capo di Ponte (Brescia), Italy; ☎364-42091; 364-42572; e-mail info@ccsp.it and www.ccsp.it. Non-profit research institute for the study of prehistory and tribal art. Takes on about ten volunteers and apprentices a year to help explore sites, lab work, mapping, graphics, editing, translating, computer data input. Fieldwork in Alpine area. All volunteers work at their own expense but help in finding lodgings given.

CTS-Centro Turistico Studentesco e Giovanile: Via Nazionale 66, 00184 Rome; tel-06 4679317; fax-06 4679252; www.cts.it). The largest Italian youth association, CTS organises research activities and expeditions which use paying volunteers to work in the field and fund different projects carried out by scientists. Some of the projects are in Italy in the Alps, Apennines and National Parks. Membership is required to join the expeditions. Further details from the above website.

Emmaus: Via Castelnuovo 21/B, Segretariato Campi Lavoro, c/o Parr, 59100 Prato; ☎0574-541104; fax 055-6503458. Social and community work camps. At the time of press www.emmaus-international.org is aiming to list all Emmaus groups online including those in Italy.

Gruppi Archeologici d'Italia: Via Baldo degli Ubaldi 168, 00165 Rome; tel/fax 06-39376711; www.gruppiarcheologici.org; e-mail for summer work camps segretaria@infinito.it.

Kalat Project: Information from Archeoclub, Progetto Kalat, Emilia Bella, via Trieste, c/o Centro polivalente, Campobello di Licata (Ag), Agrigento, Sicily 92023; ☎0922 883508; www.kalat.org; e-mail campi@kalat.org. Environmental and archaeological camps in Sicily during July and August. 2 weeks €200, less for longer stays. The Kalat project has discovered more than 170 new archaeological sites up to now.

Legambiente: Via Salaria 403, 00199 Rome; ☎06 862681; fax 06 86 21 84 74; www.legambiente.com; e-mail legambiente@legambiente.com. Non-profit organisation. Volunteer opportunities include work camps, currently these are: restoration and protection camps on small islands off Sicily, bear research project in the Apennines, underwater archaeology and ecology in Sicily, etc.

LIPU (Lega Italiana Protezione Uccelli): Via Trento 49, 43100 Parma; ☎0521-273043; fax 0521-273419; www.lipu.it; e-mail info@lipu.it. The Italian equivalent of the RSPB publishes a list (in Italian) of their programme of summer working holidays protecting birds. Camps last one or two weeks and cost from €130 per week.

La Sabranenque, Centre International, rue de la Tour de l'Oume, 30290 Saint Victor la Coste, France (+33 4-66 500505; www.sabranenque.com). French-based organisation uses voluntary labour to restore villages and monuments in Altamura (inland from Bari in Southern Italy) and Gnallo (Northern Italy). The cost of participation is £180 for three weeks in July/August.

Mani Tese: P. le Gambara 7/9, 20146 Milan; ☎02-407 5165; fax 02-4812296; www.manitese.it. Collects and recycles objects for profit to finance department projects. Their summer projects include a study of development issues for which a knowledge of Italian is necessary.

Mediterranean Fin Whale Programme: Tethys Research Institute c/o Aquario Civico, Viale Gadio 2, 20121 Milan; ☎02-72001947; fax 02-72001946; www.tethys.org. Volunteers to assist with study of Fin Whales during the summer in the western Ligurian Sea and off Corsica. Volunteers must be able to swim and their tasks are varied from helping run the camp to collating data and observing.

OIKOS Via Paola Renzi 55, 00128 Rome; ☎06-5080280; www.oikos.org/ecology/volunteer.htm. Environmental organisation that has, since 1979, organised work camps to work on ecological projects to the south west of Rome.

Organizzazione Internazionale Nuova Acropoli: Via Roio 43, L'Aquila; ☎086

262860; www.nuovaacropoli.it. Environmental protection organisation that organises various projects in Italy. Information, in Italian only, on their website.

WWF Italia: Ecotourism Division, Via Orselo 12, 20144 Milano; ☎02-831 33245; fax 02-831 33222; e-mail turismo@wwf.it; www,wwf,it/vacanze. Manages about 130 wildlife refuges in Italy. Volunteers are recruited for field study projects, restoration activities and fire prevention workcamps.

ASPECTS OF EMPLOYMENT

SALARIES

Each industry in Italy has a national labour contract stipulating minimum wage (set every three years) and salary levels. However, workers in the North would never dream of being offered (let alone accepting) work paid at the minimum wage level and it is only in the most depressed areas of the Mezzogiorno where the minimum wage is a working reality. A major bone of contention between employers and unions continues to be Italy's adherence to the *scala mobile* when negotiating salary levels. Although the *scala mobile*, whereby wages are indexed to inflation, no longer passes on 100% of inflation but instead around 47% of the official inflation rate, the principle remains and the unions are reluctant to forgo it.

Italian salaries have a reputation for being lower than the European norm for individual jobs, and there is a tendency in the south to do two or three jobs to make ends meet or increase take home pay dramatically. Managerial jobs (*dirigenti*) in particular are well paid with managing directors, marketing, personnel and financial executives and other senior employees earning wages comparable to anywhere in Europe, though this is likely to be lower than in the USA. Middle level staff will earn slightly less than a UK employee at about €1,300-€1,500 monthly net 13/14 times a year (much less than a US employee) and office staff and manual workers (*operai*) a lot less than UK employees at about €900-€1,200 net per month 13/14 times a year. These guidelines will, however, depend on the area and individual qualifications. In southern Italy all of these salary rates will be significantly lower than in the north.

Peculiar to some West European countries (but not the UK) and some countries in the Far East is the practice of employers distributing from one to a maximum of four extra payrolls each year. All employees are entitled to an additional month's remuneration (the so-called 13th month) payable in December, though the collective bargaining contracts for certain sectors provide for additional payments. For example, in banking, monthly salaries are paid 16 times a year and, in the petroleum industry, 15 times. In commerce, a 14th month salary is payable in June of each year. These extra payments unsurprisingly comprise one of the greatest perks for UK and North American nationals when working abroad. Remember, however, that the base annual salary offered by the employer is usually divided by fourteen, fifteen or sixteen, rather than twelve so any feeling of extra wealth is unfortunately illusory.

WORKING CONDITIONS

The statutory working week in Italy is 40 hours except for public sector employment where it is 36 hours (but employees may have to work six days a week). Firms can ask employees to work more than 40 hours per week but the hours will be subject to higher social security contributions. Any hours exceeding 40 per week are classed as overtime and therefore paid at premium overtime rates. Overtime cannot be demanded of any employee and must be paid at a rate of between 130% and 150% of the normal hourly rate, depending on the number of hours worked and whether it is on a weekend or holiday. However, many unions do not permit overtime and are not convinced either that the 36-hour week (which is supposed to create more jobs), is at all a good thing. This suggestion followed the initiative set by France, which encouraged employers to make actual working hours coincide with the 35-hours per week adopted in France. Many complained it meant employees often being expected to do the same work in less time, though recent reforms in France have introduced more flexibility and fewer financial sanctions to get round the 35-hour week. Executives and senior managers in the private sector are still more likely to work longer hours whichever country they are in.

Italian business hours vary from the Mediterranean working day of 9am-1pm and 3pm-7pm (maintained particularly in the south) to the more familiar 9-5 working day, followed by most of the larger companies and institutions. As in France, most Italian businesses simply close down for the entire month of August as the country takes its month-long summer holiday. Every employee is entitled to an annual holiday of between five and six weeks, depending on the length of service, in addition to the ten statutory days of holiday (see *Daily Life Holidays*), which are celebrated nationally.

HIDDEN JOBS

There are about 24,000,000 individuals who are working in Italy and of these approximately one sixth, or almost four million of them, are working black (*lavoro nero*). In other words they are unrecorded and do not pay tax or social security payments. This unofficial workforce comprises housewives, retired people, the 'unemployed' (those on redundancy funds and work mobility schemes), students, and people who already have another job. Having two jobs, but only declaring one or none, is most common in the south, where illegal work is virtually a permanent form of employment. The result of such a huge percentage of illegal workers is a boon to the Italian economy and general prosperity, as companies and businesses have benefited from irregular workers boosting their productivity and profits, while not having to pay the heavy social security costs.

PENSIONS

One of the reforms that made Italy ready for the Euro was an assault on Italian pensions which until 1997 represented the highest percentage of GDP (14%) when compared to France, Germany, the UK and Ireland. At one point in the last decade the number of pensioners had slightly outnumbered workers at 1.03 pensioners per worker. One of the main problems tackled by the reforms was the number of people receiving pensions in Italy before reaching the maximum retirement age. Included in this was the fact that civil servants had the right to receive a pension after 16 years service.

Reforms have been making private sector workers ineligible for a long service pension until they are 57 years old with a minimum of 35 years of contributions. Public sector pensions have been brought into line with private ones gradually over a period of years until by 2004 they were bound by the same age and period of contributions limits as the private sector.

BUSINESS ETIQUETTE

Anyone used to Northern European or North American business practices will find the Italian way of doing things somewhat less thrusting. Contrary to what you may be used to, the Italians consider it uncivilised to race through a deal in one day and positively barbaric to hustle at a working lunch. As in France, working lunches in Italy are as much to see if you are someone that they want to work with as a time to do any actual business. Instead, once you realise that business is likely to be indivisible from pleasure, and produce a flurry of lunch and dinner invitations, at which you should use as much of the Italian you have succeeded in mastering, you are going to do better at business the Italian way than you think. The down side of this business mixed with pleasure scenario is that you may not see as much of your spouse and family as you were used to – which is probably why the French and the Italians take so many holidays and the whole of August off.

Although seemingly relaxed and easy going, most Italian offices and all business procedures are far more intensely hierarchical than Britons and North Americans are used to. This is largely because of the Italian's status-conscious psyche and to err on the side of safety it is often wise to adopt the blanket title of Signor or Signora, rather than breach the familiarity of Christian names.

TRADE UNIONS

Italy's three most important trade unions (*sindacati*) are grouped by political identity rather than profession. The CGIL, *Confederazione Generale Italiana del Lavoro* is predominantly Communist with a Socialist minority faction, while the UIL, *Unione Italiana dei Lavoratori* has a strong affiliation with the Socialists. The CSIL, *Confederazione Italiana Sindacati Lavoratori*, is Christian Democrat while the CISAL is affiliated with the right wing Italian social movement. There are also trade unions formed on the basis of an industry or sector of economic activity, mainly in the public sector and transportation industry. The most important of these are the General Confederations of Industry, Commerce and Agriculture. Although harbouring a history of radicalism and turbulence during the post-war decades of the 50s and 60s, the 80s saw a taming of the Italian trade unions to some of the more peaceable and compliant in Europe.

Union membership is not compulsory in Italy and membership figures have fluctuated considerably from 60% membership at the union's most militant post-war period in 1947 to an all time low of 33% membership in 1967. However, after the UK, Italy remains the most strongly unionised country in Europe.

The unions tend to work through a cycle of relative peace (with the exception of sporadic strikes on such national issues as housing, schools, unemployment, etc.) until the negotiation for the renewal of the two or three yearly labour contracts (*il rinnovo del contratto*) comes around. Then whole sectors of different industries are protesting simultaneously during the arduous negotiation process. The situation is not eased by the frequency with which *La Confindustria* (the Italian employers' confederation, the equivalent of the CBI in the UK) deliberately allows the contract expiry dates to overrun and so gain bargaining power over the unions, whose workers are technically without employment contracts during this interim period. Most recently large scale union turnouts have been prompted by Berlusconi's pension reforms and labour law reforms to make hiring and firing less totally protective of the employee by introducing new types of contracts allowing firms to reduce employee number in times of reduced output.

WORK CONTRACTS

Italian labour laws have tended to protect the employee to an excessive level and those protecting permanent workers against dismissal are still very stringent. However, laws have been gradually loosened up over the last eight years and new laws passed in 2003 and 2004 were formulated to encourage the hiring of part-time employees by allowing the creation of commercial job agencies and reducing the employer social security contributions for part-timers, and introducing new flexible types of contracts. 90% of Italian employee contracts are for fixed jobs.

The new laws give companies other contract options including: Job-on-Call contract (the employee works only when and if the employer asks him/her to), a new collective bargaining agreement on Teleworking (employee teleworks only if she/he agrees to, and has the same contract as employees working on the firm's premises), and a Job Sharing contract (two employees share the same job equally and if one resigns or is dismissed the contract automatically terminates unless the remaining employee wishes to take on the whole obligation, in which case the contract becomes a normal employment contract).

Further information on all types of work contract and other employment matters can be found at www.internationallawoffice.com/overview.cfm?country=Italy&workareas=Employ.

Fixed-Term Contract

A Fixed term contract can be drawn up for less than five years but the employee can withdraw after three years provided that the employee gives a period of notice and adheres to other formal contractual obligations for quitting. A fixed contract can also be extended for one time only and for a period not exceeding three years.

Apprenticeships

This is a special work contract where the employer is required to provide the young employee with sufficient training for the acquisition of skills comparable to a qualified worker's experience, while taking advantage of the apprenticeship. These types of contracts may last from 18 months up to 4 years. It is important to note that apprenticeship wages are less than those of a normal employment contract.

WOMEN IN WORK

Statistics concerning the female working population in Italy show that with a roughly identical female population to the UK, slightly fewer (just over 40%) women work overall. The position of women in the Italian work place is ambiguous. Italian females have yet to penetrate the highest and most elite echelons of Italy's political and business establishments; as yet there is no Italian equivalent of France's Edith Cresson, Britain's Margaret Thatcher or America's Condoleezza Rice. However, increasingly, women are reaching the forefront of the major professions (journalism, medicine, law and architecture in particular) and commanding the respect that their influential positions warrant. Moreover, the Italian social services are not geared to the working mother; there is a serious shortage of free nursery schools and of company and state-funded crèches. Ironically then, it is often only those who can afford babysitters and private nursery school fees who are able to have a career or even work outside the home if they wish to. Many Italian women go further and say that they have to choose between a career and children because of the lack of care facilities. Evidently, many are choosing the career option as birth rates are amongst the lowest in Europe.

Depending on whom you speak to, Italian male chauvinism is a resilient dinosaur that working women still have to contend with, or Italian men are still gentlemen who protect and provide for their women. Many of these old-fashioned Latin prejudices are connected to the woman's perceived role within the family.

Italy has a law entitled 'Positive action for the achievement of male-female equality at work' (*Azioni positive per la realizzazione della parità uomo donna nel lavoro*). This was designed to remove all obstacles and give women free access to professions and types of work where they were under-represented and introduced the concept of indirect discrimination, where discrimination is unseen but evidenced by the facts. If a woman were to bring a case against an employer, the onus would be on the employer to demonstrate that there was no discrimination and not the other way around. It also allowed for the setting up of a series of organisations to oversee the administration of the law.

However, judges who rule that a slap on the bottom is not harassment, as long as it is a one-off and lacks sexual connotations (as happened in January 2001) do not help judicial protection of women harassed in the workplace! Similarly, the appeal court ruled in 1999 that a woman could not be raped if she was wearing tight jeans, as their removal required consent.

Also in 1991, a special law (number 215) was passed aimed at helping women to start their own businesses. Further information can be obtained from local chambers of commerce, regional co-operatives and artisan associations and *Centri Bic* (Business Innovation Centres).

Useful Addresses for Women

Differenza Donna: listing of regional offices at www.fpcgil.it/aree_att/donne/donneind.htm. Women's organisation providing help and advice to working women suffering harassment and abuse.

Telefono Rosa: viale Mazzini 73, 00195 Rome; ☎06-375 18261/2; fax 06-375 18289; www.telefonorosa.org. Monday to Friday from 10am to 1pm and 4pm to 7pm. Women's association that can offer advice to working women on subjects such as sexual discrimination and harassment and legal, banking, psychological counseling, and family mediation. Offices in various Italian cities – see website for addresses.

Ufficio Speciale della formazione Professionale: These are located in most areas and can be found via the Chamber of Commerce. Provide professional training courses for women, regardless of age, designed to provide the skills that employers are looking for. Further details can be obtained from the above address. The courses are designed for Italians and will therefore be conducted in Italian.

Contacts for business start-ups by women:

Impresa Femminile Singolare: c/o Federlazio viale Libano 62 Rome; ☎06-549121; www.federlazio.it.

Professional Women's Association in Milan: www.pwa-milan.org/ is an excellent English-speaking club for working women and for networking.

La Societa per l'Imprenditorialita Giovanile: via Mascagni, 160 Rome; ☎06-862641.

Sentiero Impresa: Providing online advice on finance, e commerce and business: www.sentieroimpresa.it.

BUSINESS AND INDUSTRY REPORT

The 1980s saw a decade of enormous economic and industrial success for Italy. After entering the decade with the highest strike record in the West, lame-duck industries and layer upon layer of ill-concealed political corruption, Italy succeeded in emerging from them as the capitalist world's fifth strongest economy, poised to overtake France and rise into fourth position. However, the successes of the manufacturing industry during this time belied an ominous lack of any overall economic policy and a national debt greater than the country's GDP, with a budget deficit running at over 12%. By mid-1990 to 1991 Italy's recession marked the end of one of the longest and most prosperous periods of expansion ever experienced by the industrialised economies since the reconstruction years following the Second World War. In 1993-94 the recession was still biting with rising unemployment (25% in the south). However, in addition to the political upheaval in the late 1990s that saw the ignominious demise of the Christian Democrats in a sea of corruption allegations, an economic upheaval took place as Italy tightened its welfare belt ready for joining the single currency. There is still high unemployment, but this has shown a downward trend in recent years and averages 9% though still higher than that in the south. Unfortunately for Italy, the general world economic slowdown that started in 2001 is expected to affect its growth and budget plans; as Silvio Berlusconi admitted in the autumn of 2001 when actual tax revenues fell below estimated income.

High-tech industries in Italy have grown greatly in recent years due to increased demand and to the availability of skilled labour. Fast-growing sectors include telecommunications, electrical appliances and the machine tool (industrial robots) industry. Within the service sector, business services and financial services and insurance companies in particular are expanding. Further information on the Italian business scenario is provided in the chapter *Starting a Business*. Many of the multinational companies which dominate Italian industry provide good potential for well skilled job hunters. These companies are to be found predominantly in the motor vehicles (Fiat, Ford, Renault) and electrical appliances (Merloni, Zanussi, Electrolux) sectors.

The level of state-run industry in Italy has gone down quickly from being the highest in the EU, thanks to a massive sell off in recent years that has brought deregulation in that most dynamic of sectors, telecommunications. There is still however a large state interest in a variety of industries, especially those which are considered of strategic importance, such as raw materials, transport, defence, power generation, telecommunications and banks. Istituto per la Ricostruzione Industriale (IRI) is Europe's largest single company (excluding oil companies) and directly or indirectly employs huge numbers of people and controls hundreds of companies, including three major banks, RAI (the radio and television network), Alitalia (airways) and companies belonging to groups such as Finsder (steel), Finmeccanica (engineering), Fincantieri (shipbuilding) and Telecom Italia (electronics). Ente Nazionale per gli Idrocarboni's (ENI) interests include oil, raw and derived chemicals, petrochemicals, mining, energy engineering and services, textiles and financing. It has a share in some 285 companies, employing around 100,000 people. Finally, Ente Participazioni & Finanziamento Industria Manifattureriera (EFIM) has shares in 137 companies employing 60,000 workers. Its subsidiaries include aluminium, glass, food, engineering, transport and railways, aircraft and diesel engines companies. Although state-controlled industry includes many well-managed and technologically advanced concerns, it is suffering from huge accumulated debts and the effects of political interference and mismanagement in past years. The origins of all three mega-companies date back to the years following the Second World War, when the state intervened to rescue many companies with the proposed objective of selling them back into the private sector once they had been restructured and revitalised. This, however, rarely happened. Recently, some companies have been sold back into the private sector, though the government often holds a 'golden share' that basically means it still own more than 50% of the company.

Small businesses have dominated Italian industry over the last decade, and comprise one of its most distinctive features. Only 19% of the workforce is employed in companies which have more than 500 staff and over 59% of the manufacturing workforce is employed in companies where the total number of workers is less than 100. By contrast, these percentages for Britain and Germany are nearly a complete reverse. At the last count there were approximately three million registered small businesses functioning in Italy. Thus, small businesses are responsible for a large share of industrial output, especially in sectors where size is not a strategic feature, e.g. the retail trade, clothing and furniture and other areas requiring not large investments but substantial entrepreneurial ability. Most businesses in Italy are owned by a family or a partnership and this is typically true of farms, most retail and service establishments and many small manufacturing concerns. Gaps in the market exist (e.g. health food shops, pet shops and services for expats) and are there to be taken advantage of by expatriates with hands-on experience of the relevant market in their own country. See the Chapter, *Starting a Business* for more ideas for new businesses. Although it will take perseverance to find a gap and to establish a presence in the Italian market, once you have made contacts and established your foothold the rewards, both financial and in terms of job satisfaction, can be immense. Of course fluency in Italian is a prerequisite for most of theses opportunities.

The widely-held belief that the whole of the Mezzogiorno is an area lacking potential for industrial development and to be avoided at all costs on account of Mafia infestation is misleading. Admittedly, some areas in the far south, e.g. parts of Sicily and Calabria, are not ideal areas for industrial investment, dominated as they are by organised crime and hampered by a ludicrously inadequate system of infrastructure, communications and transport. However, some areas of the south – the mountain region of Abruzzi, Puglia and parts of Molise – have factories which function as efficiently as in the north, while benefiting from impressive government tax and credit incentives.

Finally, the opportunities of the single market are being taken very seriously by Italy (as her wholehearted endorsement of the Euro shows), even if her observance of EU directives is not quite so assiduous. Italy has been one of the most frequent offenders in the European Court for non-implementation of European directives – though France is also a major defaulter it rarely seems to get taken to court over it. However, harmonising trade will probably be a lot easier for Italy than harmonising banking standards and practices which still lag behind as do financial services providing private pensions and life assurance.

The following section provides an alphabetical guide to the most important Italian industries. The current prosperity or otherwise of each industry is discussed with a view to its employment and business potential for the expatriate. The most powerful companies in each sector have been listed wherever possible and the Italian contact addresses for these and many other Italian and international companies can be found in the *Directory of Major Employers* at the end of this chapter.

AEROSPACE

The aircraft and defence electronics group, Alenia, was formed in December 1990 from the merger of the Selenia electronics and Aeritalia aircraft subsidiaries of IRI and is Italy's leading aerospace group. Italy has joined the UK, Germany and Spain in participation in the Eurofighter programme. However, despite general buoyancy at the time of press there is cause for gloom in the defence business owing to a decline in other orders from the military services as defence budgets continue to shrink. Funding difficulties for the Italian air force have put a ceiling on the number of Tornado jets being purchased and there are doubts about how many other aircraft will be needed.

Bright spots on the industry's horizon include aerospace electronics, concentrated in the former Selenia group, which continues to flourish. Alenia in particular has also expanded on the space side. Combined with Aerospatiale and Alcatel Espace of France, it spent has spent millions of dollars on a stake in Space Systems/Loral, the satellites business controlled by Loral, the US defence group.

On the commercial aviation front, Alitalia the national carrier is seeking a state subsidy to finance its reorganisation plan. However, dubious management practices have resulted in a delay in the subsidy going through and the airline is the subject of investigations. As the airline industry suffers the after-effects of the September 11 terrorist attacks in the US and experts talk about consolidation of the numerous European airlines into three or four large groups, Alitalia's future does not look rosy. The profitable small airline, Air Dolomiti, like many low-cost European airlines is likely to continue its recent successes.

AGRICULTURE

Italy has a total land area of 30,127,874 hectares of which 24% is classified as mountainous (i.e. above 600m or 700m according to region). Forty-five percent is hill land and the remaining 31% is plain. Average rainfall is 43 inches in the north, 37 inches in the centre and 33 inches in the south. There are more than 3,200,000 agricultural holdings, with an average farm owning 7.2 hectares of land of which 4.8 hectares is usable. The main agricultural area is the large fertile Po Valley, which is responsible for about 40% of Italy's total grain production. Other important, though less fertile plains are on the Tyrrhenian coast from Pisa down towards Naples and the coastal plains in Puglia.

About 8% of Italians work in agriculture which is considerably higher than the EU average of 2% which means that there is no shortage of experienced workers for agricultural enterprises. About half of the value of Italy's total agricultural output is derived from Mediterranean produce grown largely in the southern regions: wine, olive oil, and especially fruit and vegetables; Italy is the most prolific grower of fruit and vegetables in Europe. The remainder of Italy's agricultural output is farmed in the north and mostly comprises meat, dairy products and cereals. Farms in the south tend to be smaller, more labour intensive and much less fertile than those in the north. Additionally, the level of mechanisation and investment is lower in the south, communications are relatively poor and marketing less developed. Agricultural contribution towards the GDP fluctuates but represents about 7% on an average year. Sugar beet, grapes for wine and maize are the three largest agricultural crops in Italy, while sheep, pigs and cattle are the most profitable forms of livestock. Of those working in agriculture, approximately 63% are self employed and 35% are women. However, the interest in agriculture and the opportunities offered within it have declined and Italy's youth are now opting increasingly for the more attractive conditions offered by industry.

Italian farmers have embraced organic farming much more than other European countries and consequently organic produce in Italy is often no more expensive than chemically fertilised food. Italy banned the import of biotech seed in 2000 and has maintained this ban on GM food even though some are now approved by the EU. A number of expatriates have bought and now operate vineyards in Italy, combining business and pleasure in an Italian idyll.

THE AUTOMOTIVE INDUSTRY

The Italian automotive industry is led by Fiat of Turin, which dominated Italy's automotive market in the last century along with Piaggo, Magneti Marelli, Brembo and Pirelli. The success of the Fiat mega-corporation and other Italian makers, has been more than challenged in recent years by the Italians' growing love of foreign cars, the purchase of which now embraces over a third of the domestic market. Other major manufacturers include the Fiat subsidiaries of Lancia, Alfa Romeo and high class makes. This last accounts for only minimal shares of the market and includes the glamorous and ostentatious marques Maserati, Ferarri and Lamborghini. Fiat's serious decline began in 1991 when it laid off between 20,000 and 50,000 workers for one week each month when foreign competition and the recession dampened demand within the Italian market. However, over a million cars are still being produced in Italy every year for the international market, and Italy is one of the top five car producers in Europe. The Italian automotive industry gives 173,000 top engineers, designers, technicians and other specialists employment.

Japanese-badged cars (many of which are constructed in Europe) have become popular and pose a threatening presence in the Italian market. Ford and Renault have also made vast inroads into the Italian market.

Piaggio and Greave's of India formed a joint venture to produce the three-wheeled 'Ape' in India to be marketed in undeveloped markets in Asia and Latin America.

The DIY sector has been the centre of increased interest, with the number of outlets selling parts and accessories growing. As Italy has the world's highest number of cars per thousand inhabitants (533 against the US's 469) this market still has great potential for growth.

CHEMICALS

The outlook for the Italian chemicals sector is not a rosy one. If the industry is to catch up with its principal rivals and to be a competitive international force it will have to carry out large-scale structural reforms or suffer the alternative of continued decline or being taken over. The chemicals sector has always been subject to political manipulations and has suffered directly as a result of this. Moreover, the industry has moved against international trends by becoming more rather than less state-controlled and by relying heavily on the domestic market for sales and plant location. The industry is now dominated by EniChem, the industrial chemicals subsidiary of the state-controlled ENI. In an effort to turn around its poor economic situation, EniChem had to weather a strong union protest as it closed some of its plants in the south and cut some 4,500 jobs from its 50,000 strong workforce. Almost 55% of new investment in the chemical industry is in the south, Sardinia and Sicily.

However, EniChem still represents a significant percentage of world chemical production and a larger percentage of European production. The industry employs approximately 230,000 workers. Major foreign multinationals with a strong presence in the Italian industry include Unilever, Esso, Dupont, BASF, Ciba Geigy, Hoechst, ICI, Henkel and Alusuisse.

In pharmaceuticals, the highly successful Menarini group makes over 40% of its sales abroad and has spent heavily to develop foreign interests. The group's current priority is to develop a market in the UK. Many small and medium sized companies also flourish in this sector; 60% of Italian chemicals companies employ less than 50 staff.

CLOTHING AND TEXTILES

Italy is one of the world's largest textile and clothing producers but now, with increasingly strong competition from low-cost producer countries (notably, Portugal, Romania and certain countries in the Far East; lately China is posing a serious threat to the Italian textiles industry) and a turndown in the home market, Italy is striving to maintain its position and reputation within the market. Biella and Prato in northern Italy are the two centres of the Italian textile trade. Some of the most powerful Italian textile companies include Marzotto, Montefibre,

Gommatex, Snia-fibra, Lanerossi and Legier Industria Tessile. However, after three decades of spectacular growth the industry had its first crisis. During the 90s a number of well-known family-run concerns had to look to outside investors to survive – some families had to concede control in order to survive at all. The number of textile companies has fallen by many thousands from a peak of 17,000 and employment levels have dropped to fraction of the all-time high of 60,000 jobs in the 1980s. In an effort to cut costs, the industry employs an immigrant and largely illegal work force (mostly Chinese and North African).

The unpredictability of the fashion business is partly responsible for these cutbacks, combined with the small size of the majority of the companies which means that financial structures are weak. Moreover, as mentioned above, the Portuguese textile industry has emerged as a major competitor, and more recently Romania and a number of Asian producers including Turkey; although China is the main problem now. Today a large percentage of activity is still concerned with recycling textiles and producing for the mass market. Roughly half of total productivity is taken up with supplying the ready-to-wear business and department stores; while the remaining 15% focuses on the production of up market fashion garments. However, the textiles industry is under no serious threat of extinction and some of its greatest supporters even argue that the decline in the number of companies during the last five years is a part of a dynamic process whereby the industry is being strengthened and modernised.

Italian designers are also struggling to find a new focus. A centuries-old artisan tradition in working endless variations of fabric and leather, added to extensive recent research on novel ways of treating or developing various fabrics, allows Italian designers to adopt a unique look which constantly eludes and frustrates foreign designers. However, as competition from new rivals (e.g. USA, Germany and Japan) grows more intense and the pressure is maintained from traditional rivals (e.g. France), Italian designers are exploring all available avenues in order to survive and prosper; market flotation, expansion into other manufacturing fields via franchises – even the financial market. Some of the largest Italian clothing manufacturers of international renown are Benetton, Max Mara, Stefanel, Miroglio Tessile, Linea Sprint and Confezioni di Matelica. The top Italian fashion designers include Valentino, Versace, Armani, Ferre, Trussardi, Krizia, Enrico Coveri, Laura Biagiotti and Missoni.

COMPUTERS AND PERIPHERALS

The Italian computer industry, in line with the industry worldwide, has experienced dramatic fluctuations in orders and profits over the last few years. Olivetti, the former champion of Italy's computer industry tried and failed to compete in the worldwide, and particularly against the US market. It even moved production to cheaper plants in the Far East amidst an inevitable storm of protest from trade unionists and politicians. After a complete reorganisation in 2003, the company now makes office peripherals (digital copiers and printers) and provides systems services under the brand name Olivetti Tecnost which is a subsidiary of Telecom Italia. Olivetti has moved some of its production plants to cheaper plants in Singapore and Mexico causing another flurry of protest from trade unionists and politicians. Sales of laptops were up 14% in 2004.

A continuing growth area for the industry in Italy is in software and services, where margins remain relatively high. Finsiel, the former software subsidiary of Telecom Italia is the main agent for the Italian public sector in software development and is a powerful force in the Italian computer software industry. Telecom Italia has sold off 80% of Finsiel to Gruppo COS, which carries out business processing and outsourcing.

ELECTRICAL HOUSEHOLD APPLIANCES

Italy's white goods sector counts among one of the country's greatest successes in terms of innovation, productivity, quality and sheer financial success. At its peak, Italy was responsible for approximately 40% of total European production of electrical appliances – as is obvious if you walk around any European show-room admiring the rows of sleek washing machines and dryers sporting 'Made in Italy' tags. The success of the industry is not only due to innovative thinking and personal leadership by the industry's giants e.g. Lino Zanussi and the Fumagalli brothers (from Candy), were responsible for the industry's meteoric rise to fame and success in the 1950s and 1960s. The industry's export market is thriving and exports represent nearly three quarters of the market. In particular, the Eastern European market presents growing potential for Italian exports. Italy's white goods producers have sold hundreds of thousands of appliances to former eastern bloc countries and are well placed to sell more. The home market is also thriving, helped by the Italians' propensity (by British standards anyway) to feverishly change their entire kitchen armoury with great regularity.

The industry's largest companies include Merloni (the largest Italian-owned company in the industry whose brands include Ariston, Indesit and Colston), Zanussi (now owned by the Swedish Electrolux group), Elettrodomestici, Ocean, Rancilio, Framec and Nilox.

FOOD AND BEVERAGES

Although Italy is traditionally regarded as being an agricultural country self sufficient in foodstuffs, food and agricultural produce account for the largest percentage of Italy's import bill and this percentage seems to be increasing. The main imports are meat, milk and dairy products and fish.

The average Italian family spends around 30% of its income each year on food.

The following unlikely assortment of food products are recognised as potential growth areas in the Italian retail market: health food, breakfast cereals, high quality biscuits, processed sliced cheese, pork, mayonnaise and beer. The general trend of this industry is one of increased profitability achieved through the application of high technology production methods to traditional products and the adoption of high-quality advertising campaigns. IBP (Buitoni Perugina), De Cecco, Gardini, Barilla, Galbani, Illy, Sagit, Ferrero (the inventor of Nutella) and Parmalat are some of the largest Italian food companies. European and American multinationals such as Kraft, Nestlè, Danone, Unilever have also made large inroads into the Italian market. The main Italian beverage companies include Martini & Rossi I.V.L.A.S., Fransesci Cinzano and Gio Butoni.

The change in eating and drinking habits of Italians is seen best in the drinks market – beer consumption has grown so much that wine producers have to resort to advertising their product.

HIGH TECHNOLOGY

Italy features well in various high technology sectors e.g. robotics, radar systems and aerospace. Fiat's Comau subsidiary makes industrial robots which are used worldwide (General Motors is a major client), as well as in Italy where they have successfully automated much of the Fiat auto production line and the gigantic Benetton warehouse stock systems. Italy's hi-fi industry is fairly buoyant – Brionvega radios, Seleco-Formenti audio and video equipment and Autovax car stereos all have as good a name as imports from Northern Europe or Japan, as does the entire Olivetti office equipment range.

For non-EU citizens this has proved one of the best sectors to look for employment as there has been a great shortage in skilled workers for this industry in Italy and throughout Europe.

HOUSING AND CONSTRUCTION

In recent years high interest rates and strict legislation on rents and building permits have troubled the construction sector. The result has been an unsatisfied demand for both rental property and accommodation for outright purchase and a parallel proliferation of illegal building work. However, subsidies are available to facilitate access to finance and thereby encourage construction activity.

As foreigners continue to buy old Italian property for renovation, there will be a continued demand for skilled workers who can restore and rebuild old property and also speak English.

IRON AND STEEL

Industrial development in Italy is a very recent phenomenon and the iron and steel industry only dates back as far as 1958. This was when new ventures mushroomed while existing industries underwent a solid period of consolidation and marked a boom period in the iron and steel industry which lasted until the arrival of recession in 1974. The industry has never really returned to its former heights although steel-pipemaking is doing well In 1993 the European Commission elected to cut the EU's capacity for hot steel production by subsidising shut-downs. In Italy this resulted in a 43.8% reduction in capacity up to 1996. Generally speaking, however, there has been a shift in focus away from the manufacturing to the service sectors in industry, Italy's current fastest-growing sectors are all steel users e.g. the machine tool, automobile, industrial equipment and household electrical appliance sectors. Italian iron and steel foundries have invested heavily in plant and equipment to help fend off increasing competition from outside Italy.

INFORMATION AND COMMUNICATION TECHNOLOGY

Italy's ICT sector is one of its biggest markets in Europe and demand for ICT specialists, which outstripped supply for several years, is now being filled by home-grown science and high technology/engineering graduates coming off the production line at the rate of over 45,000 a year. Italy was slower than other major European countries to jump onto the broadband/internet bandwagon, even though conversely, Italy embraced mobile telephone technology almost up to the limit in a much shorter timespan. Italy is now Europe's fourth largest ICT market with a growth rate of 4.5% (2004). There are an estimated 23 million internet users and 53 million mobile telephone subscriptions in the country. There are now 70,000 companies in Italy operating in the ICT sector, and a number are internationals. Another radical development in recent years is the setting up of ICT companies in southern Italy, particularly in Campania, Puglia and Sicily, as well as Tiscali in Sardinia, thanks to government incentive schemes for these regions. In the more established regions of Piemonte, Lombardia and Veneto a very high level of specialization has been achieved, meanwhile the information highway is reaching into southern Italy as large amounts of government finance are being dedicated to bringing the South of Italy on to broadband.

Other growth areas include data switching and line leasing services and internet and online services for commerce. Business in Italy was much slower than in other countries to get online. Internet-linked services are currently growing at the rate of 30% a year.

MACHINE TOOL INDUSTRY

The machine tool sector continues to thrive and Italy is the third most successful manufacturer and exporter of machine tools in the world, exceeding even the United States. The machine tools industry is comprised mainly of small-sized industries (the watchword of Italian industry), which are able to meet the requirements and adjustments of individual demand; about 85% of the industry's approximately 500 firms have fewer than 70 employees. Especially successful are the metal-bending equipment firm Pedrazzoli and the food-processing machine firm, Braibanti-Golfetto, now part of the GBS Group. The industry is represented by the national machine tools, robot and automation manufacturers' association, UCIMU. The association's membership of nearly 220 companies accounts for about 80% of total industry-wide turnover. The industry's particular stronghold is its export market which it is expanding slowly, especially in Germany, France, the US and Russia. UCIMU considers that Italian machine tool makers are well positioned in Europe, particularly in the German, Spanish and French markets. In addition, the industry has good sales networks in Portugal, Switzerland, Eastern Europe and Russia.

MINING

Italy is poorly endowed with mineral resources, although sizeable quantities of pyrites, lead, zinc, magnesium, bauxite and coal are mined. Europe's only significant deposits of sulphur are found in Sicily, but extraction is uneconomic. Output of metallic materials has been in long-term decline, although surveying is now being intensified. Domestic coal production accounts for less than 10% of total consumption of coal.

OIL AND GAS

ENI is Italy's mega enterprise in oil and gas which is 30% government owned. Through its subsidiaries it is involved in oil and natural gas, petrochemicals and services for oil and gas fields and has expanded into power generating in recent years. ENI's primary subsidiaries are: EniPower (power generating), Italgas (natural gas), Saipem (oil field services), Snam Rete Gas (gas pipelines) and Snamprogetti (contracting/engineering). The American petroleum company American Agip is also a subsidiary.

The largest non-Italian oil company is Esso, followed by MonteShell (a conglomerate of the privately-owned, home-grown Montedison and Royal Dutch Shell) and Mobil, while the largest Italian concerns are Erg and Api. All non-Italian oil companies used to have to follow the rigid regulatory framework laid down for all ENI state subsidiaries which set limits on the opening and closing times of service stations and any changes of services a service station could introduce, but these restrictions have, however, been liberalised and opening hours extended in recent years.

TOURISM

Italy's tourism industry is one of the world's largest providing approximately two million visitors' beds. It contributes over 11% of GDP and the growth rate is about 4% annually. However, whilst the luxury end of the market is being strongly cultivated and proving profitable for other countries, Italy has lagged behind in this sector despite being the Western world's greatest cultural treasure trove. One causal factor is that compared with other countries Italy has fewer of the electronic systems that allow countries such as the USA and France to manage tourism through global distribution systems that allow tourists to book a flight and hotel room through one online booking system. In the USA 57% of travellers use the internet to book hotel rooms; in Italy the figure is a meagre 4%. The Italian home tourist industry is however in a progressive state of computerisation.

REGIONAL EMPLOYMENT GUIDE

In the *General Introduction* the main cities and regions of Italy were discussed with a view to residence. In this section, the same regions and major cities are covered, but this time with a view to the employment prospects available in the major industries in each area. The information provided gives some idea of the industries which are dominant and the types of jobs which are most readily available in each area.

A very useful website giving details of jobs in cities all over Italy from Agrigento to Viterbo is www.offrolavoro.com.

PIEDMONT AND AOSTA

Regions: Piemonte, Val d'Aosta in north west Italy.
Main Cities/Towns: Aosta, Cuneo, Turin, Novara, Vercelli.
Regional Newspaper: La Stampa (national paper published in Turin).
Chamber of Commerce: Union of Chambers of Commerce of Piedmont, Via Cavour 17, 10123 Torino; ☎011 5669230; fax 011 5119144; e-mail euroservizi@pie.camcom.it
Major Employers: Alenia Spazio, Fiat Avio, Microtecnica (aerospace), SKF, Sofitem, Comau, Fata, Dea .

Employment Prospects: Piedmont is one of the most industrialised parts of Italy and one of the most technologically oriented. Main sectors include metal-mechanics, industrial robotics, automotive and telecommunications. A key feature of businesses in the area, as with the rest of Italy is that businesses are mostly SMEs with fewer than 50 employees, so only those with specialist skills, who speak Italian are likely to find jobs in these sectors.

Piedmont forms Italy's main industrial and commercial heartland and the Valle d'Aosta, although not a major international trading market, is important as a tourist area and attracts many millions of visitors each year, chiefly in the winter months during the ski season. The Valle d'Aosta also exports over 75% of its annual production of electricity to meet the industrial demands of nearby Piedmont. As Italy lacks indigenous sources of fossil fuels, substantial investment to achieve a further increase in the hydro-electric generating capacity of the region is planned. Torino is also set to be the host town for the Winter Olympics in 2006, which will attract investment and tourist attention to the region.

The region of Piedmont boasts a wealth of distinct, diverse and prosperous commercial features within its six provinces. From the Fiat-based automobile industry of Turin to Olivetti computers at Ivrea, textiles in Biella, wine, soft fruits and agricultural produce from Cuneo, Asti and Vercelli and light precision engineering in Alessandria and Novara, the area is richly endowed as a source of potential wealth. Piedmont has succeeded in motivating its industries through a level of automation and technological innovation that necessitates a labour force of only 1.8 million – less than 9% of the Italian total. Turin is however moving away from its almost exclusive industrial base towards finance, service and technology. The area encompassing the cities of Turin, Ivrea and Novara has been designated Italy's 'Technocity' to signify the wide range of new industries developed in the region i.e. robotics, aerospace, telecommunications, computers, bioengineering and new materials. The Technocity is responsible for much of the national production of robots, computers and by far the majority of its aerospace products.

Notable industrial corporations located in the Technocity area include Aeritalia (aerospace and aviation), SKF (ball and roller bearings), Microtechnica (aviation and space research), Prima Industria, Bisiach and Carm (robotics), BICC/CEAT (cabling) and Pirelli (tyres). As far as the other major provincial towns are concerned, Biella is a prime textile centre processing wool products. Ivrea is the home of Olivetti, famous for its office machinery and communications products while the province of Cuneo is one of the largest market gardening areas of northern Italy. The soil and climatic conditions that exist here are ideal for the cultivation of a wide range of vegetables and soft fruits while Alba and Asti are renowned for their high-quality wines, especially the effervescent Asti Spumante. As part of Technocity, Novara is notable for its hi-tech, precision engineering companies, many of which serve the industrial needs of Milan.

Alessandria and Valenza are famous for their jewellery trade while Vercelli is noted for its rice and maize cultivation.

Useful Information

Turin: International Airport (☎011 5676 361/2; www.turin-airport.com) is located 16 kms/10 miles north of the city centre. Shuttle buses (☎011-30 00 611) and train services (☎011-691 0000; www.satti.it) operate to the city centre. A bus service to Aosta (☎0165-262 027) is also available.

Turin tourist information, Via Viotti, 2, CAP 10128; ☎011-5541111; fax 011-554 1122; www.regione.piemonte.it/turismo.

British Chamber of Commerce, Turin; Mrs Jocelyn Holmes (Hon. Regional Secretary for Piemonte), c/o Musci & Holmes Architetti, Via Genola 3, 10141 Turin, Italy; tel/fax 011-331216.

LIGURIA

Region: Liguria, coastal region north west Italy.
Main Cities/Towns: Genoa, Savona, La Spezia, Portofino, Rapallo, Imperia.
Regional Newspaper: Il Secolo XIX (www.ilsecoloxix.it).
Chamber of Commerce: Unione delle Camere di Commercio della Liguria, Via San Lorenzo 15/1, 16123 Genova; ☎010 248521; fax 010 2471552; e-mail unione.liguria@lig.camcom.it.
Major Employers: Elsag, Piaggio Aero Industries, Siemens Automations (technology), Lameter, Tecnica (metallurgical), APV Ratto, Ansaldo Energia, FIMA (electro-technical), Panarello, Perla (local food products).
Employment Prospects: the main industries are metallurgical, shipyard, petro-chemicals, electro-technical and food. The trading port of Genoa, one of the largest in the Mediterranean, employs 60,000 workers. When the big shipbuilding and steel industries, centred on Genoa, went into decline two decades ago, Liguria was slower than many regions to adapt to the newer technological industries but has now progressed to become one of Italy's key technology centres. Other business revolves around companies building commercial and recreational sailing craft, electronic businesses, tourism and the protection and marketing of local products (mainly foodstuffs). The best prospects for employment probably lie within the tourism sector, or the new technologies research based in various high-tech centres and universities.

Liguria essentially forms the Italian Riviera and is a small and densely inhabited region which is mainly mountainous and hilly. Genoa saw the start of the industrial revolution in Italy, albeit almost a century after Britain's. The region produced the first motorcar, the first military field tank and the first aeroplane. The region's traditional wealth stems from its steel, port handling and ship building industries in the port city of Genoa as well as from the tourist industry in the whole region.

Investment in the port facilities is aimed at boosting capacity for container handling, ferry activities and improving handling of a still active oil and petrochemicals sector. This compensates for some of the thousands of jobs lost due to the decline of the steel industry and may signify a general revival in the regions fortunes. The ship building facility of Fincantieri, has also borne heavy financial losses like much of the worlds shipbuilders due to a cutback in military budgets and competition from the Far East. Tourism, once the main money-spinner of the whole region, has also declined and the current major downturn in tourism will exacerbate the problem. Visitors to the region are mostly Italians rather than foreigners. The fact that the Italian Riviera has to some extent lost its fashionable reputation of the past and is seen as expensive compared to Spain and Turkey, has further reduced the number of visitors to the region.

However, on the more positive side of life, Genoa offers a high quality of life – often ranked head of Milan, Rome and Turin. The purchasing power of the local population is high, boosted by a large number of wealthy people who are in retirement or who own holiday homes in the region. Although there have been some disappointments in overall economic performance, this can be attributed mainly to the poor performance of state sector industries, and regional GDP is almost in line with the national average.

The established oil and associated petrochemicals industries are located in and around Genoa and the small industries sector is also strong. Interestingly, a large percentage of businesses registered with the Genoa Chamber of Commerce are run by women. Finally, the highly developed infrastructure of the area includes an efficient motorway system, the Munich-Verona railway line and a gas piping system which covers almost all the industrial development zones of the region.

LOMBARDY AND EMILIA-ROMAGNA

Regions: Lombardia, Emilia-Romagna, north central Italy.
Main Cities/Towns: Bergamo, Brescia, Como, Milan (Lombardia); Bologna, Emilia, Ferrara, Modena, Parma, Reggio (Emilia Romagna).
Regional Newspapers: *Affari Italiani, Avvenire, Il Giorno, Internazionale, Marketpress, Milano Finanza, Quotidiano.net* (portal site), *Il Mondo* (Lombardia); *Il Resto del Carlino* (Bologna),*Il Corriere della Sera* (national newspaper based in Milan and has a regional edition).
Chambers of Commerce: Camera di Commercio di Milano, Via delle Orsole 4; ☎02 8515 5790; e-mail urp@mi.camcom.it; Bologna Chamber of Commerce, Piazza Mercanzia 4, 40125 Bologna; ☎051 609 3111; www.bo.camcom.it.
Major Employers: multinationals include Campari, Feruzzi Group, Luxottica (spectacles), Montedison (chemicals), Recordati (pharmaceuticals), Tetra Pak (cartons), Trussardi, Armani and Prada (clothes).

Employment Prospects: a quarter of the Italian workforce for industry is concentrated in Lombardy which is Italy's number one region for productivity, where the main industries are based around metallurgical products, mechanics, chemicals, food, clothing and textiles, furniture, publishing, fashion and construction. Milan has the highest employment level in Italy and of the 340,00 Milanese firms, 14,000 do business abroad, which could offer good prospects for some bilingual employees. There is a very high concentration of successful, family-run businesses in the region. Furthermore, the majority of Lombardy's high concentration of inhabitants are in their 50s and 60s so that there is also potential for jobs in many service industries (financial, banking, insurance, consulting, advertising and tourism).

Unlike most of northern Italy, which was predominantly agricultural until the end of the Second World War, Lombardy boasts an industrial history dating back to the nineteenth century. Although Rome attracts many foreign business people and professionals as the country's capital, Milan, the regional capital of Lombardy, functions as the true economic and financial centre of Italy. A major trading and manufacturing centre for centuries, Milan has maintained a business tradition placing it at the forefront of the European business scene. The income that the Milan area generates is responsible for a sizeable percentage of the Italian gross industrial product and employs a similarly disproportionate percentage of the Italian workforce. Greater Milan alone, with a population of more than four million, has more than 70,000 industrial units employing more than a million people. The most important of the confusingly wide range of industries to be found in Milan include steel, heavy engineering, machine tools, transport equipment, chemicals, oil refining, plastics, textiles, clothing and shoes, electronics and domestic appliances. The food industry as a whole is especially strong in Milan and throughout the entire region. Milan is also home to Agusta, the Italian helicopter manufacturer.

The industrial importance of Emilia-Romagna has escalated over the last fifty odd years. At one time solely agricultural, the region, particularly in and around Bologna and Modena, has become extremely influential industrially, particularly in the areas of light engineering, food processing and ceramics. The city of Modena is now estimated to have the highest per capita income in Italy while the 3.9 million citizens of the region as a whole have come to enjoy the second highest per capita incomes in Italy. The number of expatriates in the Modena area is demonstrated by the opening of the International School of Modena. With an unemployment rate of 3.8% set against a national average around 9.2%, the region has the rare problem of facing a shortage of labour. The region boasts 45,000 highly successful small and medium-sized businesses operating in agriculture and food products, industry and tourism. Modena's contribution is in the form of farm machinery, luxury sports cars and Tetra Pak cartons. Bologna is famous for its electronics, packaging and mechanical industries while Forlì is the centre of an important fruit and vegetable processing industry. Ravenna is an important port as well as being the hometown of the Ferruzzi Group which has a whole range of interests from oil seed, cement and sugar production to a controlling interest in one of Italy's largest chemical companies, Montedison. The total group turnover rivals that of the Fiat group.

Together these regions produce a third of Italy's gross industrial production. A large portion of this derives from the small and medium-sized manufacturers that abound in Italian industry.

Useful Information

Milan: Linate Airport is 7km from downtown Milan. Malpensa Airport is located 50km from the city. Information about both airports can be obtained from ☎02-7485220 and www.sea-aeroportimilano.it/Eng/. Both airports are served by shuttle buses (Malpensa – 02-58583185; Linate – STAM ☎02-717106, STAB ☎035-318472, Air Pullman ☎02-4009 9260) to/from Milano Centrale Railway Station and Malpensa is also served by train from Milan Central and Milan Garibaldi stations. A shuttle service between Linate and Malpensa is also operated by STAM, STAB and Air Pullman.

Milan tourist information, Galleria di Testa Stazione Centrale FF.SS., CAP 20124; ☎02-7252 4360/370.

British Chamber of Commerce, Bergamo; Mr Arnold Attard (Hon. Area Secretary for Bergamo), c/o British E.L.T., Via Taramelli, 52, 24121 Bergamo, Italy; tel/fax 035-249150.

British Chamber of Commerce, Bologna; Mr Roger Warwick (Honorary Regional Secretary for Emilia Romagna), c/o Pyramid, Viale Masini, 20, 40126 Bologna, Italy; ☎051-254568; fax 051-254948.

British Chamber of Commerce, Brescia; Ms Julia A. Jones; C.S. International, V.le. della Bornata 42, 25123 Brescia, Italy; ☎030-3366811; fax 030-3366098.

VENETO, FRIULI-VENEZIA GIULIA, TRENTINO-ALTO ADIGE

Regions: Veneto, Fruili-Venezia Giulia, Trentino-Alto Adige, north eastern Italy.
Main Cities/Towns: Belluno, Bolzano, Cortina, Padua, Verona, Udine.
Regional Newspapers: *Alto Adige, Dolomiten, Corriere della Alpi, L'Arena* (Verona), *Il Gazzettino* (Venice, Padua).
Chamber of Commerce: Centro Estero CCIAA, Via delle Industrie 19/D, Edificio Lybra, Vega-Parcoscientifico Technologico, 30175 Venezia Marghera; ☎041 252 6211; e-mail uvcamcom@ven.camcom.it.

Major Employers: Generali (insurance), Benetton, Diesel, Marzotto, Stefanel (clothes and textiles), Autogerma Societa (automotive), Glaxosmithkline (pharmaceuticals), AIA Agricola Italiana Alimentare, Agricola Tre Valli Societa Cooperativa (food processing), Supermercati PAM (retail), Luxottica (spectacles), de Longhi, Zanussi (domestic appliances).

Prospects for Employment: the Veneto region has over 400,000 companies, mostly SMEs which between them contribute more than 14% of Italian exports worldwide. There is some heavy industry but most business revolves around life-style products and includes hide tanning, marble and granite production, clothing production and especially eyewear (80 of Italian eyewear manufacturers are located in the Veneto), footwear, ski boots, furniture, goldsmithing, agriculture and food and tourism. Employment prospects are likely to be greatest for those with specialist skills. Teachers of English are also in demand in this export-mad region. It would however also be a fantastic area for foreigners to do apprenticeships as this is one of the best creative craftsmanship regions of Italy where the acquisition of specialised skills could be a useful precursor to finding jobs there.

The concentration of economic activity is not entirely limited to the north-western regions of Italy. In the past 25 years the Veneto region in Italy's north-east has become one of Italy's most successful business regions, especially with small to medium-sized companies producing high quality, hand-crafted goods such as shoes, clothes, spectacle frames, medical equipment and mechanical components. This is the territory of Benetton, Stefanel and Carrera Jeans. Other commercial activities include speciality cakes and foods, printing and publishing, natural stone, wine, banking, light and heavy engineering, advertising, consultancy and research. Verona is the area's commercial hub and is strategically placed to take advantage of the good communications to central Europe and the Balkans now that they are emerging as economic entities one again. Verona is also home to Italy's third largest exhibition centre. Verona focuses on pharmaceuticals, transport, engineering and publishing, while Vicenza is famous for its tanning, textiles, industrial jewellery, ceramics and steel and mechanical engineering. Names of international stature in the area include Benetton in the Treviso province, the Vicenza-based Marzotto (the biggest wool manufacturer in Europe). This region was largely agricultural until after the Second World War, the main exceptions being the textile, jewellery, tanning and ceramic manufacturing industries around Vicenza which date back to the eighteenth century. Treviso specialises in textiles, sportswear, ceramics and mechanical engineering and Venice in glass, heavy industry and fishing. Padua is known for mechanical engineering, finance and services distribution. Fish farming is an important new industry in the lagoons and around the Po Delta. As for the newer technology industries there are cutting edge developments in the field of nanotechnology based around the universities of the region and their research departments.

The Friuli region is made more attractive to potential investors by the various financial and tax incentives offered here by the Government. However, most likely due to the area's somewhat isolated position geographically, investments by foreign and Italian companies were slow to build up but are now booming. Ironically, the area's position tucked into the north-east corner of Italy was traditionally its downfall, but now makes it its biggest advantage in years to come with its strategic closeness to the rapidly changing economies of new EU members in Eastern Europe and the Balkans. At the very least it is well-placed to profit from the through traffic that will have to transit the area. The industrial area of Porto Marghera in the Venice lagoon was established in the 1920s and shipbuilding takes place along the coast near Trieste. However, now these traditional, large industries are at least equalled in importance by a firmament of young medium and small enterprises, producing an extensive range of capital and consumer goods. Belluno is noted for its spectacle manufacturing industry and Pordenone for its white goods and steel engineering sectors; Zanussi have a large base in Pordenone. Pordenone is the main town in the province of the same name and is a dynamic economic and cultural centre. There is an annual international business Fair (*fiera*) held in September and throughout the year there are many other events based around various sectors: machine tools, horticulture, food and catering, electronics and hi-fi, optical equipment, design and more. Significant trends in the region include a much stronger decrease in the number of agricultural workers than the national average and a much higher rate of increase in industrial workers. Thus, the economic outlook is rosy and industrialists and traders, aware of the blossoming of opportunities that the EU has brought, are ready to collaborate with British firms.

Trentino-Alto Adige, the alpine area to the north of Verona, has succeeded in implementing a miracle of long-term planning and efficient administration over the past two decades. The largely German-speaking population enjoys a wide-ranging regional autonomy from Rome and its mountain farming population is actually increasing and prospering while everywhere else in Europe such populations are in decline and the indigenous farming population leaves its homes in droves. This is thanks to very generous regional contributions to local farming which keeps alive the traditional way of life ('heimat' and all that this word connotates). The Trentino-Alto Adige area is often favoured by large German and Japanese companies setting up in Italy, both for its northern European mentality and its easy accessibility and efficient infrastructure. The highly developed infrastructure of the area includes the motorway system, the Munich-Verona railway line and a gas piping system which covers almost all the industrial development zones of the region. Proximity to Austria and Slovenia (and therefore much of Eastern Europe) means it is well placed to attract further inward investment.

This region also offers highly attractive tax and investment incentives which, though less weighty than those offered in the south, can be approved by the efficient local bureaucracy in a very short period, often in little more than three months. Incentives include significant tax concessions, cheap land, subsidised infrastructure development and training courses with the prestigious University of Trento.

Useful Information

Venice: Marco Polo Airport (☎041-541 6397; www.veniceairport.it) is 13km north of Venezia and direct transfers are available by boat (Motorboat Service – ☎041-541 5180; water taxis – ☎041-541 5184), bus (041-541 5180) and taxi.

Venezia tourist information, Santa Lucia (Stazione Ferroviaria), CAP 30122; ☎041-529 8711; fax 041-523 0399.

Vicenza tourist information, Stazione FF.SS., CAP 36100; ☎04-4454 0355.

British Chamber of Commerce, Trieste; Prof. John Dodds, Università di Trieste, Via F. Filzi 14, 34132 Trieste, Italy; ☎040-6762322 or ☎040-6762385; fax 040-6762301; dodds@sslmit.univ.trieste.it.

British Chamber of Commerce, Pordenone; Mrs Susan Clarke (Hon. Regional Secretary for Friuli Venezia Giulia), c/o Overseas Language Consultancy, Corso Vittorio Emanuele 54, 3170 Pordenone, Italy; tel/fax 0434-29089.

British Chamber of Commerce, Gorizia; Mr D. Katan, Via F. Filzi 14, 34132 Trieste, Italy; ☎040-6762322 or ☎040-6762385; fax 040-6762301.

British Chamber of Commerce, Verona; Mr Peter Eustace (Hon. Regional Secretary for Veneto), c/o CSA snc – via Pigna 14/a, 37121 Verona, Italy; ☎045-592482; fax 045-597629.

British Chamber of Commerce, Venezia; Mr Ivor Neil Coward, Lexicon Translations SAS, Via Caneve 77, 30173 Mestre, Italy; ☎0422-780505 or 041-5348005; fax 0422-782821 or 041-5349720; lexivor@tin.it.

British Chamber of Commerce, Udine; Mr C. J. Taylor, Via del Torso 41/8, 33100 Udine, Italy; tel/fax 0432-600397.

TUSCANY, UMBRIA & MARCHE

Regions: Toscana, Umbria, Le Marche, central Italy.

Main Cities/Towns: Florence, Grosseto, Livorno, Lucca, Pisa, Siena (Toscana); Orvieto, Perugia, Terni (Umbria); Macerata, Urbino (Le Marche).

Regional Newspapers: *La Nazione* (Florence), *Il Tirreno* (Livorno); *La Nuova* (Torrino).

Chambers of Commerce: Firenze: Piazza dei Giudici 3, 50122 Firenze; ☎055 27951; fax 055 2795259; www.fi.camcom.it. Perugia: via Cacciatori delle Alpi

40, 06100 Perugia; ☎075 57481; fax 075 5748205; Pesaro e Urbino: Corso XI Settembre 116, 61100 Pesaro; ☎0721 3571; fax 0721 31015; www.ps.camcom. it.

Major Employers: Berloni, Febal, Scavolini, Poltrona Frau (furniture), Geox, Roberto Cavalli, Tods (shoes), Teleunit (broadband), .

Prospects for Employment: the northern Marche around Urbino and Pesaro has developing economies based on the manufacture of kitchen utensils, aluminium fixtures, textiles, clothing and fibre-glass yachts, and a world famous cluster of firms producing furniture. Also shoes, which have been a large part of the local economy for over 30 years. More than 43% (2,700) firms in Le Marche are involved in shoe-making with the majority of these having fewer than a dozen employees. Larger operations are now outsourcing their factory work to eastern Europe where labour is cheaper so employment prospects are not good for the time being. Umbria is not as highly industrialised as other regions of Italy because of the lack of good transport communications. The main industrial regions are around Terni and Perugia

About 57% of the total population of these three regions is concentrated in Tuscany, of which Florence is the much-loved and tourist saturated capital. Close to Florence, at Prato, is the centre of the largest textile area in Italy which involves some thousand companies and nearby at Santa Croce sull'Arno is Italy's largest tanning industry which supplies the local shoe and leather industry. Other important industrial areas include Pisa, Lucca (home to a large papermaking industry), Livorno (which boasts the main Italian container port) and Empoli (renowned for its glass and pottery). Other important industries in Tuscany include steelworks, electronics, furniture, medical equipment and the famous Chianti wine and olive oil as well as Carrara marble. Umbria, home to approximately 23% of the regional population, is mainly agricultural although important steelworks exist at Terni and ceramic, food, textiles and clothing production and the telecommunications company Teleunit are near Perugia. Le Marche is again predominantly agricultural although the prospering Merloni group (producer of white goods) is based in this area.

Also important are the needs of the large numbers of foreigners who own homes in the region.

Useful Information

Florence: Florence airport tends to just receive regional flights as the nearby mountains prevent larger planes from landing. Passengers for Florence normally go to the larger Pisa airport.

Pisa: Aeroporto Galileo Galilei (050-500707; www.pisa-airport.com) is only 20km from Lucca and Livorno and 80km from Florence. Trains run directly to

Pisa airport from Firenze SMN station and it is possible to check in at the air terminal inside on platform 5. Compagnia Pisana Trasporti (www.cpt.pisa.it) run regular buses to and from central Pisa. Tickets for buses and trains can be bought from the information office in the arrivals hall. Car rentals are available through the major companies such as Hertz, Avis, Europcar, Sixt and Thrifty.

Firenze, tourist information, Piazza Stazione, 4, CAP 50121; ☎05-521 2245; fax 05-5238 1226.

Pisa tourist information, Via Pietro Nenni, 24, 56124 Pisa; ☎050- 929777; fax 050 929764.

Florence; Maria Grazia Antoci, Viale Milaton 33, 50129 Firenze, Italy; ☎055-4625049; fax 055-486463; mgantoci@videosoft.it.

LAZIO, ABRUZZO AND MOLISE

Regions: Lazio, Abruzzo, Molise, southern central Italy.

Main Cities/Towns: Rome, Viterbo, Rieti, Latina (Lazio). L'Aquila, Chieti, Pescara (Abruzzo). Campobasso, Isernia, Teramo, Termoli (Molise).

Regional Newspapers: *La Repubblica* (national paper published in Rome), *Il Messagero* (Rome), *Il Centro Quotidiano dell'Abruzzo*.

Chambers of Commerce: Lazio: Camera di Commercio di Roma, Via de' Burrò 147, 00186 Rome;   ☎06 520821; fax 06 6791 309. Abruzzo: Camera di Commercio L'Aquila, Via del Guastatore 7, 67100 L'Aquila; ☎0862-6671; fax 0862-413543. Molise: Camera di Commercio Teramo, via Savini 48/50 64100 Teramo; ☎0861-3351; fax 0861-246142.

Major Employers: Alenia Spazio, Telespazio, Finmeccanica (aerospace), Cinquina (food products Abruzzo).

Prospects for employment: there are many foreigners employed in the Rome area, which is probably one of the most popular places amongst foreigners looking for temporary work. Longer-term work for specialists is harder to find. Abruzzo has fast become a source of jobs in the technology industries and is also attractive as a place to live as it seems to have the best of two worlds, ancient and modern. Molise is a pretty poor prospect jobwise as there is little development of industry or spare jobs.

This area is significant for the strong presence of service industries, especially in Lazio. The three regions of Lazio, Abruzzo and Molise together account for around 10% of the GNP and slightly more of the total national expenditure on goods and services. Rome, besides being the administrative and governmental capital of Italy is also home to the main offices of the state holding companies, IRI, ENI, and EFIM. The head offices of the main Italian banks are also found in Rome, in cosy proximity to the majority of state agencies and public utilities e.g. RAI, the state television company; ENEL, the national electricity board; CNR, the national research council; the Italian State Railways and the Southern Italian Economic Development Board (Agenzia per la Promozione dello Sviluppo del Mezzogiorno). Industrial activity in the capital is low in comparison with the service industries. However, a number of towns near the capital have become centres of intensive industrial production e.g. Frosinone, Latina, Aprilla, Pomezia, Civita Castellana and Rieti which specialise in the electronics, telecommunications, light engineering, pharmaceutical and chemical industries. Rome is also at the centre of Italy's aerospace and information and communications technology industry and has two science parks the Tiburtino and Technopolo di Castel Romano; both of them are managed by the Rome Industrial Technology Park Company.

Abruzzo has been traditionally an agricultural area. Amongst its produce wine and olives are still prized. It is an area that has taken some time to catch up with the twenty-first century but thanks to government incentives which have made l'Aquila, Pescara, Chieti and Teramo hotbeds of technology production, research and education it is now one of the fastest developing areas for technology jobs. One of the main physics laboratories in Europe is located beneath the Gran Sasso and together with the Fucino Space Centre this has provided large numbers of jobs in the region while Telecommunications and pharmaceutical companies are attracted by financial incentives to set up there. Tourism is also a major growth area and Abruzzo has three national parks. Temporary voluntary jobs are available in the national parks (see *Temporary Work* section). Whereas the population of Abruzzo used to migrate to find jobs the reverse is now true and people looking for jobs are moving to Abruzzo.

Molise is a land that time has just caught up with. For most of its existence its inhabitants have been leaving to seek their fortunes elsewhere in Italy or further afield. Mountainous areas have recently been developed for tourism; for instance the ski resort at Campitello Matese and this means some seasonal job openings. The only real industrial area is around Termoli and there is a science park (PST Innovazione Molise) at Campobasso. The service sector employs just under half the adult population.

Useful Information

Rome: Leonardo da Vinci International Airport (☎ 06 65953640; www.adr.it), at Fiumicino, is located 35km /22 miles from the city centre. Taxis take about 40 minutes. Regular trains run from Termini Station (www.fns.net/termini/fseng. htm) and Tiburtina (☎ 848-888088). A night shuttle bus (☎ 800 431784) runs between Tiburtina and the International terminal. Ciampino Airport (☎ 06 794942) is twenty minutes from the centre of Rome and a bus service connects the airport to Ciampino railway station and Anagnina underground station, which have frequent connections to the centre of Rome.

Roma: tourist information, Via Parigi 5, CAP 00185 (☎06 488 991; fax 06 481 9316; www.romaturismo.com).

British Chamber of Commerce, Rome; Andrew Colvin, Via Acherusio 18, 00199 Roma, Italy; (☎06 86206459; fax 06 86383162); acolvin@tin.it.

THE SOUTHERN ITALIAN MAINLAND

Regions: Campania, Puglia, Basilicata Calabria, southern Italy.

Main Cities/Towns: Napoli, Amalfi (Campania). Bari, Brindisi, Foggia, Lecce, Taranto (Puglia). Matera, Potenza (Basilicata). Catanzaro, Cosenza, Crotone, Reggio Calabria (Calabria).

Regional Newspapers: *Il Mattino* (Naples), *La Gazzetta del Mezzogiorno* (Bari).

Chambers of Commerce: Napoli: Via S. Aspreno 2, 80133 Napoli; ☎081 7607111; fax 081-5526940; www.na.comcom.it. Brindisi: Via Bastioni Carlo V, 4, 72100 Brindisi; ☎0831 521436; www.pug.camcom.it/IT222000.html. Matera: via Lucana 82, 75100 Matera; ☎0835 2471. Cosenza: via Calabria 33. 87100 Cosenza.

Major Employers: Alcatel, Vodafone, Wind, Bull, Getronics, Sema Group, EDS Italia, Italdata, Oracle Italia, Nortel Networks (computers and information communication technology).

Employment Prospects: The total working population of all four southern regions is around 4 million and unemployment is traditionally 20% or higher in some parts. Campania, the exception has just had its fortunes boosted further by a three-year EU grant to set up high tech centers of excellence to fund product start-ups and economic development, and further funding provided from 2005, especially to SMEs to help promote their high tech and other products to the international market Job prospects for those at the forefront of technology and communications are very good but with the area producing many suitably qualified graduates of its own, foreigners will have to work hard to get a look in. An internship might be the best way as. Not so good are the prospects in Calabria and Basilicata, which are still lagging far behind the rest of Italy in development of industry. The best prospects for work are probably in tourism or ICT, but with such high unemployment locally, it is unlikely that foreigners will find it easy to get jobs.

The four southern regions of the Italian mainland are traditionally the poorest in Italy, with the exception of Campania. Campania is where most of the industry of the south is located along with the major share of tourism in the south and the commerce that accompanies a major influx of visitors. This makes the average income of Campanians higher than those elsewhere in the south.

Campania has the largest concentration of industry in the south and this region's economic growth has been only slightly below the national average over the last few years. Campania's main interests include traditional industries such as food processing, canning, tanning and leatherwork, ship building and steel railway rolling stock and chemicals, but also more advanced and potentially prosperous sectors such as aerospace, electronics, telecommunications and motor vehicles. The latter are the areas in which there has been the greatest amount of new investment in recent years, largely by the major national companies. The older industries, and particularly the myriad small artisan-type industries which abound in the Naples area, have however, been slow to invest in new technology and risk being left behind by their international rivals.

Calabria and Basilicata, comprising approximately 20% of the area's population, are relatively undeveloped with few industries and remain largely dependent on agriculture and a growing tourism industry.

In Puglia, the highest concentration of population is around Bari, which also has a high concentration of relatively small but energetic industries and every year the *Fiera del Levante* is held, while in Foggia, there is an agricultural fair. Taranto is a major steel production centre, with a number of ancillary industries but had to cut back production to meet EU directives, which did not help the local economy as other industrial regions in Europe found with same EU directive. The main agricultural products of the region are hard wheat, wine, olive oil, chestnuts and hazelnuts, tomatoes, vegetables and fruit (citrus fruits and kiwi fruit in particular). Agriculture accounts for around 20% of the total local gross product and around half the population still depends directly or indirectly on agriculture for a living. Though the number of people directly engaged in agriculture is declining, land holdings still remain relatively small. The average per capita income in the south is official much lower than in the north and the disparity in wealth between the north and south are widening – though this low level should be considered in the context of the large black economy of the region. To demonstrate the size of the black economy, there is no lack of money in the south and a large consumer market exists for luxury items. There are approximately 4,000 wholesalers and 99,000 retailers in Campania; 4,500 wholesalers and 42,000 retailers in Calabria and 700 wholesalers and 11,000 retailers in Basilicata.

Useful Information

Naples: a fifteen-minute drive from the centre of Naples, there are bus connections between *Aeroporto Internazionale di Napoli* (☎081 789 6259; www.gesac.it) and Piazza Garibaldi (Azienda Napoletana Mobilità – ANM, (☎081-763 2177, or Piazza Municipio (CLP, (☎081-531 1706).

Bari: tourist information, Piazza Moro, 32/A, CAP 70122; (☎080 5242244).

British Chamber of Commerce, Naples: Roy Boardman, St Peter's ELC, Riviera di Chiaia 124, 80100 Napoli, Italy; (☎081-683468; fax 081-682721).

British Chamber of Commerce, Taranto: Stefania Lo Cascio, Worldwide Trusts Consultants Srl, Via Nitti 45/a, 74100 Taranto, Italy; (☎0348-3851033 or (☎099 4590880; fax 099-4590809); staff@trustsitaly.com).

DIRECTORY OF MAJOR EMPLOYERS

Additional employers and employers in certain fields can be found through the online Italian Yellow Pages, Chamber of Commerce Directories and internet search engines.

Accountants

Coopers & Lybrand Spa: Via delle Quattre Fontane 15, 00184 Rome; ☎06-4818565; fax 06-48146365.

Deloitte and Touche Spa: Palazzo Carducci, Via Olona 2, 20123 Milano; ☎02-88011; fax 02-433440.

KPMG Peat Marwick Fides Snc.: Via Vittor Pisani 25, 20121 Milano; ☎02-67631; fax 02-67632278.

Pricewaterhouse Coopers Spa: Corso Europa 2, 20122 Milan; ☎02-77851; fax 02-7785240.

Reconta Ernst & Young SaS di Bruno Gimpel: Via Torino, 68, 20123 Milano; ☎02-722121; fax 02-72212037.

Advertising Agencies

CiTieSHoldingsSrl, Viadell'Artigianato 2, 20044 Bernareggio, Milan.; ☎03 96900570; fax 03 96901201.

Saatchi & Saatchi Spa, C.so Monforte, 52, 20122 Milano – (Mi); ☎02 77011; fax 2781196.

Aerospace Manufacturers and Suppliers

Aerea S.p.A., Via Cefalonia, 18, 20156 Milano (MI); ☎02 33 4831; fax 02 3340 2676.

Aermacchi S.p.A., Via Ing. P.Foresio, 1, 21040 Venegono Superiore (VA); ☎03 3181 3111; fax 03 3182 7595; www.aermacchi.it.

Agusta S.p,a,, Via G. Agusta, 520, 21017 Cascina Costa (VA); ☎03 3122 9111; fax 03 3122 2595; www.agusta.it.

Alenia Aeronautica, Un'Azienda Finmeccanica, Via Giulio Vincenzo Bona, 85, 00156 Roma; ☎06 417231; fax 06 411 4439; www. aleniaerospazio.com.

Alstom Ferroviaria S.p.a., Via Fosse Ardeatine, 120, 20099 Sesto S. Giovanni (MI); ☎02 2442 3211; fax 02 244 23400; www.alstom. com.

Aviointeriors S.p.A., Via Appia Km. 66,400, 04013 Tor Tre Ponti (LT); ☎07 73 6891; fax 07 73 631546; www.aviointeriors.it.

Bonetti Aircraft Supports S.r.l., Via Sottoripa 1/a, 16124 Genova; ☎01023 501; fax 010235 0222.

Elettronica S.p.a., Via Tiburtina Valeria Km 13, 700, 00131 Roma;

☎06 41541; fax 06 415 4924.

Galileo Avionica S.p.a., Via di S. Alessandro, 10, 00131 Roma; ☎06 418 831; fax 06 4188 3800.

GSE - Ground Support Equipment S.r.l., Viale del Vignola, 44, 00196 Roma; ☎06 322 2877; fax 06 361 1715; www.g-s-e.it.

Lital S.p.a., Via Pontina Km 27, 800, 00040 Pomezia (RM); ☎06 911 921; fax 06 912 2517.

Logic S.p.a., (Gruppo Aeronautica Macchi), Via Brescia, 29, 20063 Cernusco Sul Naviglio (MI); ☎02 922 4401; fax 029210 2528; www. aermacchi.it.

Mecaer Meccanica Aeronautica S.p.a., Via per Arona, 46, 28021 Borgomanero (NO); ☎03 2283 7173; fax 03 2284 4081; www. mecaer.it.

Moreggia S.p.a., Via Bardonecchia, 77/10, 10139 Torino; ☎011 385 5635; fax 011 4028436; www. moreggia.com.

Piaggio Aeroindustries S.p.a., Via Cibrario, 4, 16154 Genova Sestri; ☎010 64811; fax 010 6481234.

Secondo Mona S.p.a., (Aircraft equipment), Via Carlo Del Prete, 1, 21019 Somma Lombardo (VA); ☎0331 756111; fax 0331 252334; www.secondomona.com.

Airline and Associated Companies

BAA Italia, BAA GESAC – Capodichino Airport, 80014 Napoli – (Na); ☎081 7896528; fax 081 7896201.

bmi british midland c/o SAS, Via Albricci 7, 20122 Milano – (Mi);

☎0272435211; fax 0272021945.

British Airways Plc., Corso Italia, 8, 20122 Milano – (MI); ☎02 724161; fax 02 8055806.

Buzz c/o B. & D.P. Srl, Piazza Bertarelli, 1, 20122 Milano – (Mi); ☎02 72022466; fax 0272020162.

Cathay Pacific Airways Limited, Via Barberini, 3, 00187 Roma – (RM); ☎06 4820703; fax 06 4741297.

Gandalf Airlines Spa, Via Aeroporto 13, 24050 Orio al Serio – (Bg); ☎035 4595011; fax 035 4595083.

Go Fly Ltd, Enterprise House, Stansted Airport, Stansted, Essex CM24 1SB, UK; ☎+44 (0)1279 666333; fax +44 (0)1279 681762.

Banks

Banca Popolare di Novara Scrl, Via Quintino Sella 5, 28100 Novara – (No); ☎0321 662736; fax 0321 662017.

Banca Toscana Spa, Via Pancaldo 4, 50127 Firenze – (FI); ☎055 4391374; fax 055 4360061; www. bancatoscana.it.

Banca Woolwich Spa, Via Pantano, 13, 20122 Milano – (MI); ☎02 584881; fax 02 58488511.

Barclays Bank Plc (Corporate clients only), Via Moscova, 18 20121 Milano – (MI); ☎02 63721; fax 02 63722925.

Credito Emiliano Spa, Vicolo Santa Margherita, 20121 Milano – (MI); ☎02 88131; fax 02 8813340; www. redem.it.

Credito Italiano Spa, Via Arsenale, 23, 10121 Torino – (To); ☎011 57131; fax 011 57131.

HSBC Bank Plc, Via Santa Maria alla Porta 2, 20123 Milano – (Mi); ☎02 724371; fax 02 72437402.

Ing Barings (Italia) Srl, Via Brera, 3, 20121 Milano – (MI); ☎02 809271; fax 02 809007; www.ing-barings.com.

National Westminster Bank, Via F.Turati, 16/18, 20121 Milano – (MI); ☎02 6251; fax 02 6572869.

Robert Fleming Sim Spa, Via Manzoni, 12, 20100 Milano – (Mi); ☎02 760361; fax 02 76008107.

SBC Warburg Dillon Read, Italia SIM Spa: Via Santa Maria Segreta 6, 20123 Milano; ☎02-725271; fax 02-72527773.

UBS Warburg (Italia) Sim Spa, Via Santa Margherita 16, 20121 Milano – (MI); ☎02 725271; fax 02 72527772.

Chemicals and Pharmaceuticals

Chr. Lechler & Figlio Succ.ri S.p.a., Via Cecilio 17, 22100 Como (CO), ☎03 1586211; fax 03 1586206; www.lechler.it.

Nuncas Italia S.p.a., Via G.di Vittorio, 43, 20017 Rho (Mi); ☎02 9317961; fax 02 93179630; www.nuncas.it.

Reckitt & Benckiser Italia S.p.a., Via Lamedusa, 11A, 20141 Milano (MI); ☎02 844751; fax 02 8464810; www.reckitt.com.

Segix Italia Srl, Via del Mare 36; 00040 Pomezia; ☎06 911 801; Fax 06 912 2882. Manufacturer of pharmaceutical products.

Unilever Italia S.p.a., Via N. Bonnet 10, 20154 Milano (MI); ☎02 623380; fax 02 6552310; recruitment.milan@unilever.com; www.unilever.com.

Clothing and Textiles

Coats Cucirini S.p.a., Via Vespucci, 2, 20124 Milano (MI) ☎02 636151; fax 02 659 6509. Also: Viale della Costituzione, Isola A/3, 80143 Napoli (NA); ☎081 562 5004; fax 081 562 5200; www.tamtamitalia.com/coats/.

Samar S.p.a., Via M. Libertà 68, 13874 Mottalciata (Bi); ☎0161 872111; fax 0161 857782; www.samar.it.

Techwear S.p.a. (Production and worldwide distribution licencee of Gianfranco Ferre' Men's Underwear and Homewear), Via Vivaio 11, 20122 Milano (Mi); ☎02 7733 0150; fax 02 7733 0155; www.gianfrancoferre.com.

Construction and Contracting

J & A Consultants Italia Snc, Piazza San Fedele, 4, 20121 Milano (Mi); ☎02 869 15041/2/3; fax 02 8901 1120; info@jacons.com.

Turner & Townsend Project Management Italia, Corso Monforte 39, 20122 Milano (Mi); ☎02 7639 4760; fax 02 7639 9973; www.turnerandtownsend.com.

Estate Agents & Relocation Services

Bonaparte Spa, Via Clerici 11, 20121 Milano – (Mi); ☎02 8855161; fax 02 88551660; www.bonaparte.it.

CB Richard Ellis Spa, Via dei Giardini, 4,

20121 Milano – (MI); ☎02 6556701; fax 02 65567050; www.cbrichardellis. com.

Eres Srl – European Real Estate Service, Via Urbano III, 2, 20123 Milano – (Mi); ☎02 89408373; fax 02 89408413.

Healey & Baker, Via Turati, 25, 20121 Milano – (MI); ☎02 637991; fax 02 653254; www.healey-baker.com.

Immobiliare Internazionale Mina Mothadi Broszio, Residenza Sagittario T2, Milano 220090 Segrate – (Mi); ☎02 2640582; fax 02 26410393.

Jones Lang LaSalle Spa, Via Durini, 28, 20122 Milano – (MI); ☎02 776971; fax 0277697232.

Property International Srl, (Estate & Relocation Agent), Via Correggio, 55, 20149 Milano – (MI); ☎02 4980092; fax 02 48194170.

Vigano' Giorgio Srl, Via Maggiolini, 2, 20122 Milano – (Mi); ☎02 76003914; fax 02 783618.

Electronics and Computing

3G Electronics S.r.l., Via Boncompagni, 3b, 20139 Milano (MI); ☎02 539 0441; fax 02 569 0243; www.3gvideogroup.it; www.3gelectronics.it.

Ariete S.p.a., Via Toscana 57A/B, 59100 Macrolotto, Prato (Po); ☎054 5281; fax 054 528400; www. ariete.net.

Arteleta International S.r.l.: Via Pelizza da Volpedo, 57, Postbox 26, 20092 Cinissello Balsamo; ☎660 1541; fax 02 612 2573.

BBJ S.r.l., Piazza Sicilia 6, 20146 Milano (Mi); ☎02 3650 4650; fax 02 3650 4662; www.bbj.it.

*Comestero Sistem*i S.r.l. Via Bolzano, 1/E, 20059 Vimercate (Mi); ☎039 625 091; fax 039 667479; www. comestero.com.

Control Techniques Spa: Via Brodolini 7, 20089 Rozzano, Milano; ☎02 575 751; fax 02 5751 2858. Electronic speed and position controls.

Easynet Italia S.p.a. Viale Fulvio Testi 7, 20159 Milano (MI); ☎02 3030 1500; fax 02 3030 1590; www. it.easynet.net.

Human Technology S.r.l., Viale Masini, 4, 40100 Bologna (BO); ☎051 254 988; fax 051 244 208; info@humantechnology.it; www. humantechnology.it.

Kontron Instruments Spa: 25, v. Madonna degli Angeli, 84019 Vietri Sul Mare (SA), Campania; ☎08 976 1488. Electromedical equipment.

Rigel Engineering S.r.l., Piazza Attias, 21/C, 57125 Livorno; ☎0586 210222; fax 0586 210255; www. rigel.li.it.

Tecnimex S.r.l., Via A. Corti, 28, 20133 Milano (MI); ☎02 7063 5924; fax 02 7060 0412; www.tecnimex.it.

Vision Engineering Ltd Italia, Via Roma 72, 20037 Paderno Dugnano (Mi); ☎02 9904 9973; fax 02 9904 9973.

Financial and Business Services

American Express Bank Ltd., Piazza San Babila 3, 20122 Milano – (Mi); ☎02 77901 – 800651520; fax 02

7790582.

Invesco Europe Ltd., Via Cordusio, 2, 20100 Milano – (Mi); ☎02 880741; fax 02 88074391.

Norton Rose, Via Visconti di Modrone 21, 20122 Milano – (Mi); ☎02 799144; fax 02 77331538.

Reuters Italia Spa., V.le Fulvio Testi, 280, 20126 Milano – (Mi); ☎02 661291; fax 02 66101498.

Rothschild J., Via E. Panzacchi, 6, 20123 Milano – (Mi); ☎02 72002111; fax 02 8693727.

St. James International (Offshore services), Via Lazzaretto, 6, 20124 Milano – (Mi); ☎02 29516108; fax 02 2914615; www. stjamesinternational.com.

Thomas Cook Italia Ltd., Viale Marche, 54, 00187 Roma – (Rm); ☎06 48782316; fax 06 48782330.

Towers Perrin Group, Via Pontaccio, 10, 20121 Milano – (MI); ☎02 863921; fax 02 809753; www. towers.com.

Scottish Equitable Italia Srl., Via Turati, 9, 20121 Milano – (MI); ☎02 655821; fax 02 65582500.

Insurance Services

Commercial Union Italia Spa., Viale Abruzzi 94, 20131 Milano – (MI); ☎ 0227751; fax 02 2775204.

Generali Assicurazioni Spa, Piazza Duca degli Abruzzi, 2, 34132 Trieste – (TS); ☎040 671111; fax 040 671600.

Lloyd Italico Assicurazioni Spa., Via Fieschi 9, 16121 Genova – (GE); ☎010 53801; fax 010 541221.

Lloyd's of London, Via Sigieri, 14,

20135 Milano – (MI); ☎02 55193121; fax 02 55193107; www. lloyds.it.

Marsh Spa, Pal.Carducci, Via Olona, 2, 20123 Milano – (MI); ☎02 485381; fax 02 48538300; www. marsh.com.

Marsh Spa, Via Cavour, 1, 10123 Torino – (To); ☎011 565471.

Royal & Sun Alliance Assicurazioni, Via Martin Piaggio, 1, 16122 Genova – (GE); ☎010 83301; fax 010 884989; www.rsa-ass.it.

Royal International Insurance Holdings Ltd., Via F.lli Gracchi, 30/32, 20092 Cinisello Balsamo – (Mi); ☎02 660791; fax 02 66011760; www. royal.it.

SAI – Società Assicuratrice Industriale Spa, Corso Galileo Galilei, 12, 10126 Torino – (TO); ☎011 6657111; fax 011 6657685.

Lawyers

Ashurst Morris Crisp Studio Legale Associato, Via Finocchiaro Aprile 14, 20124 Milano – (Mi); ☎02 620227225; fax 02 620227226.

Colvin Andrew, Via Acherusio, 18, 00199 Roma – (Rm); ☎06 86206459; fax 06 86383162.

Grimaldi e Clifford Chance, Via Clerici, 7, 20121 Milano – (Mi); ☎02 806341; fax 02 80634200; www.cliffordchance. com.

Lovells Studio Legale, Via F.lli Gabba 3, 20121 Milano – (Mi); ☎02 7202521; fax 02 72025252; www. lovells.com.

Simmons & Simmons Grippo, C.so Vittorio Emanuele, 1, 20122

Milano – (MI); ☎02 725051; fax 02 72505505.

Studio Legale Associato Freshfields, Via dei Giardini, 7, 20121 Milano – (Mi); ☎02 625301; fax 02 62530800; www.freshfields.com.

Worldwide Trusts Consultants Srl, Via Nitti, 45/a, 74100 Taranto – (Ta); ☎099 4590880; fax 099 4590809.

Management Consultants

Andersen Spa, Via Della Moscova, 3, 20121 Milano – (MI); ☎02 290371; fax 02 6572876.

ASI Consulting Italy Srl, C.so Venezia 16, 20121 Milano – (Mi); ☎02 76003138; fax 02 795659; www. asigroup.net.

Beavan C.P. Christopher, Via Leopardi, 21, 20123 Milano – (MI); ☎02 4815369
fax 02 48108133.

O'Donnell & Associates Srl, Via Stradon 5, 35010 Borgoricco – (Pd); ☎ 049 9336275; fax 049 9338847; www. odas.it.

Management Recruitment Consultants

Chayo & Partners Executive Search, Viale Bianca Maria 10, 20129 Milano – (Mi); ☎02 5460499; fax 02 55186540.

DPA Srl, Corso Magenta 56, 20123 Milano – (Mi); ☎02 48020668; fax 02 48020540.

Egon Zehnder International Spa, Piazza Meda, 3, 20122 Milano – (MI); ☎02 770791; fax 02 76021063.

MacCormick Hamilton International Italia Srl, Via Conservatorio,

17, 20122 Milano – (Mi); ☎02 7742171; fax 02 76012379.

Mindoor Srl, Via Santa Maria Segreta 7/9, 20123 Milano – (Mi); ☎02 45485800; fax 02 45485188; www. mindoor.com.

Nicholson International Italia Srl, Via Cino del Duca 5, 20122 Milano – (Mi); ☎02 7722961; fax 02 798349; www.nicholsonintl.com.

RRA Srl, Via A.Appiani, 7, 20121 Milano – (MI); ☎02 6231121; fax 02 6552837; www.russellreynolds. com.

Manufacturers and Equipment Suppliers

Audco Italiana S.r.l., (Hydraulic equipment), Via D. Cucchiari, 30, 20155 Milano (MI); ☎02 317241/2; fax 02 313464.

Fiat S.p.a., Via Nizza, 250, 10126 Torino; ☎011 686 1111; fax 011 686 1723; www.fiat.com.

Hodara Utensili S.p.a., Viale Lombardia, 16, 20090 Buccinasco (MI); ☎02 457721; fax 02 48842783; info@hodara.it; www. hodara.it.

Indemar S.r.l., Via Guido Rossa, 40, 16012 Busalla (GE); ☎010 9641927; fax 01 09641920; info@indemar.com; www.indemar. com.

JCB S.p.a., Via Enrico Fermi, 16, 20090 Assago, Milan (MI); ☎02 48866401; fax 02 488 0378; www. jcbitalia.com.

Sede SCALA S.r.l., (Home interiors manufacturer), Via Caboto 18/20, Zona Ind. Ranaro, 46046 Villanova

Di Reggiolo (RE); ☎0522 973112; fax 0522 974016; www.scalasrl. com.

Sistema Compositi S.p.a., Via Casilina Km. 57, 500, 03018 Paliano (FR); ☎07 7553 8511; fax 07 7553 8158; www.sistemacompositi.com.

SKF Industrie S.p.a., Via Dante Alighieri, 6, 10069 Villar Perosa (TO); ☎0121 312111; fax 0121 514304; www.skf.it.

Special Metals Services S.p.a., Via Assunta, 59, 20054 Nova Milanese (MI); ☎0362 4941; fax 0362494224; www.specialmetals. com/europe.htm.

Metal Sud S.r.l., Via Nazionale Appia - Località Crisci, 81021 Arienzo (CE); ☎08 2380 5397; fax 08 2380 5089.

Oil and Pharmaceuticals

B.P.Italia Spa, Milano Fiori Palazzo E/5-Strada 6, 20090 Assago – (MI); ☎02 822741; fax 02 57500709.

British Gas Italia Spa: Piazza Cavour 2, 20121 Milano; ☎02-777941; fax 02-77794440.

Enterprise Oil Italiana Spa, Via dei Due Macelli, 66, 00187 Roma – (RM); ☎06 699561; fax 06 69956600.

Glaxo Wellcome Spa, Via A. Fleming, 2, 37135 Verona – (VR); ☎045 9218111; fax 04 59218388; www. glaxowellcome.co.uk.

Smithkline Beecham Spa, Via Zambeletti, 20021 Baranzate di Bollate – (MI); ☎02 38061; fax 02 38200536.

Unilever Italia Spa: Via N Bonnet 10, 20154 Milano; ☎02-623380; fax 02-6552310.

Miscellaneous

Cable and Wireless Spa: via Ferrante Aporti, 26, 20125 Milano; ☎02-268181; fax 02-26141504.

Christie's of London: Piazza Navona 114, 00186 Rome; ☎06-6872787; fax 06-6893080.

P & O Container Europe Srl Strada 4, Palazzo A, Scala 7, 20090 Assago, Milano; ☎02-575681; fax 02-57512614.

STARTING A BUSINESS

CHAPTER SUMMARY

○ There are over 6.5 million micro-enterprises (which have fewer than 10 employees) which make up 97% of total enterprises in Italy; Some 300,000 new ones set up each year, but many of these fail.

○ Only a third of micro-enterprises in Italy have a website and only 3% undertake e-commerce.

○ Personal relationships are especially important in Italy when conducting business transactions so knowledge of Italian is essential.

○ There is official encouragement for new businesses but it can be difficult to raise finance and there is much red tape to be waded through.

○ Help for prospective entrepreneurs can be obtained from the British Department of Trade and Industry, the British or American Chambers of Commerce in Milan and elsewhere, and the network of Euro Info Centres established by the European Union.

○ Although the north of Italy is the most dynamic business region there are various state incentives for those considering investing in the south.

○ Raising money can be difficult as British banks will not provide start-up loans for Italian businesses, and even if an Italian bank can be persuaded to help the interest rates will be high.

○ An individual setting up in business in Italy must establish a proper business structure, for which professional advice is essential.

○ Possible fruitful types of business to establish include health food stores, car repair, estate agencies; doctors and dentists may do particularly well in areas where there are numbers of other expatriates.

○ The Italian tax system is complex, and so expert fiscal advice is essential for the self-employed.

The single European market has made citizens of EU countries increasingly aware of the possibility of starting a business in another Community country. In the case of Italy in particular, the close historical and family links of many North Americans to Italy has made many of them consider doing so too. The experience can be a rewarding one for those who have the appropriate skills and know how, and who know how to use the support and resources that are at their disposal and that are often needed. There are, however, many challenges in starting a business and many more that only manifest themselves when doing so in a foreign country.

John Matta warns that setting up a business is not a quick process

Setting up a business in Italy is definitely not as easy as the UK where you can buy an off the peg company one day and be trading the next. Here, you have to allow at least four months for all the processes to be completed. It is a big mistake to think you can do it all on your own. You should start by using one of the specialist companies that make their living from company start-ups. They charge a fee yes, but in the end it will save you a lot of time and be worth it. Also, unless you can communicate freely in Italian you cannot expect to make a success of business here.

Before setting up business in a foreign country it will undoubtedly be an advantage to have already run, or helped to run a business in your own country or Italy. Many entrepreneurs have already had a successful business or professional career working for someone else when they set out on their own and this experience is even more useful when setting up in a foreign country.

The possibilities in Italy are certainly as wide-ranging and in some fields (e.g. financial services, computer consulting and high quality consumer goods) are more promising than they are in Britain and the US where there is already much competition. Self-employment as a medical or dental practitioner, artist, writer, mechanic, manufacturer, retailer, house renovator, personal trainer or farmer are just some of the successes notched up so far.

Italy is known as the land of mainly small business and there are over three million of them. Estimates put the number of new enterprises started annually at an astonishing 300,000, though the number of failures is also high. This explosion of Italian entrepreneurial activity is often linked to the difficulty in finding an employer willing to offer long-term job security, so skilled workers have opted to go into business for themselves, whether they have an aptitude for the chosen business or not. It is therefore small wonder that this exceptional volume of entrepreneurial activity leads to a high failure rate. Studies show that the majority of Italian businesses fold in the first five years of their existence. In fact in some recent years the number of firms that ceased activity has exceeded the number newly registered. Part of the reason for this historic high failure rate is that while Italy encourages people to set up in business, the necessary support structures including bank finance and even training for potential entrepreneurs is lacking. Mainly owing to the intimidating failure statistics for new business, franchising has experienced an explosion of popularity in the last few years as it reduces start-up costs considerably, training and ongoing support are provided and brand recognition already exists and has a known market.

Another potential hurdle is the bureaucratic one, which is less burdensome than it used to be, especially for small, or one-man/woman businesses. There has been some recent progress on bank support for start-ups and banks are now permitted to lend in the medium-term for commercial projects (though applications are certain to be strenuously scrutinised). Some banks, notably Credito Italiano have a corporate finance and mergers and acquisitions department.

Evidently, the process of setting up an Italian business is not for the faint-hearted. To sum up: Italy offers two extremes to the prospective foreign entrepreneur. On the one hand Italians are some of the world's best business people and are excellent to deal with. On the other hand problems that you might encounter getting a business up and running in your own country are heightened in a foreign country where you have to cope with unfamiliar bureaucracy, culture, language and business practices. If your company is going to be incorporated, you will need the services of a lawyer to draw up the statute. Larger companies take the headache out of the whole process by employing a professional advisors or a relocation agency, the majority of which are based in Milan. The services offered by each vary from helping to form a network of contacts to completing the formalities necessary to start trading, and from complete corporate relocation (including finding accommodation for foreign executives to helping find offices and staff for your business.

Italian Fabio Ausenda, whose publishing business is based in Genova, gives an idea of the different start-up procedures for small businesses

I have participated directly in the start-up of about ten companies in Italy, both sole traders and ltd. For a limited company it takes a maximum of 15 days to incorporate the company, register at the VAT office and chamber of commerce and open a bank account. A simple sole trader can open to business within a day, the time it takes to register at the VAT office and get a VAT number. Shops used to need a licence to prevent excess competition in an area. Until the mid 1990s the number of the same kind of shop was restricted one area to prevent an excess of competition; a regulation strongly supported by shopkeepers. Now only pharmacies, bars serving alcohol and tobacconists need licences. The main problem is that the comuni can impose zoning restrictions on shopping areas. For a bar or restaurant there are extremely strict hygiene and disabled access regulations. Bear in mind though, that opening a business particularly as a small trader or small limited company is the easy part; finding clients to make your business grow is much harder. As in any other country, you need to find the right product or service and produce or supply it at the right cost. You also need to be a good salesperson; personal contacts and networking are very important components for a successful business but if your product is not as good as, or is more expensive than the competition, then even if you are a personal friend of the Pope, you will not sell it.

As already mentioned, it would be unthinkable to attempt going into business in Italy without finding learning the language, mainly because being a commercial success in Italy probably relies more on socialising than in most other countries. The ability to communicate in Italian is therefore imperative for anyone contemplating an Italian business venture. In addition to speaking Italian, as when starting a business in any country checking off the following is important:

- Have a sound business plan.
- Carry out an in depth feasibility study on the practicalities of running your proposed business in the area you are considering.
- Have a thorough knowledge and experience of the type of business you are intending to run.
- Have the personal stamina and determination and the capacity to the handle risk of losing everything.
- *Pensare in grande, cominciare in piccolo* (think big, start small).

The following sections outline the various processes involved in setting up different types of businesses.

PROCEDURES INVOLVED IN STARTING A NEW BUSINESS

The predicament facing foreigners who wish to operate a business in Italy is whether to acquire an existing business or launch their own and there are compelling arguments for both options. Taking over an existing concern avoids the bureaucracy (more relevant for some types of business than others), and having to build up custom. On the other hand you don't have to deal with existing problems such as demotivated employees; more importantly, it is often difficult to ascertain with certainty the exact financial state or standing of the package you are acquiring. If the package includes staff, then Italy's protective labour laws may make a shake up, or dismissal of staff extremely difficult. However, companies with fewer than 15 employees can dismiss staff with a 'just cause' which can include restructuring. On balance there is probably more to be said in favour of starting up an entirely new business.

Preparation from Scratch

Before launching yourself into the necessary formalities for setting up a business in Italy, exhaustive preparation is essential. For instance thorough research should enable you to determine accurately whether a proposed business has a reasonable prospect of succeeding. This often means finding a gap in the market that the Italians have not yet exploited, or which is underexploited. An example of niche-making is that of Abbey National, which having noted the lack of an Italian equivalent of building societies, ensconced itself in northern Italy where it had ten branches selling mortgages to Italians until it sold on the mortgage business to Unicredit Banca per la Casa in 2003. However, most entrepreneurs in Italy will not be creating niches on such a grand scale. More likely for them is a shop selling English, Swedish, American or other foreign-made products not easily obtainable in Italy, or working as an independent consultant in an area where there is a growing demand. Anything to do with pets is currently such an area. There is also scope in providing different services for the expatriates some of which are included in *Ideas for New Businesses* below.

Preparation is not only about spotting a gap in the market. Other considerations include whether or not the prospective business person or organisation feels that the Italians will be able to relate to them. The best way of finding out is undoubtedly to spend as much time there as possible, on holidays, business prospecting trips etc. making friends and useful contacts who will form your network of advisors and allies if and when you finally decide to take the plunge. Many entrepreneurs who have already successfully negotiated the bureaucracy say that, initially, advice from the DTI in London, the British (or American) Chamber of Commerce in Milan, proved invaluable.

Another starting point for those thinking of setting up business in Italy is the Italian Chamber of Commerce for Great Britain (1 Princes Street, London W1B 2AY; ☎020-7495 8191; fax 020-7495 8194; www.italchamind.org.uk) which exists to promote two-way trade between Britain and Italy and to promote UK investment in Italy. They can supply a list of British firms operating in Italy and can also provide contact addresses in Italy and information on Italian government incentive schemes. They also organise an annual promotion event, Viva Italia, at Earl's Court Exhibition Centre, London in September which aims to be a shop window for Italian business and commerce. Categories represented at the event include tourism, health and beauty, food and wine and property and everything for the home. However, the most productive groundwork will undoubtedly be that carried out in Italy itself. Foreigners who have located their market pitch in Italy report that growth is usually meteoric, such is the buoyancy of the Italian market. There are numerous Italian Chambers of Commerce in North America and they can be located through www.italchambers.net and www.italbiz.net.

Euro Info Centres (EICs)

One of the first steps before moving to Europe to start doing business is a visit to one of the network of Euro Info Centres established in 1987 by the European Commission. There are now hundreds of EICs in fifteen European countries and more around the world. The Info Centres are linked directly to the European Commission's databases and are an up-to-date source of information on European standards, EU initiatives for small businesses, and new opportunities arising from the single market. By linking up with other Centres throughout Europe, information about national and local opportunities and regulations can be obtained. The cost of services is partly borne by the European Union and partly by the client.

A list of the UK EICs is below and most of them can be contacted by email. Up-to-date contacts for EICs can be found at www.euro-info.org.uk/centres or through http://europa.eu.int/comm/enterprise/networks/eic/eic_uk.html. A directory of all EICs in Europe and around the world can be found at: http://europa.eu.int/business/en/advice/eics/index.html,

Belfast: EIC, Invest Northern Ireland, Upper Galwally, Belfast BT8 6TB; ☎02890-239090; fax 02890-490490; eic@investni.com; www.investni.com.

Birmingham: European Business Centre, 75 Harborne Road, Edgbaston B15 3DH; ☎0121-455 0268; fax 0121-455 8670.

Bradford: West Yorkshire Euro Info Centre, Investinbradford, The Bradford Design Exchange, 34 Peckover Street, Bradford BD1 5BD; ☎01274-434262; fax 01274-432136; eic@Bradford.gov.uk; www.Bradford.gove.uk/euroinfocentre.

Bristol: EIC, Business West, Leigh Court Business Centre, Abbots Leigh, Bristol, BS8 3RA; ☎01275-373373; fax 01275-370706; eic@businesswest.co.uk.

Cardiff: Wales Euro Info Building, UWCC Guest Building, P O Box 430, CF1 3XT; ☎02920 229525; fax 0290-229740.

Durham: North of England EIC, Rivergreen Centre, Aykley Heads, Durham DH1 5TS; ☎0191-383 7317; www.northeasteic.com.

Glasgow: Euro Info Centre, Small Business Gateway, 150 Broomielaw, Atlantic Quay, Glasgow G2 8LU; ☎0141-228 2797; fax 0141-222 2327; euroinfocentre@scotent.co.uk; www.Scottish-enterprise.com/euroinfocentre.

EIC: Brynmor Jones Library, University of Hull, Cottingham Road, HU6 7RX; ☎01482-465940; fax 01482-466488.

Essex: Essex County Council, Aquila House, Waterloo Lane, Chelmsford Essex CM1 1BD; ☎01245-702460; fax 01245-702461; eic@essexcc.gov.uk; www.essexeic.org.uk.

Hull: EIC Humberside, The University of Hull, Brynmor Jones Library, Cottingham Road, Hull HU6 7RX; ☎01482-465940; fax 01482-466488; euro-info-centre@hull.ac.uk; www.hull.ac.uk/euroinfo.

Inverness: European Business Services, 81A Castle Street, Inverness, Scotland; ☎01463-702560; fax 01463-715600; eic@euro-info.co.uk; www.euro-info. co.uk.

Kent: Kent Euro Info Centre, 26 Kings Hill Avenue, Kings Hill, West Malling, Kent ME19 4AE; ☎0345 226655; fax 01732-841109; eic@kent.businesslink. co.uk.

Knutsford: The Forum of Private Business, Ruskin Chambers, Drury Lane, Knutsford, Cheshire WA16 6HA; ☎01565-634467; fax 0870-241 9570; neillmarrs@fpb.co.uk.

Leeds: Mid-Yorkshire Euro Info Centre, The Learning Centre, Leslie Silver Building, Leeds Metropolitan University City Campus, Leeds LS1 3HE; ☎0113-283 3126; fax 0113 283 6779; eic@imu.ac.uk; www.imu.ac.uk/Iss/ eic/.

Leicester: Leicester EIC, 10 York Road, Leicester LE1 5TS; ☎0116-2559944; fax 0116-2553470.

Liverpool: EIC North West, The International Trade Centre for Greater Merseyside, No 1, Old Hall Street, Liverpool, L3 9HS; ☎0151-237 5005; fax 0151-237 5000; www.eicnw.co.uk.

London I: EIC 33 Queen Street, London EC4R 1AP; ☎020-7489 1992; fax 020-7203 1812.

Manchester: Euro Info Centre, UK564, Churchgate House, 56 Oxford Street, Manchester M60 7HJ; ☎0161-237 4020; fax 0161-236 1341; euroinfo@c-b-e/co.uk; www.c-b-e.co.uk/eic.

Nottingham: EIC, Nottinghamshire Chamber of Commerce, 309 Haydn Road, Nottingham NG5 1DG; ☎0115-962 9633; fax 0115-985 6612; info@nottschamber.co.uk; www.nottschamber.co.uk/EIC.

Sheffield: South Yorkshire EIC, SYITC, c/o Sheffield Chamber of Commerce, Albion House, Savile Street, Sheffield S4 7UD; ☎0114-201 2595; fax 0114-201 2552; g.r.wade@shu.ac.uk.

St Albans: EIC, 45 Grosvenor Road, St. Albans, Herts. AL1 3AW; ☎01727-813693; fax 01727-813404; www.hertseic.co.uk.

Southampton: Southern Area Euro Info Centre, Civic Centre, Southampton S014 7LW; ☎02380-832866; 02380-231714.

Useful Addresses

British Chamber of Commerce for Italy: Via Dante 12, 20121 Milan. ☎02-877798/8056094; fax 02-86461885; www.britchamitaly.com. Has a Small Business Guide on its website.

Direzione Generale della Producione Industriale: Via Molise 2, 00100 Rome, Italy; ☎010-39 6 47051.

DTI London: Kingsgate House, 66-74 Victoria Street, London SW1E 6SW;

☎020-7215 58000; UK trade and investment section has a department which covers export market information. Further information from www.invest.uktradeinvest.gov.uk; e-mail: enquiries@dti.gsi.gov.uk. Statistics, directories, market research reports, mail order catalogues, country profiles may only be available in libraries owing to DTI downsizing. Contact the DTI for more information.

Italian Chamber of Commerce for Great Britain: 1 Princes Street, London W1B 2AY; ☎020-7495 8191; fax 020-7495 8194; www.itallchamind.co.uk.

Accountancy Firms: Anyone planning to start a business in Italy would be advised to seek the advice of accountancy firms in Britain which have branches in Italy. A list of international accountancy firms with offices in Italy can be found in the list of *Major Employers in the Employment* chapter.

Chambers of Commerce in Italy

In the initial stages of setting up a business in Italy you will probably be dealing with the British Chamber of Commerce in Milan (☎02-877798; bcci@britchamitaly.com; www.britchamitaly.com) or the American Chamber of Commerce (☎02 8690661; amcham@amcham.it; www.amcham.it). The chamber can provide you with contacts, make introductions and advise on offices if you need a physical base in Italy. In addition to the head office in Milan, there is a branch of the British Chamber of Commerce in Bologna, Brescia, Cagliari, Firenze, Napoli, Novara, Padova, Pordenone, Roma, Taranto, Torino, Trieste and Verona. In addition to all its other services the British Chamber of Commerce for Italy produces *Britaly*, an online newsletter available to subscribers. It also prints:

Focus on Italy: the guide to business and pleasure in Italy with facts, figures, articles contacts and information on doing business in Italy.

Speak to the World: an annual brochure of the Chamber's English Language Consultancy Service. It has a print run of about 5,000 copies.

Trade Directory and Members' Handbook: is a bi-annual publication which lists all chamber members and is now on-line on their website (www.britchamitaly.com). Print run of some 1,500 copies.

To advertise in any of the above you can phone (02-877798) or fax (02-86461885) or email bcci@britchamitaly.com.

The branches of the British Chamber of Commerce throughout Italy will be able to provide local advice and information for prospective entrepreneurs.

The Italian Chamber of Commerce (www.chamberofcommerce.it) has its seat in Milan (via Meravigli, 12-20124 MI, Italy; www.mi.camcom.it). There are 103 chambers of commerce throughout Italy. You can locate your nearest chamber of commerce via the above website, or contact the Milan chamber and they can refer you to a local chamber of commerce (*camera di commercio*) to complete your paperwork. Local Chambers of Commerce can also be found through the Yellow Pages (www.paginegialle.it) or from overseas branches of the Italian Chambers of Commerce. The website of the Chamber of Commerce has links to various investment authorities in Italy who may be able to assist with financing and other incentives. During the 1990s the chambers of commerce were reformed and given a totally independent status in their role of supporting and promoting business interests for their area.

Italian businessman Fabio Ausenda explains when company registration is necessary and when it is not:
CCIs also act as a public registry of all existing companies, (except if you are an independent consultant) so when you start a new company you need to register with the Chamber of Commerce and Industry and pay an annual tax which depends on the size of the company and the number of locations where it operates. I am a sole trader publisher with one location and I pay 80 euros a year; my wife, who is an independent human resources consultant, only needs a VAT number and does not need to register with the Chamber of Commerce.

CHOOSING AN AREA

In addition to market research and preparing the ground, one also has to choose an area. As mentioned, northern Italy is the most dynamic business region of Italy. This does not mean however that the Mezzogiorno should be totally ignored. Generous incentives have resulted in a rush of both foreign and Italian companies to the south. However, the deep south (Naples to Sicily) is traditionally the least-favoured region because of mafia activity and poor infrastructure.

The type of business envisaged will also have a bearing on the choice of area. Some foreigners find themselves partly or wholly dependent on other expatriates for clientele, while others will rely on Italian consumers and yet others on an international clientele. Medical and dental practitioners prefer the Milan area where there are an estimated 30,000 expatriates. For the Lombardy region as a whole the number is probably triple that. Those in the real estate business once only thought of being based in the north, Rome, Tuscany or Umbria but now might be in Le Marche, Puglia, Sardinia, and other regions.

Italian Regional Incentives

In 2006, following five years of investment, the regions of southern Italy will have received 45 billion euros from the EU and the Italian regional governments. Regions in north and central Italy which have been recognised as disadvantaged will also receive substantial investment. The stated aims for this spending programme in the south include improving law and order, encouraging innovation, reducing the black economy and promoting tourism especially in Naples and along the Amalfi Coast and Sorrento peninsular. Half the EU funds spent in the south have been split between Campania and Sicily. By far the largest portion of investment is going into tourism so any businesses in Campania that support tourism are likely to benefit from regional investment and promotion.

Fabio Ausenda on where the incentives can be particularly good, and where there are downsides

Chambers of Commerce do assist entrepreneurs in finding opportunities and with funding. Some of the regions where subsidies and help with access to markets are particularly good are the German-speaking South Tyrol where you get substantial help to start a business, but you need South Tyrolean partners who speak German. In the South of Italy too, there are generous funds, but the prospects of success are often low, and the danger of attracting the attention of criminal gangs, at least in some areas, is very high.

Useful Resources

English Yellow Pages: these are nothing to do with British Telecom. They are a source guide for the English-speaking foreign community in Rome, but with supplements for Florence, Milan, Naples, Genoa, Palermo and Catania. Available from international bookshops and news-stands in the above three cities and also online at: www.intoitaly.it.

The Informer: Buroservice SNC, Via Tigli 2, 20020 Milan; ☎02-93581477; fax 02-93580280; www.informer.it. An online magazine aimed at expatriates in Italy. Provides regular updates on changes in the legislation regarding tax, businesses etc. plus the best ways to tackle the bureaucracy. Subscription payable.

The Italian Business Review: Founded in 1967. Published monthly (except August) by The Italian Business Review Inc., European address: Suite 693, 2 Old Brompton Road, London SW7 3DQ; ☎020-7413 9554; fax 020-7581 4445.˙Subscription US $510 annually. Comprehensive reporting of Italian business news and a good way to keep in touch with developments in Italy; includes forecasts and indicators and focus and analysis sections.

Opportunities for Investment and Joint Ventures in Southern Italy: published by IASM (see below), Via Ariosto 24, Milano; ☎02-481 76 36.

Wanted in Rome: (www.wantedinrome.com) An online magazine aimed at the expatriate community. Has a large classified advertisement section listing accommodation, jobs and other services needed by expats.

RAISING FINANCE

Those contemplating opening a business in Italy should note that UK banks in Britain will not be able to provide start-up loans in cases where the prospective proprietor intends to be resident abroad. As already mentioned Italian banks are unlikely to lend money to small businesses for start-ups without guarantees. The obvious way for prospective proprietors to raise money is by selling their UK home. If this proves insufficient then it should be possible to raise a mortgage on an Italian property using a mortgage provider such as Unicredit Banca per la Casa, Banca Intesa, or the Woolwich Bank (now a brand of Barclays), both of which have branch offices around Italy (see *Mortgages in the Setting up Home* chapter).

Alternatively one could investigate the potential of the Italian government business incentive schemes (see below).

Investment Incentives

If raising finance is a problem, it may be worth investigating whether or not your proposed business could benefit from a government or EU incentive programme. Government schemes are heavily biased in favour of the Mezzogiorno (the provinces south of Rome, and Sicily and Sardinia), however certain small islands and specially designated zones in Tuscany, Umbria and the north of Italy also come with inducement packages, albeit less munificent ones. The government agency that handles new investment is Sviluppo Italia (www.sviluppoitalia.it) and the areas currently eligible for investment incentives are Campania, Puglia, Basilicata, Calabria, Sicilia and Sardegna. There is an English version of Sviluppo Italia on their website and you can also consult Invest in Italy (via Calabria 46, 00187 Rome; e-mail info@investinitaly.com; www.investinitaly.com) which is another source of guidance to investment incentives in eighteen regions. You can see which provinces are eligible for grants and incentives at www.territory.sviluppoitalia.it. Note that investment incentives from the EU are likely to dry up after 2006 when newer and poorer EU countries will have the bulk of EU development finance directed to them. The British and American Chambers of Commerce in Italy can also put you in touch with local offices that handle regional investment.

Tax Incentives: Certain of the employer's social security contributions are refunded in the case of new investments.

Non-tax incentives: The governent also offers grants and low-interest loans up to the level of 70% to 75% of total investment. For joint ventures, regional and state agencies in the Mezzogiorno will put up half the share capital and then give the private partner the option to buy out the state's shares when the company is over the start-up period. Small and medium-sized businesses valued at not more than about 30,000 Euros are entitled to loans at 10.3% interest (lower in the south). The maximum loan is 2,000,000 million euros.

Research and technological assistance: All businesses engaged in research projects 60% based in Italy are eligible for incentive grants subject to government approval.

Specific Activity Incentives: Companies engaged in certain types of business activities are eligible for grants throughout Italy:

Agriculture	Shipping yards and ship repairs
Cinema	Waste Disposal
Machine Tools	Publishing
(retail and wholesale)	Mining
Aircraft	Energy Saving
Publishing	Hotel and Catering
Maritime Fishing	Handicrafts

European Union Incentives: Europeans carrying out business activities in Italy are entitled to grants and soft loans under aid programmes operated by the EU. The main programmes are:

The European Regional Development Fund: the ERDF exists to redress regional imbalances within the EU.

European Social Fund: aims to facilitate employment of workers through increasing their mobility.

European Agricultural Fund: aims to improve agricultural structures.

Other EU incentives are obtainable for the coal and steel industries and research and technology development.

RELOCATION AGENCIES AND BUSINESS SERVICES

Inspired by an increasing awareness of the business potential of Italy but deterred by the idea of coping with the setting up formalities and practicalities in a foreign country, newcomers can turn to a relocation or business assistance agency. There is an expanding number of such agencies, particularly in the north and Rome, which can help aspiring business people not only with commercial contacts and guidance through the formidable procedures for setting up, but also the equally frustrating domestic problems of finding somewhere to live and arranging connections to the utilities, telephone, internet etc. In addition to the addresses provided below, a list of such agencies can be obtained from the British Chamber of Commerce for Italy (Via Camperio 9, 20123 Milan; ☎02-877798; www.britchamitaly.com – directory online) and The English Yellow Pages at www.intoitaly.it.

Useful Addresses

At Home, Specialty Relocation and Real Estate Services, via del Babuino 56, 00187 Rome; ☎06 321 20102; fax 06 178 274 0479; www.at-home-italy.com.

CORE (Cocchini Relocation S.r.l)., Via Sirtori 13, 20129 Milan; ☎+39 02 29512793; fax +39 02 29513075. Relocation services (securing of documents, school registration etc.) and location of homes and offices for individuals and businesses. Agents also in Rome, Florence, Turin, Genoa and Venice.

Crown Relocations, Milan: Via Edison 118, Settimo Milanese, Milan 20019; ☎+39 02 4891 0971; fax +39 02 4891 4957; italy@crownrelo.com. Rome: V. Salaria 161 - 00016 - Monterotondo , Rome, ☎06 90085244; fax 06 90085060; www.crownrelo.com.

Milligan & Milligan Rentals, via degli Alfani 68, 50121 Florence; ☎055 268256; fax 055 268260; www.italy-rentals.com; e-mail milligan@dada.it. Villas and apartments in Tuscany of interest to foreigners wanting to buy properties, or who are relocating to Italy.

Property International, Via Correggio 55, 20149 Milan; ☎02-49 80 092; fax 02-48 19 41 70; also Rome office at Viale Aventino 79; ☎06 47 43 170; fax 06-57 43 182. Provides a wide range of services from rentals and sales of residential and commercial property to obtaining the necessary documentation for an expatriate to live and work in Italy.

Relocation Enterprises Srl, Rome; ☎06 824060; fax 06 824055; info@relocation enterprises.com; www.relocationenterprises.com/italy/individual.htm. Rome and other cities in Italy.

Studio Papperini: 114 Via Ugo Ojetti, 00137 Rome; ☎06-86895810; fax 06-86896516. Comprehensive relocation service headed by Giovanni Papperini, a solicitor specialising in immigration and nationality law. Based in Rome, but with offices in Milan, Naples, Genoa, Palermo, Florence, Bologna and Catania. Offers a pre-move service and cost effective, tailor-made package to suit employer or employee.

Turin Relocation, via Bognino 14, 10024 Moncalieri (TO); ☎+39 011 6485033; + 39 011 648739; info@turinrelocation.com; www.turinrelocation.com. Contact Aida Bernabei Chauvie.

Business Services & Business Consultants:

Abacus Serviced Offices Worldwide, ☎ 07074-847882; fax 01483-200221; enquiries@serviced-offices-europe.com; www.serviced-offices-europe.com, searchable online database of available offices.

English Yellow Pages, www.intoitaly.it has an extensive list of service providers.

British Chamber of Commerce in Italy, online database of service providers at: www.britchamitaly.com.

CSA snc: Via Pigna 14/A, 37121 Verona; ☎045-592482; fax 045-597629. CSA provides a full range of commercial services from set-up and relocation to providing essential contacts throughout northern Italy and is a member of the British Chamber of Commerce in Milan.

Regus Business Centre Srl: Via Torino 2, 20123 Milano; ☎02-725461; fax 02-72546400; www.regus.com. Fully furnished offices at five locations in Milan and four in Rome, contact detail can be found on their website.

Start in Italy: Via Saffi 30, 20123 Milano; ☎02-8905416; fax 02-89054190; e-mail info@startinitaly.it; www.startinitaly.it. Start in Italy helps foreign companies that want to enter the Italian market and gives legal and fiscal support.

Stelnet.com: Telecentro Stelnet, Via del Canneto 10/A, 09134 Cagliari, Sardinia; ☎070 503093; fax 070 520959; www.stelnet.com; e-mail info@stelnet.com. Assists foreign businesses to do business in the Italian market place by arranging introductions to Italian entrepreneurs and partners. Stelnet also supports small and medium-sized Italian businesses with their foreign deals. Has a network of Stelnet Infobrokers throughout Italy.

Business Incubators

Business incubators can help small businesses develop, provide physical space, help with networking and offer other kinds of support. Not all categories of business are appropriate for this kind of help; for instance they are not usually suitable for retail businesses. On the other hand most types of business concerned with high technology and research and development are suitable candidates for an incubating service. The aim of the incubating organisation is to help produce a viable business that can expand on its own.

A list of small business incubators can be found www.smallbusinessnotes.com/incubation/italy.html.

BUSINESS STRUCTURES

In order to operate commercially in Italy, an individual or a company must have a recognized Italian business structure. The equivalent of a UK Limited Liability company is a *Società di responsabilità limitata* (SrL). Individuals may prefer a simpler entity, the *Società in Accommandita Semplice* (SAS). The *Società per Azioni* or SpA is a larger Incorporated Company with many shareholders. The formalities of setting up a business structure are normally entrusted to a legal or fiscal advisor. Large international accountants such as PricewaterhouseCoopers, Andersen, KPMG, Ernst & Young etc. who have offices in Italy will sometimes recommend local consultants. Alternatively, the British Chamber of Commerce in Milan will be able to suggest ways of locating possible advisors.

The different business entities and the steps required to form them are as follows:

SpA. A SpA is a largish incorporated company that corresponds roughly to a UK Plc. To create an SpA specific information regarding the company, its shareholders and directors must be incorporated into a public deed. Before an SpA can be formed two thirds of the capital must be underwritten by two or incorporators and deposited with the Banca d'Italia until the company is officially registered. It is also possible to establish an SpA as a single incorporator. If there is a sole shareholder, the entire capital is required. Within 30 days of incorporating the company memorandum (*Atto Costitutivo*) and Articles of Association/Statutes (*Statuto*), they must be submitted to the registrar at the local Chamber of Commerce. After ascertaining that the necessary legal requirements have been fulfilled, the court will enter the company in the business register. Following incorporation, it is necessary to apply immediately for a VAT number (*numero di partita IVA*), You will also be given a company number (*numero REA*) by the chamber of commerce and company register details (*registro imprese*).

In order to be quoted on the stock exchange an SpA must have a minimum capital of around €120,000. Stock exchange flotation is not however compulsory once this level of capital is reached. Once an SpA has gone public it is required to submit its accounts to outside auditors. Formation procedures for an SpA are very costly: an SpA with capital of €260,000 will cost approximately €16,000. SpAs are large companies not usually suitable for small investors.

Srl. An Srl is a private (limited liability) company. The procedures for an Srl are similar to an SpA. The minimum authorized capital is €10,000. Liability is limited to the paid-up company capital. The capital contribution of a participant in an Srl is referred to as a quota. Unlike SpAs, Srls are not required to appoint an outside auditor if their capital is less €50,000.

Italian entrepreneur Fabio Ausenda has set up several Srls
To set up an Srl is not difficult. You incorporate the company in the presence of a notary (the same official as for house purchases). The notary also prepares the statute, so you don't even need a lawyer for that. Before going to the notary you

deposit a third of the company capital at any bank, and that will be the starting capital that you can use for the business. The bank gives you a receipt for the money deposited, and with that you go to the notary to establish the company. The notary himself applies to the chamber of commerce for the registration, and with a copy of the Atto costitutivo *(enabling act), witnessed by the notary, you go to the VAT office and obtain a VAT number on the spot.*

Partnerships. Partnerships of various kinds are suitable for the self-employed as the setting up procedures are less complicated and there are no minimum capital requirements as there are for companies and corporations. The main disadvantage of partnerships is that participants are personally liable for company debts. The types of partnership structures are:

- *Societa in nome collettivo (Snc):* A general partnership with unlimited liability, (ie. all the partners are liable for the debts of the partnership).
- *Societa in accomandita semplice (Sas):* An incorporated partnership in which the main partners' liability is without limit.
- *Societa in accomandita per Azioni (SapA):* A partnership in which the liability of individual participants is restricted by agreement to the amount of their capital input.

All partnerships have to be incorporated in a deed, which gives details of the partners including their duties and responsibilities, and the aims of the partnership. The registration procedure is the same as for an Srl

There is a minimum limit of two partners, but no maximum. Companies, including Italian companies may be partners. Partnerships are required to keep a company journal and an inventory register, with invoices of all purchases and copies of all correspondence sent and received. There is no legal requirement for an audit.

Sole Proprietor. A sole proprietor has to register within 30 days with the business registry of the town where his or her business is located – i.e. with the registrar at the local Chamber of Commerce. It can take one hour to set up a sole proprietorship. You fill out a simple form at the VAT office and there is no charge for this formality. You also register at the chamber of commerce where you pay 25 euros. Sole proprietorship income is taxed as personal income. (see *Taxation* below).

Freelance Consultant. For this kind of commercial activity you need only go to the tax office to get a VAT number. There is no need to register at the chamber of commerce.

IDEAS FOR NEW BUSINESSES

Unlike Spain and Portugal where the majority of expatriates are concentrated in specific areas of the country, in Italy they are more widely dispersed. This makes it difficult to start up bars, restaurants, shops etc. that are largely dependent on expatriate patronage. As already mentioned, the Italians are avid, but very discerning consumers, so competition in the food and other retail businesses is likely to be keen, and in the case of fashion, unbeatable. It is for this reason that newcomers may feel happier taking over an established and profitable business through which new products can be gradually introduced on a trial-run basis. This can be a less risky way of creating a new business ie. by introducing new products with existing ones rather than starting from scratch.

Some ideas that have proved successful so far include: running a boutique luxury guesthouse/hotel, offering cookery, yoga or painting courses in Tuscany, Umbria, Puglia and anywhere picturesque that is no more than an hour from an airport that has cheap flights (ditto for other types of holiday, horse-riding, holistic, cycling, walking etc.), running an English book/video shop, or one that sells typically English products that the Italians will also buy and perhaps combining this with an English tea shop or restaurant. Other types of business that have worked include: organic farming, winemaking and running some kind of property related business including letting out your own property.

Starting a Business Versus Taking Over an Existing One

By European standards the majority of Italian businesses are on a small scale employing fewer than 100 staff; only 19% of the workforce are employed in companies with over 500 workers. This means there is probably no point in opening a business of which there are several of a similar kind in your area, unless you can offer something different and if possible unique. There is potentially no shortage of small commercial concerns available in the in the market place and it is tempting to think it may be the easier option and that it will save start-up costs. If taking over an existing business you should make absolutely sure that it is profitable and that it will be money well spent. You may find that it is cheaper to start up your own business and build it up as you go along.

Foreign Professionals in Italy

Foreign professionals who have relocated in Italy and who have set up successful businesses include lawyers qualified in international law, accountants, veterinarians, landscape gardens and interior designers. An area where foreigners are likely to succeed, sometimes beyond their wildest dreams, is in the professions where their training, particularly in the dental fields, is acknowledged to be vastly superior to those acquired by many of their European colleagues. Italians and expatriates alike prefer to trust their teeth to private practitioners, despite the enormous fees charged, rather than suffer the drawbacks of underfunded public health and dental services. Under EU reciprocity regulations, doctors' and dentists' qualifications obtained in one EU country are recognised throughout the EU. There is therefore little difficulty for foreigners establishing a lucrative niche in private healthcare for expatriates who prefer to deal with an English-speaking professional.

Estate Agents

Estate Agents used to be in short supply in rural areas of Italy but their number has exploded and there are now very few regions where you cannot find an estate agent doing business. In the last couple of years Italian estate agents have also been moving into the market that involves selling rural properties to foreigners. Although there are also a few British, Dutch, Swedish, American etc. estate agents their clientele is mainly amongst their own nationals. Now that currency restrictions have been abolished in Italy, Italians are also buying up property in France, Spain, Portugal, Eastern Europe etc. and it would certainly be worth the while of estate agents with international contacts looking into this area of business. There is definitely a gap in the market for estate agents to sell property outside Italy to Italians.

Letting Out Italian Property

This can be done as part of an estate agency business, whereby once you have sold several properties you can then offer the owners a management and letting service, especially if they are only using their property infrequently for holidays.

Alternatively, once your Italian property is furnished, letting it out can be a useful way of helping to pay off the cost, particularly if you are not living in it for much of the year. It is worth remembering that if your property is in a rural area of Tuscany, Umbria etc. the main letting period will be from spring to autumn. The income you can expect will vary according to the degree of luxury offered and whether the let is in high season (July and August), mid-season (June and September) or low (April, May and October). Rentals range from about £300 for a studio apartment to upwards of £6,000 a week in high season for a luxury seaside villa with a swimming pool and cook/cleaner. Rentals are usually a week or longer. In the main season two weeks is usual while out-of-season lets tend to be shorter. It is possible to let to Italians or foreigners. Of course not everyone relishes the idea of a constant stream of strangers marching through their property inflicting additional wear and tear, but most tenants behave responsibly and you can always stipulate no animals, small children or pop stars if you are particularly fastidious about your furnishings.

Considerations Before Renting Out. Before you place an advert for your property in a newspaper or magazine you must make sure that you meet all the requirements that make your house/apartment a suitable rental.

- A swimming pool is fairly essential
- If your property is near a major city or place of interest you can charge more rent.
- Well-equipped kitchen
- Provide bed linen and towels
- Have a cot and highchair for young children
- Central heating or another form of adequate heating
- Washing machine/dryer (laundry room)
- Place to hang washng
- TV, radio, CD player
- Bicycles, badminton, table tennis etc.
- Garden space with private corners for guests to sit
- Barbecue area - eating area suitable for up to 12 diners equipped with crockery, cutlery and fridge for cold drinks.

With holiday letting you are free to make your own rules e.g. period of rent, deposit and number of occupants.

> You will be liable to pay tax on your rental income in Italy; and long-term rentals over a month should be registered with the authorities. Some *comunes* require all guests whatever their length of stay to register. This is a requirement of Italian bureaucracy which some *comunes* will not waive.

Advertising Your Property. If you decide to act as your own agent there are many ways you can advertise your property. The newspapers in the UK which contain holiday rental classifieds from homeowners in Italy are, *The Sunday Times*, *The Sunday Telegraph*, *The Observer*, and *Dalton's Weekly* and niche magazines such as *The Gay Times*. Another possibility is to create your own website but this is costly. A well produced brochure with internal/external photographs and a few paragraphs about the local information, the attractions, the facilities and shops etc. A map on how to get there is also a good idea and of course your contact details, and clear instructions about the cost, paying the deposit and balance.

There is also no shortage of holiday villa rental companies that can be approached – the Italian State Tourist Office can provide a list. On the internet it is easy to find sites where you can advertise your property. When you have had a satisfied client – then word of mouth will be your best advert.

Agents. If you don't have much time to arrange the renting out yourself you can use an agent or (agents). The agent takes care of everything, They deal with the clients and they sort out any problems affecting the visitors during their stay. The agent charges commission of about 10% of the gross rental income. If you are charged more than that then there should be extra services provided. The agent often has a catalogue/brochure or internet site on which they advertise properties. If you are considering renting out, contact the rental company the summer before you want your renting to begin. Letting agents turn down as many as nine out of ten properties that are sent to them. Needless to say it is of the utmost importance to employ an agent who is conscientious, efficient and honest and comes recommended.

> You do not have to have a special licence to set up as a holiday rental agent in Italy and some have gone bust owing their customers thousands of euros.

A company that has been trading for a number of years and can show you other villas and apartments on their books is the best bet. It is usual to sign a contract with the agent and this is renewed annually. The services of the agent should include:

- Meeting the guests – handing over the keys.
- Tour of the property and how main appliances work.
- Arrange for cleaners and linen changes between rentals.
- Arrange for a gardener and for the pool to be cleaned.
- Give guests contact phone number for emergencies.
- Check property occasionally when not rented during contract period.
- Arrange for payment, deposit etc.

Because of the immense competition in renting your villa, farmhouse or apartment in Italy it is possible that all your vacancies will not be filled. At best you can expect 8 to 12 weeks (if you are lucky) especially if your property is of a high rental standard and with good staff. However, geopolitical problems and changing fashions can have a devastating effect on a rental season. At the moment Italy is extremely popular because of its abundance of history and art treasures combined with good food and *simpatico* people. But it is also very expensive for Americans who usually provide the bulk of holiday renters, and who have virtually disappeared. Additionally, there is huge range of competition in holiday hotspots from Italians' renovated farms and private homes.

Health Food

Health food is becoming increasingly popular in Italy and there is potential here for frozen and pre-packed diet meals (Italian children are becoming increasingly overweight) and other health foods.

Natural and organic food is also a growth sector as wide publicity has been given in Italy to food safety crises such as BSE and other food problems related to intensive farming.

Restaurants

Restaurants are another possibility although it will have to be something exotic to the Italians, for instance Indian or Thai restaurants and be in a big city where tastes are cosmopolitan. Another food-related area is food-travel, where tourists come to sample real Italian food, shop in the markets and learn to cook the food for themselves.

Il fast food on the other hand has probably had its heyday in Italy. McDonalds seems to have ceased expanding there. Additionally, the anti-global movement of which McDonalds is an acknowledged target has as many young supporters in Italy as elsewhere in Europe. The Slow Food movement, which began in Italy is now a small but growing international movement, so organic restaurants using local produce are likely to be more popular than fast food.

Franchising

Although not strictly a new business, it is worth mentioning as Italy has seen a regular and sustained growth in franchising in the last few years. Growth was concentrated in the north of Italy, where there is more disposable income but has spread to the south of Italy where it is seen as a way of getting round the lack of jobs there as If you can't find a job, you can work as a franchisee for a franchisor and it is like running your own business but with much reduced set up and running costs. However, you are also subject to strict guidelines provided by the franchisor and to split profits with the franchisor as you are normally obliged to pay them royalties.

An Italian franchising law was passed in May 2004 and an English version can be found at www.buyusa.it. In Italy franchising is governed by laws governing commercial contracts and trademark licensing and the most usual duration of a franchising contract is five years, but it can also be three or six years. An entry fee is required to join a franchising operation and most franchisors offer comprehensive training programmes, manuals and regular workshops for their franchisees. The minimum cost of setting up is around €10,000. The Italian franchising organization is Assofranchising (Viale Majno 42, 20129 Milano; ☎ 02 29 00 37 79; fax 02 65 55 919; www.assofranchising.it). Successful franchises in Italy include: Italiana Immobiliare (property agency), Zoo Planet (pet products and petfood), KA International (home décor), Kiron (financial advice and mortgage broker) and Nissolini Corsi (preparation for competitive public exams).

The Garage Trade

There are no national chains of car repair centres in Italy and the trade is dominated by thousands of small, family-run businesses specializing in supplying services to the motorist: mechanical maintenance (*auto riparatori*), *body shops* (*carrozzieri*) and tyre supply and maintenance (*gommisti*). Such businesses are supplied by small local wholesalers who supply individual businesses with minimal quantities of parts. Italy has one of the highest rates of car ownership in the world with approximately 35 million vehicles on the road, which is approximately five million more vehicles than in the UK.

Pet Products & Accessories

This area of business has grown faster in Italy than in any other European country in the space of the last few years and presents great opportunities for the entrepreneur as the market is still wide open and with a long way to go before saturation. One of the reasons Italians may be taking to pet animals is that the human birth rate has dropped to one of the lowest in Europe and Italians need something to dote on and also to provide psychological comfort. However, as with all trends Italian, the fashion aspect plays an important part. For a certain type of Italian the dog is a fashion accessory and their cat some exotic breed that looks like a miniature leopard. Having said that, there are also many appealing muts that are adopted from local municipal kennels as strays and giving adoring homes. The pet then has to have its own accessories for which there is great potential business. Apartment bound Italians are also splashing out on other smaller, exotic, low maintenance creatures including, birds, rodents, reptiles and fish. Just over half of all pet food is imported but only 20% of accessories are.

Wine-making

It is the dream of many expatriates to be the proprietor of a vineyard but often they do not know where to begin and what it involves (or the huge cost of buying a vineyard). In fact being the owner can be the easiest part and it is very common practice in Italy to sub-contract production (crop maintenance, harvesting, wine-making, bottling, labelling) in part or in full which is fine if all you want is to see your name on a wine label but not if you want to try to make a profit. Unless you are an experienced viticulturist you will probably need some outside help while you learn more about the art of wine-growing.

One company which specialises in properties with vineyards in the unspoilt

Piedmont region is Piedmont Properties, the British trading agent for the Azienda Agricola Ute de Vargas. The eponymous Ute is a retired opera diva who has lived in Italy for 30 years and owned and run a successful vineyard in Piedmont since 1987. She has been marketing property, especially vineyards, in the region since 1989. The UK and USA marketing operations can be contacted online at www.piedmont.co.uk or telephone 01344-624096. Prices start at £60,000 for a small (1.5 hectare) vineyard on its own, and from £120,000 for a small vineyard with a period farmhouse.

Other

Other foreign professionals who have located a demand for their services in Italy, and who have set up successful businesses include lawyers qualified in international law, accountants, veterinarians, landscape gardeners and house restorers.

Exporters

Areas of high demand for imports into Italy include high quality paper products and stationary, meat, electro-medical equipment (with technical support services) and security systems. The Italy Desk of the Overseas Trade Services of the Department of Trade and Industry (DTI) in London (Kingsgate House, 66-74 Victoria Street, London SW1E 6SW; ☎020-7215 4385; fax 020-7215 4711; www.tradedepartment.gov.uk) and the regional Business Link offices (see below) provide help and information specifically for exporters in a number of ways. They are able to provide basic market information, commission status reports on specific companies and find suitable representatives for UK firms as well as giving current information on tariff rates and import procedures. Fees are charged for most of these services. Although this service will only be of use to those considering exporting to Italy, the DTI also publishes several booklets focused on Italy including *Italy Trade Brief* and *Italy, an Overseas Trade Supplement*. It can also advise small businesses thinking of venturing into Italy. All of these publications are available free of charge from the DTI by calling the above number and asking for the Italy Desk.

In addition, the Trade Partners UK Library at Room 150, First Floor, Ashdown House, 123 Victoria Street, London SW1; ☎020-7215 5444; www.tradepartners.gov.uk) is worth a visit for anyone researching into business opportunities in Italy. The library boasts a mine of statistical information and business and industry reports as well as an extensive supply of the Italian *Yellow Pages*. The library is open from 9.30am-5.30pm Monday to Friday and visitors may use the library at any time within these hours (you will have to sign in with a business address), although students are mysteriously required to make appointments in advance.

An alternative to the DTI's Italy Desk in London are the Business Link offices set up around the country as one-stop-shops for businesses. They can also advise on exporting to other countries including Italy. To find your nearest, look up Business Link in the telephone directory.

RUNNING A BUSINESS

Employing Staff

Employer and employee relations in Italy are controlled by a mass of social and labour legislation, parts of which may vary according to the employer's principal industrial activity and the work status of the employee. The three main categories of staff are *dirigenti* (managers), *impiegati* (white-collar staff) *and operai* (workmen/women). Depending on their category, conditions of employment, including the level of employer/employee social security deductions, minimum salary, holiday allowance and minimum advance notice of dismissal, retirement and death benefits, will vary.

Successful small companies run by foreigners in Italy are unanimous in exhorting newcomers to take enormous care in the selection of staff. The Italian labour laws are significantly more protective towards employees than in other EU countries like Britain, and a small employer can be ruined by his or her virtual inability to dismiss inefficient staff.

Workers' rights. Italian workers' rights are guaranteed by Law number 300 of 20 May 1970. They are as follows:

- Freedom of opinion.
- The installation of audiovisual equipment is not permitted for checking workers' activities.
- Employers are not permitted to check on a worker's fitness to work.
- Personnel searches of unskilled workers may only be made by automatic selection systems and must respect the dignity and privacy of the worker.
- Disciplinary action is only permitted under laid-down procedures.
- Opinion surveys by employers are not permitted.
- Employees may ascertain that safety regulations are being adhered to.
- Employees may not be downgraded; no worker may be transferred from one unit to another, except for proven technical, organizational or production reasons.
- Workers have the right to form and join unions and carry on union activities on work premises.
- The courts may reinstate a worker judged to have been unfairly

dismissed.

○ Companies may not suppress union activity.

Trade Unions: Apart from the major trade unions (see the chapter, *Employment*) which are unified into political rather than work-type categories, there are others which spring from a particular industry or sector of activity. Working hours lost through strikes have halved since 1984 thanks to Italy's economic boom which has brought prosperity to a large number of Italians. Nowadays, strikes are most likely to occur in the public sector and transportation industries. The continuing influence of Italy's trade union movement should not be underestimated at worker level although its powers have declined considerably since the 1970s. Workers are not obliged to belong to a union and an estimated 70% are non-unionized.

Employer Associations: Most of the employers' associations were set up in the aftermath of the First World War. The main ones are: The General Confederation of Agriculture *(Confagricoltura)*, The General Confederation of Commerce *(Confcommercio)* and The Confederation of Small Firms *(Confabi)*. These Associations represent their members in discussions with the government. The largest and most influential is Confidustria entrepreneurs' association. The current president of Fiat, Luca Corderdo di Montezemolo, is also president of Confidustria.

Employee Training. There is no obligation for employers to provide employee training programmes but they may enhance the employer's activity. As an incentive to employers to engage young people, the 1986 Contract of Training and Work was passed. Under this, employees of less than 30 years of age can be engaged for a period of two years on normal salary rates but with minimal social security contributions. After two years the employer may confirm or terminate the contract with no further obligation.

Wages and Salaries. For each Italian industry there is a national minimum wage and salary scale. However most employers are obliged to pay way above the mininum, except in the most deprived regions. In common with many other European countries employees are entitled to an additional month's salary ('the thirteenth month'), payable in December. In commercial industries it is also customary to pay a further additional month's salary in June.

Social Security Contributions. The government social security system provides old age and disability pensions, sickness and unemployment benefits, healthcare and medical treatment. Only very high up manager types also have private insurance (that includes dental care) as part of their company employment packages. The quality of public health service is extremely variable but mostly adequate for most employees who rarely opt to pay out for private treatment plans. Nevertheless social security and welfare contributions are obligatory on the part of the employee and employer, the latter paying the major share of the employee contributions.

Paid Holidays: In addition to a statutory annual vacation, variable between five and six weeks according to the employer's activity, and the employee's category and length of service, staff are entitled to the ten statutory public holidays (see the chapter *Daily Life*). Women are entitled to six months' paid maternity leave beginning in the last month of pregnancy, or earlier if the pregnancy is regarded as 'at risk', and five months after the birth, regardless of the number of months taken before.

Taxation

Italian tax rates are some of the highest in Europe after the Scandinavian countries. Although tax evasion is still widespread amongst the self-employed, it is virtually impossible for the salaried employee to evade taxes as they are deducted at source. Even large companies, particularly those quoted on the stock exchange are now subject to more controls, particularly since the Parmalat scandal which involved massive financial malpractice. Tax evasion is more common amongst very small enterprises such as a mechanic or plumber, or restaurant that does not give out receipts. For the foreign entrepreneur the temptation to follow the Italian smaller examples is great, but probably not worth it, as the Italian tax authorities are likely to be far from lenient with foreign tax dodgers.

Once a business structure has been registered in Italy, the company becomes liable for Italian taxes. Unlike the UK, the fiscal year for companies can begin or end on any date in a period not exceeding twelve months. However since it is easy to overlook the dates when tax instalments fall due and thus become liable for a 15% surcharge plus 6% interest charges per annum, it may be advisable to stick to the calendar year ie. 1 January to 31 December which is easily remembered.

Each corporation must file an annual tax return on Form 760, giving company results. The tax return must be accompanied by a balance sheet, a report from the statutory auditors (*sindaci*) if your company is big enough to have them, and the directors' reports and resolutions approving the accompanying financial statements. The tax return covers both Corporate Income Tax and Local Income Tax (see below). The main company taxes are:

Imposta sul Reddito delle Personne Giuridiche (IRPEG). IRPEG, or Corporation Income Tax, is levied on corporations at the fixed rate of 33%.

Partnerships will either pay IRPEG, or in some cases personal (IRPEF) income tax.

IRAP a local income tax payable by businesses: it is levied at the base rate of 4.25%. It is currently being challenged by the EU.

Imposta sul Valore Aggiunto (IVA). The Italian equivalent of VAT is charged at the standard rate of 20%. Other rates 4% and 10%. There are a few VAT exemptions. The main categories of exemption are sales and leasing of both land and buildings (except newly constructed buildings and leasing of buildings used as fixed assets by a business), insurance, banking and financial services, certain health services and education.

The payment and collection of VAT is separate from other taxation. Traders are required to produce monthly computations of the VAT payable and the VAT receivable. Small businesses can make quarterly payments. If the balance is in favour of the payable this must be paid to the tax authority by the sixteenth day of the following month. If the balance is in favour of the trader, the amount is carried forward to be offset against future payable amounts. If, at the end of the calendar year, the balance still shows in the trader's favour the amount may be reclaimed from the authorities.

For small businesses with a turnover of less than €180,000 there is a simpler administrative procedure.

Note that the Mezzogiorno is a VAT-free zone for newly established companies. Other VAT-free zones abut on Livigno, Trieste and Gorizia.

Imposta Comunale sugli Immobili (ICI): An annual tax on the value of property that varies from 0.4% to 0.65%.

Tassa di Concessione Governativa. This is a company registration tax payable annually to the chamber of commerce. The tax varies according to the capital and legal entity of the company.

Accountancy Advice

Owing to the complexity of the Italian tax system it is essential to have expert fiscal advice from an accountant *(commercialista)*.

Useful Addresses – Accountants & Legal Advisors

Claudio del Giudice: Avvocato and Solicitor, Rivington House, 82 Great Eastern Street, London EC2A 3JF; ☎020 7613 2788; e-mail delgiudice@clara.co.uk; www.delgiudice.clara.net. Specialises in Italian property work and conveyancing.

Conti, Costanzo, Palladino e Associati, Studio di Consulenza Aziendale:, L.go Augusto 3, 20122 Milano; ☎ 02 79 61 41; fax 02 796142; info@scaonline.it;

www.scaonline.it. Chartered accountants.

The International Property Law Centre: Unit 2, Waterside Park, Livingstone Road, Hessle, HU13 OEG; please contact Ugo Tanda, Italian Avvocato, on ☎0870-800 4591 (e-mail ugot@maxgold.com); or Stefano Lucatello, Italian Solicitor on ☎0870-800 4565 (e-mail Stefano@maxgold.com); fax 0870-800 4567; general e-mail internationalproperty@maxgold.com; www. internationalpropertylaw.com. Specialists in the purchase and sale of Italian property and businesses, wills and probate, and litigation.

John Howell & Co: The Old Glassworks, 22 Endell Street, Covent Garden, London WC2H 9AD; ☎020-7420 0400; fax 020-7836 3626; e-mail info@europelaw.com; www.europelaw.com. Law firm specialising entirely in foreign property purchase.

Lanaia & Partners Accountants: Via A. Saffi 29, 20123 Milan; ☎ 02 48 00 65 14; fax 02 46 01 15; info@lanaia.com; www.lanaia.com. Accountants that specialise in business start-ups and ongoing support.

Rosauer Studio Legale: Via Umbria 7, 00187 Rome; ☎ 06 4818321; fax 06 487 1242; studiolegale@rosauer.it. www.rosauer.it. Commercial lawyers.

Studio Associato Caramanti Ticozzi & Partners: Via F. Casati 20, 20124 Milano; ☎ 02 29521641; fax +39 02 27791122; e-mail Francesco.mangiameli@ctep. it; www.ctep.it/index_html?cl=en. Accounting and auditing.

Studio Legale Sutti, Tax Department: Via Bigli 4, 20121 Milan; www.sutti.com. Independent business law firm. Contact company commercial department.

APPENDIX 1

PERSONAL CASE HISTORIES

CHARLES BUTTERNO

Charles Butterno is a freelance writer and wine consultant in his 50s and originally from Capetown, South Africa. He now lives in the Tuscan town of Valdarno and finds a town dwelling secure, and easy to care for and to leave empty when his work takes him away from Italy.

How long have you lived and worked in Italy?

Almost twenty years. For fifteen years I lived in a place lifestyle magazines habitually write about; a restored 400-year old barn on a remote olive farm, 450 metres above a Tuscan valley with the pre-Appenines as a spectacular, sometimes snowy, backdrop. I lived there as a tenant and felt perfectly at home, having (albeit laboriously) established an acceptance within the tiny local community, a harmony with the environment and a highly productive vegetable garden.

Despite being seemingly cemented to the place I had the delicious option of being able to pack up and leave at any time I chose, having few cumbersome possessions and even fewer obligations. So why I bought a house in Italy I don't know as I am among those of us who believe (believed?) that if you truly love country environments you don't go and live in them. But it doesn't really matter why, I'm just glad I did.

With barely time to plan or consider the consequences I found myself owning a small second floor apartment smack bang in the main thoroughfare of Valdarno in the valley below. From the natural serenity of the Tuscan woodlands I was faced with neighbours, traffic, urban noise....in other words, all those things most people want to leave behind.

How did it happen?

A non Italian-speaking foreign friend had asked for some help in finding a property 'somewhere in Italy', firstly for his family to live for a year, secondly to rent out when they weren't here. He had ideas of life deep in rural Arcadia, the 'real' Italy, communing with nature and the locals, interrupted only by idyllic picnic lunches in the fields. However, knowing his manual clumsiness and his chronic and dominating urban habits, I had other ideas about what he needed i.e. to be close to shops, restaurants and the autostrada. The search therefore concentrated on medium-sized typical Tuscan towns and ultimately on a 70 square metres apartment in the process of restoration, above a grocer's chop and opposite a bar in the main street of an historically famous town built on the banks of the Arno river 700 years ago. But instead of him buying it, I did.

What about the buying process?

Simple, particularly because I had no need of a mortgage: cash on the contract. Luckily the agent from whom I had bought it was a trusted, capable and credible friend and the architect overseeing the restoration soon became one. Had I not had such assistance, nor spoken the language, undoubtedly, it would have been an exercise riddled with misgivings, mistrust and fear of falling into a ruinous bureaucratic, legalistic morass. My friends handled it all, presenting me with strangely worded and formatted papers to sign and suggesting procedural short cuts which would make it easier for all of us. Trusting them implicitly to do the right thing I calmly signed on all the dotted lines.

How do you feel about your purchase now?

I've been here several years and in that time the value of the property has gone up by over 25%. I could sell it tomorrow, or easily rent it, but I have no intention of doing either. An extra advantage is that it has a single entrance on the second floor, and has neighbours on all sides. With a security door, the likelihood of burglaries is minimal, and so when I leave the country for months on end, I close and lock the door in a state as near peace of mind as you can get.

ERIN McCLOSKEY

Erin was raised in Canada but has a British passport. Now in her mid-thirties she went to Italy on a sabbatical from university (where she studied biology). She came across an Italian-published book (in English) on conservation volunteers and because it dealt with her field, she wrote to the publisher and was offered a job in Genova. She went to Italy with no Italian-speaking ability and five years later she is living in Turin having made a career for herself as a freelance editor, writer and most recently, as a translator. We asked her:

How did you find somewhere to live?
I was very lucky: the publisher had a flat I rented from him for six months. I then acquired an Italian boyfriend and he had a flat too and I moved in with him.

How much did your lack of Italian affect your job prospects after you decided to stay on in Italy?
Well I work only on English-language publications or write in English. I have recently acquired additional work as a translator from Italian to English so my Italian has come on, although I do not use it much for work, apart from the translating. It is very easy to learn Italian if you want to. Every comune offers free Italian lessons to foreigners. I attended these free local classes.

Did you have problems with the bureaucracy?
As I have a UK passport I got a ten-year *Permesso di Lavoro* straight off. If you are not from the EU the bureaucracy involved in staying here is much more time wasting. I believe you have to renew your work permit every six months, which must be daunting. Italy is extremely bureaucratic.

What is the social life like?
You have to make an effort to get to know people who are here long-term and locals. It is all too easy to socialise with expats who are only here for a short while. This is a big mistake, as when they leave and you stay on, you are temporarily isolated.

Is it easy being freelance in Italy?
It is very complicated being in business in Italy. There are big differences in the business culture. For instance, Italians often take several hours off from 1pm and then work until 10pm at night. Personally, I don't think that is very healthy as they have little time for after work activities such as visits to the gym or sports. As regards the way your business operates, there are so many options that you have no way of knowing how to choose what is the right one for you and the same applies to tax regimes. If you were on your own without any Italian help I don't see how you would manage. For instance, I do not have a business code which you get by registering at the chamber of commerce as freelance consultants do not need to do this. But because I am not registered I cannot claim expenses connected with running a business. Tax is another problem to deal with. You absolutely must have an Italian friend to help you, or an accountant with international experience. You cannot expect to understand the implications of everything each choice involves, on your own. Even with all the help I get, I am still anxious. In some ways, I think it must be much better being a *dipendente* (employee) so that all the formalities are dealt with for you.

Have you any advice for those thinking of going to work in Italy?
Make friends with Italians as fast as you can. You cannot have too much help in this country. I have been amazingly lucky and I couldn't have done without them. That is my best advice.

SARAH RASMER

As an expat expecting to spend only a few years in Italy, life is very different to that experienced by a retiree in Tuscany and the experience will be very different to someone who speaks Italian and has decided to relocate to Italy to start a business. Sarah Rasmer, an American, accompanied her partner to Ferrara in northern Italy and has the following comments and advice to pass on to those who follow her to Ferrara, or Italy. We asked her:

How important is speaking the language?
It has been essential for us to study Italian as few people speak English in Ferrara. My husband must speak Italian at work, and was surprised that some people he works with do not speak in Italian, but in the local dialect. We find Italians to be very friendly, they have gone way out of their way to help us, even before we could speak any Italian.

What is the most infuriating part of living in Italy?
The most frustrating thing that I have found about living in Italy has been the Italian bureaucracy system. We were advised to hire a translator to go with us when obtaining the necessary paperwork when we first arrived. We are very glad we followed this advice, as it took away some of the frustration involved due to our lack of Italian at the time. One thing that has been a source of confusion for me when dealing with the bureaucracy is that I took my husband's name when I got married. Italian women keep their maiden names when they marry and every office where I had to get paperwork assumed I did the same. It has been easier for me to use my maiden name on my paperwork, because they didn't understand when I tried to explain it to them.

Did you find it hard to acclimatise to Italian working hours?
Business hours are improving, but can still be frustrating. Many government offices are only open for a few hours in the mornings. It is always a good idea to call ahead to check business hours. Banks are open from 8:30-12:30 or 1pm and again between 3 and 4pm. Most shops are open from 9am through tp 12:30 or 1:00 pm, and open again from 3:30 or 4 to 7pm (4:30 or 5-7:30/8pm in summer). Each city designates one morning or afternoon a week that the shops close, Ferrara's is Thursday afternoons. Small, family run businesses close for funerals and vacations; they will leave a note on their door to notify their customers. Most businesses

close for at least a couple of weeks in August. Many shops are open on Sunday afternoons; and some do not close for lunch. All *tabacchi* shops, which sell various items like stamps and prepaid phone cards in addition to cigarettes, remain open for lunch. There are two large shopping centres outside of Ferrara, which have large grocery stores. These stores are called *supermercato* and they have the best selection and prices for groceries. They also carry household items like appliances and clothes. There are fruit and vegetable shops in most neighbourhoods in the city where they pick out the produce for you, so it is best to find one you like and frequent it as they give the best selection to regular customers.

How did you find motoring in Italy?
Buying a car was more complicated than we expected. We were able to buy a used car from a dealer and dealers offer warranties with used cars. The dealer seemed reluctant to sell us a car at first, even though my husband's colleague, who also speaks English, was friends with the owner and accompanied us. They told us that there is more paperwork for them to fill out because we are foreigners. They were also concerned with the fact that we are here on a temporary basis. My husband's employer had to call the dealer to 'put in a good word' for us. We were only able to finance the car for 18 months, I think because we told them we were going to be here for 2-3 years. The whole process took a few weeks, but we did manage to buy the car we wanted in the end! We were advised to buy either German or Italian made cars because they are the easiest to resell, diesels are also popular.

Many streets in the historic centres of cities are closed to traffic except for taxis and buses. We live on such a street and had to get permission to drive on it, and can only drive on part of the street.

Have you found any Italian websites particularly useful?
The website I use most is the Italian railway's website: www.fs-on-line.com. This is the best place to find current train schedules and you can also look up the fare. It is now possible to purchase train tickets online, but only for tickets that have reservations and that depart between the hours of 6:30-11:30pm. Ferrara's train station is not a full service station, so sometimes it is easier to purchase tickets at a travel agent; the website above lists authorised travel agents.

For good information about shopping and factory outlets see: www.made-in-italy.com. The International Women's Forum is a group located in Bologna for international women who speak English; their website is www.iwfbologna.org. They also provide a job bank for members.

GEORGINA GORDON-HAM (JINKS)

Georgina has an Italian-French mother and an English father and so, apart from being trilingual from an early age she has always had familial links with Italy, and some of her schooling took place there. After finishing a PhD in Languages at the University of Rome in 1975 she did a Postgraduate course in translating and interpreting at the University of Westminster. For six years she was the permanent staff translator/interpreter for the ENI Group (Italy's National Petroleum Board). She is a Member of the Institute of Translating and Interpreting and the Institute of Journalists, London and has been a freelance translator/interpreter/journalist since 1982. She has lived in Italy for about 20 years and her husband who is English, is in the IT business. We asked her:

How do you find the Italian red-tape?
It is very irritating. For instance the *Permesso di soggiorno* has to be renewed every five years even if you have lived in Italy for 20 years. However belonging to the European Union has caused some improvements. Things do move a bit faster.

I suppose you had a head-start setting up in business with your connections?
Well yes, but you still have to work very hard at it, especially the international marketing aspect. To be taken seriously you should also become a member of the Chamber of Commerce and belong to a recognised professional body.

What about your work?
Being an interpreter/translator is an ongoing process as you have to maintain contact with all your languages, which in my case are English, Italian and French. Interpreters charge fees on a per day basis. Translations are generally charged by the page in Italy although sometimes by words which works out at about £75-90 per 1,000 words.

What is the social life like?
Here in Rome there are clubs for the British, Canadian and Americans. Actually they tend to be mixed nationality as there are a lot of Italian husbands. It's not so easy for a newcomer to socialise with Italians who although open and welcoming are reserved. Playing sports is another good way to socialise. Also, there are two types of foreign communities, those *en passage* who are here for two or three years and those who live here permanently.

Is it pleasant living in Rome?
Yes, apart from July and August when it is very humid, the climate is very pleasant and mild, especially in winter. The area around, particularly the hills are beautiful

and in winter you can go skiing for the day at Terminillo and Campo Felice about one and half hour's drive away. The sea is also close and there are some lovely resorts such as Sperlonga, Circeo, Friggene, Santa Marinella.

Have you any advice for those thinking of going to work in Italy?
I would advise that you don't have too many romantic ideas about Italy, coming here to work is not like coming here on holiday when you are free from all cares. You need to have a pragmatic approach. If you don't already know the country and the language very well then I would recommend that you start by working here on a full-time basis because then the company posting you, or the employer recruiting you does all the paperwork and sometimes fixes up your accommodation as well. This way you get to know your way around the procedures so that it is all familiar when you come to do it for yourself and you feel less like an outsider.

MARIA MAKEPEACE

Maria Makepeace, a freelance artist and teacher, moved from the UK to Siena in 1988. In 1997 she moved to Florence. She is a qualified teacher of art, English and geography and has over 20 years' teaching experience. Despite being half Italian she did not learn to speak Italian properly until she arrived in Italy and has now made contact with the Italian side of her family who live in Tuscany. She has had over 30 exhibitions of her work in Italy. Her 'bread and butter work is Tuscan landscapes and she paints to commission including animal portraits (☎055-223819). She also writes poetry based on the history, traditions and/or culture of Tuscany. Her exhibitions have been very successful with a large part of her work going to clients abroad including the United States. We asked her:

Is it difficult to survive on painting alone?
It would be, but I do some teaching as well. For instance I have given private English lessons, and taught art in *elementari and scuola media* schools in extra-curricular classes paid for by the parents. I also taught at the *Università Populare* (a kind of Italian WEA) in Siena. Also, I have just recently done my first simultaneous translation.

How do you find the Italian bureaucracy
It is very irritating. For instance when I have to send one of my paintings to a client abroad there are forms to be filled out in triplicate and I have to take an actual painting (and they can be very big) to the Belle Arti inspector in the main national gallery for checking that I am not illegally exporting anything. The other thing you have to do is register for tax. Freelances have to register for *partita EVA* (VAT), but I am not generally earning enough for this. I am now also registered

with the British Chamber of Commerce in Milan.

Another small niggle concerns publicity. Posters have to be stamped by the *comune* and each stamp costs money. I have been known to make myself a T-shirt instead of a poster and walk around Siena for a few days before an exhibition – wearing my publicity! Permits from the *Vigili Urbani* (Traffic Wardens) to transport exhibitions into central pedestrian areas are yet another bureaucratic nightmare – unless you know someone who knows the chief traffic warden.

How do you find social life and the Italians
In Siena I was living just outside the town in the countryside and met a lot of Italian country people. In Florence I tend to meet only English people. I am not a club person at all and the nature of my work is such that I need to be alone quite a lot of the time. I go to lectures at the British Institute here in Florence and use their wonderful library. I am also going to life-drawing evenings occasionally to keep my drawing 'in form'.

How do you find a place to exhibit?
You usually have to ask the *Comune* (town hall). Sometimes they will rent you space and sometimes it will be provided free. Another possibility is to 'pay with a picture', for example in hotels.

Have you any advice for anyone, particularly artists thinking of setting up in Italy?
Firstly, don't come to Florence thinking it is the art centre of the world. In one sense it is – for art from the past, but definitely not for modern art.

Another tip is about exporting. If you sell to foreigners make sure that you charge enough so as not to make a loss on the carriage abroad which can be very expensive if you go to *spedizionari* (specialised freight companies), especially if they have the local monopoly. You have to have special wooden crates for packing. You need a friendly carpenter to make the crates at a fraction of the price and then take them to the freight company's office yourself, having been to Belle Arti yourself with the picture first, so that it is ready packed.

You can save a lot of money by doing your own framing and publicity (see above). You need adaptability, imagination, staying power....and a knowledge of several languages, not just Italian, is useful; as is an interest in the history and cultural heritage of Italy.

JOHN MATTA

John Matta, originally from London had an Italian-British father who ran a wine importing business (F.S. Matta Ltd) in the UK. In the 1960s his father bought into a Chianti vineyard and John began to shuttle back and forth between London and Italy which meant he could spend a total of four to five months a year there. He did a three year course in oenology at the Istituto Tecnico Agrario Umberto Primo, (a state-run college that specialises in oenology) located in Alba in Piemonte. He now runs the family vineyard, Castello Vicchiomaggio (75 acres) and produces, a Chianti Classico DOCG. As well as being a wine producer, he also exports worldwide, lets holiday apartments and owns a restaurant. He has been permanently resident in Italy since 1980. We asked him:

Obviously you had a head start, but how difficult is it to set up a business in Italy?
Setting up a business in Italy is definitely not as easy as the UK where you can buy an off the peg company one day and be trading the next. Here, you have to allow at least four months for all the processes to be completed. It is a big mistake to think you can do it all on your own. You should start by using one of the specialist companies that make their living from company start-ups. They charge a fee yes, but in the end it will save you a lot of time and be worth it. Also, unless you can communicate freely in Italian you cannot expect to make a success of business here.

What about foreigners in the wine business. Are there any British-run vineyards here?
I don't believe so, though there are a couple of Swiss and Germans and one American that I know of. Also, the big American company Kendall-Jackson from Napa Valley have taken over the vineyard of San Leonino which is a Chianti Classico.

What would your advice be to prospective wine-growers?
You need at least fifteen hectares (about 45 acres) if you want to bottle and market your own label. Less than 15 hectares would be a 'hobby vineyard and you could sell your grapes to the local wine co-operative. If one person wanted to grow, harvest and sell the grapes themselves then four hectares is manageable if you wanted to do the picking yourself (though there is always local help willing to come and pick for you).

Any final words of advice?
You must realise from the outset that Italy is a different country and that things are done quite differently here in a more time consuming way and there are procedures for everything. The UK is different from most European countries in this respect and it stems partly from the fact that Britain was never invaded. Napoleon invaded Italy and imposed the Code Napoleon which affects the laws and systems here. So if you are planning to come here and earn your living then

think very carefully about it and the cultural adaptation it involves.

If you want to come here as a retiree, then things are quite different and it's much less of a big decision than coming here to start a business. Italians are so friendly and helpful and you can get by with conversational Italian.

ROGER WARWICK

Roger Warwick who is in his late forties has been based in Italy for about twenty years. He settled in Italy, after a period of taking extended holidays there, because he knew it better than other countries. He grew to like northern Italy and he preferred the climate to that of Britain. He was at one time manager of the duty-free facilities at Heathrow Airport and during his trips to Italy in the 1970s he taught English at private schools. In 1978 he and his Italian wife set up a business offering financial investigative services, which includes everything from assessing companies prior to merger or acquisition, to advising on counter industrial espionage tactics. Roger is also the regional secretary of the local Chamber of Commerce for Bologna and Emilia Romagna. He lives just outside Bologna on a modern development. We asked him:

Was it difficult to set up a business?
Yes it was. We are the only British-run organisation offering investigative services that has a licence from the local *prefetto* (magistrate). It is extremely difficult to obtain such a licence.

How do you find living and doing business in Italy compared with the UK?
Obviously I prefer it in Italy, or I wouldn't be here. Northern Italy is fine because it is efficient and things work well. I'm talking about the private sector; the public sector and the bureaucracy are Kafkaesque. I'm lucky enough to have found a niche and doing business here amongst normal people (i.e. not bureaucrats) is enjoyable, partly because a high standard of education is more widespread than in the UK. Italians are very good at pulling something out of the hat. When you ask an Italian engineer to produce something unusual or new he can do it. In Britain, it would be damned on the drawing board. On the other hand Italians are extremely bad at marketing their products whereas the British, French, Germans etc. are very good marketers. I think this is partly due to the poor image the Italians have abroad. English promoters use Englishness and French promoters Frenchness and the world recognises these as something chic. There is no similar regard for Italianness; in fact you'd be hard put to think of anything except *The Godfather* and stilletto murders. There is definitely scope for British experts in marketing techniques to promote Italian products in the UK.

The cost of living in Italy is greater than in the UK. In Bologna it is particularly high – the highest in Italy I believe, because there is no unemployment in this region and so there is no need to lower the prices. Bologna is one of the most pleasant towns in Italy. It is small enough to be human and big enough to be a city.

How do you find the social life and the Italians?

I live on a modern development of fifteen houses and all the couples there are Italian and of a similar age to us; much of our social life revolves around them. I speak fluent Italian which is essential. I know foreigners who have lived in Italy for twenty years and can only mumble a few words in Italian which severely limits the possibilities of making friends with Italians as hardly any of them speak English well enough to have an interesting conversation. The other part of my social life revolves around the events organised by the local Chamber of Commerce.

Have you any advice for those thinking of taking the plunge?

Forget your preconceptions about all Italians being gangsters and come to the north of Italy: realise you are going to be up against a bureaucracy like something out of Kafka's *The Trial*: learn to speak Italian.

APPENDIX 2

READING LIST

Buongiorno Italia! Coursebook, £10.99 plus three cassettes £6.99 each). A BBC beginners' course (1982) in Italian comprising 20 lessons. The textbook, teacher's notes and cassettes can all be purchased individually from the Italian Bookshop in London (e-mail Italian@esb.co.uk) or online at the BBC website www.bbcshop.com.

A Concise History of Italy, Christopher Duggan, Mark Duggan, Cambridge University Press (1994), 334 pages, £15.99 (US$23). Italy from Roman times to the present.

Excellent Cadavers: Alexander Stille, Vintage, £8.99 (US$15.00). The story of the mafia. Made into a film of the same name in 1999.

Getting it Right in Italy, William Ward, Bloomsbury (£9.99): a combination of insight into and practical advice on, all aspects of Italian life including money, family life, sex, politics and the economy, by a journalist and broadcaster who has made Italy his home for over ten years. Full of fascinating facts and figures in an easy access format. 390 pages. Unfortunately now out of print but still worth a look if you can buy it secondhand.

The History of the Decline and Fall of the Roman Empire (Abridged), Edward Gibbon, David Womersley, Penguin Books, 848 pages, £10.99 (US$16.00).

A History of Contemporary Italy: Society and Politics 1943-1988, Paul Ginsborg, Penguin, £12.99 (US$24.95): Ginsborg's book charts the success of Italy's transformation from a war-torn country to the success story of the late 1980s and also traces the failed and repeated attempts at much-needed political reform. 425 pages. Also, the more recent *Italy and Its Discontents: Family, Civil Society, State: 1980-2001* by the same author, published by Penguin (2003).

The Honoured Society, Norman Lewis, Eland, £9.99: the journalist Norman Lewis writes absorbingly and authoritatively about the development of the Mafia's power and influence in Italy. First published in 1964, this book is kept in print by classic publisher Eland. 266 pages.

The Italians: Luigi Barzini, Penguin, £10.99 available from the Penguin online bookshop (www.penguin.co.uk) or in the US for (US$14.00) from Longitude

Books (www.longitudebooks.com). First published in 1964 and considered a classic insight into the Italian character.

Lonely Planet produce a number of Italian guides, including Italy, Rome, Venice, Sicily, Tuscany and Walking in Italy. Lonely Planet phrasebooks are also a good source of the slang Italian that crops up in everyday life but never appears in traditional language courses. Lonely Planet books can be found in most bookshops and also ordered from their website www.lonelyplanet.com.

The New Italians: Charles Richards, Penguin, £9.99 (1995). An account of contemporary Italians and Italy.

Rough Guides produce a number of Italian guides, including Italy, Rome, Tuscany and Umbria and Sardinia. Rough Guides can be found in most bookshops and also ordered from their website www.roughguides.com.

Burton Anderson's Best Wines of Italy: (US$29.95): an exploration of the source of some of the country's finest wines, unveiling the products of esteemed winemaking traditions.

A Traveller's Wine Guide to Italy: Stephen Hobley, Interlink Press (2001), £9.62 on Amazon.co.uk (or US $19.99). a wealth of practical information on Italian wine, some reflections on cultural and gastronomic points of interest in Italy, and some suggested itineraries for visiting wineries. 144 pages.

The above books can be obtained through the Italian Book Shop (7 Cecil Court, London WC2N 4EZ; ☎020-7240 1634; www.eurobooks.co.uk). Nearest tube Leicester Square. The majority of the books listed above can also be bought from online booksellers such as www.amazon.co.uk, www.amazon.com and www. bn.com who will deliver worldwide.

Complete guides to life abroad from Vacation Work

Live & Work Abroad

Live & Work in Australia & New Zealand £12.95
Live & Work in Belgium, The Netherlands & Luxembourg £10.99
Live & Work in China £11.95
Live & Work in France £11.95
Live & Work in Germany £10.99
Live & Work in Ireland £10.99
Live & Work in Italy £11.95
Live & Work in Japan £10.99
Live & Work in Portugal £11.95
Live & Work in Russia & Eastern Europe £10.99
Live & Work in Saudi & the Gulf £10.99
Live & Work in Scandinavia £10.99
Live & Work in Scotland £11.95
Live & Work in Spain £12.95
Live & Work in Spain & Portugal £10.99
Live & Work in the USA & Canada £12.95

Buying a House Abroad

Buying a House in France £11.95
Buying a House in Italy £11.95
Buying a House in Portugal £11.95
Buying a House in Scotland £11.95
Buying a House in Spain £11.95
Buying a House on the Mediterranean £13.95

Starting a Business Abroad

Starting a Business in Australia £12.95
Starting a Business in France £12.95
Starting a Business in Spain £12.95

**Available from good bookshops or direct from the publishers
Vacation Work, 9 Park End Street, Oxford OX1 1HJ
Tel 01865-241978 * Fax 01865-790885 * www.vacationwork.co.uk**

**In the US: available at bookstores everywhere
or from The Globe Pequot Press (www.GlobePequot.com)**